THE ABILITIES OF GIFTED CHILDREN

Edwina D. Pendarvis
Marshall University

Aimee A. Howley
University of Charleston

Craig B. Howley
Appalachia Educational Laboratory

PRENTICE HALL, *Englewood Cliffs, New Jersey 07632*

Library of Congress Cataloging-in-Publication Data

Pendarvis, Edwina D.
   The abilities of gifted children / Edwina D. Pendarvis, Aimee
Howley, Craig Howley.
      p.   cm.
   Bibliography: p. 357
   Includes index.
   ISBN 0-13-002072-9
   1. Gifted children.   I. Howley, Aimee.   II. Howley, Craig B.
III. Title.
LC3993.P38   1990
371.95—dc20   89-8789
                                                  CIP

Editorial/production supervision and
   interior design: Shelly Kupperman
Cover design: 20/20 Services Inc.
Manufacturing buyer: Pete Havens

For our parents:
Marionette and Edward
Roberta and Aaron
Lorna and Jim

© 1990 by Prentice-Hall, Inc.
A Division of Simon & Schuster
Englewood Cliffs, New Jersey 07632

Printed in the United States of America
10 9 8 7 6 5 4 3 2 1

ISBN 0-13-002072-9

Prentice-Hall International (UK) Limited, *London*
Prentice-Hall of Australia Pty. Limited, *Sydney*
Prentice-Hall Canada Inc., *Toronto*
Prentice-Hall Hispanoamericana, S.A., *Mexico*
Prentice-Hall of India Private Limited, *New Delhi*
Prentice-Hall of Japan, Inc., *Tokyo*
Simon & Schuster Asia Pte. Ltd., *Singapore*
Editora Prentice-Hall do Brasil, Ltda., *Rio de Janeiro*

Contents

Part II: Kinds of Talent

Part III: Talent Development

8   TYPICAL GIFTED DEVELOPMENT   212

9   PRECOCIOUS DEVELOPMENT   242

10   INHIBITED DEVELOPMENT: UNDERACHIEVEMENT   265

11   UNFAIR DISCRIMINATION, POVERTY, AND MINORITY GIFTED CHILDREN   294

Part IV: Implications

Preface

One of us was recently asked by a state agency to speak to a group of teachers and administrators about the conclusions of research on acceleration. The talk took place at an annual statewide meeting, and the new state regulations, which for the first time specified this strategy by name, were on the agenda.

At the end of the talk, however, an official of the agency rose to make this statement: "Acceleration should be used with only a small fraction of gifted students." This remark would have had the intended effect, had not an outspoken educator from one of the universities conducting research on acceleration challenged the remark. According to this educator, the strategy was appropriate for 85 percent of gifted students.

This anecdote illustrates that supposition and sentiment, rather than informed judgment, too frequently guide the evolution of school programs. In the hectic climate of the classroom, it is, in fact, not easy to consult research. Intuition necessarily plays a valuable role in helping teachers make the countless decisions that each day demands of them.

Whereas this pattern of intuitive response makes sense in the press of classroom events, it *does not* make sense for planning either lessons or programs. Planning for lessons and programs requires knowledge more than intuition. Three types of knowledge apply: knowledge of subject matter, knowledge of students, and knowledge of teaching methods. There are no substitutes; neither sentiment nor supposition will do.

We wrote this book to give teachers the second kind of knowledge, knowledge about what gifted children are like. In the last decade a great deal of research has examined this topic. Our goal was to make sense of it. First, we wanted to make sense of it for ourselves. Without a clear personal understanding, we could not make sense of it for others. Second, on the basis of that understanding, we wanted to present the research in a way that would help teachers and administrators make rational decisions about bright students.

Not only did we think it important to bring together the conclusions of the best research, we also saw the need to provide a context for interpreting the findings. Such a context acknowledges both the value and the limitations of empirical research, for empirical research makes sense only in light of well-reasoned theory.

The Abilities of Gifted Children is designed as the primary text for courses that consider the nature of giftedness. Some such courses emphasize the characteristics of gifted children, and others focus on the psychological constructs that determine talent. This book is relevant to either conception. In addition, it offers a strong introduction to the study of gifted education. Because the text is highly readable, it is accessible to both undergraduate and graduate students.

ACKNOWLEDGMENTS

Writing a book is a selfish act. It deprives your children of attention; it bores your friends; it puzzles your colleagues; and—as your grass goes unmowed—it must secretly irk your neighbors. Therefore, we think it is fitting to express thanks to all of these people for their forbearance.

We also want to thank others for their help with the manuscript: Susan Willig and Carol Wada, our editors at Prentice Hall, for their sense of perspective and their optimism; Shirley Ferguson, for reading both of our textbooks back to back; Pat Cahape, the mother of two mathematically talented girls, for her review of Chapter 7; Kathy Showen and the teachers of the gifted in Jackson County, West Virginia, for their enthusiasm and support; and the staff of the Appalachia Educational Laboratory, for their persistence in bringing research and practice together. We greatly appreciate the helpful reviewer comments and suggestions: Steven Christopherson, United States Air Force Academy; Dean K. McIntosh, University of South Carolina–Columbia; Mark Pitts, Seattle Pacific University; Avis J. Ruthven, Mississippi State University; Beverly D. Shaklee, Kent State University; and Terry A. Thomas, California State University–Sacramento.

Earlier versions of material in Chapter 5 and Chapter 11 have appeared in the *Journal for the Education of the Gifted* and the *Rural Special Education Quarterly,* and we wish to thank these publications for their permission to use this material here.

This book has claimed three years of our lives. Its progress has paralleled our children's travels through various school experiences and our own progress through various professional experiences. This background is a constant accompaniment to our writing; the experiences and the writing have taken meaning from each other. We hope you will find this book's connections to your life—as a student, teacher, parent, researcher, and writer.

1

The Study of Gifted Students

Focusing Questions

1. How do theoretical and functional views of giftedness differ? Which is more likely to result in a coherent definition? Why?
2. What role has business played to support the development of programs for gifted students? Which kind of ability receives this support, general intellectual ability or creative ability?
3. What are the differences among the various types of empirical studies of gifted students?
4. In what way do the resources of a school and community determine how a school district will address the problem of talent development?
5. What constitutes a healthy respect for measurement error? Why is it so important for teachers to understand?
6. How is gifted education related to the more general notion of school improvement?

WHAT IS THE STUDY OF GIFTED STUDENTS?

This book is about what gifted students are like. It is not about how to teach gifted students, although the two topics have a good deal in common.

As a result of our work in gifted education, the authors came to realize that the topic of what gifted students were like was not well understood. Whereas nearly everyone believes that gifted students are concerned with theoretical and aesthetic matters, no text seemed to pull together in one volume the *empirical* literature on such students. Since the 1960s, that literature has grown substantially, and we felt it was time to attempt a synthesis of this literature.

Furthermore, it seemed to us that adults who were preparing to teach gifted students were the ones most in need of knowledge about the research concerning the characteristics of gifted students. Hence, we wrote this book for teachers who are now or will soon be working with such students. We hope it prompts teachers to arrive at new insights, and we hope it challenges widely held misconceptions effectively.

This first chapter is an introduction to the issues and methods described in the rest of the text. As you can tell from the focusing questions, it ties several themes together. It begins with a discussion of different types of definitions and concludes by noting the connection between the improvement of schools and the improvement of programs that address the needs of very talented students. It covers a lot of ground.

Our synthesis of what is known about teaching gifted students is briefly summarized in the last chapter of this text. In this text our main point is that instruction should have a lot to do with the kinds of students served in a particular program. We believe, therefore, that a text whose intention is to consider characteristics would be incomplete without a brief introduction to methods. For this reason, we not only include a chapter that provides an overview of issues related to instructional methods but also conclude many chapters with a section that discusses the instructional ramifications of the type of giftedness considered in the chapter.

DEFINITIONS

Definitions of giftedness reflect two perspectives: the theoretical and the functional. Each of these perspectives serves different purposes. Definitions of giftedness that are interested only in theory usually guide research or innovative programming. Functional definitions are usually designed for funding and regulating gifted education programs in the schools.

Theoretical Views of Giftedness

Theoretical definitions ascribe giftedness to individuals who possess two attributes: (1) a particular kind of ability and (2) a high level of that ability. The first attribute has been a greater source of controversy than the second, and it depends on the theoretician's perspective. Some psychologists (e.g., Terman, 1925) have argued for a single, broad ability, such as "intelligence." Some (e.g., Gowan, 1978) have argued that "creativity" is more important. Many psychologists (e.g., Guilford, 1967; Gardner, 1983) believe that there are a number of important mental abilities that exist independent of one another. These psychologists would include many different types of abilities in their definitions of giftedness.

Social attributes. Paul Witty (1958) recognizes the social importance of giftedness when he defines giftedness as remarkable performance in any potentially valuable human endeavor. Tannenbaum (1983) discusses types of giftedness that meet society's explicit, implicit, and latent needs. They are, respectively, skills that are important in meeting current manpower shortages, skills that are important for newly emerging specializations, and skills that are related to cultural enrichment, such as artistic skills.

Another way of looking at giftedness as a social attribute, however, involves interpreting giftedness as a status rank (Goodnow, 1984). According to this view, certain individuals are invested by others with the characteristics of giftedness. They are thought of as gifted and treated as though they were gifted. From this perspective, giftedness is not a characteristic of the individual at all. Instead, it is a trait ascribed—rather arbitrarily—to the individual by a social group. For example, students who dress better than other students are perceived by their teachers to be brighter (Good & Brophy, 1987).

Psychological constructs.   Some theoretical views entail models of psychological reality, or "constructs." The work of several theoreticians involves such constructs.

Galton (1869/1962), in *Hereditary Genius,* described intellectual performance in terms of the concept of deviation from the mean. He included many types of ability in his notion of giftedness: musical ability, athletic ability, and writing ability, among others. According to Galton's view, however, ability alone was not sufficient for genius to emerge. He maintained that "genius" was the interaction of ability, zeal, and stamina. Galton believed that mental traits were inherited, and given the three necessary ingredients, genius would emerge no matter what the environmental conditions.

Galton would not have used these three elements to locate gifted school children, however. He proposed no practical applications based upon his description of genius. For Galton, the issue of genius had more to do with politics, economics, and empire than with schooling. In fact, the idea that schools could work to develop a high level of talent in students from many backgrounds would probably have struck Galton—like many others of his era—as quite foolish.

A recent definition, based on the work of Galton and on more recent research on adult success, includes two of Galton's standards. Renzulli's (1978) definition of giftedness requires above average ability, creativity, and task commitment: characteristics of *adults* who make significant contributions to society. Unlike Galton's definition, Renzulli's is intended to guide *identification* of gifted children. However, because it is based on adult characteristics, its applicability to school children is questionable. Children who show the combined characteristics of high ability, high creativity, and task commitment may indeed be talented, but the definition overlooks many children with uncommon potential for academic achievement.

Robert Sternberg's (1981) perspective on intelligence has also been applied to the problem of defining giftedness. His approach, based on the construct of information processing, places a premium on the *efficiency* of cognitive processes, rather than on their rarity. Sternberg (1982) is particularly concerned with the individual's ability to handle unfamiliar (i.e., "non-entrenched") tasks and concepts.

Terman's (1925) definition of giftedness has both theoretical and functional ramifications. He applied Galton's notion of the comparative rarity of talent to the study of highly intelligent school children, and developed an instrument capable of distinguishing comparative rarity. In his definition, giftedness is "the top 1% level in general intellectual ability, as measured by the Stanford-Binet Intelligence Scale or a comparable instrument" (Terman, 1925, p. 43). Both Terman's definition and his instrument have been very influential in psychological research and in school practice. The focus of Terman's work, however, like that of Galton, was to describe talent and to draw conclusions about the utility of gifted children to society. The description of talent is the aspect of Terman's work that makes it theoretical. His interest in the utility of talent is the aspect that makes it functional.

FUNCTIONAL VIEWS OF GIFTEDNESS

Functional views of giftedness apply more directly to the practical issues of schooling. Hence, they tend to embody cultural values more explicitly than the theoretical views discussed previously. For example, functional definitions often serve as policy statements to help secure funding and provide a basis for regulations. Sometimes, however, functional definitions that accomplish the goals of society are not stated explicitly. These functional views represent implicit, common-sense ideas about talent. Such implicit ideas are strongly influenced by popular views of the economic and political forces that shape the schooling of children and the work of adults.

Pedagogical Definitions of Giftedness

Pedagogical definitions specify the population of children who are legitimately served through special programs funded by the school system. These definitions must agree with the philosophy of the school system and with the views of school administrators and the community. Pedagogical definitions typically emphasize the mission of the school to develop the potential of each individual student. Students' needs figure prominently in these definitions.

Federal definition. In the 1970s the U.S. government provided two definitions of giftedness. These federal definitions of giftedness illustrate the pragmatic nature of institutional definitions in two ways: (1) they have been constructed to suit political realities and (2) they are not theoretically coherent. In other words, such definitions are creations of the moment; they can be revised periodically, and often are.

The 1972 definition of giftedness (Marland, 1972, p. 2) reads as follows:

> Gifted and talented children are those identified by professionally qualified persons who, by virtue of outstanding abilities, are capable of high performance. These are children who require differentiated educational programs in order to realize their contribution to self and society.
>
> Children capable of high performance include those with demonstrated achievement and/or potential ability in any of the following areas, singly or in combination:
>
> 1. General intellectual ability,
> 2. Specific academic aptitude
> 3. Creative or productive thinking,
> 4. Leadership ability,
> 5. Visual and performing arts,
> 6. Psychomotor ability.

The 1978 federal definition eliminated "psychomotor ability" from among the areas of giftedness. The reason for this exclusion was economic; experience showed that funds earmarked for gifted programs could be used for athletic programs. Since there was already a great deal of money available for athletic programs, and because the other kinds of giftedness in this functional definition were relatively neglected, "psychomotor ability" was removed from the definition.

The recent definition, given in Section 902 of PL 95–561, The Gifted and Talented Children's Education Act of 1978, is worded slightly differently, but it includes the other five areas that are found in the 1972 definition:

> The term "gifted and talented children" means children and, whenever applicable, youth who are identified at the preschool, elementary, or secondary level as possessing demonstrated or potential abilities that give evidence of high performance capabilities in areas such as intellectual, creative, specific academic, or leadership ability, or in the performing and visual arts, and who by reason thereof, require services or activities not ordinarily provided by the school.

The 1972 federal definition has been criticized for its internal inconsistency (e.g., Renzulli, 1978); and the 1978 definition has the same problems. The different types of ability listed in the definition include three hypothetical, content-free ability areas: intellectual ability, creative ability, and leadership ability. The two other types of ability are associated with disciplines: specific academic ability, and ability in the performing and visual arts.

The federal definition has also been criticized by Renzulli (1978) for the lack of direction it provides local school personnel. He contends that the definition is often misinterpreted. Some school districts treat the six areas as mutually exclusive and set up different identification procedures for each. By contrast, other districts require only a high IQ score, regardless of the type of ability listed in their definition. Renzulli's criticism calls into question both the theoretical coherence of the definition and its functional utility. Nevertheless, many states have adopted definitions like the federal definition (Council of State Directors of Programs for the Gifted, 1985).

Because so many states have adopted definitions similar to the federal definition, we have chosen to organize the characteristics sections of this book on the basis of that definition. The chapters on intelligence, academic aptitude, creativity, leadership, and ability in the visual and performing arts elaborate the concepts identified with each of these kinds of talent and the characteristics associated with individuals who demonstrate superiority in them.

State definitions. Major pragmatic considerations for school systems and other agencies serving gifted children are (1) priorities regarding the type or types of ability the system is most concerned with developing and (2) budgetary constraints. These considerations determine both the content of the definition and the eligibility criteria that limit the scope of the definition. State and local definitions of giftedness determine who will receive special instruction. Different definitions suggest different identification procedures that locate different, if overlapping, populations of children.

One school system may define giftedness as exceptional academic ability and give scope to its definition by requiring scores above the 95th percentile on standardized individually administered achievement or aptitude tests. Another system, with different educational priorities, may define giftedness as exceptional ability in any of several areas, including, for example, academics, performing arts, or visual arts. Given the same proportion of funds to spend on gifted education, the school district with the broader definition could limit its gifted population by establishing a higher criterion level in each area. In general, the more limited the funds, the higher the level of giftedness required for eligibility for special programs.

Well over half the states' definitions include most of the abilities included in the federal definition. Forty-four states include intellectual ability, 42 specific academic ability, 36 creative ability, 32 ability in the arts, and 23 leadership ability (Council of State Directors of Programs for the Gifted, 1985). The highest priority is intellectual ability, perhaps reflecting the long history of research interest in that area. Of those states that include an

IQ cutoff in their definition, the most commonly named level is two standard deviations above the mean, or about the 97th or 98th percentile (Council of State Directors of Programs for the Gifted, 1985).

Marland (1972) estimated that in applying a broad definition of giftedness, such as that of the federal definition, *at least* 3 to 5 percent of the total school-age population would be considered gifted. It may be that states with mandates that require special education for all identified gifted children tend toward narrower definitions, such as the high-IQ definition, because they cannot afford to serve 5 percent of the school-age population in gifted programs. Where there is no mandate, and where local school systems determine whether or not to serve gifted children and how many and what kind to serve, a broad definition is more likely to be adopted, even though it will probably not be implemented very well (cf. Mitchell, 1981).

Instrumental Definitions

Two rationales support the provision of special programs for gifted students. The first is concern for the development of individual potential, a concern that strongly influences pedagogical definitions of giftedness. The second rationale is development of talent as a national resource.

The United States is not alone in expressing its concern for national security through efforts to find and use the talents of gifted individuals; all societies choose to nurture gifted individuals in accordance with the society's perceived values and needs (Kitano & Kirby, 1986). Indeed, concern over the interests of business and national security help to turn away some of the suspicions that gifted education arouses in citizens. Without such a compelling rationale, it is unlikely that the public would allow the expenditure of any funds for gifted programs.

National security.   According to Laycock, society must have the contributions of gifted individuals. It needs them for survival and for cultural enrichment. Laycock's book, *Gifted Children* (1979, preface), begins, "Gifted children are any society's prime asset." This sentiment, held by many citizens, offsets their resistance to gifted education. This feeling is confounded, however, with the suspicion that gifted children are not only an asset to society, but also *threatening* to the status quo. Such fears seemed justified during the late 1960s: The leadership of the student protest movement was composed largely of uncommonly talented (and uncommonly advantaged) students.

Gardner (1961) explains society's mixed feelings toward excellence. Such feelings probably condition the public's reactions toward gifted individuals. According to Gardner, the critical lines of tension in our society are between the emphasis on individual performance and the restraints on individual performance. These conflicting interests help to create what Kirk and Gallagher (1983) have called the love-hate relationship that exists between American society and its gifted individuals.

During times of political crisis, attention to the development of talent increases and consequently so does programming for the gifted. Tannenbaum (1981) has identified two peaks of interest in gifted children: the five years following the 1957 launching of Sputnik and the five years following the 1975 withdrawal of U.S. troops from Vietnam. Between those times, there was little interest in the gifted. In 1983, *A Nation At Risk,* published by the National Commission on Excellence in Education, reported troubling findings: U.S. students seemed to compare unfavorably with students from other world powers. The report emphasized the need for more attention to academic subjects, and it recommended that the federal government help fund and support efforts to meet the needs of the gifted and talented.

Business definitions.   Economic supremacy is considered by many to be essential to national security, and business has had a determining influence on education in the United States. This influence is documented by Raymond Callahan (1962) in *Education and the Cult of Efficiency.* According to Callahan, the influence of business over education has grown steadily since the early twentieth century. One of the first indications of business influence was change in the composition of school boards. They changed from large, mixed-interest groups to small groups of businessmen. This change, it was hoped, would enable schools to be run more like businesses, efficiently and economically.

At the same time, there was an effort to make the curriculum of the schools more practical. Vocational schools and courses were established, classical studies declined, and a strong current of anti-intellectualism began to appear, evidenced by such phrases as "mere scholastic education" or "mere book learning" (Callahan, 1962, p. 8).

Andrew Carnegie was one of the leading critics of the traditional curriculum and one of the strongest proponents of practical education. In his view, the secret of his own success and that of other business leaders was not book learning. He saw more value in ingenuity and common sense. Carnegie's view and that of other businessmen put pressure on school superintendents to develop practical curricula.

Historical records confirm that the superintendents responded to the pressures by making changes in the schools. Callahan (1962) quotes proceedings from the National Education Association that document such changes. For example, he quotes a bank president's congratulatory address to a group of school superintendents for their contribution to America's material progress. The bank president maintained that such progress was "a result of getting away, to an extent, from the mere scholastic education, and developing the practical side, making the school the place to learn how to manufacture. . ." (NEA Proceedings, 1901, cited in Callahan, 1962, p. 9).

Given the businessmen's interest in ingenuity and industry, business perspectives on giftedness have focused more on creativity than on intelligence. Divergent and productive thinking are important commodities in the business world, which has to keep marketing novel products and developing more efficient ways to solve problems. Programs for increasing creativity have emphasized industrial and technological applications. Osborn (1953), for example, devised a number of techniques, such as brainstorming, to help advertising personnel solve problems. Such programs and techniques have been imported directly from business to gifted education.

CHARACTERISTICS: EMPIRICAL VIEWS OF GIFTEDNESS

As the preceding discussion indicated, there is little consensus about what constitutes giftedness. Diverse interests view giftedness in rather different ways. How can one possibly know which view of giftedness is correct? Surely, theoreticians and practitioners can debate the matter indefinitely.

Can a perpetual debate be of much use to educators who want to help talented children get the most out of their years in public schools? The answer to that question is a qualified yes. Over the long term, knowledge is advanced by such debates in every field. On the other hand, the ambiguities of that debate complicate the educator's immediate job. The debate offers little in the way of practical guidance for designing good school programs or for developing further the ones already in existence.

One way to learn more about the concept of giftedness as it pertains to children in schools is to review the empirical research on gifted children. This section of the chapter begins by discussing the various kinds of empirical research about the characteristics of able students. Then it discusses the more difficult question of interpreting empirical results.

Research About Students' Characteristics

Studies of the characteristics of individuals who are said to be gifted can be classified into three groups: (1) case studies, (2) quantitative cross-sectional studies, and (3) longitudinal studies. Such studies will be reviewed throughout subsequent chapters, so a brief introduction to these general types of study follows.

Readers should remember that empirical research cannot ultimately determine which theoretical view of giftedness is best in general. It *can* help thoughtful readers decide the question for themselves, and it can help them make better-informed practical decisions with respect to children in schools.

Case studies. Case studies describe particular individuals or a number of individuals in depth. An empirical case study stays very close to verifiable observations (there are many other types of case studies). Hence, such a study typically includes a wealth of factual data and comparatively little critical analysis. Most case studies make rather interesting reading. Reading a number of case studies, however, ultimately yields only an impressionistic view of a category of individuals. Techniques other than the simple case study are needed if hypotheses about a category of individuals are to be examined carefully.

Case studies are reported throughout this textbook. Most of them are anecdotal in nature, and a number of them were gathered before inferential statistics became established in the social sciences.

Perhaps the most famous American case studies in gifted education are those prepared by Leta Hollingworth (1942). Intrigued by the use of the Stanford-Binet Intelligence Scale, Hollingworth described in detail 12 children who scored very high (above 180 IQ) on the test. (Hollingworth had also done earlier work with very low-scoring children.) She reported a variety of data about these high-scoring children, including information about their birth and infancy, school progress, and later development.

Two European scholars, Jean Piaget and Vad'im Krutetskii, have produced substantial research using what might be termed case study methods. Neither of these scholars, however, has used very sophisticated statistical techniques.

Jean Piaget was a renowned Swiss psychologist. His unit of analysis was an idealized *typical* child, rather than actual *exceptional* individuals (Fisher, 1987). Piaget's interest seems abstruse, remote, and impractical to many American educators, but it reflects his European intellectual background. He was interested more in philosophical and metaphysical questions (e.g., how is knowledge related to human growth?) than in practical pedagogical questions (e.g., what is good instruction in our schools?). Since the early 1970s American scholars, however, have adapted Piaget's techniques to the American context of research. Some of the work that has been influenced by the Piagetian method is reported in Chapter 8.

The most original use of case studies in research about *exceptional* talent is probably a Soviet achievement. To investigate mathematical talent, the Soviet psychologist Vad'im Krutetskii used a method of case study with over 200 children. His work, which began in the early 1960s, became available in the United States in the mid-1970s, largely through the efforts of Irving Wirszup and his colleagues at the University of Chicago. American researchers have just begun to exploit the methods developed by Krutetskii.

Case studies are used in enterprises other than basic research. Sometimes they are used to present the results of research in an anecdotal fashion. The Study of Mathematically Precocious Youth, for example, has often published case studies to dramatize the accomplishments of the talented students it serves. Case studies are also sometimes recommended as a means to develop program plans for gifted students (e.g., Baldwin, 1978; Maker, 1982).

Studies of the sort conducted by Krutetskii and Piaget are very expensive. They require intense interaction with each subject and equally intense analysis of the data accumulated during the interactions. Often the work takes decades to complete; in a sense, the scope of case study projects like these is so great that the work can never be considered complete.

Case studies are, in the United States, typically reserved for instances in which it is difficult to obtain a sufficiently large sample to permit quantitative analyses. In the United States, studies typically employ research designs that involve many subjects, a short time frame, and produce results at substantially less cost per subject than the European case study research cited previously. American empirical studies usually opt for efficiency of data collection and analysis, whereas European studies often opt for a complex theoretical analysis of data. Case studies offer more opportunity for such analysis than the *quantitative* methods favored by empirical researchers in the United States.

Quantitative cross-sectional studies.   Most of the studies reviewed in this textbook are based on quantitative analyses of the performance of selected samples on a variety of formal tests. Of these studies, most are *cross sections* of the performance of the individuals in the sample.

Quantitative methods are based on the statistical notion of generalizability. A number of conditions—most of which can be measured numerically—must be met before obtained findings can be said to represent a general finding. Two of these conditions are especially important.

First, the sample must be representative of the larger group for which it will be claimed that the findings are *characteristic*. Second, the sample must be large enough so that the researchers can say the findings are not due to chance. This second condition means that if the researcher is studying a large number of characteristics, or looking at small differences in characteristics, the sample must be rather large, perhaps including several hundred or several thousand subjects. These conditions are virtually impossible to meet in typical case study methods.

The cross-sectional studies reported in subsequent chapters are of several sorts. Among these are correlational studies. Many correlational studies were conducted in the earlier part of the century, following the development of the technique by Karl Pearson.

A "Pearson product-moment" is the most common type of correlation. It measures the strength of one variable's relationship to another, on the assumption that the relationship can be displayed graphically as a straight line. The more closely the relationship resembles a straight line, the stronger the correlation. High correlations between two conditions (e.g., performance on an IQ test and success in school) can be interpreted as indicating a *characteristic* relationship. The results of correlational studies are reported throughout this textbook. For example, the relationship between IQ and early reading is a topic in both Chapter 3 and Chapter 6; the relationship between academic performance and professional performance is a topic in Chapter 5.

The patterns among correlations of related characteristics have also intrigued quantitative researchers working with cross-sectional data. These studies are of basically two types. One method, developed very early in the twentieth century, is called "factor analysis" and has been applied widely to the study of individual characteristics. The goal of factor analysis is to create a kind of *synthetic characteristic* from a number of correlations among real characteristics.

Early researchers who used factor analysis gave many tests to a group of subjects and correlated all the subjects' performances on each pair of tests. Then they could construct a "factor" (a synthetic measure) with which most of the tests correlated highly. In this textbook factor analysis figures most strongly in discussions about creativity, intelligence, and academic talent (Chapters 3, 4, and 6). Stephen Gould has developed a very understandable explanation of factor analysis (Gould, 1981, pp. 243–250).

Another method of examining patterns of correlation is called "multiple regression." This method is used when researchers want to assign the sources of influence in one measure (called the "dependent variable") to a number of other measures (called "independent variables"). This technique has been used less frequently to study psychological and educational characteristics than to study the effectiveness of instruction or to examine the relationships among sociological characteristics. Some works that use multiple regression, however, are referenced in Chapters 2 and 11.

Longitudinal studies. Longitudinal studies follow a sample (called a "cohort") for a long period of time in order to chart their development. Lewis Terman identified such a cohort in the early 1920s, and he and his associates followed the progress of the cohort throughout their years in public school, in college and graduate school, in their professions, and into retirement.

The Terman study is the most extensive longitudinal study in educational research; and its topic is, of course, gifted students. The study illustrates very well the difficulties of conducting longitudinal research of this scope. For example, standards of research changed dramatically between 1920 and 1980. Terman would have designed a much different study, if, in 1920, he had had access to the tools and techniques (including computers) that were available even so long ago as 1960.

Nonetheless, the Terman study has collected masses of data that other researchers have begun to reanalyze. Some of this research is reported in Chapters 3, 10, and 11. In general, however, longitudinal studies are rare not only because of the technical problems mentioned previously, but also because the logistical problems of staff continuity and continual funding are difficult to resolve.

INTERPRETING EMPIRICAL RESULTS

Readers should remember that the basic material used in this textbook (American quantitative research) strongly influences the presentation. The empirical view presented here is a peculiarly American view. We believe that fact makes this research particularly applicable to the schooling of very talented students in the United States.

American researchers are often concerned with testing carefully defined hypotheses that seem to have clear implications for practice. The way in which hypotheses are defined and the way in which results are derived also convey the impression of practicality.

Hypotheses are designed to be tested statistically so that they can be shown to be either true or false within specified limits. Hence, both the hypotheses and the results of study can be stated simply. These facts help lend the status of objectivity to obtained results. There is another sense in which quantitative research methods can be said to be practical. They make possible the use of more subjects at lower cost in a shorter time period.

Recognizing Assumptions

Empirical study carries with it assumptions that those who use it must understand. Too often, educators are unaware of these assumptions. For a variety of reasons they may be unaware of the intellectual traditions that shape empirical social science research. Sometimes, teacher preparation programs include little theoretical work; sometimes introductory courses include no perspective other than that of empirical social science.

Here we want merely to point out some of the major assumptions of most American empirical science and to alert the reader to the existence of more complex views of education in general. These assumptions entail (1) a focus on the individual, (2) faith in the measurability of behavior as well as of invisible traits and constructs, and (3) faith in the utility of research as a guide to practice.

Focus on the individual.   In a pedagogical specialty like gifted education, virtually all the empirical research focuses on individuals. Teachers and other educators want to know what particular children who are said to be "gifted" are like; and they want to know, on the basis of such findings, how such children should be treated in schools. Hence, in gifted education, it seems especially natural that individuals should be the focus of research.

The values of our culture stress the importance of the individual, and they tend to deny the importance of other entities, such as social class, that might serve as "units of analysis." It is important to remember this point when one interprets the empirical view of giftedness.

Faith in measurability.   Most of the studies reported in this textbook are quantitative cross sections. They are often large studies of the performances of many individuals on tests. The tests assume that the behaviors, traits, or constructs they reflect are measurable. A critical requirement of such research is that the instruments used be valid and the measurements obtained be reliable.

There are two main problems with measurability. First, there is an important technical problem. The requirements of validity and reliability are not always met. (Some critics would say they are seldom met.) Research instruments are often "technically inadequate." That is, they are not good enough to perform some of the tasks for which they are used.

Second, there is an important theoretical problem. In defining hypotheses very narrowly—so that they can be tested statistically—researchers usually exclude from consideration much that might be relevant to the question. Intelligence tests are a good case in point. Alfred Binet, the real originator of intelligence tests, did not himself believe that a phenomenon so complex as intelligence could be measured easily. He certainly did not believe his test measured intelligence. It did, he believed, measure the likelihood that a student would benefit from instruction in the regular classroom. The test had a narrow practical purpose. When scholars and educators use IQ tests to define intelligence, they are straying very far from the original purpose.

The very great controversy that has emerged around this sort of misapplication of IQ tests is considered at length in Chapter 2. The discussion in that chapter is really a "case study" about the limitations of empirical research in the social sciences.

Faith in research as a guide to practice.   American educational researchers expect that their work will help shape what goes on in classrooms. They are, however, often frustrated in this expectation. It is no wonder. Researchers study a wide assortment of problems, using a wide variety of methods, and they often reach conclusions that are contradictory. It is probably accurate to say that research influences what goes on in classrooms only indirectly (Buchmann, 1987).

Although every research study that appears should *not* guide practice, it is true that understanding the reading, thinking, and writing that others have done about education can be a very good guide to working with students in schools. Teachers must be active participants in this endeavor, however. They cannot be told what to do: They must read, think, and decide for themselves. Disciplined inquiry cannot yield a formula for operating the schools. Too many things change in the course of a decade; schools and children are too different from one another, and so are teachers.

Hence in reading this textbook, educators should understand that we have tried to present empirical research about gifted students in a way that will help them think and decide for themselves what may make sense in the classroom. Chapter 12, however, presents our own interpretation of what makes sense in the classroom.

Applying Research About Characteristics

Research about characteristics addresses the question of what gifted students are like. In general, the phenomenon of concern to educators interested in gifted children is uncommon (or "exceptional") talent. Many kinds of exceptional talent, and many circumstances under which exceptional talent exists, are discussed in subsequent chapters. Of what use is this knowledge?

Since the report Sidney Marland made in 1972 about gifted students to the Congress, programs for gifted children have grown rapidly. The rate of increase in these programs seems to be slowing. A great deal needs to be done to improve these programs (Cox, Daniel, & Boston, 1985). Some programs are elitist (Weiler, 1978) or even anti-intellectual (A. Howley, 1986; C. Howley, 1986).

The source of these problems, it seems to us, is a mismatch between the kinds of students identified (i.e., the characteristics of identified students) and the types of programs that are offered to students. This problem cripples the effectiveness of many programs. These programs do not supply the kind of instruction required by the students they serve.

Across the nation, many states have adopted a definition of giftedness that includes many of the types of talent described in subsequent chapters of this textbook. At the same time, the programs they offer serve primarily high-IQ children (Council of State Directors of Programs for the Gifted, 1985); and the high-IQ children served in these programs do not have access to the flexible pacing most appropriate for them (Cox et al., 1985).

If the schools are serious about serving a wide variety of talent— general intellectual ability, specific academic talent, artistic talent, creative talent, leadership ability, and manual talent (e.g., gifted students in vocational schools)—then educators will need to know much more about students who are talented in each of those categories.

This is a mammoth undertaking; it is as if educators concerned with mentally retarded children advocated five or six subcategories of mental retardation, with differentiated programming required for each subcategory. In gifted education, this plan has not only been proposed, but it has been translated into state and local regulations.

In applying empirical findings about creative individuals, artists, high-IQ students, early readers, and precocious math students, educators need to consider several problems simultaneously:

- Which instruments select students who exhibit these characteristics?
- Which characteristics can be addressed by instruction?
- What kind of instruction is needed?
- How can instruction be arranged efficiently?

Chapter 12 deals with some of these questions, primarily for students who demonstrate general intellectual ability and specific academic talent. In general, however, we note that although other kinds of talented students can be *described*, it is impossible to locate technically adequate instruments to *identify* particular individuals who exhibit those characteristics.

Despite this impediment, however, the empirical literature on the characteristics of gifted children suggests that many gifted children possess multiple talents. Perhaps the tendency to possess multiple talents is the reason multicategorical definitions of giftedness identify so many high-IQ students and so few students with specific talents. If this is the case, then most gifted programs, as Cox and colleagues (1985) note, also need to improve the comprehensiveness of their offerings.

TALENT IN THE SCHOOL SETTING

The development of talent seems to be a logical concern of schools. Most school districts state goals such as this: to enable each student to develop to his or her fullest potential. Such goals are ambitious in the context of universal schooling. Perhaps the difficulty of accomplishing these sorts of goals leads schools to identify only a small group of students who show the greatest promise. If schools view a minority of students as talented, then the development of talent becomes a more limited, and hence, more manageable enterprise.

Global definitions of talent, however, suggest a different perspective. If schools cannot predict the adult contributions that will be made by children, then they should prepare all children to perform optimally. Common sense suggests that a well-educated majority will collectively accomplish more than a well-educated minority. In spite of this logic, schools may be unable, in practice, to accomplish such an encompassing goal. Political, economic, and even pedagogical realities militate against this goal.

This section of the chapter examines the schools' role in cultivating the potential of school children. It considers issues related to (1) the identification of talents, (2) the social context of talent development, and (3) the educational response to talent.

Finding Talent

The method that a school district uses to identify its talented students depends, in large measure, on its definition of talent. It also depends on the resources available to the school district, though this dependency is less obvious. Resources govern the quality and quantity of services available to those students who are considered to be talented. They also govern the size of the group that can be identified as talented.

In wealthy, suburban school districts, for example, a large number of students are presumed to have the academic talents needed for the successful completion of undergraduate programs in selective colleges and universities. Such districts provide students with the rigorous educational experiences that will prepare them for success in college. This sort of preparation depends on the district's ability to bring together a number of pedagogical resources: excellent teachers, a challenging curriculum, supportive guidance counseling, and a community of receptive students. Uncommon leadership can help other districts provide these things.

On the other hand, poorer districts have in general a *much* more difficult task, and not only because they lack material resources. Such districts may not expect to send a majority of students to college. The expectation of these schools mirrors the expectation of the communities they serve. College attendance may not be a value of such communities; it may not even be perceived as a promising avenue for economic advancement. Such districts may identify only a small percentage of students as talented, or they may fail to identify *any* students as talented.

Most school districts, however, are neither wealthy nor impoverished. Instead, they serve students from a variety of economic backgrounds. In these districts, the identification of talent often reflects, though not perfectly, the social structure of the community: The children of local professionals are often placed in the school's gifted program. Less often are the children of unskilled workers selected for such programs.

The following interpretation is one way to synthesize the preceding observations: The wealthier the district, the more is talent perceived as universal; and the poorer the district, the more is talent considered a rarity. Some hereditarians (e.g., Jensen, 1973) explain this educational disparity as a difference in the structure of reality. According to their argument, society rewards talent through its economic structures. Hence, wealth is a proximate measure of talent. The logic of the hereditarian position leads to the following conclusion: Wealthy school districts identify more talented students than poorer districts because such districts contain more talented students.

Psychometric definitions of talent have been used to support the hereditarian position. After all, high socioeconomic status (high-SES) students *do* score higher on intelligence tests than do low-SES students. A more generous view of talent, however, accords environment a much greater role. Such a view suggests that children's social environments condition their performance on standardized intelligence tests and other measures of performance. Even more important, this perspective emphasizes the role of schooling in the cultivation of talent.

Rarity and universality. Definitions of giftedness vary dramatically in their scope. According to some definitions, giftedness represents excellence in *any* area of human endeavor. Other definitions relate giftedness much more closely to academic knowledge. Both perspectives, however, have important ramifications for schools.

Although schools might want to develop all of the talents of all their students, very few of them have the resources to accomplish this goal. Given these conditions, schools may wisely opt to identify as gifted the students who are least likely to benefit from grade-level instruction in the regular classroom. At the same time, however, schools can increase their responsiveness to the needs of all students. The literature on school effectiveness reiterates this position: Certain school practices are capable of cultivating higher achievement, even in schools in the poorest communities.

Significant changes in the priorities of our society are necessary before schools can attempt to develop all talents. Universal schooling has limited effects—imparting basic skills and propagating the knowledge believed necessary for good citizenship. In schools designed to accomplish these minimal outcomes, it can be difficult to nurture some kinds of uncommon talent. In spite of their limited resources, however, public schools can address certain types of uncommon talent. In particular, the development of *academic* talent does seem possible in our educational system as presently structured.

Practical methods of identification. When schools choose to identify academically talented students, they have several alternatives. They may base their identification on students' grades, intelligence test scores, or achievement test scores.

Many districts attempt to identify students who are talented in areas other than academics. For example, talent in sports is an area addressed by most public schools. School athletic programs provide an interesting model of identification practice. Large groups of students are provided with training in basic skills through the school's physical education programs, and those who perform well or who enjoy the sports activities choose to try out for teams. Usually the district supports a hierarchy of teams: Intramural teams are the least selective, whereas varsity teams are the most selective.

Students who are selected for teams are drilled in the skills and strategies of the sport. From among those who are trained, the most excellent are selected to perform in competitive events.

Few other school endeavors give so much opportunity for talent development. In schools that support excellent drama, dance, music, and art programs, however, the selection process resembles the one for athletics. Talented students audition for parts in plays or for places in the orchestra. Art students prepare portfolios of their best work. In such programs, an expert in art, drama, dance, or music, or panel of such experts, selects the students with the most potential.

Some districts use a relatively broad definition of giftedness to select students to participate in gifted programs. They may use multiple selection criteria in order to *restrict* the number of students who are identified or they may use multiple selection criteria in order to *increase* the number of students identified.

In either case, however, the identified group will be composed of students with a variety of abilities and needs. Students identified on the basis of one type of measure vary considerably from those identified with another type of measure. Because these students do not have similar educational needs, they cannot be served well in a single gifted program; yet rarely do districts maintain separate gifted programs for intellectually gifted students, creatively gifted students, and students with leadership potential.

Error and equity.   Educators pay more or less attention to issues of equity depending on their purposes for identifying talented students (e.g., development of individual potential or a concern for the national security). Ensuring equity complicates fulfillment of these purposes. In order to ensure equity, educators must develop identification procedures that account for social *inequities*. Such procedures can be perceived as impractical.

Some educators recommend using subjective measures of talent in order to offset the cultural bias of standardized tests (cf. Council of State Directors of Programs for the Gifted, 1985). Districts that use subjective measures reason that, if they avoid using standardized tests altogether, they will be free to include more poor and minority students in programs for the gifted. Although this observation is correct, it means that identification depends solely on the good will of those who administer the program. This situation forces districts to rely on unreliable measures that may have little relationship to talent.

There is no reason to believe that subjective measures of leadership ability, creativity, or accomplishment will identify the most talented students from among poor, black, or Hispanic families. Depending on the good will of the subjective evaluators, districts are free to include more poor students in gifted programs; however, they are also free to exclude all poor students when they use subjective measures. This degree of uncertainty is inherent in the practice of subjective measurement.

Given what is known about cultural and racial prejudice, it is probably very unwise to put a great deal of faith in the fairness of subjective measures, or the good will of program administrators. Objective measures (e.g., standardized tests) have the advantage of allowing educators to identify and even quantify their degree of prejudice. We know, for example, what the differences are between the black mean and the white mean on IQ tests. We are very unlikely, by contrast, to understand how or to what degree unexamined assumptions influence subjective judgments.

Critical to the use of objective measures, however, is a healthy regard for error. Educators should remember that any obtained score *always* reflects some degree of error (see Box 1–1). Once we understand the degree of test error that is reflected in the scores of a relatively heterogeneous norming sample, we can begin to appreciate the degree of error that might be reflected in the comparison of a minority student's scores to those of a predominantly white, middle-class norming group. This understanding leads to the recommendation that minority students be compared to a group of their peers. Statistical methods for making such comparisons exist. The process is sometimes referred to as *local norming*.

BOX 1–1   *How True Is an Obtained Score?*

What does it mean when a student obtains a particular score on an IQ test? Is a score of 126 significantly different from a score of 130? These questions can be answered through an explanation of the related concepts of test "reliability" and "standard error of measure."

The reliability of a measure is the degree to which successive scores obtained on an infinite number of potential administrations of a test cluster around a hypothetical "true" score. Statistically, test reliability is reported as a correlation. The dispersion of scores around the hypothetical true score can be calculated as a standard deviation. This special kind of standard deviation is called the "standard error of measure" (SEM). Using the standard error of measure, evaluators can determine the likelihood that a student's *obtained* score reflects a true score within a particular range.

Typically, test scores obtained on individually administered IQ tests are reported on a standard score scale (mean = 100, S = 15 or S = 16, depending on the test). One SEM on such a test may be 3, 4, or 5 points, again, depending on the test.

What this means about a given obtained score is that it is likely to fall within a range that is equal to twice the size of the SEM. This range is known as the "confidence interval." If the SEM is 5 points, then the likely range is 10 points. This calculation reflects the fact that we speak of a score in consideration of the test's SEM.

Usually scores are reported as the obtained score plus or minus 1 SEM. It is possible, however, to report a score in consideration of 2, or even 3, SEMs. The more error is taken into consideration in the reporting of the score, the more likely will the predicted range be accurate.

What does a score mean when it is reported in consideration of 1 SEM? It means that in approximately 68 percent of the hypothetical administrations of the test, the obtained score will fall within the range described by the SEM (i.e., the confidence interval). If, for example, a student obtains a score of 130 on a Stanford-Binet IQ test, this obtained score should be expressed in terms of the confidence interval. One SEM represents a 68 percent confidence interval. Hence, the student's score will probably fall within the range of 125 to 135. How sure can we be that the score will fall within this range? We can be 68 percent sure.

What can we do, if we want to be more certain of a score range? We can increase the confidence interval by reporting a score in terms of more than 1 SEM. With a range of 2 SEMs we can be 95 percent confident; with a range of 3 SEMs we can be 99 percent confident. Returning to our example, we find that the obtained IQ score of 130 stands a 95 percent chance of representing a "true" score that falls in the range of 120 to 140 and a 99 percent chance of representing a "true" score in the range of 115 to 145. In other words, we can be quite certain that the student's intellectual ability falls somewhere in the above average to very superior range. This degree of certainty doesn't help us decide, however, whether or not to place the student in the gifted program. In fact, it makes our decision more difficult. How can we be sure that this student is *truly* gifted? The truth is: We can't.

Rewarding and Punishing Talent

Once a school district identifies talented students, by whatever means, it must decide what to do for these students. Almost always identification is followed by placement into some type of program. The nature of the program, and how it fits into the school curriculum as a whole, depends on the way talent is viewed in the school and the community.

Scholars, including both educators and historians, differ in their interpretations of how talent is treated in the United States. According to some scholars, talent is rewarded through the economic and political structures of society. According to others, it is not rewarded at all, but is even punished. The view that talent leads to disproportionate rewards suggests that programs for developing talent are likely to support elitist aims (Feldman, 1979). The view that talent is not appreciated, on the other hand, suggests that programs for developing talent exist in an unsupportive—and even anti-intellectual—context.

Elitism.   To determine whether or not gifted programs are elitist, we need to analyze their aims. Programs that *do* make extensive provisions to cultivate talents are probably *not* elitist. They serve a well-defined group of students, their purposes are consonant with the general aims of education, and they provide instruction in response to the identification of talents. When such programs make a special effort to include poor and minority students, they probably counter elitism.

Other programs, however, offer talented students special opportunities that do not contribute in substantial ways to the development of their talents. These programs provide "enriching" experiences such as field trips and brainstorming sessions. Educators, however, would have a difficult time demonstrating that such programs are *not* elitist. Since all students would benefit from the activities included in such programs, why should only a few be permitted to participate? (For a thoughtful discussion of the elitist nature of such programs, see Weiler's 1978 article, "The Alpha Children: California's Brave New World for the Gifted." For a more theoretical discussion, see Aimee Howley's 1986 article, "Gifted Education and the Spectre of Elitism.")

Anti-intellectualism.   A number of scholars have observed the anti-intellectual character of schools in the United States. Coleman's (1961) study, *Adolescent Society,* suggests that high schools reward prowess in sports and physical appearance much more than they reward scholarship. Similar impressions emerge from the naturalistic studies of working-class and middle-class schools (e.g., Wilcox, 1982). By contrast, studies of classrooms in exclusive private schools reveal an emphasis on scholarship and critical thinking (e.g., Anyon, 1980; Jackson, 1981).

In order for talent development to be pursued systematically in U.S. school districts, communities will need to support intellectual values. Such values seem, however, to conflict with the practical values of the U.S. political economy. Until intellectual and artistic work is endorsed for its own sake, rather than for its utility, programs for talented students will be in jeopardy. Such programs will, at the whim of legislators, school boards, or school administrators, be replaced by other programs that—at a given time—appear to be of more practical value.

Developing Talent

In spite of claims that it might be elitist and in spite of the sometimes anti-intellectual context of schooling, talent development nevertheless seems a worthy enterprise for public schools to undertake. It is important work for several reasons:

- It enables individuals to achieve to their greatest potential.
- It prevents students from encountering the wasteful boredom of work that is not challenging.
- It trains even the most facile students in the ethos of hard work.
- It advances the intellectual and aesthetic legacy of Western civilization.

Schools that choose to engage in talent development can (1) implement programs that meet the needs of a small minority of students who are identified as talented and (2) improve instructional programs for all students. These two approaches need not be mutually exclusive, so long as gifted education does not provide programs that are elitist.

Gifted programs.   Gifted programs should be based on the characteristics of the students who are identified as talented, in specific, and the characteristics of schools, in general. Most manageable within public schools are programs that address the needs of academically talented students. In general, the business of public schools is to cultivate academic learning. Hence, it would be practicable for schools to identify the most academically apt students and provide them with advanced instruction. This practice would meet the needs of such students, and it would enhance the academic climate of schools.

Even when the content of public school gifted programs is academic, the instructional methods of the program may not conform to the characteristics of academically talented students. Too often advanced content is not taught at an advanced conceptual level. Since academically talented students are usually characterized by superior abstract reasoning, gifted programs should provide learning experiences that are conceptually complex. Such experiences are based on extensive involvement with textual materials. They provide the opportunity to critique, debate, discuss, and apply ideas.

School improvement.   Talent development is best accomplished in schools that use effective practices. In such schools, the need to identify a select group of the most capable students may be unnecessary. Such schools provide a climate that supports academic learning. They enable all students to progress rapidly through instruction at their level of performance, and they encourage poor and minority students to excel academically.

Even in schools where appropriate practices have a strong positive effect on academic achievement, talent development may be limited. Such schools may deliver high-quality instruction in basic skills but may neglect to provide experiences that encourage critical thinking or foster respect for intellectual endeavors. According to Timar and Kirp (1987):

> Excellence is a difficult product for educational policymakers to deliver. High academic standards may require some individuals—students, teachers, parents, administrators—to change their attitudes about schooling. One of the underlying assumptions, for example, is that students can be made to value education intrinsically. An appreciation of education for its own sake, it is thought, can be fostered with some clever policy engineering. Making class periods longer, requiring more school days each year, promoting enrollment in academic courses, creating a curriculum that emphasizes basics, and curtailing students' extracurricular activities are generally thought to be ways of redressing mediocrity. (p. 312)

Schools—even the most effective—may have a difficult time providing appropriate programs for developing certain kinds of talent. Because of limited resources, schools often cannot provide the extensive sort of training in art, music, dance, or drama that is required for the development of talents in these areas. Talent development in music, for example, requires quite extraordinary resources: private lessons, opportunities for solo performance, opportunities to perform in ensembles, ear training, instruction in music history, and instruction in music theory. Such a range of educational experiences is available in only a limited number of public schools, usually so-called magnet schools in large urban areas.

When schools are unable to provide programs for certain sorts of talent development, they should encourage capable students to seek appropriate out-of-school training. Schools with an abiding interest in providing poor and minority students with equal access to programs—even those that are offered outside of the school—should help such students obtain the necessary scholarship assistance.

Summary

This chapter introduced the notion of characteristics in gifted education. The discussion examined definitions of giftedness—theoretical views of giftedness as a social attribute or as a psychological construct, and functional views of giftedness for educational purposes and for other specific goals. The discussion showed that functional definitions had clearer implications for practice, whereas theoretical definitions offered wider scope for reflection about human nature, social interaction, and talent development throughout society in general.

While definitions provide a context for understanding giftedness, they cannot give a detailed view of what gifted individuals are like. Definitions, after all, are synthetic statements. Hence, the middle section of this chapter described the value of empirical research about various types of exceptionally talented individuals. It described broad categories of empirical research and discussed the origins and uses, in particular, of representative techniques of quantitative research. The middle part of the chapter concluded with a discussion of the interpretation of empirical results—recognizing the assumptions of empirical research and the applications of empirical research to the education of gifted students.

The final section of this chapter discussed the treatment of talent in the public schools. Discussion here contrasted the notions of rarity and universality with respect to the identification of talent, the practical methods for dealing with talent in the schools, and the related issues of testing error and equity. In particular, two empirically based ways to achieve equity in programs for gifted students were mentioned. The discussion also considered the twin issues of elitism and anti-intellectualism in gifted programs, and suggested ways in which that dilemma might be resolved. Finally, the need to develop talent was related not only to improving gifted programs, but to improving schools in general.

2

Heredity and Environment

Focusing Questions

1. Is there a difference between artificial early giftedness and real giftedness? Describe the sense in which the adage "early bloom, early rot" is true.
2. What sorts of studies have been done to investigate the degree to which levels of intelligence can be attributed to genetic or environmental causes? What are some of the specific problems of these studies? Some of the general problems?
3. How is it possible—in both hereditarian and environmentalist perspectives—for children to be more intelligent than their parents? What evidence supports this phenomenon in each case?
4. If the source of all variability in individuals' IQs could be attributed to genetic cause, could we therefore infer that group differences in IQ were caused by genetic differences?
5. How are the preceding questions related to the identification of giftedness in minority children? What advantages and disadvantages are associated with alternative methods of identifying minority children?
6. If giftedness is not genetically determined, are gifted programs defensible? Why not, or in what way?

THE NATURE AND NURTURE OF THE DEBATE ABOUT NATURE AND NURTURE

The terms of the nature-nurture controversy form the subject of this chapter. Discussion considers the hereditarian and environmental views about the relative influence of genetic endowment and social circumstance on the acquisition of intelligence. This controversy is important to gifted educators for several reasons:

- Identification of giftedness most often depends on high IQ scores.
- Few black, Hispanic, and American Indian children have been placed in gifted programs.
- Elitist conceptions of giftedness rest heavily on the belief that intellectual ability is both genetically determined and unchangeable.
- One's view of the controversy leads to certain conclusions about the degree to which talent development is possible.

Whether gifted children are born gifted or whether they are gifted because of their environment has long been a matter of controversy. Most teachers and parents in the United States, however, assume that children's intelligence is inherited. In fact, they tend to see obvious environmental advantage as inducing an *artificial* kind of ability, not real giftedness.

They may, for example, believe that kindergarten students whose parents have helped them learn to read display an artificial ability. They often predict that such artificial abilities will disappear as the special conditions of the home are replaced by the normal conditions of school. They see the environmental advantages as a kind of crutch that truly bright children can do without.

This viewpoint sometimes appears to be confirmed by experience. To a certain extent, the adage "early bloom, early rot" is correct. School can equalize children's abilities, and in the case of gifted children, the equalization means a *drop* in achievement. The leveling influence of a curriculum designed for the average student often does have an adverse effect on gifted students' achievement, regardless of early advantages in their environment.

Research Difficulties

This issue is troublesome. There appears to be no feasible experimental design that can answer with certainty the question of the relative influence of heredity and environment on human cognitive behavior. In laboratory studies of animals, genetically related individuals can be raised in carefully controlled environments, but the environment cannot be controlled very effectively in experiments with humans. Thus, studies to determine the major influences on human intelligence cannot sort out the effects of environment from those of heredity. Scientists, of course, keep trying even in the face of this difficulty. Their continued efforts attest to the significance of the question.

Difficulties in accounting for sources of variability in IQ.   The social implications of the issue of nature and nurture are suggested by the position of scientists on the controversy, which virtually always reflects their politics and social status. One study (Pastore, 1949) found that among 24 scientists, 11 of the 12 liberals were environmentalists and 11 of the 12 conservatives were hereditarians. Another study (Sherwood & Nataupsky, 1968) showed a relationship between opinion on this issue and socioeconomic factors. Of over 80 scientists studied, those who had been the first-born, who had grandparents born in the United States, who had parents with higher educational levels, who had higher grades in college, and who had grown up in rural communities tended to interpret intelligence test scores in a hereditarian fashion.

As Gage and Berliner (1975) point out, the results of these studies weaken researchers' claims of scientific objectivity on this controversial issue. Gould (1981) carries this point even further in his book, *The Mismeasure of Man*. He provides examples not only of biased results, but of fraudulent results used to support hereditarian arguments. (If the advocates of environmental sources of superior intelligence have fudged their results as much as the other side, they have been very fortunate in not getting caught.)

Practical value of the research question.   Researchers have repeatedly tried to discover how much variation in individual behavior on IQ and other academic tests is explained by hereditary factors and how much is explained by environmental factors. Although this question is not one that can be answered without qualification, the literature includes a wide range of estimates.

Arthur Jensen, perhaps the most well-known proponent of the hereditarian view, opted for an 80 percent heredity figure in his 1969 article, "How Much Can We Boost IQ and Scholastic Achievement?" Christopher Jencks (Jencks, et al., 1972), an equally well-known proponent of the environmental explanation of intelligence, estimated the heredity figure to be about 45 percent. Some researchers believe that the percent contributed by heredity may be even smaller (e.g., Lewontin, Rose, & Kamin, 1984).

Some, on the other hand, (e.g., Hunt, 1961) don't even think we should ask the question. They have recommended that, instead of investing resources in attempts to make better guesses, specific influences should be investigated. Such investigations have been undertaken, but they are not likely to get the same attention that studies of the more controversial question get. The broader studies deal with an ideological question that reflects predominant views of the mainstream culture.

RESEARCH ON THE NATURE VERSUS NURTURE QUESTION

The types of research studies that have been used to argue for innate differences in the intelligence both of individuals and of different racial or ethnic groups are (1) comparisons of twins' and other siblings' intelligence test scores, (2) comparisons of intelligence test scores of adoptive and natural parents with the test scores of their adopted and natural children, and (3) comparisons of the test scores (both IQ and achievement) of different racial and ethnic groups with the scores of the white majority.

Twin Studies

Studies of identical and fraternal twins have served as a mainstay for research on hereditary versus environmental factors in cognitive development for over a century. Galton's *Inquiries into Human Faculty and Its Development* (1883) included studies of monozygotic (identical) twins and dyzygotic (fraternal) twins. As one of the most eminent English scientists of that time, and a staunch proponent of heredity as the exclusive source of human abilities, Galton influenced the thinking of both English and American scientists. One of the most prominent among them was Cyril Burt, whose twin studies formed the foundation for even later studies, such as those of Arthur Jensen. Burt's results, however, which supported a hereditarian view of intelligence, have been discredited because they were falsified.

Most twin studies have found that the strength of the correlation between IQ scores tends to increase with both genetic and environmental similarity. For identical twins raised together, the correlation coefficient is, on the average about 0.85. When identical twins are raised separately their IQ scores tend to correlate about 0.75 (Gage & Berliner, 1975). The fact that both of these correlations are higher than correlations between either fraternal twins or nontwin siblings has been used to argue that heredity is more important than environment.

The argument proceeds as follows: If identical twins—whose heredity is identical—are more alike in IQ test scores even when they are raised in different environments than fraternal twins raised in the same environment, then heredity must influence IQ scores more than does environment. Kamin (1981), however, suggests alternate explanations for the twin study findings.

Alternate interpretation of findings from twin studies. According to Kamin, one reason identical twins *raised together* show a higher correlation of IQ score than fraternal twins is that identical twins are treated similarly and tend to spend a great deal of time together. In other words, their environment is more similar than that of fraternal twins and nontwin siblings. Kamin found that the IQ scores of identical twins whose parents reported that they had tried to treat them the same were higher than between identical twins whose parents reported that they had not tried to treat them the same.

In further support of his argument, Kamin notes that the similarity of IQ scores varies with gender, whereas the similarity in height does not. Female twins' IQ scores are more similar than male twins' scores. Kamin believes that this result is obtained because female twins are usually closer together more of the time (for example, they usually sleep in the same room) than are male twins. There is no gender difference in correlations of the height of female twin pairs and male twin pairs, however. Kamin thinks this different correlation pattern stems from the fact that height is highly heritable and IQ score is not.

On the other hand, nontwin siblings are treated less similarly than identical or fraternal twins. Moreover, their environments are less similar: they are born at different times and have different age-mates, for example. Kamin claims that these differences, not different heredity, explain the lower correlation of non-twin siblings' scores.

Cyril Burt's influence. Burt's discredited study (e.g., Burt, 1966) is the largest study correlating the IQ scores of separated identical twins. This study formed the foundation of many hereditarians' belief in the profound influence of heredity in determining IQ score. Cyril Burt's articles were supposedly based on 53 twin pairs. The IQ correlation of these separated twins was very high, higher than that reported in other studies. More significant, however, was his assertion that the environments of the separated pairs were totally dissimilar. This meant that their similar scores were due only to similar heredity.

According to the authors of *Not In Our Genes* (Lewontin et al., 1984), there are several objections to conclusions favoring heredity as a factor in the high correlation of IQ scores of separated twins. Lewontin, Rose, and Kamin cite the ready acceptance of Burt's study by other professionals as a reason to doubt the hereditarian thesis. According to these authors, such ready acceptance raises questions about the objectivity of the scientists who incorporated Burt's results into their work.

They contend that the implausibility of Burt's reports should have been noted at once: Burt failed to provide a description of *how* he collected his data, *when* it was collected, or *where* it was collected. He did not even *name the IQ test* he used. More critical readers observed that some of Burt's correlations were "impossibly consistent." Further investigation led to the discovery that Burt had collected *no data at all* during the time period when he was purportedly studying separated twins. Once Burt's results were impugned, so were the results of those who had based much of their argument on his findings.

Problems with the research design. Lewontin, Rose, and Kamin (1984) also raise questions about the validity of all separated twin studies. Weakening the validity of other such studies is the fact that the research design yields inevitably biased results. Twins who have truly been raised apart—that is, separated from birth—may not know of each other's existence. These twins cannot respond to the appeals of scientists for volunteers. Inspection of the data on most "separated" twins reveals that they were not actually raised separately.

For example, Shields's (1978) study included "separated" twin pairs that had been reared in related branches of the same family. There were only 13 pairs in which the two twins had been reared in unrelated families. The most common pattern shown in the study was for the biological mother to rear one of the twins and the maternal grandmother or aunt to rear the other. The IQ correlation of the pairs reared in the same family network was significantly higher than the correlation of the pairs reared in unrelated families. This difference is an environmental effect because the twin pairs are genetically identical. Also, there is probably an environmental influence even on the twins who were reared in unrelated families because they were reared by close family friends. The Shields study required only that at some time during childhood the twins had been reared in different homes for at least five years. Many of their subjects had spent most of their lives together.

Parent-Child Studies

The other mainstay of research on genetic and environmental sources of intelligence is the study of correlations between the IQ scores of adopted children and the scores of their natural and adoptive parents. Most of the research from this approach shows higher correlations between children and their natural parents than between the children and their adoptive parents. However, Kamin (1981) questions the results of these studies. He notes problems with the socioeconomic status (SES) classifications and reports that the Munsinger (1975) study, one of the most famous of recent studies, has been discredited and should be discarded.

Methodological problems. There are some problems inherent in the design of all of the studies of adoptive parents and their children. First, adoptive parents constitute a special group that, in general, differs on variables that are not adequately "captured by demographic measures of environment" (Kamin, 1981, p. 118). This restricted range of environmental variance alone can account for lower correlations between adopted children and their adoptive parents than between adopted children and their natural parents. Kamin cites improved studies (e.g., Horn, Loehlin, & Willerman, 1973; Scarr & Weinberg, 1976) that suggest a higher correlation between the IQ scores of children and their adoptive parents. The improved designs and improved statistical analyses of these more recent studies result in a significantly lower estimate of heritability than earlier studies; so low, in fact, that, according to Kamin (1981), even behavior geneticists who conduct adoption studies have begun to point out that some of the data suggest *zero* heritability.

Reanalysis of early studies. McAskie and Clarke (1976) have reanalyzed data from two major early studies, Snugg (1938) and Skodak and Skeels (1949). In these studies, adopted children were found to have much higher scores than their natural parents. The reanalysis of these data also produced quite low correlations between parent and child IQs.

Snugg reported a regression of 17 points toward the mean for a sample of 312 foster children. Average natural parent IQ computed from the Snugg data was 78, while the mean IQ of the offspring was 95. The correlation of parent-offspring IQ was 0.13.

In the Skodak and Skeels data, average natural parent IQ was 86, and mean offspring IQ was 106, a regression of 20 points, which overshot the mean. The correlation of natural parent-offspring IQ was 0.38. In addition, three of five comparative cohorts in the original study regressed from 1 standard deviation below the mean (parent IQ) to 1 standard deviation above the mean (offspring IQ). Regression is not predicted by the genetic model in the case of average parent IQ (McAskie & Clarke, 1976), and these extreme differences in the scores of children and their natural parents argues for a large environmental influence on intelligence.

McAskie and Clarke (1976) also reported the very low correlation coefficient (r = 0.08) of Terman and Oden's comparison of the IQs of their gifted subjects with the IQs of their parents. The mean parent IQ was 152 and the mean child IQ (parent and offspring were of the same chronological age at testing) was 133. A restricted range helps to explain this low correlation, however.

When we consider that Terman and Oden (1959) argued that their subjects provided a relatively homogeneous environment for their children, this figure is still surprising. Genetic theory says that as the environment becomes more stable, or homogeneous, the proportion of variance attributable to genetic causes becomes greater. A high correlation between IQ scores of parents and their children cannot answer the question of whether the correlation reflects environmental or hereditary factors. Given valid and reliable tests, however, a low correlation is evidence against strong hereditary influence.

Group Differences and Studies of Test Score Differences

Do different groups of students display systematic differences in IQ? Can such differences, if they exist, be ascribed to differences in the genetic background of the groups? These questions are among those most often asked in the nature versus nurture debate. These questions are still asked, despite the fact that the popular hereditarian view is now known to rest on shaky findings (i.e., Burt's discredited studies). In addition, as Gould (1981) points out, even if IQ differences in individuals could be ascribed to genetic causes, it would still be difficult to ascribe *group differences* to genetic causes. Samuda (1975) states four premises about IQ tests that limit the validity of any hypothesis about racial differences in intelligence:

> The scientific basis for the existence of racial differences in intelligence rests on four premises. (1) The concept of intelligence is well understood. (2) Intelligence tests provide a true and reliable measure of intellectual functioning, and the differences in scores reflect differences in intellectual potential. . . . (3) Both whites and blacks represent separate but homogeneous groups racially distinct. (4) The effects of the variance in physiological, sociocultural, and economic conditions of both groups can be ignored. (p. 40)

These unsound premises are not just the province of hereditarians. Some researchers who subscribe to environment as a major influence in *achievement* subscribe to all but the last of these four unsound premises. Usually such researchers attribute the mean differences in the IQ scores of black and white children solely to the debilitating effects of minority attitudes and habits. Hence, the investigations of intellectual inequality (e.g., Coleman, 1966; Mosteller & Moynihan, 1972; Passow, Goldberg, & Tannenbaum, 1967; Williams, 1970) attempt to discover those features of the culture of the disadvantaged that make them appear intellectually deficient. Such analyses are more cogent, however, if they acknowledge that disadvantage may be a function of the way in which "disadvantaged" groups are treated by "advantaged" groups.

Jensen's research.   The influence of disadvantaged status has been reported even by hereditarians. Jensen (1969), for example, found that socioeconomic status (SES), not racial or ethnic origin, produced IQ differences. Of course, Jensen believes that differences in intelligence are inherited. Hence, he believes that the poverty of blacks is a result of their lower intelligence. Those who believe the environment has the greater influence usually advocate the opposite causal relationship, that is, that the low intelligence test scores are the effect of poverty.

In his research, Jensen also found that children from middle-class families earned higher scores on tests requiring reasoning than did poor children; he observed less difference in their ability to memorize. Jensen cites the difference in reasoning scores to support the hereditarian position. The difference in reasoning ability, however, can be explained as a result of differences in schooling. Lower-SES children are schooled differently from middle- and upper-SES children (Anyon, 1980; Oakes, 1985; Wilcox & Moriarity, 1977); and one of these differences is that wealthier children are encouraged to reason and to consider the implications of their actions, whereas lower-SES children are encouraged to do what they are told without questioning authority (e.g., Wilcox, 1982).

Jensen (1973, 1980) reports that white-black differences are slightly larger on nonverbal tests than on verbal tests. Jensen (1980) also reports that the magnitude of the white-black differences depends on the extent to which these tests reflect general intelligence (i.e., in the vocabulary of factor analysis, the extent to which the verbal and nonverbal tests "load" on the general intellectual factor, g). Jensen incorrectly assumes that the omnipresence of g in factor analyses of tests indicates that it is a real psychological factor. There is more reason to interpret g as a characteristic of the tests and the statistical methods of analysis than of the psychological makeup of those who take tests (Gould, 1981).

Individual and group differences.   The controversy about group differences in intelligence is long-standing. However, it derives from a misunderstanding of the implications of research findings on individual differences in intelligence and a misunderstanding of the nature of IQ tests. Lewontin, Rose, and Kamin (1984) try to clear up the confusion by likening IQ test scores to the growth of corn seed:

> Suppose one takes from a sack of open-pollinated corn two handfuls of seed. There will be a good deal of genetic variation between seeds in each handful, but the seeds in one's left hand are on the average no different from those in one's right. One handful of seeds is planted in washed sand with an artificial plant growth solution added to it. The other handful is planted in a similar bed, but with half the necessary nitrogen left out. When the seeds have germinated and grown, the seedlings in each plot are measured, and it is found that there is some variation in height of seedling from plant to plant within each plot. This variation within plots is entirely genetic because the environment was carefully controlled to be identical for all the seeds within each plot. The variation in height is then 100 percent heritable. But if we compare the two plots, we will find that all the seedlings in the second are much smaller than those in the first. This difference is not at all genetic, but is a consequence of the difference in nitrogen level. So the heritability of a trait within populations can be 100 percent, but the cause of the difference between populations can be entirely environmental. (p. 118)

Hereditarians often fail to understand that the causes of the differences *between* racial, ethnic, or socioeconomic groups are not the same as the sources of variation *within* the groups. If the environments of the groups are truly different, then there is no way to reason from a conclusion of genetically determined individual differences to a conclusion of genetically determined group differences (Lewontin et al., 1984).

Coleman's research.   Another way of looking at the differences between the school performance of children from different groups is found in Coleman's (1966) *Equality of Educational Opportunity.* This study reported on students' achievement across the United States, and it found that blacks, Mexican-Americans, and lower-SES white students scored considerably lower than middle- and upper-SES white students in almost all school situations. What has commonly been identified as most significant about this finding, however, is that the quality of the schools—quantified by measures such as teachers' salaries, size of library, level of funding—did not seem to affect student achievement significantly. The report, however, suggested something quite different: that the quality of the schools (measured in dollars expended) was, in fact, nearly equal, even though blacks and whites were consistently segregated.

Ryan (1976) takes exception to the control variables in the Coleman study, however. He says that controlling for family background or socioeconomic status (SES) before comparing differences in children's achievement as a function of differences in their schools eliminated what should have been a major variable studied. It is not surprising that Coleman's findings were that school resources made little difference in achievement; he did not compare white upper-class schools with white lower-class schools. His comparisons removed the significant variable of SES. In effect, he compared the achievement of upper-SES students from different schools, and the achievement of lower-SES students from different schools.

It is no wonder then, according to Ryan, that differences in achievement bore little relationship to differences in the schools. There was very little difference between the different schools attended by white, upper-class children. In controlling for children's family background, Coleman was, in effect, eliminating the variable of greatest interest. His study simply found that there is little difference in the effectiveness of schools attended by children of the same socioeconomic class.

He certainly did *not* find that there is little difference in the effectiveness of schools attended by working-class children versus those attended by upper-class children. This latter conclusion is, nonetheless, the one most people draw from his research. Recent analyses also confirm the observation that, once SES is controlled, expenditures are an ineffective measure of the quality of schools (Walberg & Fowler, 1987).

HISTORICAL IDENTIFICATION TRENDS

Discussion of group differences in IQ focuses on the comparison of blacks and whites. In the context of the many possible comparisons that could be made between ethnic and racial groups, this focus is revealing. The characteristics of Jews, Asians, Afro-Asians, Irish, Slavs, and a variety of other "racial" groups could and, at one time or another, have been scrutinized with equal zeal.

The Immigration Restriction Act of 1924 was based on studies by Goddard, Yerkes, and others. But in the United States no comparison has received the persistent attention given to IQ differences between blacks and whites. The most consistent finding in the literature on black-white IQ differences is that the mean score for the black population is about one standard deviation below the white mean. For the population measured generally, this difference seems to have been constant for some time. That such differences have vanished for some ethnic immigrant groups indicates the intransigence of the problem that assimilation into the mainstream has posed for blacks, at least in part because of the *extreme* discrimination they have suffered at the hands of whites in the United States. Indeed, it is only recently that the black literacy rate has approached the white literacy rate in the United States.

Brain Research

The earliest attempts to test intelligence reflected the hereditarian views of the researchers. They predicted that there would be a high, positive correlation between intelligence and brain size.

Paul Broca was a nineteenth century French physiologist who studied the brain. Broca identified the area in the brain—now referred to as Broca's area—that controls speech. Broca's method for testing intelligence, however, was less reputable than his physiological studies and, consequently, is less well known.

His approach was to use the skulls of deceased men and women, some noted scholars, some laymen, and some criminals, and compare the sizes of their brains. Broca expected to find that larger brains were to be found in the skulls of male scholars (see Box 2-1). His theory was not borne out by the data, however. As Gould (1981) points out, some of the largest skulls Broca measured belonged to undistinguished persons, even criminals.

This method of research did not readily confirm the hypotheses of the investigators, and less crude methods were developed. Galton, for example, tried testing sensory and motor responses such as reaction time. This and similar methods also failed to confirm the hypotheses of the researchers. Ironically, it was the psychometric method of a non-hereditarian, Alfred Binet, that provided the measurement tool that lent itself most readily to the hereditarian hypothesis.

BOX 2-1 *Women's Brains*

Broca's predilection for measuring the size of skulls arose from his desire to test a popular hypothesis: that white, northern European males are more intelligent than other groups, particularly blacks, and particularly women, white or black. Broca believed that women were not as smart as men because women had smaller brains. He knew, of course, that part of the reason women had smaller brains was that, in general, they had smaller bodies than men. He claimed, however, that even taking body size into consideration, men were smarter and their brains larger than body proportion could account for. His reasoning, however, was circular. Gould (1980) quotes Broca:

> We might ask if the small size of the female brain depends exclusively upon the small size of her body. Tiedemann has proposed this explanation. But we must not forget that women are, on the average, a little less intelligent than men, a difference which we should not exaggerate but which is, nonetheless, real. We are therefore permitted to suppose that the relatively small size of the female brain depends in part upon her physical inferiority and in part upon her intellectual inferiority.

Many other scientists of the time agreed. One, in particular, was "horrified" (Gould, 1980, p. 155) at the idea of offering women an opportunity for higher education. He proclaimed the idea not only misguided, but dangerous to society. Though these ideas now seem ridiculous to most of us, we should not forget that they were accepted wisdom less than 100 years ago.

Gould reanalyzed Broca's data comparing the skull capacity of men and women. Using a statistical correction for the effects of height and age, he found that there is still an average difference of 113 grams. However, as he points out, his formula could not take into account cause of death, which often has a significant influence on brain size. There is, for example, a 100-gram difference between the brains of persons who have died of degenerative arteriosclerosis and those who died by violence or accident. Many of Broca's female subjects were elderly; and according to Gould, it is likely that lengthy degenerative disease is an explanatory factor in their relatively small brain size.

The best means of correcting for body size is still not certain. One nineteenth-century scientist, who argued that muscle mass and force should be considered, found that when he took this factor into account, women's brains were proportionately *larger* than men's.

The value in Gould's retelling of events in this period in science history is in recognizing the obvious use of science to confirm common prejudice. Proponents of white male superiority claimed that women and blacks were like children, and, consequently could not be afforded rights equal to those of white men. Gould takes issue, not just with Broca's conclusions and those of his modern counterparts, but with "the whole enterprise of setting a biological value upon groups. . ." (p. 159). He regards such science as both irrelevant and injurious.

Psychometric Testing

Binet, who developed the first psychometric intelligence test, thought intelligence was too complex to be represented by a single number (Gould, 1981). He cautioned users of his test that the test score was an average of performances on the various tasks in the test, not representative of an innate psychological entity. Binet had not designed his scale to confirm a hypothesis about innate ability; he designed the scale to identify children who might need special instruction in order to succeed in school.

American psychologists who imported Binet's test and popularized it disregarded Binet's cautions about his test, however. Hereditarians like H. H. Goddard and Lewis Terman promoted the test as an index of innate intelligence. Goddard used the IQ test to identify persons whose intellectual inheritance was "poor" in order to segregate them from the general population and to keep them from having children (Gould, 1981). Terman was primarily interested in studying the development of children whose intellectual inheritance was, according to his theory, superior to that of other children. Terman revised Binet's scale and developed the Stanford-Binet Intelligence Scale. He designed this test for research on the development of gifted children.

In order to identify subjects for his longitudinal study of gifted children, Terman (1925) administered his IQ test to children who were referred for testing by their teachers. His approach, say critics, limits the generalizability of the findings to gifted children from middle- or upper-class families.

Terman's method of selection (teacher referral) yielded a sample in which the representation of working-class and underclass children is low. Ten times as many subjects came from professional families as would be expected from the percentage of professional families in the population (Hildreth, 1966). This finding did not seem anomalous to Terman; rather, it confirmed his belief in the importance of inherited intelligence.

From the 1920s to the late 1960s, teacher referral followed by IQ testing was the basic approach used to identify gifted students. In the late 1960s and early 1970s, the effort to identify economically disadvantaged gifted children from ethnic or racial minority groups was a federal priority. Nonverbal intelligence tests were recommended as alternatives to the standard IQ tests, and the creativity tests developed during the late 1950s and early 1960s were also used to identify gifted children. Checklists itemizing behaviors associated with giftedness were given to teachers as guides to their referral of disadvantaged children.

These approaches are still common provisions for identifying minority gifted children. These approaches have problems, however, associated with (1) their lack of predictive validity and (2) their unreliability. There is little evidence that the disadvantaged children identified by these methods are those children who have the greatest academic potential and who, on that account, most need special attention.

Behavior checklists, especially, are of dubious worth. Most of them are so subjective that they make it likely that the children who are identified are those who are most attractive to teachers, rather than those with unusual potential for superior academic or artistic achievement. The most promising methods for identifying gifted minority children, establishing local norms or using quotas, are seldom used because they require greater effort to implement.

Local norms and quotas.   It is more difficult to establish local norms or to identify the top 3 percent of a specific population than it is to compose a behavior checklist or administer different tests as alternatives to IQ tests. Failure to use reliable identification methods is also a function of the disrepute into which IQ tests, in particular, and standardized tests, in general, have fallen. Only a few efforts have been made to use IQ tests to benefit disadvantaged children. One of the most extensive efforts is Mercer's System of Multicultural Pluralistic Assessment (SOMPA, 1981), which is a form of renorming the tests by which gifted children are identified.

By using local norms, however, educators can rely on technically adequate measures and at the same time compensate for limitations in the use of IQ tests, such as those pointed out by Samuda (1975). As Samuda (1975) argues:

> It would be remarkable if there were no such differences in the scores of different groups on test results, for some aspects of the values and content of tests are—to a lesser or greater extent—necessarily alien to a large propor-

tion of minorities. If tests are to be used for selection, if cutting scores continue to form the grounds for admission into educational institutions or to the avenues of access to employment opportunities, then it follows that without differential points of entry minorities will remain at a disadvantage, equity of educational and employment opportunities will be denied them, and the gap between the dominant majority and the striving minorities will increase. (pp. 129–130)

Unfortunately, the question of identification of gifted students is bound up with the question of IQ heritability. The practical need to find those students who can accelerate through the curriculum is confounded by the need to assert these students' innate superiority. Establishing the proper perspective from which to view identification efforts requires a sensible critique of the hereditarian viewpoint.

MISCONCEPTIONS IN HEREDITARIAN INTERPRETATIONS OF RESEARCH

Critics have pointed out the misconceptions in hereditarians' understanding of the implications of even the most extreme hereditarian case; that is, the assertion that intelligence is completely hereditary. Central to their case is the concept of "heritability."

Heritability versus Inheritability

Heritability is a numerical estimate—from measurements made in a single generation—of the likelihood that a given, genetically encoded trait, will be modified by the environment. It is, in a sense, not a measure of *inheritability* at all. It is actually a measure of what is left *after* environmental influence is accounted for. The more different the environments of the subjects—or the more unstable their common environment—the lower the heritability estimate.

Heritability is an empirical inference, not an empirical fact. In fact, estimates of IQ heritability vary widely. Researchers have, for example, computed rather low heritability estimates among black and low-SES populations (Scarr, 1981).

Another problem in equating heritability with inheritability is the questionable assignment of variables to "genetic" categories. One study (Scarr & Weinberg, 1976), for example, classifies "mother's IQ" as a genetic factor; confounding the issue further, the mothers' IQs in this study were not obtained directly but were extrapolated from the level of the mother's educational attainment. Despite this weakness, however, this study, provides evidence of the substantial effect of environment on the IQs of black children adopted by white families.

Another important misconception about the implications of differences in test scores is the notion that if IQ is inheritable, it is unchangeable.

If a trait is inheritable, however, it does not necessarily mean that the trait cannot be affected by the environment. Modern genetics has found that genic operation itself is responsive to environmental variation (Deutsch, 1968, p. 61).

The history of intelligence testing and the types of decisions that have been based on IQ tests have reflected the assumption that intelligence is both innate *and* fixed. The confusion of "inheritable" with "unchangeable" is characteristic of the hereditarian view and has had a continuing negative effect on the opportunities of minority groups in the United States. This situation is perhaps more a result of how inequality is structured in our nation than it is a result of research about group differences in IQ.

ALTERNATE CONCLUSIONS

Thus far, this chapter has reviewed the basic positions on the relative contributions of heredity and environment to intelligence. It has pointed out limitations in the popular hereditarian view. Chapter 11 discusses the impact of that view on minorities. We conclude that the implications of the hereditarian view of intelligence are no longer tenable, as scientists like Lewontin, Rose, and Kamin (1984) have pointed out.

In our view, mankind is characterized by a general human intelligence that transcends boundaries of racial and social order; this intelligence is made up of many qualities that are reflected in such human abilities as dexterity, mimesis, language, abstraction, and metaphor. None of these intellectual endeavors has been described with sufficient precision by pedagogy, psychology, or biology to relate them to the mechanisms of hereditary transmission.

This view does not rule out the possibility of differing genetic endowment. Differential developmental strengths have been consistently noted by such investigators as Bayley (1970) and Freedman and Freedman (1969). Thus it is permissible to speculate that any hereditary differences between subpopulations, differences which may eventually be confirmed by biology, will be quite specifically delineated, whereas the general genetic rule will be that of structural and functional intellectual equivalence. Our position is speculative, however. It represents an hypothesis no more testable than the opposing view: a view that has not been confirmed by study, despite the claims of hereditarians (cf. Gould, 1981, pp. 273–274).

The major implication of our view is that if gifted children are gifted in large part because of their environmental circumstances, then (1) they can be made more gifted and (2) a greater number of gifted children could be created by a change of circumstances. The key concept in this interpretation is the notion of trait plasticity (Dobzhansky & Montagu, 1975) or cognitive modifiability (cf. Feuerstein, Miller, Hoffman, Rand, Mintzker, &

Jensen, 1981). Even conservative estimates suggest significant possible change. Scarr and Weinberg (1976), for example, suggest an average IQ "malleability" of 15–20 points. This degree of change seems to have been brought about without much conscious intent on the part of the families and schools of the subjects studied by Scarr and Weinberg. It seems reasonable to predict that devoted and systematic efforts to develop children's intellectual ability could raise this average considerably.

SUMMARY

This chapter has identified the major issues in the nature-nurture debate on the acquisition of intelligence. Although the terms of this debate have not been established by gifted educators, its outcomes are critical to an understanding of gifted education.

The chapter reviewed the empirical basis of the hereditarian position and critiques of that position. Results from twin studies, parent-child studies, and studies of group differences in IQ were evaluated. The chapter also summarized the historical uses of intelligence testing and explained how the tests have contributed to the continuing debate about innate human abilities.

Finally, the chapter offered an alternate hypothesis about IQ heritability. This hypothesis is based on the notion of trait plasticity. Such an hypothesis takes account of the social realities that confront many minority students, and it accords minority students greater access to gifted programs.

3

Intelligence Constructs

Focusing Questions

1. What is the relationship between a psychological construct—such as intelligence—and psychological testing? Is intellectual giftedness merely that which is determined by intelligence tests?

2. In what critical ways do multiple-factor and dichotomous-ability theories of intelligence differ? Which do you think represent reality better? Why?

3. Explain the connections between practical problem-solving behavior and adaptive behavior.

4. Give four reasons why the achievement of gifted students is less extreme than their IQ. In your answer, be sure to show how these influences are connected to one another.

5. What evidence suggests that cultural and ethnic differences influence achievement? How are these influences related to socioeconomic status?

6. What differences did Terman and Oden (1947) find between the families of "underachievers" and "achievers"? What inferences do you draw from these findings? Defend your inferences.

7. In what ways is the construct "scholastic aptitude" a clearer guide to program planning than "intelligence"?

8. Describe seven justifiable program options for gifted students and show how they relate to the justification you have in mind.

NORMAL AND ABNORMAL INTELLIGENCE

This chapter examines views of intelligence. Psychological constructs of intelligence are of particular concern here because they have been used so widely to identify gifted students. Other constructs—for example, creativity, mathematical ability, leadership—are dealt with in subsequent chapters. We will examine the distinction between normal and abnormal intelligence since to be "gifted" is so often understood to mean "abnormally intelligent." The term "intellectually gifted" is also used as a synonym for high-IQ students, but the distinction between *intelligence* and *intellect* will also be discussed.

The education of gifted students has historically depended on four premises: (1) intelligence exists, (2) substantial individual differences in intelligence exist, (3) the degree of these differences can be measured accurately among individuals, and (4) only some students possess sufficiently exceptional intelligence to warrant altering the usual practices of schooling. Over the years all of these premises have been challenged, and many of the challenges have had some effect on opinion in the field, though their practical effect has been more limited. This section of the chapter considers the way in which giftedness reflects ranking by levels of intelligence.

Ranking

Our society prizes utility. We regard most highly those persons, ideas, or inventions which are most useful. Scientists have developed empirical methods that can rank individuals according to the degree to which they possess qualities that are believed to reflect social utility. The qualities that are regarded most highly involve verbal and quantitative reasoning. Though these qualities are prized for their utility, they are also considered to be intellectual qualities of inherent worth.

Our society also believes, like most societies, that inherent worth is mirrored in social rank. This belief, however, actually has little to do with the inherent intellectual worth of an idea or intellectual work, and even less to do with the general human worth (as opposed to the utility) of verbal or quantitative reasoning, wherever it may be found. This distinction is an important one because it relates to what we expect of individuals said to be "gifted."

We *assume* that individuals of high social rank make useful contributions to society. We also believe that as a result of these contributions such individuals should receive, or be entitled to receive, large financial rewards. The assumption works in reverse too: Failing to make the distinction between social rank and the more general human worth of thinking and reasoning, we erroneously conclude that those who reap the greatest financial benefits are by definition those who intrinsically have the most to contribute. Not only do we conclude that wealthy businessmen and successful professionals are *entitled* to great wealth and large incomes, we infer that they make an extraordinary contribution to society as a result of their extraordinary capabilities.

This belief seems quite reasonable, so it is difficult for some people to understand that apparent superiority might be the *result of*, rather than the *cause of*, high social rank. The hereditary acquisition of wealth and privilege, however, not infrequently confers high social rank to individuals who possess neither useful nor inherently worthy qualities.

Despite this important distinction, however, it is also true that social rank itself gives many individuals the chance to improve "native ability." Hence, it is very difficult to separate the empirical method of rank (based, for example, on verbal and quantitative reasoning) from the social context in which it takes place. Nevertheless, the empirical approach to the intelligence construct assumes that this separation is possible.

Much of what occurs in schools reflects and strengthens the process of social ranking. Although children may start out in school with similar levels of ability, economically and socially privileged students acquire increasingly greater benefits from school (Oakes, 1985). These benefits are reflected in higher grades, achievement test scores, and even IQ scores (Rosenbaum, 1975). By the time these children leave school, they *do* have skills that are more valuable to society. Hence, the practice of schooling inevitably perpetuates the scheme of social rank. It is natural that this should be so, but it makes the ranking of inherent worth problematic.

The authors of some intelligence tests, however, have purported to measure levels of inherent ability with their tests. Some theorists are convinced that these ability levels are not only inherent, but heritable—that is, that doing well on such tests can be passed on genetically. Others believe that, like grades, intelligence test scores reflect socialized behaviors.

At the present time, no one really knows the degree to which these tests measure heritable traits or learned behaviors. Our lack of certainty in these matters contributes to a persistent and often heated debate about the nature of intelligence and the meaning of its variability.

The Definition of Intelligence

Frustrated educators say that intelligence is what intelligence tests measure, and their circular logic is intended as irony. Any definition of intelligence, however, is based on circular reasoning because intelligence is not a thing, but a construct.

Theorists hold differing views of intelligence, in part because of their reasons for defining it. Piaget, for example, wanted to see human intelligence as an extension of biological adaptation. Hence, he defined intelligence in terms of the processes (e.g., assimilation and accommodation) that help humans adapt to their environment. For Piaget, therefore, all humans act intelligently.

Spearman, by contrast, wanted to define intelligence "objectively," which for him indicated a quantitative description. He viewed intelligence as a mental capacity that undergirds all cognitive performance, and his definition related *amounts* of intelligence to *levels* of cognitive performance. For Spearman, therefore, some humans act more intelligently than others.

It is difficult to evaluate definitions of intelligence simply—as correct or incorrect. Definitions can, however, be evaluated with respect to the way they are used. The discussion that follows considers five definitions of intelligence and the social context in which they are embedded. These notions reflect (1) behavioral theories, (2) single-factor theories, (3) multiple-factor theories, (4) dichotomous-ability theories, and (5) theories of cognitive processing.

Theories of Intelligence

Most early theories of intelligence assumed that intelligence could be measured. Some early theories measured speed. Others measured the amount of a valued trait or constellation of traits. Both approaches included tests that purported to measure the level of an individual's intelligence. Individuals could, in the one view, be more or less speedy. They could, in the other view, have more or less capacity. Many theorists, however, combined notions of speed and capacity.

The earliest quantitative definitions of intelligence related brain capacity to mental performance. The individuals with the largest brains were assumed to be the most intelligent. Theorists of the mid-nineteenth century, however, were more interested in the relative intelligence of different *groups* of people than in differences between *individuals*.

Broca, Galton, and Morton measured the size of people's skulls to confirm the correlation between intelligence and brain capacity. For these researchers the results were disappointing, however, because white males did not turn out to have the largest skulls. Consequently, these men looked for different ways to measure intelligence. They wanted to find methods of measurement that would confirm their assumptions about the superiority of European males (Gould, 1981).

Disappointed by the failure to correlate brain size with intelligence, Galton decided to explore the correlation between reaction time and intelligence. This approach was no more promising than the measurement of brain capacity. Galton did, however, contribute a memorable concept to the study of intelligence, the concept of statistical rarity.

Psychometric tests such as the one developed by Binet and Simon proved more satisfactory than physical tests as a means to rank the mental performance of individuals and groups. These tests included sequences of verbal, mathematical, and reasoning tasks. The tasks were similar to the kinds of performance required in school. When Stern (1914) expressed as a *ratio* the relationship between task performance and age, he combined the idea of speed with that of capacity.

This notion—the notion of "intelligence quotient"—implied that the early mastery of skills would predict future capacity to master more advanced skills. Henceforth, learning rate was understood to be directly related to academic potential.

Behavioral theories. Behavioral psychologists emphasize observable phenomena and resist making inferences from behaviors. Therefore, they are more concerned with the observed products of learning than with hypothetical mental abilities. This approach leads to the measurement of actual rather than potential attainment.

Measures of adaptive behavior often conform to this theoretical approach. They are very helpful in determining the actual accomplishments of developmentally delayed children. They are much less useful, however, in describing the performance of gifted children. Highly intelligent children may adapt or choose not to adapt for a variety of reasons. Gifted children may, for example, act immature in order to get attention or to blend in with other children. Whereas teachers want mentally retarded children to adjust as well as possible to a "normal" sequence of adaptive requirements, teachers should not want to make gifted children normal.

Galton's (1869/1962) *Hereditary Genius* was perhaps the first attempt to define intelligence in terms of its behavioral correlates. Galton looked at what we today would call very complex behaviors—the life accomplishments of his eminent subjects.

Recent methods of identifying gifted children rely on less complex indicators of behavior. Behavioral checklists (e.g., Renzulli, Smith, White, Callahan, & Hartman, 1977) attempt to relate observed characteristics to potential giftedness. They are troublesome because these characteristics may not correlate very well with aptitude for scholastic performance.

Single-factor theories. In the early twentieth century, Spearman (1927) postulated the existence of a global trait, g, that determined intellectual performance. According to Spearman, different individuals had different amounts of g. Those individuals who had the most g were able to perform all mental tasks better than those who had less g. Spearman (1927) explained this idea in the following way:

> [The] success of the same person throughout all variations of both form and subject matter—that is to say, throughout all conscious aspects of cognition whatever—appears only explicable by some factor lying deeper than the phenomena of consciousness. And thus there emerges the concept of a hypo-

thetical general and purely quantitative factor underlying all cognitive performances . . . *g* . . . taken to consist in something of the nature of an "energy" or "power." (p. 5)

Based on this view, Spearman determined that any test of mental performance would reflect greater or lesser amounts of *g*. Wecshler applied this view when he developed his intelligence scales. Wecshler (1958, p. 7) described intelligence as "the aggregate or global capacity of the individual to act purposefully, think rationally, and deal effectively with his environment."

There has been little empirical evidence to support Wechsler's claim, however. Researchers have found only a slight correlation between measures of intelligence and measures of life success (Baird, 1985). They have, however, found a strong relationship between performance on intelligence tests and performance on academic tasks. Although this correlation does nothing to prove the merits of the single-factor argument, it does clearly establish the *utility* of the tests that derive from this theory.

The single-factor view of intelligence is also associated with hereditarian arguments, such as those put forth by Jensen (see Chapter 2). It is easy to draw an analogy between single-factor IQ and a single, heritable *biological trait*, such as eye color or height. Intelligence tests seem to allow psychologists to measure the quantity of this trait in different individuals.

This approach, however, is misleading. Intelligence tests measure complex behaviors that are defined in a social context. It is doubtful that a single, heritable biological trait could account for the many phenomena that are classified as intelligent behavior, even that intelligent behavior described by IQ tests.

Multiple-factor theories. Because Spearman's single-factor definition did not account for much of the variability in an individual's performance of different kinds of tasks, Thorndike and other theorists suggested a multiple-factor definition. Thorndike (1927) proposed three kinds of intellectual capacities: abstract, mechanical, and social. Thurstone (1938) suggested seven primary mental abilities: verbal, number, spatial, memory, reasoning, word fluency, and perceptual speed.

Guilford (1959) developed a three-dimensional model of intelligence that accounted for 120 independent factors. The three dimensions of the model are operations, content, and products. According to Guilford, performance of an intellectual task depends on the interaction of an operation, a content, and a product. Different cognitive tasks require different kinds of interactions.

A more recent multiple-factor view of intelligence is described by Gardner (1983). Like Thorndike, Gardner believes that intelligence governs more than cognitive functioning. In fact, Gardner maintains that there are seven separate types of intelligence: linguistic, logical-mathematical, spatial, musical, kinesthetic, interpersonal, and intrapersonal.

Among the multiple-factor theories, those that include fewer different abilities have the greatest practical value. Like the tests derived from single-factor notions of intelligence, tests based on these multiple-factor views relate to academic learning. At least several of the factors in many of these theories also relate to school performance. For example, Thurstone's tests of verbal and numerical reasoning predict performance in specific school subjects because they sample behaviors similar to those expected in school.

Dichotomous-ability theories.   Similar to the multiple-factor theories are the dichotomous-ability theories that hypothesize the existence of two distinct kinds of intelligence. These theories attempt to resolve the question of the influence of heredity as compared with the influence of environment on intelligence.

Some psychologists recognized that certain questions on intelligence tests were dependent on children's previous learning. Vocabulary items, general information items, and arithmetic items were the ones most obviously sensitive to the effects of early learning. These psychologists believed that IQ tests should include items that are less sensitive to early learning. According to these theorists, such items would reveal native ability.

Cattell (1971) distinguished between two kinds of intelligence: fluid and crystallized. According to Cattell:

> Crystallized ability . . . operate[s] in areas where the judgments have been taught systematically or experienced before . . . Fluid ability, by contrast, appears to operate whenever the sheer perception of complex relations is involved. It thus shows up in tests where borrowing from stored, crystallized, judgmental skills brings no advantage. (pp. 98–99)

Cattell's tests, the Culture-Fair Intelligence Tests (Cattell, 1950; Cattell & Cattell, 1960, 1963), made his distinction operational by linking verbal performance with crystallized intelligence and by linking nonverbal (perceptual reasoning) performance with fluid intelligence. Cattell believed that the measurement of fluid ability would better represent the "true" intelligence levels of children from different races and socioeconomic backgrounds. Unfortunately, the results of his tests suggest that his assumption was incorrect. Measures of fluid ability have turned out to be no more "culture-fair" than measures of crystallized ability (Sattler, 1982).

Kaufman and Kaufman (1983) attempted to make a similar distinction with their notion of the differences between intelligence and achievement. According to Kamphaus and Reynolds (1984, p. 215–216), the

Kaufmans viewed intelligence as the process of problem solving, whereas they viewed achievement as the "application of . . . mental processing skills to the acquisition of knowledge from the environment." This distinction places "measures of what have traditionally been identified as verbal intelligence, . . . general information, . . . and acquired school skills" among the tests of achievement rather than among the tests of intelligence (Kamphaus & Reynolds, 1984, p. 215). The Kaufmans' notion of achievement clearly resembles Cattell's notion of crystallized intelligence.

The Kaufmans based their test battery, the Kaufman Assessment Battery for Children (K-ABC), on the distinction between these two kinds of performance. The battery samples abilities that reflect both perceptual reasoning, or fluid intelligence, and acquired learning, or crystallized intelligence. The test battery excludes behaviors that reflect crystallized (or verbal) intelligence from its assessment of intellectual potential. The authors of the K-ABC consider this characteristic of their test sufficient to establish its culture-fairness. There is, however, little evidence that minority students perform better on nonverbal than on verbal tasks (Jensen, 1973; Samuda, 1975). Jensen (1973), for example, reports that most black children perform better on *verbal* tests than on *nonverbal* tests.

Although the distinction between two kinds of intelligence has not been linked to differences in native and acquired abilities, the verbal portions of tests based on this theory do predict school achievement. Whether or not we call such verbal performance "intelligence" or "achievement" is moot; however, we do know that previous verbal achievement, like IQ, predicts future achievement.

Information-processing theories.   In contrast to the psychometric approaches that emphasize the *products* of cognition, the information-processing theorists focus on cognitive *processes*.

These theorists see intelligence as a sequence of events. The sequence includes phenomena such as arousal and maintenance of attention, short- and long-term recall, and transfer of learning. Even if these processes do condition intelligent behavior, they are so internal that they resist measurement.

Information-processing theorists study the influence of these mental events on the way that individuals solve problems. They attempt to establish correlations between cognitive processes and more traditional measures of aptitude, for example, the ability to work formal analogies or mazes (Sternberg, 1977).

Some of the distinctions made by information-processing theorists resemble dichotomous-ability theories. According to Sternberg (1982a), intelligence comprises the ability to acquire and to think in terms of novel concepts and conceptual systems. Intelligence involves the ability to assimilate systems that at first seem strange and then to apply existing knowledge, structure, and skills to the new system. He distinguishes between analytic intelligence and synthetic creativity.

In contrast to the dichotomous-ability theorists, however, Sternberg is not concerned with identifying children's true levels of native ability. Rather, he is concerned with the ways that individuals learn. This approach is similar to that of Piaget (see Chapter 8).

Because the theory of information-processing has limited practical application to the measurement of intelligence, theorists have expanded the scope of their work to include metacognitive processes such as those listed by Brown (1978). He identifies predicting, checking, monitoring, and reality-testing as executive processes of metacognition. Such processes are more easily measured than information-processing, and they can also be taught. The relationship of metacognitive processes to traditional measures of intelligence and to academic performance is unclear, however (Sternberg, 1977).

Rarity: Normality and Abnormality

The notion of ranking assumes that there are different levels of performance. The idea of an age-ratio (i.e., Stern's concept) postulates differences in learning rate.

Neither view, however, addresses the relationship between the levels of performance and the numbers of performers. Galton was the first to relate superior performance to its degree of rarity. In his view, the more a performance differs from the average or norm, the more rare it is. Superior performance is, therefore, a kind of abnormality according to Galton.

This statistical notion is crucial to the view that intelligence is a characteristic that is *normally distributed* in the population. IQ tests are constructed so as to confirm this analysis. Test authors include only those items that *produce* a normal distribution of scores in a representative sample.

The value of rarity.   When intelligence tests are used to identify gifted individuals, they attempt to find those whose performance is most deviant. Typical school definitions of giftedness identify the top 2 or 3 percent of students; Galton, though, was concerned with performance that was *considerably* more rare.

All efforts to identify superior performers are based on the belief that particular kinds of high-level performance are—somehow—of particular value to society. They also assume that rare performance is a "gift" that cannot be replicated. Therefore, individuals who possess gifts must be found, so that they can serve society.

Nevertheless, individuals who demonstrate high levels of intelligence may not be able or willing to serve society. In the highest range, intelligence scales cannot accurately predict socially validated performance. Within this restricted range, they are not even good predictors of school success. (That is, among children with IQs above 145, it is not in general true that a child with an IQ of 180 will perform better in school than a child with an IQ of 150.)

Although our society seems to value superiority, it values conformity at the same time. The exceptional academic performance of very high-IQ individuals may not correspond to the specialized needs of a pragmatic society. Moreover, the performance of individuals with extremely high IQs may be unpredictable. In the most extreme ranges, then, IQ scales may *lose* their utility because deviant performance is unpredictable.

ADAPTIVE BEHAVIOR

The broadest definition conceives intelligence as adaptation to the environment. According to this view, the quality of intelligence differs as environments differ. The demands of the physical or social environment establish the terms by which intelligence is determined. School learning is only a small part of the modern social environment, so measures of aptitude for school learning consider only a *narrow interpretation* of intelligence.

This section of the chapter considers the *broad* concept of intelligence. It shows the relationship between adaptation to academic expectations and adaptation to other social demands. It also examines the social adjustment (i.e., adaptive behavior) of high-IQ students.

Social Validation

A poll to determine how laypersons define intelligence (Sternberg, 1982b) found that it is commonly associated with success in any endeavor except athletics, which was seen by most of the people surveyed as not requiring extraordinary intelligence. This popular definition implies that intelligence is adaptive; and, in fact, the lay definition of intelligence is close to that of psychologists who have included in their definitions of intelligence a reference to its adaptive function (e.g., Piaget).

Extraordinary intelligence, however, is sometimes seen as incompatible with adaptive behavior. For example, the view of intelligence as successful adaptation contrasts markedly with the stereotype of the maladaptive genius. Gifted children *are* often described as having no common sense and as being social misfits.

In fact, the two views may represent judgments about adaptation to different environments: adaptation to school and adaptation to life. Because adaptive behavior cannot be defined without reference to the environment, what is adaptive behavior in one environment may be maladaptive in another. The advanced vocabulary associated with a high IQ score, for example, may represent a successful adaptation in a family that values the articulation of ideas, but using such a vocabulary may be maladaptive at recess.

Just as intelligence can be defined narrowly as scholastic aptitude, adaptive behavior can also be defined narrowly. When psychologists and educators use the term "adaptive behavior"—particularly in reference to exceptional children—they usually mean *noncognitive behaviors* that help children get along in the classroom and in public. These behaviors include a wide range of skills, literally from nose-wiping to making polite conversation.

A particular social context is, in fact, essential to the definition of adaptive behavior. In general, adaptive behavior is behavior that is validated by its congruence with social norms. Although most of us recognize that some children are "street smart," this type of adaptive behavior is not acknowledged by social norms, and it will never be taught in schools nor measured by tests.

Adaptation to peers. Gifted children, at the elementary school level anyway, enjoy the acceptance of their classmates (Gallagher, 1985). Other children perceive gifted children as dressing "preppy," wearing glasses, talking about boring things, carrying books, being polite, behaving well in public, treating others with kindness, doing well in classes, getting good grades, and having common sense (Alexander, 1985). At the preschool level, gifted children exhibit more social play forms than other children. They initiate play sessions with other children; and they play more cooperatively and share playthings to a greater extent than other children (Barnette & Fiscella, 1985).

At the high-school level, gifted students are at least as well accepted, though not so popular as some other children (Coleman, 1961; Tidwell, 1980). Solano (1977) found ninth graders of average ability used equally positive adjectives to describe precocious students as they used to describe themselves: determined, self-confident, sophisticated, serious, and cautious. Negative comments about gifted children included "dull," "conceited," and "self-centered."

Gifted children's acceptance by peers may be an acknowledgment of social distinctions. Gifted children's appearance—dressing "preppy," (Alexander, 1985) for example—reflects their socioeconomic status, a status that classmates acknowledge by their acceptance.

Adult acceptance of gifted children. Adults often attribute certain noncognitive traits to gifted children. These traits include outgoingness, perseverance, a tendency to dominate a group, and curiosity. These characteristics are probably more a function of the perceptions of children's middle-class backgrounds than of children's intelligence, however.

Other studies of adult perceptions of gifted children tend to confirm this hypothesis. Teachers, in particular, are negative about any students who do not perform classroom tasks systematically, regardless of the children's intellectual abilities. Adults' positive perceptions about gifted students are always confounded by other variables. (For further discussion, see the section on school performance that concludes this chapter.)

Similarly, adult perceptions of underachieving gifted students relate more to their views about underachievement than to their perceptions of giftedness. They describe underachievers as lacking persistence in the accomplishment of ends, lacking the integration necessary to achieve goals, lacking self-confidence, and having feelings of inferiority (Terman & Oden, 1959). At least in part, these perceptions reflect impressions of the underachievers' socioeconomic status. The gifted children in Terman's study who grew up to be underachievers were, as a group, less affluent and their parents were less well educated than the average for the gifted group as a whole.

Cultural Pluralism and Ability

Different cultural groups show different mean levels of performance on intelligence tests. When the effect of social class is not taken into account, blacks tend to score about one standard deviation lower on IQ tests than do whites. Whites, however, tend to score about two-thirds of a standard deviation below orientals.

Less well known is research that identifies different aptitude patterns in different cultural and racial groups. Stodolsky and Lesser (1967) found that Jewish children score higher on verbal tests than they do on spatial, reasoning, and numerical tests. Blacks, too, score highest on verbal tests, according to Stodolsky and Lesser. Chinese and Puerto Rican children score highest on spatial tests, according to these researchers. Moreover, Stodolsky and Lesser observed identical patterns within the same ethnic group at both lower- and middle-class socioeconomic levels. Hence, these different aptitude patterns seem to be phenomena more closely associated with culture than with class.

These different patterns of performance may reflect children's adaptation to the values of the cultures in which they are raised. Both the Chinese and the Jewish cultures, for example, have for many centuries placed a very high value on intellectual endeavors. The way in which such cultural legacies relate to findings like those cited previously is, however, obscure. The way in which such phenomena affect school performance is also obscure, though they may influence the development of cultural stereotypes, for better and worse.

Problem Solving as Adaptive Ability

Successful people seem to be those who adapt best to their environment; adaptation, however, often involves *solving problems.* Though competence in most of the endeavors of life requires much more than *academic* problem solving, this section will consider only academic problem solving.

Information-processing theory is relevant to the concerns of this section. Each of Sternberg's factors of intelligence is, in a way, construed as a category of adaptive behavior that seems to lie somewhere between achieved skill and an ability to adapt new information usefully. Two factors that influence the success of problem solving are (1) the novelty of a task and (2) the degree to which a task is performed automatically (Sternberg, 1985). Ease of adaptation relates to the second of these factors. Gifted children, who are already familiar with many of the concepts and skills required by grade-level work, perform school tasks more automatically than average ability peers. Their performance, therefore, is usually more accurate and rapid.

Speed is important in many school tasks even though the correlation between perceptual speed and IQ scores is weak. The relationship between speed of reasoning processes and IQ, however, is moderate to high: 0.70 for analogies, 0.50 for series completion, and 0.64 for classifications (Sternberg & Gardner, 1983).

Other problem-solving strategies may also be adaptive in the classroom. Three separate processes that constitute insight may relate to the performance of academic tasks. These processes are:

1. selective encoding—sifting relevant from irrelevant information,
2. selective combining—combining facts into a coherent scheme, and
3. selective comparison—making analogies between new information and previously acquired information. (Sternberg, 1985, p. 81)

Within a school setting, it might appear that solving math problems correctly is the most adaptive behavior, and children with high IQ scores are adept at such adaptations. Readers should, however, remember that heading one's paper correctly, sitting still, and being polite are *equally important* adaptive behaviors in school; and gifted children vary substantially in their willingness to meet such social obligations in the classroom.

Sternberg (1985) uses the term "practical intelligence" to connote the kinds of adaptive social skills required for life success. These skills seem to entail the ability to interpret social situations effectively for one's benefit. Sternberg calls this ability "tacit knowledge." Again, this sort of adaptation was not the focus of this section.

Intelligence, as measured by IQ tests, is a mechanism for adapting to the *cognitive* requirements of school. It may not be a mechanism for adapting to the *noncognitive* requirements of school or, for that matter, of work (Baird, 1985).

The next section of the chapter considers the relationship between high IQ and school performance.

SCHOOL PERFORMANCE

On almost any index of school performance, students with high IQ scores, tend, as a group, to score above average. Their scores on academic achievement tests are as high as those of older students and adults. They are more likely than other students to earn high grades, complete college, and win academic honors. As adults, they tend to do well in scholastic careers.

A high IQ does not, however, *ensure* superior school performance, and a remarkable number (perhaps 15 percent) of gifted children perform at or below the average level for children their age. Though the school performance of gifted children is affected by the environment, it is, you may be surprised to learn, also affected to some degree by the measures used to index school performance. The limitations of common indices of school performance—grades and group achievement tests, in particular— often underestimate the achievement of high-IQ students.

These low estimates provide false evidence in support of a common misconception. This misconception holds that the educational needs of high-IQ children are not very different from those of other children and that special provisions for them are unnecessary. Consequently, many high-IQ students are not provided the advanced schoolwork they need in order to progress academically.

Indices of School Performance

School performance is measured by indices (e.g., grades) that, in many instances, cannot portray the academic variables relevant to understanding gifted children. In fact, they often reflect variables that are irrelevant to academic progress. As a result, the contrast between a high IQ score and an average performance rating causes confusion. The contrast creates doubt about the student's abilities and causes teachers to question whether or not the child with a high IQ actually possesses superior ability.

By contrast, the validity of the most widely used indices of school performance is seldom questioned. Grades are generally regarded by parents, teachers, and school administrators as *reliable* indicators of a student's mastery of academic material.

It is rare that grades are recognized for what they are—an unreliable, "gallimaufry" measure (Hunt, 1978, p. 109), confounded by differences in teachers' biases and skills and by myriad social conditions—of the student, the school, the family, and the community. Researchers, who *do* often doubt the reliability of grades, use achievement test scores; but achievement tests, especially group achievement tests, do not always accurately represent a gifted student's achievement either.

Achievement tests. The positive correlation between IQ and achievement test scores is usually construed to mean that innately intelligent children, who are identified by their high IQ scores, learn more readily than other children and so score higher on achievement tests. This interpretation is not necessarily accurate.

IQ scores do not explain high (or low) achievement, despite their use as "diagnostic" instruments (Mercer, 1981). It is at least as likely that students who score high on IQ tests also score high on achievement tests because (1) IQ and achievement tests measure similar cognitive skills and (2) the social variables that contribute to students' high IQ scores also contribute to high achievement test scores.

Because some of the information required to score high on IQ tests is more generally available than that on achievement tests, IQ test scores depend less on students' in-school experiences than do achievement test scores. Children who have not yet received instruction in particular academic skills, who have received poor instruction in them, or who because of emotional or physical handicaps have not benefited from instruction, are more likely to score high on IQ tests than on achievement tests. However, the differences between IQ test and achievement test performance are not all due to differences in the content of the tests.

Difference in test format can result in discrepancies that have nothing to do with the child's knowledge of the content of the test. Although there are both group-administered and individually-administered IQ and achievement tests, children identified as gifted are often identified on the basis of individually-administered IQ tests. On the other hand, their achievement is typically measured with *group* tests. Perceptual, physical, or emotional problems keep a small proportion of these gifted students from demonstrating their mastery on group-administered achievement tests.

However, because of the way these tests are constructed, even bright students who are not handicapped can fail to perform optimally on group-administered tests. Tests designated for a particular age level, for example, do not have enough difficult items to allow *gifted* students of that age to demonstrate their mastery of advanced skill, that is; such tests have a "ceiling" that is too low.

Even among multilevel achievement tests, it is difficult to find tests with a high enough ceiling to assess accurately the achievement of gifted children twelve years old or older or of highly gifted children eight years old or older. In fact, the available individually-administered achievement tests also suffer from this latter limitation. Some researchers, such as

Stanley (1976b), advocate the use of achievement tests designed for older students as a means of addressing this problem.

Nonetheless, most scholars who conduct research about gifted children have failed to take the problem of the low ceilings of available achievement tests into account. The tests they use often cannot sample the full range of achievement among high-IQ students. As a result, much existing research probably misrepresents the achievement of gifted students. Again, because of the inadequacy of available tests, there has been little alternative to such misrepresentation.

Statistical regression toward the mean further confounds understanding of the relationship between IQ and achievement. Although several of the factors just discussed contribute to this effect, chance factors also make it likely that students who score high at one testing will score somewhat lower in a subsequent testing. Even if high-IQ students were retested with the IQ test on which they were identified as gifted, a slightly lower group mean often would be observed in their second scores.

In summary, most studies find high-IQ students' achievement test scores to be superior, but closer to the mean than their IQ test scores. This fact is partly a result of differences in the skills and information measured by IQ and achievement tests. The presence of confounding variables, however, such as differences in test format, low achievement test ceilings, and regression toward the mean suggests that the actual achievement level of many high-IQ students may be closer to their IQ level than existing research shows.

Grades.   In the case of high-IQ students, grades misrepresent academic progress even more than achievement test scores. In many instances, students' grades have little to do with what they know about the subject on which they are graded (Chansky, 1964; Kubiszyn & Borich, 1984). Leiter and Brown (1985) found that primary school children's mathematics grades showed a *slight* correlation with their demonstrated mastery on standardized mathematics tests; but their reading grades showed *no* correlation with their reading achievement test scores!

It can be argued—indeed, many teachers believe it—that such discrepancies indicate problems with achievement tests, not with grades. This opinion is not surprising. Despite teachers' faith in grading, however, many academically irrelevant factors enter into their evaluation of students' performance. Students' physical appearance (Ysseldyke & Algozzine, 1982), their personality (Roedell, Jackson, & Robinson, 1980), race (Leacock, 1969), socioeconomic status (Rist, 1970), and sex (Carter, 1952) can and do influence teachers' judgments about students' school performance. This observation is not a condemnation of teachers, who cannot be blind to students' characteristics. It *does* suggest problems with grades as a criterion of achievement.

Teachers evaluate positively those children who are compliant and participate enthusiastically in classroom activities (Roedell et al., 1980). These traits appear to be more prevalent in girls than in boys; a circumstance which may help to explain why teachers award girls higher grades than their performance warrants (Carter, 1952; Edmiston, 1943; Stockard, Lang, & Wood, 1985). The prevalence of these traits in girls may help account for the fact that about 60 percent of honor students are female whereas about 60 percent of students who make D or F averages are male. It may also help explain why boys are about twice as likely as girls to score higher on aptitude tests than on teacher ratings (Sexton, 1969).

Compliance is also more prevalent in middle-SES than in low-SES students, and it is more prevalent in anglo students than in students from ethnic and racial minorities. Teachers' reactions to gifted students may depend, in part, on the students' race and SES. In some classrooms of low-income students, teachers take a more negative view of *bright* black students than black students of average or low intelligence (Leacock, 1969). Rubovits and Maehr (1973) found that teachers praised white gifted children more than other children, but criticized gifted black children more than any of the others.

High-IQ students who are independent and especially interested in theoretical and aesthetic issues sometimes make lower grades than other gifted students with lower IQ scores (Drews, 1961, cited in Tannenbaum, 1983). Teachers often consider bright but independent students to be less bright, less creative, lower in social acceptance, and more dogmatic than other gifted children.

In a comparison of several indices of superior academic ability, Pegnato and Birch (1959) found that grades did not discriminate well between high-IQ students and students with average or slightly above-average IQ scores. When teachers used a 3.0 grade point average (GPA) as the criterion for referrals for the gifted program, most of the students who were referred, about 86 percent, scored lower than 136 IQ, the minimum score for identification as gifted in the study. Among all of the children in the school who *did* score 136 IQ or higher, a large minority—about 25 percent—had a GPA lower than 3.0.

Discrepancies between IQ scores and grades are not due solely to the technical inadequacy of grades. Mediocre instruction, a slow pace, and academically irrelevant curricula may contribute to gifted children's underachievement. In general, when support for academic effort is not provided by the community, school, or home, achievement suffers. Of course, negative influences can also lower gifted children's achievement test scores; their effect on grades is more pronounced, however.

Grades are more sensitive to compliance issues; and gifted children, like other children, sometimes refuse to conform to academic requirements. They may fail to turn in assignments, or they may make careless errors. They may wander around the classroom, daydream, or read rather than do their class work. If, as frequently happens, these gifted children nevertheless learn the academic concepts and skills that are measured by achievement tests, their teachers are likely to regard the test scores as erroneous.

Learning Rate

High-IQ children's early mastery of academic subjects is well documented. The reasons for their early mastery may vary, but they include quality of instruction, motivation, and effort; no doubt an important contributor to learning rate is the effect that accumulated knowledge has on the speed with which students can comprehend new material. Although there are "late bloomers," these are the exception rather than the rule.

Most research that describes gifted students' early mastery of academic skills is summative. It tells how advanced their skills are at various age or grade levels. A smaller body of research is devoted to the speed with which gifted students perform academic tasks.

Research on early mastery of academic skills.   The results of a statewide study reported by Martinson (1972) typify the findings about high-IQ students' mastery of school subjects (e.g., Gallagher & Crowder, 1957; Terman & Oden, 1947; Witty, 1930). Based on comparisons of students' performance on standardized achievement batteries, the report shows gifted children to be much further advanced in achievement than other children who have been in school an equal length of time.

Gifted kindergarteners scored as high as second graders on reading and mathematics tests. Gifted fourth graders and fifth graders scored higher than seventh graders; in fact, the upper quartile of gifted fifth graders scored above the tenth-grade level. Most of the gifted eighth graders scored at the twelfth-grade level, and a sizable percentage scored as high as the average college freshman. Most of the gifted tenth graders and eleventh graders scored as high as average college sophomores. A group of gifted high school seniors who were given the Graduate Record Examination (GRE) in social sciences, humanities, and natural sciences scored as high as average college seniors. In the social sciences, the gifted high school students' average was higher than college seniors who were *social science majors* (Martinson, 1972).

The higher their IQ scores, the more rapidly children master academic skills. Hollingworth and Cobb's (1928) comparison of two groups of third graders, one with IQ scores ranging from 130 to 150 and one with IQ scores above 150, found that the children with higher IQ scores mastered third-grade skills faster. Case studies, biographies, and autobiographies of individuals with estimated IQ scores of 180 and above (e.g., Grost, 1970;

Hollingworth, 1942; Wallace, 1986) supply anecdotal evidence that highly gifted children can, at the age of nine or ten, easily compete with average college students.

 Research on speed of performance on academic tasks. Whether or not gifted students complete individual academic tasks more rapidly than other children and the degree to which the speed of performance contributes to early mastery has not been established. In fact, the question has not even been studied very extensively. Speed of performance on academic tasks, in itself, may be too trivial to be a useful predictor of academic achievement.

 One study (Duncan, 1969) purports to show a positive correlation between the speed of accomplishment of academic tasks and IQ. Duncan compared the oral reading rates, verbal fluency rates, and arithmetic calculation rates of gifted fourth-, fifth-, and sixth-grade children with those of other students in the intermediate grades. She found that, on the average, gifted pupils had higher performance rates than other pupils. The greatest difference in performance rate on an academic task was in arithmetic calculations. The gifted sixth graders were able to perform correctly 28.4 multiplication operations per minute while the average sixth graders calculated correctly 17.5 operations per minute. The sixth-grade gifted students differed more from the norm for their grade than did the gifted fourth- and fifth-grade students.

 A problem with Duncan's study is that the scoring procedures factored accuracy into the rate score; the reported rates are rates of *correct* responses. Even if the gifted children's accuracy was greater than that of other children, it is still possible that they worked no faster. Some of the materials used by Duncan were above grade level, so this explanation is likely. In fact, an earlier study (Klausmeier & Loughlin, 1961), which did not confound accuracy and rate, discovered no significant difference in problem-solving rate among high-, average-, and low-IQ students.

Family Support

 Parents of high-IQ students assist and guide their children's scholastic efforts. Because parental support is a consistently positive correlate of superior school performance, the nature and extent of the support are important issues in gifted education. Since family socioeconomic status (SES) influences the way parents bring up their children (Jencks et al., 1979), SES and related variables may help explain superior performance. Conversely, these variables may also help account for the failure of some high-IQ individuals to succeed in academic endeavors.

 Intellectual environment. The home environment of many high-IQ children is characterized by intellectual activity: reading; writing; listening to music; visiting libraries and museums; and attending movies, plays, and concerts. Cornell (1984) found that, compared with other middle-class families, families with identified gifted children scored higher on an intellectual-cultural orientation scale designed to measure the extent to which a family engages in political, social, intellectual, and cultural pursuits.

Cornell also found that family "togetherness" was stressed to a striking degree in the families with gifted children. Parents of the gifted reported being closely involved with their children in family activities. Terman and Oden (1947) found that gifted children were more likely than other children to come from two-parent homes. Their finding may reflect the additional time and resources two parents can commit to their children's intellectual development, or it may reflect the high SES of their group. At any rate, the incidence of divorce and separation was lower in this group of parents than in the general population even in the 1920s.

Anecdotal evidence also supports the positive influence of families on gifted children. Rhodes Scholars describe their families as strong and supportive. Their parents report that they were involved in their children's schooling and encouraged them to assume difficult tasks. Reading and books were frequently mentioned as part of the families' shared recreation (Denbow, 1984). Similar findings are reported for MacArthur Fellows (Cox et al., 1985). In retrospect, these high-achieving adults attribute their success to their parents' support of their intellectual development. They report that commitment to learning, to literature, and to the discussion of ideas was an important part of their childhoods. Although their educational levels varied, the parents shared an exceptional commitment to supporting their children's intellectual efforts, both in and out of school.

Socioeconomic status and family support. Family background accounts for about half the variance in children's educational attainment; and economic status is a major determinant of the family's overall impact (Jencks et al., 1979). The odds are against low-income families having the ability to offer the intellectual and financial support that can be provided by parents with high education levels and adequate incomes. Identified gifted children are predominantly members of middle- and upper-class families.

Only 18 percent of the children identified as gifted in Terman's study were the children of laborers (Terman & Oden, 1947). Of those, only a few were the children of semiskilled or unskilled laborers. Of the gifted children who came from low-income families, a large proportion were underachievers.

In 1947, Terman and Oden determined that on average, parents of children in the gifted group had completed four to five more years of formal schooling than the average person of the same generation in the United States at that time. The parents of the underachievers, however, averaged far below the achievers' parents in education; half of the most successful group's fathers were graduated from college as compared to only 15.5 percent of the fathers of the least successful men. The occupational status of the underachievers' fathers was also markedly lower.

Other family variables may relate to SES. These variables include intactness of the family unit, mothers' employment, family religion, race, and ethnicity. Research that relates the absence of a father to children's cognitive performance is mixed. Some studies have found no difference in school achievement as a function of the father's absence from the home (Bronfenbrenner & Crouter, 1982); but a recent review of the literature found small, consistent differences favoring children from two-parent families (Hetherington, Camara, & Featherman, 1981). Bachman (1970) found slight detrimental effects on boys' verbal IQ when the father was absent because of divorce or separation, but no effect when the father had died. The incidence of separation and divorce was about twice as high for parents of Terman and Oden's (1959) "least successful" men as for the "most successful" group. The proportion of deceased fathers was also considerably larger for the underachieving group.

Mothers' employment, whether in a single-parent or two-parent household, does not have consistent or large effects on children's achievement either. Related factors, such as income, however, do affect achievement (Hayes & Kamerman, 1983). Some studies find that mothers of gifted children are more likely to be employed than those of other children, particularly if the mothers are themselves gifted (Groth, 1975); but among most white, middle-class families, mothers' employment has little effect on children's achievement. Among black, single-parent families, however, employment of the mother is positively correlated with achievement (Milne, Myers, Rosenthal, & Ginsberg, 1986).

The family's ethnic, racial, and religious group membership may also influence children's school performance. In the United States, Jewish and Oriental families seem to value their children's educational achievement most. In 1986, Asian-American students, who comprised only 2.1 percent of the college population, constituted 11 percent of the freshman class at Harvard and 18 percent of the freshman class at the Massachusetts Institute of Technology (Butterfield, 1986). Jewish children also are strongly represented in select colleges as well as in gifted programs. About twice as many Jewish children as would be expected based on California's population at the time were identified as gifted by Terman in 1925. Students from other ethnic (e.g., Mexican-American) or racial (e.g., American Indian) backgrounds, on the other hand, are underrepresented in gifted programs.

Catholic children, as a group, score at the mean of IQ tests; Baptist children score the farthest below the mean of any religious group (Bachman, 1970). These effects, like those of ethnicity, can be attributed in part to SES. The family's economic status does not, however, explain all of the differences between Jewish, Catholic, and Baptist children's mean IQ scores; nor does it explain all of the difference between Asian-American and other immigrant children's scores. Educational attitudes and aspirations vary to some degree with the groups' different cultural histories, and these or similar differences may influence school performance beyond the influence of SES.

An example of a difference in attitude that is significant for their children's intellectual development was found in a study of mothers' views about academic achievement (*New York Times*, 1986). Japanese mothers were most strongly convinced that academic achievement was the result of hard work; Chinese mothers were nearly as convinced; but American mothers usually attributed academic achievement to inborn ability.

The mean IQ of black students is usually reported to be 10 to 15 points lower than the mean IQ of caucasian students (Bloom, 1964). This difference is often construed to represent genetic differences in intelligence between the races. However, Bachman (1970) found that differences between whites and blacks disappeared when he excluded from his analysis black students from segregated southern schools. When whites and blacks from integrated schools were compared, the black students' mean IQ score was only 3.3 points lower than the white students' mean IQ. This difference is about the same as the 3.4 point difference found between whites in the Northeast and whites in the West when SES was controlled. Even these slightly lower scores may be a function of SES. Bachman (1970) comments:

> Even though we have invested much in our measurement of SEL [socioeconomic level], we surely are not completely successful in our attempts to control it statistically. Moreover, we cannot say that the black students in integrated schools have received "equal" treatment throughout their school experience. Some spent their grade school years in segregated schools; and some spent their high school years in course programs that are largely segregated. In short, statistical controls for SEL and school experience are at best only approximations; and because of this, we cannot conclude that even the small difference of 3.3 QT would remain if other factors were fully and completely controlled. (p. 83)

Nearly every family variable shown to affect achievement is related to SES. When SES is controlled, differences between the mean IQ scores of minority groups and white, middle-class children are practically eliminated.

The effects of the family's SES on children's school performance appear to be cumulative. Durkin (1966) found that socioeconomic status was not as influential in early reading achievement as in later reading achievement. Early reading related more to the mothers' willingness and ability to involve their children with books than it related to SES. Although many studies have found that parental involvement and support has a positive effect on low-income students' school achievement, these studies are often looking at differences *within* a particular SES group (e.g., Dolan, 1983).

Bloom (1964) found that at Grade 2, there was no correlation between reading comprehension and the father's occupational level; at Grade 8, the correlation was 0.50. He attributed this increase to the accumulated effects of socioeconomic status on school performance. These effects include not only the nature and extent of the *family's influence* on children's educational efforts, but also the nature and extent of the *teacher's influence* on children's educational efforts (cf. Anyon, 1980).

Attainment

Children who have high IQ scores when they are eight years old or older can be expected to have high IQ scores when they are adults (Bloom, 1964). This phenomenon is partly related to their longer period of school attendance. Although being smart does not make them rich, it does predict that they will be more than ordinarily productive in academic and professional fields. Their above-average academic performance, in many instances, continues throughout adulthood.

Adult IQ of high-IQ children.   In order to determine the stability of high IQ scores, Terman developed a verbal intelligence test with items difficult enough to assess the vocabulary and general information acquired by his highly able adult subjects. The Terman Concept Mastery Test (CMT) is a multiple-choice test of the ability to recognize synonyms and antonyms and to recognize verbal analogies (Terman, 1973).

The mean CMT score of the group of gifted subjects in Terman and Oden's (1947) study was 137; and the median was 141. The mean score of subjects with 170 and above childhood IQ scores was highest: 155.8 on the CMT. Those with childhood IQ scores of 135–139 had a mean of 114.2.

Schooling also related to the subjects' CMT scores. Those who had doctorates scored a mean of 159.0; those who had medical degrees scored a mean of 143.6; those with master's degrees, 143; and those with bachelor's degrees, 135.7. These scores are much higher than the scores of other groups who took the test. The mean of graduate students at the University of California, most of whom were completing their doctorates or medical degrees at the time they took the test, was 118. Engineers and scientists in a Navy electronics laboratory, all college graduates, including several doctorates, had a mean of 94.

Scholarship.   Terman and Oden (1959) report in *The Gifted Group at Mid-Life* that the high-IQ students in their study tended to stay in school longer than others. About ten times as many gifted students in their study were college graduates as were unselected students. About 14 percent of the men and 4 percent of the women completed doctoral programs at a time when less than 3 percent of the population completed them. Among the subjects with 180 IQ or above, about half received academic honors, such as membership in Phi Beta Kappa or Sigma Xi (Feldman, 1984). Of Feldman's (1984) sample of the 140 IQ group, about one-quarter were awarded such honors.

There were exceptions to the rule, however. The 150 "least successful" men in Terman's study were less likely to attend college, and those who did made poorer grades than the most successful 150 men in the study. Twenty-five percent of the most successful group had an "A" average while only 5.8 percent of the least successful group had an "A" average. Only 7 percent of the most successful averaged "C" or lower, compared with 30.8 percent of the least successful group. Half of the most successful group were graduated with honors; only 14 percent of the underachievers were.

This section of the chapter has reviewed the relationship between high-IQ giftedness and school performance. A more complex view of academic expectations is presented in the next section. The expectations that result from an emphasis on the development of intellect implicate certain school practices. These recommended practices, together with typical school provisions for the intellectually gifted, are considered in the final section of the chapter.

INTELLECT

As implied in earlier sections of this chapter, definitions of intelligence are "culture-bound" (see e.g., Gallagher, 1975), because they are defined by cultural values. Very little, however, has been done to examine those values and traditions that have determined our particular culture's notions of intelligence.

These culture-bound notions are, essentially, historical phenomena, and this section briefly examines the historical development of the institutions, values, and ideas that give meaning to the construct, "intelligence." Through this analysis, the discussion contrasts the notion of intelligence with the notion of intellect. It applies these two notions to the discussions of (1) the role and nature of scholarship and (2) the relationship between progress and thought.

Western Cultural Tradition

Two trends in the Western cultural tradition have influenced our conception of intelligence: rationalism and literacy. Rationalism is reliance on a way of thinking (reason) that emphasizes the abstraction of general laws from experience. It relies not on a framework of fate or deity, but on a framework of purely human autonomy. Sense-data and empirical methods are, in this sense, tools of reason, not reason itself. Literacy is familiarity with the written word. In addition to denoting the ability to read, it also connotes a sense of form and content in the expression and comprehension of ideas.

Literacy and reason constitute the intellectual substance of scholastic aptitude, and they play a prominent part in the identification and education of gifted children in an industrial culture. The following brief discussion of history is intended to suggest the ways in which social forces shape our work as educators.

The rise of literacy and reason.   Literacy and reason were not always accessible to many people. In ancient Athens, for example, literacy was the prerogative of citizens, but only 10 percent of the total population of the Athenian state were citizens (Butts, 1973). The extent of literacy in the Roman empire is unknown (Bowen, 1972), but it was probably quite narrow.

Between the fall of Rome and the European Renaissance, a great deal happened that would help literacy spread. As cities became established in barbarian Europe, universities emerged as centers of formal learning, and trade also increased. Increased trade brought the West knowledge and products that have helped shape the world as we know it. From North Africa came algebra—the foundation of modern mathematics—and from China an important product for the future of literacy—paper. Literacy was strongly influenced, too, by the religious reform movement that swept northern Europe and caused major changes in the status of the Church of Rome. Among the reforms proposed was an idea that was quite radical for its time: the idea that men and women should be free to read the bible in their own languages.

Bibles appeared for the first time in German, English, and other "vernacular tongues." Sometimes the translators paid for their heretical work with their lives, so great was the fear of literacy. Although the advent of paper, printing, and the publication of bibles in languages other than Latin helped extend literacy, still, in all likelihood, less than one-half of 1 percent of the general population (1 person in 200) was literate in 1700. Modern readers, of course, need to remind themselves that, at that time, reading was not much of a practical advantage in life.

The Renaissance established the relevance of human beings as a fit object of study (humanism), but the Enlightenment that followed firmly established humanity, rather than God or Church, as the *primary* subject of this world. The West was on the verge of a new literacy—a new sense of its power in the world and a new sense of the role of thought—of observation, of reflection, and of imagination—in that world.

By 1800 basic literacy was becoming an established phenomenon even outside governments, churches, and universities. Still, the absolute number of readers was surprisingly small even in 1800, no more than 2 percent of the total population (Watt, 1957). This is a fact we tend to forget in an era when nearly everyone can read a little. (Of course, reading only a little is today a much greater handicap than not reading at all was in 1800!)

The Role and Nature of Scholarship

Educators should understand the role of literacy and reason in Western civilization, because, sustained partly through the scholarship of intellectuals, literacy and reason contribute significantly to the making of new meaning and the stewardship of wisdom.

Scholarship, however, involves more than intelligence; it involves intellect. Richard Hofstadter (1963), a noted historian, distinguished between intellect and intelligence. Hofstadter saw intellect as "critical, creative, and contemplative," and intelligence as "manipulative, adjustive, and unfailingly practical." Hofstadter (1963) looked at how our society views intellect and intelligence when he wrote:

> The man of intelligence is always praised; the man of intellect is sometimes also praised, but he is often looked upon with resentment or suspicion. It is he, and not the intelligent man, who may be called unreliable, superfluous, immoral, or subversive; sometimes he is even said to be, for all of his intellect, unintelligent. (p. 24)

Hofstadter's remarks help us see why intelligence is not always used to enhance intellect. Schools may have a vested interest in making sure that high-IQ students in the end put their talents to work in enterprises where intelligence can make an immediate, practical contribution. Scholars, after all, have an unwelcome habit of asking embarrassing questions.

Scholarship and scholastic aptitude.   More than native intelligence, scholastic aptitude is what IQ tests measure. Scholastic aptitude is the *capacity for scholarship.*

A child who arrives at school with a "high IQ" has an internalized ability to do academic tasks well. Schools, however, may ignore this ability. Instead of promoting habits of scholarship and, hence, involvement with literacy and reason, schools may instead promote habits of deference, orderliness, self-restraint, and regular attendance. They may bend students' talents to the application of socially acceptable work that promises reasonable practical benefit. The emphasis placed on mathematical and scientific training for gifted students is in some ways a good example of this tendency (cf. Tannenbaum, 1981, 1983).

In this way schools may, in fact, damage the talents of their most academically able students. Schools may also fail to recognize the scholastic aptitude of many students—especially those in ethnic, racial, or regional minorities—who do not perform well on IQ tests. These students may nonetheless be demonstrably apt, even though their aptitude has not been bent to academic tasks. By characterizing these students as unintelligent, schools may exclude them from any experiences that would enhance their intellect. Stereotyping of these students' educability is usual, and it may, in fact, serve to deprive them of access to literacy and reason.

Progress and thought. Certain political and economic premises of our society depend on the belief in human excellence. This belief supports a meritocratic view of the distribution of wealth and power (see Chapter 2). Even though this view is not based on an accurate representation of our political economy, it nevertheless explains the propensity to see intellectuals as symbols of human excellence. As a society, however, we respond defensively toward intellectuals; we seem to like them a lot better once they are dead. After their deaths, we are safe from their personal influence, their embarrassing questions, and their immediate example— all of which make us uncomfortable—and we can safely regard them as symbols.

But society also regards intellectuals as dangerous. Intellectuals challenge the status quo. They are critical of society, and they are hard to control. Intellectuals also tend to concern themselves with issues that do not relate directly to the practical endeavors of our economy, which are seen as the development and the distribution of goods and services that have the potential to make money.

As a society, we put a lot more of our resources into the promotion of business and government than we do into the promotion of literacy and rational thought. Many Americans see progress only in terms of economic and technological advancement. They do not regard ideas as significant contributions to the progress of our culture.

Nevertheless, the intellectual legacy is very important to the future of our society. Western civilization may *need* a vital cultural legacy in order to save itself. We may need some powerful ideas to help us resist or recover from the destructiveness and alienation produced by unrestrained technological development (Leontief, 1982; Read, 1960; Thurow, 1987). In the long run, progress may depend more on careful thought than on the manufacture of tangible and marketable products.

Intellectually gifted students have demonstrable aptitude for scholarly work, and programs for them should address this aptitude, above all else. The section that follows provides a basis for understanding the current status of such programs and for evaluating their relevance.

SCHOOL RESPONSES TO HIGH-IQ CHILDREN

Of the constructs of giftedness, IQ is the easiest to measure. It is also the construct that is most closely related to the academic requirements of school. Consequently, programs for high-IQ students were instituted earliest and continue to be most prevalent. This section of the chapter first provides an historical review of programs for high-IQ students. Next, it recommends educational approaches that involve such students in the intellectual traditions of literacy and reason.

Historical Overview

Acceleration was probably the earliest school response to intellectually gifted students. In one-room schools, acceleration took place when a child mastered the curriculum of a particular grade level. The advent of graded schools, however, made acceleration seem less natural. Nevertheless, grade skipping took place often. Some districts conducted graded schools in terms of one-half year. Students could, therefore, skip half a grade at a time.

In the early twentieth century, educators began to organize special classes for high-IQ children. Leta Hollingworth helped establish one of the earliest classes for such children. Public School 500 (also known as the Speyer School) in New York City had special classrooms for both gifted and highly gifted children. These classes combined acceleration and enrichment (Hollingworth, 1926). They also provided a more progressive curriculum for the gifted than the curriculum offered in that era to average students. Other classrooms were established in major cities such as Cincinnati, Cleveland, and Los Angeles. The Major Works Program, which started in Cleveland in 1921, exemplifies these efforts.

The influence of progressive education.   Enrichment, as an alternative to acceleration, resulted from the concerns of progressive educators (e.g., Osburn & Rohan, 1931). Progressive educators were interested in more than the academic development of children; they were interested in the development of the "whole" child. These educators viewed enrichment as a means to allow high-IQ students to develop appropriate academic skills without having to leave their age group peers (Fowlkes, 1930). This view dominated gifted education from the 1930s through the 1950s; it became popular again in the late 1960s and continues to influence programs for high-IQ students.

Not only did the aims of enrichment programs result from the notions of progressive educators, the content of such programs also reflected progressive beliefs. For example, interdisciplinary instruction was implemented by progressive educators (Cremin, 1961) and continues to characterize enrichment programs (see e.g., Cox et al., 1985; Martinson, 1968; Renzulli, 1977).

Progressive views of education also influenced other characteristics of programs for high-IQ students. Programs to develop critical and creative thinking skills were recommended by progressive educators (e.g., Stedman, 1924). Progressive educators also noted the importance of individualization, independent study, consideration of real problems, student-directed learning, and out-of-school learning for high-ability children. These instructional approaches are still prominent among contemporary recommendations for intellectually gifted students.

The influence of Sputnik.   The 1957 launching of the Russian satellite, Sputnik, altered U.S. priorities for the education of intellectually gifted students (Tannenbaum, 1981). In the late 1950s and the 1960s, educators stressed instruction in science and math. This priority prompted the development of innovative and challenging curricula (Gallagher, 1975). The earlier emphasis on enrichment yielded to a new focus. To organize the efficient delivery of difficult curricula in science and math, schools began increasingly to group students by ability or achievement levels.

Equal opportunity and back to basics.   In the mid- and late 1960s educational programs were guided by the concern for equity. Programs for disadvantaged children proliferated. Programs for high-IQ children were seldom funded. Nevertheless, many intellectually gifted students continued to receive relevant academic instruction. Many schools continued to use the innovative curricula developed in the late 1950s and early 1960s. The theoretical orientation of "new math," for example, challenged bright students even where special programs were not provided. In addition, schools persisted in grouping children by ability until law suits in the early 1970s discouraged this practice.

In response to the concern for cultural and individual self-determination that dominated educational thinking in the mid- to late 1960s, educators in the mid-1970s and 1980s showed a renewed concern for "basic skills." Whereas instruction in basic skills is intended to help more students pass minimum competency tests, it fails to teach literacy and reason. "Basic skills," unfortunately, do not include the habits of critical thinking and inquiry.

The educational legacy of the last 30 years has influenced the most current recommendations for the education of intellectually gifted students (e.g., Bennett, 1986; Cox et al., 1985; Stanley, 1981). These recommendations advocate:

1. acceleration,
2. rigorous coursework and emphasis on academics,

3. foreign language instruction,
4. cultural literacy,
5. high expectations, and
6. advanced instruction in math and science.

Contemporary Practices

Programs for intellectually gifted students have not always addressed the cognitive strengths that these students demonstrate. If educators choose to design programs on the basis of the recommendations above, however, they will be more likely to develop these strengths. To put these recommendations into practice, educators will need to establish practical routines of identification, program planning, and instruction. The discussion below describes practices that will be most likely to correspond to the academic needs of intellectually gifted students. These practices should make it possible for high-IQ students to cultivate habits of scholarship and, thereby, to understand and, perhaps more important, to develop our intellectual legacy still further.

Identification. Intellectual giftedness is most often determined on the basis of IQ test scores. Typically, students qualify for programs on the basis of scores that are at least 2 standard deviations above the mean on tests of intelligence. IQ tests measure intellectual potential—that is, how well individuals *can* perform academic tasks.

In an earlier part of the chapter we termed this capacity "scholastic aptitude." Tests that measure scholastic aptitude are, therefore, also appropriate for determining intellectual giftedness.

Measuring academic achievement is also a way to determine intellectual giftedness. It is impossible for students to score 2 standard deviations above the mean on valid and reliable *achievement* tests without having the *potential* to do so. If such a case arises, the accuracy of the student's IQ test score needs to be questioned; it may be an unreliable measure of the student's giftedness.

An important consideration in the use of any of these sorts of tests is their fairness to children from minority groups. Both in Chapter 2 and in this chapter, we stated that students from minority groups score lower than white, middle-class students on standardized tests. Because their lower scores reflect variables other than intelligence, educators must use identification procedures that assure the equal access of minority students to programs for the intellectually gifted.

A promising approach to culture-fair assessment involves the use of local, regional, or minority-group norms. Educators can use local or minority-group norms to identify the children with the highest scholastic aptitude or achievement in a particular school or from a particular subgroup of the population.

Another approach is to modify the operational definition of giftedness to allow for the variability of scores among children from minority groups. The model definition given in Box 3-1 reflects the concern for equity. It also bases eligibility on either an intelligence or an achievement test score.

BOX 3-1   A Model Definition

Except in the case of a nonadvantaged student, a student shall be declared eligible to receive special services under the auspices of gifted education if either of the following conditions obtains: (1) the student scores two standard deviations above the mean on any major portion of a comprehensive evaluation-level test of *achievement* (e.g., the mathematics cluster of the Woodcock-Johnson Psychoeducational Battery, Part II Tests of Achievement) in consideration of one standard error of measurement, *OR* (2) the student scores two standard deviations above the mean on a comprehensive evaluation-level test of *intelligence* (e.g., the Stanford-Binet Intelligence Scale) in consideration of one standard error of measurement. *In the case of nonadvantaged students,* a declaration of eligibility shall occur in consideration of three standard errors of measurement. The term "nonadvantaged" refers to ethnically different students, to students for whom English is not the native tongue, and to students who are eligible to receive free or reduced-price meals. (Howley, 1986, p. 23)

The most appropriate operational definitions of intellectual giftedness depend on measurement. Although there are many instruments that purport to measure intelligence or achievement, the most valid and reliable ones are comprehensive and are administered individually. These tests are classified as *evaluation* instruments. They are contrasted with *screening* instruments, which are useful only for identifying children who *might* score at a particular level on an evaluation test. *Evaluation instruments are the only kinds of tests that should be used to determine eligibility for placement in a special program.*

Two scales of intelligence are most often used to determine intellectual giftedness. They are the Stanford-Binet Scale and the Wechsler Scale.

The Stanford-Binet Scale is based on a definition of intelligence that equates IQ with scholastic aptitude. For this reason, the Stanford-Binet scale includes a preponderance of verbal items (Sattler, 1982). It includes items that measure vocabulary, abstract words, sentence building, similarities and differences, analogies, sentence completion, verbal absurdities, and reasoning.

By contrast, the Wechsler Scale is based on the view that intelligence is the global ability to solve problems. It samples two broad domains of cognitive functioning, the verbal domain and the performance domain.

There are many other intelligence scales that are useful for special populations. The scale developed by the Kaufmans was intended to help identify intellectually gifted students from culturally different backgrounds. Unfortunately, the K-ABC has not been as successful at this endeavor as was first hoped.

Evaluators can also find a number of tests that measure scholastic aptitude. Most of these tests, however, are designed for group administration. The aptitude test that is most often used to identify intellectually gifted students is the College Entrance Examination Board's (Educational Testing Service, 1926–1987) Scholastic Aptitude Test (SAT). SAT scores are used by *selective* colleges (many colleges are not selective) to make decisions about admissions. They are also used for determining the eligibility of younger students (seventh and eighth graders) for special programs (Stanley, 1977).

Individual tests of achievement, unfortunately, often do not have a high enough ceiling to measure reliably the achievement of intellectually gifted adolescents. With younger children, evaluators can, however, use one of several tests. Some of these tests are batteries that measure achievement in a number of different areas; others measure achievement in only one subject. Most prominent among the multiple-subject batteries is the Woodcock-Johnson Psychoeducational Battery (Woodcock & Johnson, 1977). This test includes measures of achievement in four areas: mathematics, reading, written language, and knowledge.

Program planning.   Regardless of whether an individual teacher or a committee plans the instructional program for an intellectually gifted student, certain principles should be considered. First, the program should address the student's demonstrated propensity for academic learning. Second, the program should guide decisions about placement. The student should be placed in environments where his or her needs can best be met. The gifted resource room often is not the optimal environment for a student who exhibits advanced skills in academic subjects. Finally, the program should account for long-range planning. A student who is placed in advanced classes in elementary school should *not* have to repeat similar classes at a later point in his or her education.

The availability of a number of program options facilitates planning for intellectually gifted students. Unfortunately, most school districts endorse only one or two options (Cox et al., 1985). The twelve options listed in Box 3-2 describe the range of services required for planning appropriate instructional programs.

BOX 3-2   *Effective Program Options*

- First Option (Elementary Level): Each elementary school provides special accelerated reading and mathematics classes for gifted primary students.
- Second Option (Elementary Level): Each elementary school provides a review process to consider yearly, or more frequently upon request of teachers, parents, or students, which

accelerative strategy or strategies (e.g., cross-class placement, special accelerated classes, early entry, dual attendance, combined grades, grade skipping) are appropriate for each gifted student.

• Third Option (Elementary Level): Each elementary school offers a choice of three years of either of two foreign languages to gifted students.

• Fourth Option (Elementary Level): Each elementary school offers an accelerated literature and writing class that prepares students to write good ten-page essays by age 13. (A good essay conforms to high standards of grammar, diction, and style. High standards for gifted students aged 13 shall approximate the best efforts of average first-year undergraduates.) Such a course will provide 1 Carnegie Credit in high-school English.

• Fifth Option (Elementary Level): Each elementary school provides an advanced mathematics class to deliver the complete Algebra I content (linear and quadratic equations through the derivation and application of the quadratic formula) to gifted students in Grades 4–8. Such a course will provide 1 Carnegie Credit in high-school mathematics.

• Sixth Option (Elementary Level): Each elementary school provides an accelerated science class in biology or chemistry that will provide 1 Carnegie Credit in high-school science.

• Seventh Option (Secondary Level): Each secondary school develops procedures that allow students to earn course credit by examination (initially in a limited number of courses).

• Eighth Option (Secondary Level): Each secondary school develops an accelerated (3 or 4 years in 2 or 3 years) mathematics sequence that includes geometry, a second course in algebra, trigonometry, and integral and differential calculus to begin in the ninth grade. Such a sequence provides 3 or 4 Carnegie Credits in high-school mathematics.

• Ninth Option (Secondary Level): Each secondary school develops an accelerated (4 years in 3) literature program that requires the reading of a major work each month and frequent writing about works read. The course sequence should cover British and American literature, foreign literature in translation, and philosophy (using original sources). Such a sequence provides 4 Carnegie Credits in high-school English.

• Tenth Option (Secondary Level): Each secondary school develops a strategy to enable gifted students to complete the science sequence that provides 3 Carnegie Credits in biology, chemistry, and physics by the end of Grade 11.

• Eleventh Option (Secondary Level): Each secondary school develops an advisement system that ensures that an increasing number of gifted students attend very selective institutions of higher education.

• Twelfth Option (Secondary Level): In cooperation with other institutions each secondary school develops an internship program that gives interested gifted students a substantive experience with an outstanding community sponsor during the senior year of high school (for those gifted students who elect a four-year high school program). (Howley, 1986, pp. 24–25)

Appropriate instruction. One notable omission from the range of services listed above is the resource room. Although this method of delivering special education is the most common for high-IQ children, it is the least effective (Cox, et al, 1985). Resource room programs most often provide enrichment, a kind of instruction that, by definition, is tangential to the content of the regular curriculum (Vernon, Adamson, & Vernon, 1977).

There are two reasons why enrichment, as commonly practiced, is an inadequate alternative for high-IQ children: (1) enrichment activities lack substance and (2) other options are much more relevant to the education of high-IQ students (Stanley, 1981). Though some progressive educators of the gifted in the 1920s and 1930s had quite specific activities in mind, enrichment today is often so broadly conceived that it is actually suitable for all children, regardless of IQ (Weiler, 1978). Like extracurricular activities, enrichment programs often do provide positive and enjoyable experiences. Special programs designed for high-IQ children ought, however, to provide a lot more: They should provide substantive instruction in academic subjects.

Two instructional strategies are suited to the needs of high-IQ children: acceleration and special curriculum. Acceleration allows intellectually gifted students to progress academically at a rate that approximates the rate at which they learn. Because acceleration is a modification of the regular curriculum, it is easy and inexpensive to use. A special curriculum is more expensive and more complicated to organize. This approach, which combines acceleration and ability grouping, provides the only comprehensive way to address all of the academic needs of high-IQ students. Such a curriculum can be delivered exclusively to gifted children, or it can be offered to high achievers as well.

SUMMARY

This chapter viewed the psychological construct of intelligence from several perspectives. It examined theories of intelligence including behavioral theories, single-factor theories, multiple-factor theories, dichotomous-ability theories, and information-processing theories. The chapter contrasted the more limited construct of scholastic aptitude with the broader construct of adaptive behavior.

By reviewing the literature on the school performance of high-IQ children, the chapter showed the relationship of intelligence to indices of academic attainment. This section indicated that, in spite of some limitations, IQ tests can be used for predicting school performance. Because of the strong correspondence between intelligence and scholastic aptitude, the chapter also emphasized the importance of intellectual work for individuals with high IQs.

Finally, the chapter provided a review of schools' options for educating high-IQ children. It suggested a definition of intellectual giftedness and suitable methods for measuring IQ. It also discussed program alternatives that seem to be most effective for high-IQ students.

4

Creativity Constructs

Focusing Questions

1. Is it always possible to distinguish convergent from divergent
    questions?
2. What actual personality traits and personal values lie behind the
    stereotype of the wild and rebellious artist?
3. In what different ways has creativity been operationalized as a
    psychological construct?
4. Why do some researchers believe there is a low correlation
    between IQ and creativity, whereas others believe there is a
    high correlation? Which researchers do you think are right?
    Why?
5. Educators often express a commitment to meeting the
    intellectual, physical, social-emotional, and spiritual needs of
    students. How does creativity training serve this commitment?

INTELLIGENCE AND ADULT PRODUCTIVITY

The investigation of eminent individuals in the nineteenth century had an
important influence on gifted education. Chief among the reasons for
investigating eminence was the perceived need for more of the kinds of

products developed by the eminent. The industrial world was emerging rapidly, and the need to cultivate talent in science, industry, and commerce was keenly felt. The early researchers asked *why* their eminent subjects were able to produce more and better works than other people. They answered that their subjects were more intelligent in general, more talented in their particular work, and that they worked harder than other people (cf. Galton, 1869/1962). By 1910, psychology had emerged as a science, and both psychologists and educators felt that the time had come to find and to train exceptional talent.

Although Terman (1925) established that his test did, in fact, predict achievement in school, he was subsequently unable to prove that his test predicted adult eminence (Feldman, 1984). What had gone wrong? One answer that seemed likely to many psychologists and educators had been apparent to most skeptics of the IQ all along: IQ tests fail to measure all the components of intellect. Another answer that seemed likely was that IQ has little to do with real-life achievement.

ISSUES OF CONVERGENCE AND DIVERGENCE

According to Guilford (1950), for example, IQ tests measured *convergent* thinking, a process that results in finding a correct answer to a certain type of problem. The tests, claimed Guilford, fail to measure *divergent* thinking, a process that results in producing many possible solutions for a certain type of problem. Guilford's observation intrigued E. Paul Torrance, a wartime colleague. Torrance had already been puzzling out the notion of creativity for some time (Torrance, 1984).

Torrance (1984) reports that as early as 1943 he had developed a creativity test. Guilford's notion of divergent thinking influenced Torrance's construct of creativity, and in his creativity tests Torrance used four subskills reputed by Guilford to characterize divergent thinking. These subskills are (1) elaboration, (2) flexibility, (3) fluency, and (4) originality (see Box 4-2). Not all interpretations of creativity have adopted Guilford's model. His notion of divergent thinking is nonetheless the historical beginning of the empirical study of creativity.

Questions and Answers

Despite their important differences, convergent and divergent thinking are similar because they both answer questions. The differences in convergent and divergent thinking often lie in the kind of question answered. They always differ, however, in (1) the kind and the degree of response that is acceptable, and (2) the kind of product that may be implicit in the response.

Kind of question.   Convergent questions have an answer that is logically correct or that some *authority* has determined to be correct in advance. An unambiguous example is "What is the square root of nine?" A more ambiguous example is "What is the chief cause of the Civil War?" followed by answers in a multiple-choice format.

Divergent questions do not have a correct answer as determined by the logic of some discipline or some authority. Divergent questions are by nature ambiguous. In fact, a divergent question may be rephrased in the process of being answered. For example, "Where shall we go this afternoon?" may evoke the response, "Nowhere—let's stay here and make ice cream!" or even, "I'm not going anywhere with *you!*" depending on the circumstance. In the first case, the reformulated question is "What shall we do if we stay here?" and in the second, "Would you like to go somewhere with me?"

Simple divergent answers often beg the question. Elaborated divergent responses provide a more complete context in which the reformulated question and the thinking behind it become explicit.

A more ambiguous example of a divergent question is "How can you trisect an angle with compass and ruler?" Though the judgment of history has thus far been that this task is impossible, the correct answer may still be some undiscovered set of instructions. On the other hand the answer may be "You can't." The latter response challenges the question and might be either convergent or divergent.

Notice that an unsound convergent question (i.e., one that does not, indeed, have a correct answer) resembles a divergent question, and that a predetermined divergent question (i.e., one that specifies results) resembles a convergent question. The critical distinction between convergence and divergence seems to involve authority.

When a question is treated convergently, both the person putting the question and the person answering it treat the question as sound. The person answering the question *necessarily* accepts the soundness of the question on the *authority* of the person asking the question. The authority of the questioner is *not necessarily* accepted when a question is divergent. Many questions can easily be approached convergently or divergently, depending on the respondent's view of the question.

Kind and degree of response.   Simple convergent responses resemble the solutions to puzzles or riddles. They fit into a predetermined context. Convergent responses must also be interpreted as making unambiguous sense in such a context. They are *concise and analytical.* Thus, responses are *objectively* evaluated as part of a respondent's convergent thinking.

Simple divergent responses, however, resemble lists or puns. They reveal connections, commonalities, or contrasts. They are *fluent and synthetic.* Rather than fitting into a predetermined context, simple divergent re-

---

BOX 4-1   Contrasting and Comparing Convergent and Divergent Thinking

A DIVERGENT VIEW

Many commentators see convergent and divergent thinking as opposites. Most of the adjectives below are taken from the discussion in this chapter.

Adjectives that may describe convergent thinking:

- objective
- normative
- analytic
- concise
- hard-working

Adjectives that may describe divergent thinking:

- subjective
- autonomous
- synthetic
- elaborate
- playful

Lists of adjectives might be said to be a *divergent* description of divergent and convergent thinking. This description is merely suggestive; the original list from which these adjectives were drawn contained 15 items.

A CONVERGENT VIEW

Divergent and convergent thinking can be distinguished by one sufficient feature:

> The feature that distinguishes convergent from divergent thinking is submission to external authority and objective evaluation. Convergent thinking submits, whereas divergent thinking does not. By operating autonomously, divergent thinking acts subjectively, whereas by operating normatively, convergent thinking acts objectively.

This statement distinguishes between divergent and convergent thinking in a convergent mode. It purports to be logical and concise.

---

sponses suggest a new, altered, or extended context. This suggestive fluency means that elaboration may be necessary for a complete response. Fluency seems, however, to be the minimum observable characteristic needed to distinguish a simple convergent from a simple divergent answer (cf. Hocevar, 1979, 1980; Perkins, 1981).

Originality is also said to be another significant characteristic of divergent thinking (cf. Guilford, 1959; Koestler, 1964). Originality, however, is usually inferred from the novelty of divergent responses. This inference does not necessarily mean that all novel responses are divergent. Novel responses *can* be produced by convergent thinking, as we shall see. Truly *original* (not merely novel) responses cannot be produced by convergent thinking, however, because original responses cannot be submitted to objective evaluation during their formulation. Original responses must be *subjectively evaluated* by the respondent during their production.

The subjective quality of originality (as opposed to novelty) indicates again the degree to which divergent thinking proceeds on its own authority. Originality is in this sense *autonomous*. Marcuse (1978), for example, believes that works of art portray an autonomous vision of the world inherent in artists' manipulation of aesthetic form.

Objectivity and divergent production.   The one sense in which it is possible to attribute objectivity to a divergent response, however, is the case in which an object is made. The creation of an object may constitute a *fully elaborated divergent* response, if the object is evaluated only subjectively by its creator(s) during production.

Observers can subsequently make a normative (i.e., objective) comparison of the object with other objects to determine its utility, novelty, or beauty. An inference about the divergence of the producer's thinking may be made from the object's utility, novelty, or beauty. Many useful, novel, or beautiful objects are, however, in no way creative, or even the product of divergent thinking (Perkins, 1981). In particular, it seems strange to expect *original* products to conform to *conventional* standards of utility, novelty, and beauty. Nonetheless, definitions of creativity typically expect original products to conform to such standards, and most creativity research specifies that utility and novelty constitute necessary characteristics of *creative* (not merely divergent) products (see, e.g., Keating, 1980a; LaChapelle, 1983; Pearlman, 1983; Weinstein & Bobko, 1980; but cf. Marcuse, 1978; Perkins, 1981).

Historical Notions of Creativity

The preceding discussion gives us a contemporary vantage point from which to examine the act of creation. However, it is interesting to see how the concept of creativity has changed historically since the nineteenth century. During the first half of the twentieth century, it was commonly assumed that creativity was the province of comparatively few individuals, that these individuals were primarily artists, and that creativity was not necessarily a desirable attribute, at least from the standpoint of objective social norms (LaChapelle, 1983). By the mid-twentieth century, the concept of creativity changed (LaChapelle, 1983; Pearlman, 1983), and creativity was found to be a potential ability of all individuals, applicable to *all* fields of human endeavor (see, e.g., Rogers, 1959, p. 71).

Most subsequent empirical work on creativity has, in fact, contributed to a broadened definition of the term. According to LaChapelle (1983, p. 132), the broadened definition "allows for the possibility that almost anyone under almost any circumstance can be creative." The construct of creativity has thus come to resemble the construct of intelligence. One may be intelligent or act intelligently without ever significantly engaging the intellect; similarly, it seems in the broadened definition that one may be creative or act creatively without ever creating anything.

Nonetheless, recent programs for *developing* creativity have applied the broadened notion of creativity especially to industrial and scientific productivity. Osborn (1953), an advertising executive, devised techniques of "creative problem solving." His training program was intended to foster the inventiveness and productivity of industrial research and development teams. Osborn's thesis was "that the economic supremacy of our country [is maintained] by the creative ability of our citizens" (Osborn, 1963, p. x). Together creativity and patriotism became the province of business and industry, much as high IQ and patriotism became the province of math and science education in the 1960s (cf. Tannenbaum, 1981).

Useful novelty.   The change in focus from the arts to business and industry is quite dramatic. Is there a link between industry and art that might help account for this historical change in focus? One link may be the notion of originality, or novelty (measured empirically as uniqueness, but cf. Perkins, 1981, pp. 282–283 and Welsh, 1975, pp. 3, 69, for different notions of originality). With the help of vigorous advertising, industry induces new markets to buy new products. Novelty represents a competitive advantage in the marketplace.

Novelty also has a place in the arts, where originality, like beauty, is sometimes valued as an end in itself. Novelty is characteristic of artistic modernism (Read, 1959). It can help an art dealer establish a market by relating the works of new artists to the dominant aesthetic of the times. Mere novelty, however, is *unlikely* to be an adequate proxy for originality.

The sort of novelty shared by commercial and artistic products is *novelty in trade*. This similarity does not establish the originality of an artistic or commercial product, nor does it establish commercial and artistic production as equally creative fields.

Productivity and Creativity

Creativity research has devoted comparatively little attention to the creative product (Perkins, 1981). It is difficult to see why. After all, the presumed need for such products is the motivation for this research. Perhaps the evaluation of created objects is considered to be the territory of art critics and scholars alone.

Instead of assessing products, much of the creativity research, at present, assesses divergent thinking. The most serious flaw in such a choice is that divergent thinking is *not* synonymous with creativity. Some researchers are aware of the importance of this distinction (e.g., Hocevar, 1980; Klein, 1982; Perkins, 1981) but others are not (e.g., Torrance, 1963, 1984; Wallach & Kogan, 1965).

Two serious problems are caused by a failure to consider the distinction between divergent thinking and creativity. First, the concept of divergent thinking does not account for the *act of making a product*. Empirical research into divergent thinking struggles to characterize the internal states that precede the behavior of making a product (e.g., Wallas, 1926). Second, failure to distinguish productivity from creativity occurs when researchers are unable (e.g., MacKinnon, 1962/1981) or theorists refuse (e.g., Rogers, 1959) to distinguish *the qualities that characterize products.*

Of the terms, creativity and productivity, "productivity" is the more general term. It refers to the provision of goods or services *in abundance.* Such goods and services are typically useful, especially in trade. Concern for productivity reflects the entrepreneur's objective of increasing profits. Osborn (1953) noted explicitly that the primary function of his creativity training program was to increase the profits of industry and commerce. This analysis shows why the term creativity was broadened to include business and to include *being and doing* as well as *making.* Business includes manufactures (making) and services (being and doing), and its chief concern is profit.

As Perkins (1981) notes, however, even quite worthwhile products need not be creative. He sees the quality of products (kind and excellence) as determining what is creative.

Making Sense of Creativity

Recent theoretical work has recognized that both convergent and divergent thinking are components of creativity. The central importance of a "creative" product (whatever it may be) has also been recently acknowledged (e.g., Pearlman, 1983; Perkins, 1981).

Both Pearlman and Perkins, however, neglect the important concept of autonomy. The reasons for this neglect are inherent in the nature of ordinary commerce and scholarship. In commerce, practical restraints place severe limitations on autonomy. Osborn's (1953) version of creativity training respects such limitations in its *group method.* The group method maximizes the benefits of divergent thinking, while minimizing the risks of true autonomy (see e.g., Abelson, 1967). The group method is a practical restraint on autonomy in the service of profit (Wiener, 1954).

In scholarship the limitations on autonomy are inherent in intellectual tradition. As Perkins (1981) notes, scholars work according to established theories and methods. Creative scholarship is comparatively rare simply because it involves changing well-established theories and methods. The mixture of talent, training, and chance necessary to effect a change in conventional methods and theories is necessarily quite rare (Abelson, 1967; Perkins, 1981).

Autonomy, however, is *characteristic* of the arts. In the arts, an authentic statement (a creative product) is possible via the imaginative vision of the artist alone. Aesthetic form is the aspect of art that embodies artistic autonomy, according to Marcuse (1978). Even inept art is thus, by definition, a divergent view of the world, and *authentic* art is necessarily creative. This view of creativity helps explain why excellent works of art are much more common than creative scholarship or creative commercial products.

PERSONALITY TRAITS ASSOCIATED WITH CREATIVITY

In contrast to the limited research on creative products, analysis of the creative person has been a typical means of investigating creativity. The results of these investigations and speculations are voluminous, if not definitive. This research has ranged from Lombroso's (1891) quasi-scientific study of human behavior, through Freud's work in psychoanalysis, to the empiricism of contemporary psychology. This brief discussion can not do justice to the diverse and complex theories developed to account for correlates of creativity. However, it offers an outline of the ideas and research findings that are most relevant to educators of gifted students.

Early Studies of Creative Genius

It was only when American psychologists began to define intelligence in terms of IQ that creativity came to be treated as distinct from intelligence and even contrasted with it. Until the twentieth century, the concept "creativity" was subsumed by the concept "genius." Lombroso's *The Man of Genius* and Galton's *Hereditary Genius,* both published in England in the nineteenth century, made no distinction between the two concepts.

Lombroso's characterization of geniuses as physically and emotionally degenerate instigated one of the major controversies in the study of giftedness: the relationship between genius and insanity. Lombroso's list of characteristics (e.g., pallor, stammering, left-handedness, amnesia, and early death) contrasts sharply with contemporary lists, which tend to characterize the gifted in glowing terms (e.g., energetic, outgoing, funny). However, the belief that creativity and insanity are close relatives has not been dispelled. Psychologists still debate the existence of a relationship between the two (cf. Eysenck, 1983).

Noticing that brilliant men seemed to share certain traits, Lombroso proceeded to look for more examples to support his hypothesis. The problem with this method of collecting data is that it could establish only the occurrence of certain traits among men of genius. It could reveal nothing about the relative frequency of occurrence. It certainly could not establish, as Lombroso claimed, that the traits occur more frequently in the brilliant than in the normal population.

Lombroso's influence must be attributed not to the quality of his argument, but to the concordance of his findings with popular sentiment. Many people were convinced that genius and madness were closely associated; and a spate of biographical case studies, mostly documenting the psychological aberrations of eminent geniuses, were published.

Although Francis Galton's *English Men of Science* and his *Hereditary Genius* were among these biographical works, Galton did not subscribe to

Lombroso's view. At least he did not see the creative genius as unbalanced. In fact, creative accomplishment, in Galton's view, demands emotional balance. According to Galton, even though the eminent poets, artists, and musicians that he studied were ". . . exceedingly irregular in their way of life" (Galton, 1869 p. 278), they combined intellect, rigor, and earnestness with "delight in the exercise of their affections." This observation foreshadowed, and perhaps influenced, contemporary psychologists' findings that creative adults seem to combine psychological vulnerability and *exceptional* psychological strength.

Psychoanalytic accounts of creativity. Sigmund Freud's concept of creativity as a means of resolving personal, unconscious conflicts formed yet another association between mental disturbance and creativity, although Freud did not imply that *abnormal* needs and conflicts were the source of creative work. Freud contended that creative endeavor is only one of several mechanisms for coping with the unhappiness and frustration that everyone experiences. The unconscious desires underlying creative activity require sublimation, the redirection of basic psychosexual drives so that they are not frustrated by the external world (Strachey, 1961). However, according to Freud, the pleasure of creative work is not accessible to everyone; it requires special dispositions and abilities.

C. G. Jung, in reaction to Freud, held that the individual unconscious does not inform the content of creative works, but only of self-indulgent or neurotic exercises. According to Jung, the artist must raise images, not from the personal unconscious, but from the *collective unconscious*. From this part of the *psyche*, which he says is less accessible than the personal unconscious, come archetypal images that reflect universal experiences rather than personal history. Artists transform these images into symbols that can be understood by their contemporaries (Campbell, 1971). The creative personality is, for Jung, necessarily maladaptive because only dissatisfied misfits are sufficiently inured to conventional ideas and mores to be receptive to the archetypal images of human experience.

Jung's account is generally denigrated as mystical, but it nonetheless seems to corroborate the accounts of some artists. Although such accounts do not demand a supernatural source, they are often attributed to one. Consequently, Jung's theory of the source of creative work is regarded by most scientists as an inappropriate line of inquiry; scientific methods cannot legitimately be applied to mystical accounts of behavior.

In Jung's account, artists must be introverted in order to resist external influences. This resistance to external influences and attention to internal ones is essential to the creative process in Jung's view. Empirical investigation does support the hypothesis that artists are introverted (e.g., Barron, 1963; Barron, 1969), but these findings do not, of course, validate Jung's theory of the source of creativity.

Humanistic psychologists' view of the creative person. Alfred Adler belongs to the psychoanalytic tradition, but his view of personality, more optimistic than the traditional Freudian view, is a precursor of humanist psychology. Adler's psychology posits a kind of psychological upward mobility, that is, a drive toward superiority or, in humanistic terms, self-actualization.

Adler believes that creativity is an individual's healthy response to physical inferiorities. According to Adler's theory, creativity is a form of compensation for inferior physical organs: Poets and artists are compensating for inferior visual structures; musicians for auditory weaknesses; and actors, singers, and speakers for inferiority of the vocal apparatus (Ansbacher & Ansbacher, 1956). This theory of creativity, though certainly interesting, is, like many psychoanalytic theories, very difficult to test empirically.

Much of Adler's influence is indirect and is seen in the work of Abraham Maslow (1954), who elaborated the concept of the self-actualizing individual. Maslow's development of this idea included a hierarchy of needs basic to all humans (i.e., a need for satisfaction of primary physical drives, a need for physical and psychological safety, and a need for a sense of belonging and love). In addition to these fundamental needs, Maslow hypothesized the human need to actualize potential. Using a case study approach similar to that used by Lombroso and Galton, he identified characteristics of persons whom he considered to be self-actualizing (e.g., Albert Einstein, William James, Eleanor Roosevelt). The characteristics he found these people to share included (1) a more efficient perception of reality and more comfortable relations with it; (2) acceptance of self, others, and nature; (3) spontaneity; (4) a problem-centered rather than ego-centered orientation; (5) preference for solitude and privacy; (6) autonomy; and (7) creativeness (Maslow, 1954).

The creativeness to which Maslow refers when he describes self-actualization is different from the "special-talent creativeness of the Mozart type," (Maslow, 1954, p. 223). As he points out in his description of self-actualizing individuals, his subjects did not show special creativity through writing fiction, painting, or composing music; rather, they manifested an originality of outlook and an open, spontaneous approach to both their work and their play. According to Maslow, this style, born out of satisfaction of basic physical and psychological needs, lends freshness and inventiveness to their ideas.

Maslow's findings provide a rationale for student-centered teaching, counseling, and a psychologically supportive classroom environment: strategies that are conducive to openness and inventiveness. There is no evidence from his work, however, that these strategies are effective in developing the creative talent needed to produce outstanding novels, musical compositions, poems, paintings, and dramas. Application of Maslow's findings to the education of gifted students often disregards the distinction between a flexible, spontaneous (i.e., "creative") approach to life and the actual creation of significant scholarship or works of art. However, Maslow himself was not optimistic about influencing the making of excellent products:

> We may as well face the fact that the so-called geniuses display ability that we do not understand . . . they seem to be specially endowed with a drive and a capacity that may have rather little relationship to the rest of the personality and with which, from all evidence, the individuals seem to be born. (Maslow, 1954, p. 233)

Whether giftedness is innate or learned is still a matter of controversy, but various sorts of research do *suggest* a relationship between some personality qualities and creative genius.

Recent Research Findings on Creative Adults

Humanistic psychology cultivated an interest in the exceptionally healthy personality and in people who were unusually competent. During the 1950s and 1960s, several studies set out to identify cognitive and affective traits of highly reputed artists, scientists, architects, mathematicians, and businessmen. These studies have much in common with the approaches of Maslow, Galton, and Lombroso to the study of creativity. However, the recent studies differ from the earlier biographical studies in several ways: Subjects were selected on a more random basis, sample size was larger, and measures of personality were more objective. Among the variables found to distinguish creative persons from others were their interest in abstract ideas, lack of interest in socializing, unhappy childhood experiences, emotional intensity, emotional strength, and emulation of nonconformist behavior.

Interest in abstract ideas. Creative artists, writers, mathematicians, scientists, and architects prize aesthetic and theoretical pursuits (Perkins, 1981). On the Allport-Vernon-Lindzey Study of Values (1951)—a measure comparing relative interest in theoretical, economic, aesthetic, social-political, and religious ideas—creative persons usually score highest on the aesthetic and theoretical scales (MacKinnon, 1978). Architects tend to score highest on the aesthetic scale and second highest on the theoretical scale; scientists score highest on the theoretical scale, but their aesthetic score is nearly as high; and mathematicians score about equally high on both scales (MacKinnon, 1975). Gifted art students' aesthetic scores are extremely high and their theoretical scores next highest (Getzels & Csikszentmihalyi, 1968).

Commitment to aesthetic and theoretical issues was also shown to be one of the most salient characteristics of a group of renowned writers (e.g., Truman Capote, Norman Mailer, MacKinlay Kantor, Frank O'Connor, and Kenneth Rexroth) who participated in a study on creativity. Barron (1963, pp. 242–243) was impressed with the intensity of the authors' ". . . profound commitment to larger meanings of an esthetic and philosophical sort. . . ." It really should come as no surprise, however, that women and men who spend most of their lives working at art, music, mathematics, or literature report that they are devoted to the essential content of their disciplines.

Lack of interest in socializing.   Those creative persons who score high on interest in aesthetics and theoretical issues usually score low on the social scale of the Study of Values. MacKinnon (1975) found that about two-thirds of a sample of creative writers, architects, and scientists were substantially more introverted than their less creative peers. Scientists who are rated high in creative ability often describe themselves as loners (Andrews, 1975; Roe, 1952). Artists, too, are more introverted than the rest of the population (Gotz & Gotz, 1973; 1979).

There is little question that introversion predominates among the highly creative. What is not clear is whether their introversion results from insecurity about social interactions, from hostility toward others, or from enjoyment of solitude and intellectual pursuits. Some studies stress that scientists are socially competent, but simply prefer intellectual to social challenge (e.g., Roe, 1952); other studies suggest that insecurity contributes to scientists' introversion (Andrews, 1975). The tendency toward introversion may not result solely from either factor; it may, instead, reflect both preference for solitude *and* alienation. Introversion may arise from and support the process of creation (Getzels, 1979; but cf. Osborn, 1953).

Unhappy childhood experiences.   Highly creative adults are more likely to report unhappy childhood experiences than are less creative adults (MacKinnon, 1978). Whether or not these self-reports are accurate is open to question. The self-reports of highly creative adults are not so defensive as those of less creative persons (Barron, 1969), and this fact alone may account for their reports of unhappy childhoods. MacKinnon (1978) maintains that creative subjects' reports of unhappy childhood events contrasted with their apparently *favorable* childhood conditions.

On the other hand, Gardner (1973) and Simonton (1984) report that a surprising percentage of major research scientists lost a parent before the age of ten. Roe (1943) found that six of the 20 professional artists she studied had experienced the death of a parent or sibling during their teens, six of the 20 were socially isolated, and three had serious illnesses when they were children. However, this information is of little significance unless we find that such crises occur with greater frequency or have a greater effect than in the normal population. As far we know, none of the studies on creativity has compiled normative data with which to compare the experiences of creative subjects.

Emotional intensity.   Most creative artists and writers report intense emotional responses, awareness of their responses, and acceptance of their emotions. The highly creative authors studied by Barron (1969) expressed more extremes of emotion than did other authors who served as a control group. The creative authors also reported a more vivid dream life and more nightmares than the control group. They tended to be more open to experience and less judgmental; and they attached more emotional significance to objects and events. This intensity of emotional response, sensitivity to meaning, and candidness about their feelings may help account for artists' reputation for insanity and their high scores on measures of emotional disturbance.

Highly creative groups showed more psychopathology on the Minnesota Multiphasic Personality Inventory (Hathaway & Meehl, 1951) than did other members of their profession (Barron, 1969). This effect was particularly noticeable among creative authors, who scored high on all MMPI measures of psychopathology (e.g., subscales designed to identify schizophrenic, depressive, hysterical, and hypochondriac tendencies). Professional artists earn much higher psychoticism scores on the Eysenck Personality Questionnaire (Eysenck & Eysenck, 1976) than do subjects who are not artists, and male artists score higher on neuroticism as well (Gotz & Gotz, 1979). Gifted art students score higher on neuroticism than other students (Gotz & Gotz, 1973).

A number of studies have found a positive correlation between creativity and schizophrenia in different members of the same family. In a brief review of the literature, Eysenck (1983) reports that about half of the children (raised by foster parents) of schizophrenic mothers exhibited psychosocial problems; the other half, who seemed emotionally stable, had uncommon art talent. Although Eysenck and the researchers whose work he reviews tend to attribute creativity and schizophrenia to a common genetic component, that conclusion is not a necessary implication of their findings.

The literature on creativity and insanity does not document serious emotional difficulty in creative persons. One explanation for this finding is that researchers document the characteristics of *successful* creative persons. Another possibility is that the emotional intensity, candor, and nonconformity of creative individuals are exceptional. Their values differ from the ordinary, and they do not hesitate to admit it. Since labels of emotional disturbance reflect traditional values, individuals who reject those traditions are more likely than average subjects to be categorized as psychotic or neurotic regardless of their psychological competence.

Emotional health. Barron (1963) came to the conclusion that highly creative individuals are both sicker and healthier psychologically than other people. That is, though creative persons appear more troubled psychologically, they also appear to have greater psychological resources with which to deal with their problems. In contrast to the typical pattern for subjects who score high on the Minnesota Multiphasic Personality Inventory psychopathology scales, creative subjects also score high on the MMPI ego-strength scale, a measure that usually correlates negatively with psychopathology scales (Barron, 1969). The creative subjects also score high on the California Personality Index, a result that suggests they are flexible and persistent. Many informal observations of creative persons document their self-discipline, commitment, and independence (e.g., Galton, 1869/ 1962; Perkins, 1981).

Emulation of nonconformist behavior. Our review of research confirms the stereotype of the sensitive, rebellious artist (cf. Perkins, 1981). However, the stereotype is probably not just the result of artists' behavior, but also a cause of it. As Barron (1969) notes in discussing the MMPI scores of creative writers, being labeled "eccentric," or even "mad as a hatter" is considered a compliment when it is used to describe someone who is creative.

Children who aspire to artistic or scientific achievement are likely to be aware of the stereotypes of the highly emotional artist and the coldly intellectual scientist. They model their behavior accordingly. This phenomenon is suggested by art students' comments during interviews published in Barron's *Artists in the Making.* When asked if they thought of themselves as artists, two students replied as follows:

> I'd rather say I'm crazy than say I'm an artist. Because "crazy" means untold vision, infinite vision. Whereas "artist" means you have a few visions maybe. (Barron, Kraus, & Conti, 1972, p. 25)

> I think the ultimate artist is a magician, but there are lots of stages in between. I live a Bohemian life. . . . (Barron et al., 1972, p. 20)

When asked if, as a child, she felt different from other children, one of the students replied, "I'd like to think that I did" (Barron et al., 1972, p. 29). When asked who had affected his interest in art, another student responded, "My cousin. He's teaching painting now. He's a top artist. He's insane, but everyone appreciates his work" (Barron et al., 1972, p. 22).

Creative individuals value being different, and they actively deny conventional behavior and values (e.g., Marcuse, 1978). As Maddi (1975, p. 183) comments, many creative children and adults find opposition to their ideas stimulating and enjoy the role of a "lonely searcher and crusader for fulfillment amidst a multitude of drones."

Personality Traits of Children Who Are Divergent Thinkers

Children who score high on divergent thinking tests are, by definition, capable of unusual and clever responses to questions or assigned tasks. They are generally nonconformists, risk takers—intellectually playful, humorous, and known for their wild ideas (Torrance, 1962). Among bright children, Getzels and Jackson (1962) found that highly divergent thinkers value a sense of humor more than do convergent thinkers, that they tend to be less emotionally close to their parents, and that they seem less concerned about money.

Divergent thinkers in the classroom.   Teachers tend to prefer bright children who score highest on tests of convergent thinking to those who score highest on tests of divergent thinking (Getzels & Jackson, 1962). In fact, highly divergent children are often in conflict with both teachers and peers. Torrance (1963) reported that highly divergent children with whom he worked were given little credit for their contributions to group problem-solving sessions. Only those who persisted in the face of their peers' hostility finally won recognition by the group.

Divergent thinkers generally prefer to learn in settings less highly structured than those preferred by other children (Torrance, 1974). If we think of divergent and convergent thinking as learning styles rather than kinds of thinking, it is easy to see that the convergent style is more compatible than the divergent style with most classroom instruction.

Interactions between IQ and divergent thinking scores.   Wallach and Kogan (1965) categorized fifth-grade students as belonging to one of four groups: high-IQ, high-divergent thinking; high-IQ, low-divergent thinking; low-IQ, high-divergent thinking; and low-IQ, low-divergent thinking. In comparing the classroom behavior of children in the four groups, the researchers found differences by group and by sex.

Girls who scored high in IQ and divergent thinking were the most self-confident group of girls. They showed the least tendency to deprecate themselves or their work. They were more actively sought out by their peers than were girls in any other group, and they also sought out companions more actively than did other girls. They showed the highest levels of attention, concentration, and interest in academic work. They were also high in disruptive, attention-getting behavior; but this seemed to be a function of their enthusiasm for learning.

The high-IQ girls with low-divergent thinking scores were also self-confident, had a long attention span, had the ability to concentrate, and were sought after by others. They did not tend to seek companionship, however. They were the least likely of any group to seek attention in disruptive ways.

The low-IQ, low-divergent thinking girls seemed to compensate for their poor academic performance by activity in the social realm.

The girls who had low IQ scores and high divergent thinking scores seemed to be at the greatest disadvantage in the classroom. They were the least confident and the least sought after group. They avoided companionship and tended to deprecate themselves and their own work more than any of the other groups. They frequently engaged in disruptive, attention-getting behavior, which the experimenters regarded as a form of protest.

Personality differences among the boys were not so distinct as among the girls. Nonetheless, boys who had high IQ scores and low divergent thinking scores showed the least anxiety, whereas anxiety was highest for the low-IQ, low-divergent thinking boys. Probably because of sex-role stereotypes that allow more bizarre behavior from boys, low-IQ, high-divergent thinking boys seemed to have less difficulty in the classroom than their female counterparts.

Children who resemble creative adults. The characteristics of creative adults often guide the identification of gifted children. Several checklists, for example, have been compiled for teachers' use in identifying children with unusual creative ability. The Group Inventory for Finding Talent, or GIFT (Rimm & Davis, 1980), and the Group Inventory For Finding Interests, GIFFI (Davis & Rimm, 1982), are composed of items representing interests, attitudes, and family traits correlated, either negatively or positively, with creativity. The Renzulli-Hartman Scales for Rating Behavioral Characteristics of Superior Students (Renzulli & Hartman, 1971) include a section composed of items describing traits associated with creativity.

Although these and similar inventories are useful for research purposes and for finding out about children's interests and background, their use as predictors of outstanding creative talent is based on questionable assumptions. Both identification instruments and instructional programs predicated on this identification model assume a causal relationship between personality traits and creative production. The existence of such a causal relationship is only speculative, and the strength of the hypothesized relationship is entirely unknown.

CREATIVITY AND INTELLIGENCE

Earlier in the chapter, we saw that interest in eminence prompted the study of both intelligence and creativity. We also saw how the study of creativity was derived from the study of intelligence. In this part of the chapter we will examine the specific ways in which the *measurement* of creativity is related to the *measurement* of intelligence. In examining this relationship we will explore the notion of "creative potential" and compare it to the notion of "intellectual potential." We will consider the degree to which measures of creativity can predict eminence and the degree to which they can predict school achievement.

The Creativity Construct

A measurement *construct* operationalizes a concept statistically. A construct is meaningful if it (1) samples the components of an attribute and (2) distinguishes between the attribute and other attributes. The extent to which a particular test conforms to a theory explaining an attribute is a measure of the test's *construct validity*. One way to determine the construct validity of a test is to measure the degree to which the construct that it samples is distinct from other constructs. Once a test has been found to measure a discrete construct, other tests that purport to measure that construct will be correlated with the original test to determine their concurrent criterion-related validity. (See Kubiszyn & Borich, 1984, for a succinct discussion of validity.)

The construct validity of creativity instruments depends on the distinction between "creativity" and other mental attributes. However, it is difficult to interpret validity studies because the construct, "creativity," has been formulated in at least the following four ways: (1) as a noncognitive trait (e.g., Welsh, 1975), (2) as a combination of fluency, flexibility, elaboration, and originality subskills (e.g., Torrance, 1966), (3) as the ability to associate remote elements (Mednick, 1962), and (4) as a combination of fluency and uniqueness subskills (Wallach & Kogan, 1965). After looking at these four "creativity" constructs, we will examine the results of studies to distinguish each of these constructs from the intelligence construct.

Creativity as a non-cognitive trait. In one view creativity is a noncognitive (i.e., affective) trait. Such a trait falls outside the domain of the intellect and, in theory, has little to do with intellectual functioning. An affective trait explaining creative performance could relate to any of various aspects of personality, such as motivation (see, e.g., McClelland, Atkinson, Clark, & Lowell, 1953; Pearlman, 1983), or it might relate to a discrete noncognitive attribute. Welsh (1975) terms one such attribute "origence."

In the preceding section of this chapter, we summarized findings about the personality traits of creative individuals. The discussion noted the use and limitations of personality checklists to evaluate children's creative potential. Such checklists are not psychometric instruments and do not represent measurement constructs that can be contrasted with the IQ construct.

Various psychometric instruments have, however, been used to measure creativity. Most prominent among these have been projective tests that are sensitive to the noncognitive aspects of creativity. A test of this type that has been used extensively in research is the Welsh Figure Preference Test (1949). This test has been revised and is now called the Barron Welsh Art Scale (1963). It consists of 60 cards, each showing a simple line drawing. Subjects are asked to view each drawing and respond by saying either "like" or "don't like." The level of a subject's "origence" is based on his or her preference for particular sorts of figures. High origence is associated with preference for more complex and asymmetric figures (Welsh, 1975).

Creativity as fluency, flexibility, originality, and elaboration. Guilford and Torrance view creativity as a constellation of cognitive traits, including fluency, flexibility, originality, and elaboration. These skills comprise divergent thinking, the construct that Guilford and Torrance believe reflects creative potential. This view of creativity is operationalized in the Torrance Tests of Creative Thinking (1966). Each of the verbal and figural subtests of the TTCT is scored for fluency, flexibility, and originality; and several subtests are also scored for elaboration (see Box 4-2). This format differs considerably from the format of many tests that purport to measure different subskills (e.g., Wechsler, 1974). Most often, tests use separate tasks to measure different skills or abilities. Because it measures several skills or abilities with the same task, Torrance's procedure obscures the possible differences between these skills. According to some researchers, students' fluency scores are likely to confound both their originality and their flexibility scores.

BOX 4-2 *Creativity Subskills in the Style of Torrance*

Among the most frequently used tests of creativity are the Torrance Tests of Creative Thinking (originally published as the Minnesota Tests of Creative Thinking). The original Torrance battery included verbal and figural tasks that were scored for fluency, flexibility, and originality. According to Torrance (1963, p. 95), *fluency* is "the ability to produce a variety of ideas or hypotheses concerning possible solutions to problems." Torrance (1963, p. 96) sees *flexibility* as "the ability to adapt to changing instructions . . . to use a variety of approaches." He views *originality* as the ability to produce uncommon responses; remote, unusual, or unconventional associations" (Torrance, 1963, p. 96).

In the 1966 version of the battery, Torrance included an additional figural subskill of creativity. This skill, *elaboration,* has been defined as "the ability to expand, develop, particularize, and embellish one's ideas, stories, and illustrations" (Callahan & Renzulli, 1981, p. 395).

Below are some examples of the types of items used to assess students' verbal fluency, flexibility, originality, and elaboration.

Unusual Uses:	List all the possible ways in which you might use a safety pin.
Unusual Questions:	List as many questions as you can about safety pins. Try to think about safety pins in ways that people usually do not consider them.

Product Improvement:	Here is a toy fire engine. Describe all of the ways in which it might be changed to make it more fun to play with.
Ask and Guess:	Look at a line drawing showing two people engaged in what looks like a robbery of a bank; then write all of the questions evoked by the picture. Next, list as many possible causes of the events in the picture as you can imagine. Finally, list as many possible consequences of the events in the picture as you can imagine.
Just Suppose:	Just suppose all of the fresh water on earth became salty. What would happen? How would this change life on earth?

Creativity as remote association.   Mednick proposed a creativity construct based on the idea that creative individuals are those who are best able to join remote elements into "new combinations which either meet specified requirements or are in some ways useful" (1962, p. 221). According to Mednick, creative individuals are those who can join remote elements. Therefore, he devised a test that requires students to find the one word that links progressively more remote associates. A sample item from the Remote Associates Test (Mednick & Mednick, 1967) asks students to supply the one word that links the following three words: *sore, shoulder,* and *sweat.* The answer is "cold." As this sample item indicates, the items on the RAT reflect a theory of creativity that views it as both *cognitive* and *convergent.*

Creativity as fluency and uniqueness.   Wallach and Kogan (1965) developed a creativity test based on a construct that intended by *definition* to distinguish creativity from intelligence. This construct "limit[s] the term *creativity* to a narrowly defined set of variables, thereby identifying creativity with a single factor" (Anastasi & Schaefer, 1971, p. 115). Like the Torrance Tests of Creative Thinking, the Wallach and Kogan test battery includes verbal and figural subtests. The scoring procedures and attendant difficulties are similar to those discussed above in reference to the TTCT.

The Wallach and Kogan battery, however, differs from the TTCT in two important ways. First, the Wallach and Kogan battery is administered without time limits. Second, "uniqueness" scores on the Wallach and Kogan test are based on local norms rather than on norms derived from the testing of a representative sample of students. A response is judged to be "unique" *only* if no other student in the *same test-administration group* has given the same response. This procedure makes comparison of different groups, and thus development of reliability and validity coefficients, virtually impossible.

The Relationship between Creativity and Intelligence

Determining the correlation between creativity and intelligence is necessary in order to distinguish between these constructs. Theorists who maintain that creativity is a construct discrete from general intelligence (e.g, Torrance, 1984; Wallach & Kogan, 1965) support their view by show-ing the low correlations between creativity and intelligence. Psychologists who maintain that creative potential is strongly influenced by intellectual potential (e.g., Griffith & Clark, 1981; Simon & Ward, 1973) support their view by showing the high positive correlation between creativity and intelli-gence. Still other theorists who view intelligence as a necessary but not a sufficient condition for creativity (e.g., Getzels & Jackson, 1962; Schubert, 1973) support their view by showing the weakening of the correlation above a certain point on the IQ scale (cf. McNemar, 1964).

The low correlation between creativity and intelligence.   According to Fox (1981, p.231), "researchers have amply demonstrated that IQ and achievement tests measure abilities, skills, and personality traits that are essentially different from those associated with creativity." Fox (1981) bases this conclusion on a review of numerous studies in which the correlations between creativity and IQ were found to be very low.

Several of the studies discussed by Fox (e.g., McKinney & Forman, 1977; Metcalfe, 1978; Ward, 1975) used the Wallach and Kogan test as the measure of creativity. This test was *designed* to be factorially distinct from measures of intelligence. Although low correlations between this test and measures of intelligence confirm the success of Wallach and Kogan's test design, these results may be insufficient to validate a measurement construct that distinguishes "creativity" from "intelligence" (Anastasi & Schaefer, 1971). Because of the limited sample of behaviors measured on the Wallach and Kogan test, this instrument should not be construed as a measure of "creativity." A more reasonable assertion is that the Wallach and Kogan battery primarily measures ideational fluency, a skill that *has* been shown to be distinct from intelligence (see, e.g., Hocevar, 1979).

By definition, "creativity" based on a noncognitive construct differs considerably from *any* cognitive construct, including the *cognitive* constructs of "creativity," "intelligence," and "reading comprehension." Welsh (1975), for instance, reports a −0.06 correlation between the Revised Art Scale (Welsh & Barron, 1963) and the Concept Mastery Test (Terman, 1973). This low negative correlation suggests that variance in performance on a test of vocabulary knowledge has very little to do with preference for line drawings of a particular type. Viewed in these terms, we can see the limited practical value of the statistic cited by Welsh (1975). In this case, neither the measure of intelligence nor the measure of creativity is sufficiently com-plex to enhance our understanding of either construct.

The high correlation between creativity and intelligence.   Several psy-chologists suggest that there is a close relationship between intelligence and creativity. According to McNemar (1964), for example, methodological problems in many studies correlating creativity and intelligence often ob-scure the interrelatedness of these constructs. McNemar (1964, p. 879) claims that "the correlations [between IQ and creativity tests] are generally far higher than those found in typical studies with range restrictions."

The Remote Associates Test (Mednick & Mednick, 1967) is the creativity test most likely to be highly correlated with intelligence. This test, which is both cognitive and convergent, has been compared with IQ tests in a number of studies. Welsh (1975) reports a range of correlations between the RAT and various intelligence tests of from 0.19 to 0.55.

The TTCT (Torrance, 1966), however, claims to measure divergent thinking and should therefore be less highly correlated than the RAT with measures of intelligence. Nevertheless, Wallach and Kogan cite research to show that the correlations between IQ tests and the Torrance scales are as large as intercorrelations either among TTCT subtests or among IQ subtests. Thus, TTCT subtests and IQ subtests are similar enough to represent aspects of the same psychological construct.

Other researchers have noted similar results in reference to the Wallach and Kogan battery. Based on a study using the Wallach and Kogan test, Griffith and Clark (1981, p. 233) conclude that "even among subjects of relatively low creative ability, intelligence has an important impact on some aspects of creative responding."

Measurement cautions. Interpretation of the correlation studies must be tempered by an understanding of the limitations of the tests used to represent the two constructs. "Intelligence" is operationalized as IQ on any one of several tests that vary as to the number and kind of behaviors sampled. "Creativity," on the other hand, is operationalized on tests that vary not only as to the specific sorts of behavior sampled but also as to the *domain* from which these behaviors are sampled. As we have seen above, theorists do not agree about the nature of the creativity construct. Further, the creativity tests developed to date are neither as reliable nor as valid as most IQ tests (see, e.g., Thorndike, 1972).

Simon and Ward (1973) suggest a reasonable interpretation of the apparently contradictory data obtained in the correlation studies. They conclude that "significant positive correlations exist between certain kinds of creativity measures and certain kinds of intelligence tests, and . . . [that] insignificant positive correlations exist between other creativity measures and other kinds of intelligence tests" (Simon & Ward, 1973, p. 72).

Simon and Ward's conclusion is supported by Hocevar (1979, 1980) who identifies "ideational fluency" (i.e., the ability to generate many ideas) as the "creativity" factor that is distinct from intelligence. In a study using three of Guilford's creativity subtests, Hocevar (1979, p. 194) finds that "ideational fluency is the factor that causes creativity tests to be highly intercorrelated and factorially distinct from intelligence tests . . . but this does not mean that the broader category of creative thinking will be factorially distinct when the effect of ideational fluency is controlled." Thus, creativity tests that are highly correlated with IQ tests (e.g., Remote Associates Test, Mednick & Mednick, 1967) probably do not sample ideational fluency to a large degree. The creativity tests that are less highly correlated with IQ tests (e.g., Torrance, 1966; Wallach & Kogan, 1965) probably rely heavily on ideational fluency to represent creativity.

Intelligence as necessary but not sufficient for creativity. The notion that a certain level of intelligence is a prerequisite for creativity is supported by the common sense view of the creative person (e.g., Perkins, 1981). This view also recognizes the fact that not all intelligent people produce creative work. Although these notions about the nature of the creative person seem to make sense intuitively (see, e.g., Dacey & Madaus, 1971), they are not supported conclusively by the empirical evidence.

Interest in a *threshold hypothesis* concerning the relationship between intelligence and creativity was generated as a result of Getzels and Jackson's (1962) classic study. This study seemed to show that creativity and IQ were quite distinct at the upper ranges of intelligence. McNemar (1964, p. 879) stated the hypothesis more explicitly when he wrote, "at the high IQ levels there will be a very wide range of creativity, whereas as we go down to average IQ, and on down to lower levels, the scatter for creativity will be less and less."

Although several studies (e.g., Bowers, 1969; Dacey & Madaus, 1971; Schubert, 1973) seem to confirm this hypothesis, other studies (e.g., Guilford & Christensen, 1973; Marjoribanks, 1976) dispute the threshold hypothesis. According to Dacey and Madaus (1971, pp. 215–216) researchers arrive at varying conclusions about the threshold hypothesis because of the dubious validity of the currently popular measures of divergent thinking. Until the technical problems associated with tests of creativity are resolved, it is unlikely that researchers will be able to quantify the relationship between IQ and creative potential.

Creative Potential and Intellectual Potential

The definitions of the two terms *intellectual potential* and *creative potential* may help clarify an essential difference between measures of creativity and measures of intelligence. In Chapter 3 we saw that the term *intellectual potential* linked the general notion of intelligence with the narrower measurement construct, IQ. Because IQ tests effectively predict school achievement, they can be used to locate children likely to perform well or poorly on academic tasks. The intellectual potential of school children, therefore, refers to their potential for academic achievement.

Several theorists (e.g., Getzels & Jackson, 1962; Torrance, 1963) have described creativity tests as measures of potential. They maintain that although *creative potential* differs from intellectual potential, it nevertheless is as effective as IQ in predicting academic achievement. They suggest that above a certain IQ level, performance on measures of creativity predicts academic achievement as well as or better than performance on IQ tests. According to these theorists, creative potential, like intellectual potential, refers to students' potential for academic achievement. Getzels and Jackson (1962), in particular, hypothesized that high creative potential explained the apparent "overachievement" of some students.

Do creativity tests predict academic achievement? In order to support or refute the claim that creativity tests predict academic achievement, several researchers (e.g., Bowers, 1969; Bruininks & Feldman, 1970; Marjoribanks, 1976) have conducted studies of the relationship between performance on creativity tests and performance on tests of academic achievement. Rather than clarifying this relationship, however, these studies have confused the issue. For example, Marjoribanks (1976, p. 117) found that "for certain academic subjects creativity is related to achievement up to a threshold level of intelligence, but after the threshold has been reached creativity is not associated with further increments in achievement." This finding is the inverse of the relationship suggested by Getzels and Jackson's (1962) data and hypothesized by McNemar (1964).

To date no consensus has emerged about the usefulness of creativity tests in predicting academic achievement. If creativity tests are found to correlate highly with IQ tests, then they are *likely* to correlate with academic achievement. If creativity tests are found to correlate minimally with IQ tests, then it is *unlikely* that they will correlate with academic achievement. In either case, educators would be unwise to use creativity tests in place of IQ tests to predict academic achievement since creativity measures seem to lack both reliability and validity (Thorndike, 1972; but cf. Torrance, 1984).

Do creativity tests predict creative achievement in adulthood? According to several writers (e.g., Rekdal, 1979; Torrance, 1980, 1984), measures of creative potential predict creative achievement or eminence in adulthood. This claim is contested by Goodwin and Driscoll (1980) who report that, in general, creativity tests have very poor reliability and validity. The claim that a test measures *potential* depends on its predictive validity, and creativity tests that have neither adequate construct validity nor demonstrable predictive validity will not help educators identify the children most likely to be creative adults.

SCHOOL RESPONSES TO CREATIVITY

Among teachers interest in creativity seems to have been prompted historically by the observation that some pupils showed academic promise despite their troublesome antics (Torrance, 1984). Because of their behavior, however, it was sometimes difficult for these students to realize their promise. Thoughtful teachers in the early part of the century seem to have been asking, "What phenomenon can account for this constellation of apparently contradictory traits?" The redefinition of the term "creativity" after 1950 seemed to hold promise as a possible description of such students' behavior. Researchers (e.g., Torrance & Myers, 1971) tried not only to identify highly creative students who were at risk in schools, but to train teachers to respond to such students more flexibly.

Spiritual Schooling

As we implied above, creativity training is considered by some (e.g., Adler and Maslow) to provide a direct route to a more holistic, more healthy, more self-actualizing approach to life. Others have expanded this sense of creativity to include some of the data on brain hemisphericity (Myers, 1982), some of the constructs of psychotherapy (Gowan, 1978; Huff, 1978), some of the techniques of Eastern mysticism (Gowan, 1978; Rose, 1979), and an appreciation of the altered perceptions of psychedelic experience (Huxley, 1962). The leading spokesperson for the most successful creativity training program has noted that his program tries "to study and relate—even to 'force' relationships—with all areas and approaches" (Parnes, 1975, p. 24). Such a synthesis is a system of *belief*. It is grounded on faith, and it represents a largely *spiritual* view of life.

Torrance wanted earnestly to unlock the creative potential of all children (Perkins, 1981; cf. Torrance, 1963, 1984; Torrance & Myers, 1971). Other proponents of creativity training (e.g., Sisk & Bierly, 1979) came increasingly to believe that the special methods that benefited highly divergent students would benefit *all students*.

The expectation that schools could *liberate the spirits* of all students was a sentiment shared by many other educators (e.g., Lyon, 1971) in the 1960s and early 1970s. Part of the support for such a view no doubt came from articulate students who dissented during the Vietnam War (Tannenbaum, 1981). Creativity training, with its emphasis on divergent thinking and its promise of toleration for the behavior and lifestyle of nonconformists seems to have found a niche in the progressive ideology of that era.

Human beings *do need* a sense of their wholeness. It is questionable, however, whether very many of us can agree on just what sort of spiritual program would be appropriate for all children. Creativity training, however, may appeal to some educators as a spiritual program that *is* appropriate for all children.

Certainly most teachers would like their students to be happy, healthy, and productive. But construction of a sense of wholeness, of one's place in the universe, is a very private matter. Moreover, a good deal of research also suggests that the kinds of reforms imagined by Torrance and others probably depend on social changes that educators are powerless to make (e.g., Jencks et al., 1972; Wilcox, 1982; Meyer, 1977). The degree to which success in such reform efforts is possible is limited by requirements for conformity and compliance in schools and by the financial conditions that govern the way schools are run.

Creativity Training in the Schools

Schools are run as businesses are run, to provide a functional service as cheaply as seems reasonable. Part baby-sitting agency (a valuable role), part socializing institution, they mirror the structure and needs of society at large (Bowles & Gintis, 1976; Jencks et al., 1972; Wilcox, 1982; Meyer, 1977; Sizer, 1984). Many good things *can* happen in the classroom, regardless of the determining influence of social need, yet there are reasonable limits to what ought to be planned. The preceding discussion indicates that concern for bright, troublesome children is warranted, but that too grand an agenda will not serve such children—or anyone—very well.

It is possible to locate a group of children who perform very well on tests of divergent thinking. There is some question, however, whether (1) the tests reliably identify the sort of troublesome student described by Torrance (1984), or (2) the tests prompt educators to provide such students the support they need to realize their academic potential. We do know that poor divergent thinkers can improve their scores on divergent thinking tests rather quickly (Torrance, 1984). Such an improvement does not turn formerly poor divergent thinkers into troublesome students, of course, nor would we want it to. This backwards logic, though, does indicate the degree to which it is possible to forget the beginnings of interest in creativity in the schools, and to confound improved divergent thinking with improved academic performance (cf. Getzels & Jackson, 1962; Torrance, 1984).

It should be apparent that, if the definition and measurement of creativity is problematic, so too is creativity training. This observation is *not* meant to suggest that it is impossible to teach the skills of divergent thinking. Indeed, research indicates that the subskills of divergent thinking can be taught (Rose & Lin, 1984; Torrance, 1984).

As Perkins (1981) notes, however, improvement in children's scores on tests of divergent thinking hardly substantiates the cultivation of *creativity*. Unresolved questions pertain to the place of divergence in classrooms, to the role of improved divergent thinking in cultivating significant contributions in the arts and sciences, to the relationship of conformity and creativity in general, and to the comparative meaningfulness of the term "creativity" itself (Perkins, 1981). For a review and critique of classroom use of creativity training programs, including the Parnes-Osborn method of creative problem solving (e.g., Osborn, 1953; Parnes, 1981) and Gordon's method of synectics (Gordon, 1961), see Howley et al., 1986, pp. 171–181.

SUMMARY

This chapter reviewed the concept of creativity from various perspectives. It explored definitions of creativity based on the notion of divergence and examined the role of novelty in definitions of creativity. The discussion emphasized the importance of evaluating the nature and quality of the creative product rather than the cognitive or affective characteristics of its creator. The chapter summarized findings about the characteristics of creative individuals. However, it also cautioned against applying generalizations that result from this research. The intelligence of creative individuals was examined in some detail in the discussion of the creativity construct. This discussion considered the assessment problems resulting from the use of tests that purport to measure creative potential. Finally, the chapter included a brief consideration of the role of creativity training in public schools. Both the intent and the actual experience of creativity training were evaluated in light of unresolved questions about the nature of creativity, its relationship to conformity, and its proper nurture.

5

Adulthood: Eminence, Leadership, and Careers

　　　　　1. Corporate leaders
　　　　　2. Political leaders
　　　　　3. Cultural leaders
　　　　C. Characteristics of Leaders
　　　　　1. Transactional and transformational leaders
　　　　　2. Children's personality traits and leadership
　　　　　3. Identifying potential adult leaders
　　　　　4. The situational nature of leadership
　　　　　5. The interaction between personalities and situations
　　　　　6. Leadership and IQ
　　　　　7. Are gifted children destined to be leaders?
　　　　　8. Group dynamics and leadership training for gifted students
　　　　　9. What is the program of study for transformational leaders?
　　VI. Occupations and Giftedness
　　　　A. Two Views of Careers
　　　　B. Reasonable But Unrealistic Occupational Preferences
　　　　　1. Fantasy
　　　　　2. Career education
　　　　　3. Professional status seeking and gifted children
　　　　C. Giftedness and Professional Status
　　　　　1. The IQs of professional groups
　　　　　2. Careers among Terman's subjects
　　　　　3. Conclusions and cautions
　　　　D. Intellectualism and Careerism
　　　　　1. The Stanford study
　　　　　2. Implications
　　　　E. Gifted Students, Intellect, and Occupational Life
　　　　　1. Intellectualism and vocation
　　　　　2. Careerism and anti-intellectualism
　　　　　3. Occupational prospects for the gifted
　　VII. Summary

Focusing Questions

1. Which of the four views of leadership most influences the content of leadership training programs for gifted students? Why?
2. What reasons might our society have for failing to cultivate or reward eminent scholars and artists?
3. What factors limit our ability to make generalizations from the research on eminent persons?
4. How does the distinction between transactional and transformational leadership relate to the provision of special instruction to gifted students?
5. What characteristics, other than high IQ, contribute to adult economic success? Does our society value these characteristics more than it values exceptional intelligence? Why or why not?

CONCERN FOR THE ADULTHOOD OF GIFTED STUDENTS

This chapter investigates the subsequent adulthood of children identified as gifted in school. After their public schooling, most of these children, but by no means all, complete four years of college. Many acquire professional degrees of one type or another, and a minority get doctorates. What is likely to happen to them next? Should educators try to ensure the future professional success of gifted students? Do children whom the school calls "gifted" really turn out to be gifted adults? These are provocative questions, of course, and the adulthoods of able students are inherently interesting to most teachers.

In fact, many people believe that gifted children will become our future leaders. They expect that able children who have been well educated will provide the best possible national security (e.g., Bull, 1985). Although this line of thinking seems reasonable, it has not been confirmed by studies (Baird, 1985). Moreover, both Feldman (1979) and Bull (1985) have highlighted weaknesses of this thinking. But the "greatest national resource" argument will probably be around for a long time: Its truth seems self-evident to many people.

You should remember, however, that good research develops data that go beyond self-evidence. Teachers of the gifted need to examine the evidence of research so they can evaluate the place of leadership training and career education in their programs. Looking at the research evidence can also help them examine their own self-evident assumptions about what will happen to their students. The issue of adulthood is also important theoretically. Americans think that a prime purpose of education— perhaps the *main* purpose of education—is to prepare students for the "world of work" (e.g., Committee for Economic Development, 1985), and they often expect that gifted students will fare best in the job market (e.g., Hollingworth, 1926; Hoyt & Hebeler, 1974). Perhaps because we Americans maintain an optimistic view of human potential, we cherish great expectations for gifted students. What actually happens when these students grow up, however, can also help us distinguish between what education generally can and cannot do (cf. Katz, 1971).

The discussion below points out that definitions of adult "success" often leave a lot to be desired. Hence, the discussion tries to clear up some of the confusion surrounding the ideas of eminence, leadership, and careers in general. Perhaps part of the difficulty, however, is that adult experiences are far more varied than the experiences of schoolchildren. Success in adulthood may, therefore, be more common than success in school, whereas extreme success in adulthood may be considerably more rare than childhood giftedness.

DEFINITIONS

The key terms in this chapter are "leadership" and "eminence." Before proceeding, we need a brief look at how the terms are typically used and the ways in which they are related.

Leadership

Leadership has been investigated more fully than eminence as a topic of interest to teachers. The term, after all, was used to describe a type of giftedness by the federal government in 1970 (Kitano & Kirby, 1986). The endorsement of the federal government allowed schools to identify and operate special programs for schoolchildren who were believed to show special promise in leadership. Comparatively few schools provided programs, but the idea of special leadership skill still intrigues some educators, and it is frequently discussed in gifted education.

The need to identify and train leaders seems to have arisen from the perception, shared by many people, that the solution of global problems urgently requires "leaders with a vision" (Kitano & Kirby, 1986, p. 251). This sense of the mission of education, however, is not new. It has been a concern of U.S. education since before Horace Mann (Cremin, 1980; Katz, 1968; Stevens & Wood, 1987). Its association with the gifted and its expression in special programs, however, *is* comparatively new. Starting in the 1920s, Terman promoted the notion that the gifted would provide a pool from which future leaders would be selected by life. After 1968, when it became clear that Terman's claim could be contested (Feldman, 1984; cf. Oden, 1968), interest in *programs* to develop leadership quickened.

The most complete review of leadership and leadership training was completed by Stogdill (1974) and updated by Bass (1981). *Stogdill's Handbook* organized theories of leadership into nineteen categories. The identification and training of nineteen kinds of leadership is probably not something for which the federal government was prepared to provide financial support, then or now.

The scope of definitions of leadership runs from those that accord *all* authority to the individual to those that accord *none* to the individual. Some conceptions of leadership, in fact, assert that leaders make no difference (see Box 5-1).

Acceptable and unacceptable models.   Only if we can believe in individual leadership can we select individuals for special leadership training. If individual leadership is an illusion, however, then to identify and train it would be to practice deceit. Two of the previous models avoid these difficulties—the great man theory and the model of small group dynamics. Both give some importance to *individual leadership*.

The great man theory is an attractive, if not completely plausible,

BOX 5-1   Differences in Theories of Leadership

Rarely are the vast differences in theories of leadership made clear in gifted education. The differences are so great that some styles of leadership are certain to be at odds with prevailing political tendencies, whether right-wing or left-wing. Consensus on the sort of leadership training to be provided is unlikely, given these remarkable differences. Please observe that the differences discussed below represent political *ideas,* not partisan political *practice.*

The Great Man Theory. The great man theory enjoyed the most popularity in the nineteenth century. According to this theory, a transcendent and charismatic leader shapes major events. Certain types of biography and history recount political and military leadership in the framework of this theory. The great man theory of leadership is probably most consistent with a conservative interpretation of events. The reason is that the sphere of individual freedom is widest and the role of innate merit largest in this conception. Great men, of course, need not, like Napoleon, be military or political leaders or, for that matter, even *men.* They could be artists (e.g., Beethoven), philosophers (e.g., Karl Marx), social activists (e.g., Sojourner Truth), or nurses (e.g., Florence Nightengale)—all examples from the nineteenth century, please note, with equal representation to women and to left-leaning heroes.

Small Group Dynamics. This view of leadership is of mid-twentieth century origin. Its relevance pertains to professional life, which often requires us to take part in committees or work teams. Often such small groups *do* function poorly (e.g., Boss & McConkie, 1981; Mitchell, 1976; Ysseldyke, Algozzine, & Mitchell, 1982). Committee work does not entail the scope of mission that preoccupies "great persons." The restricted scope reflects a narrower sphere of individual freedom, and it assumes innate merit is a less significant influence on events. The model of small group dynamics might be identified as the liberal view of leadership. A sizable literature explaining how to influence such groups does exist, and skills can be taught to gifted students (Feldhusen & Kolloff, 1979). The degree to which such skills are effectively transferable has, however, been questioned (Woodman & Sherwood, 1980).

The Group Attribution Theory. This theory of leadership, like the next, is a more critical interpretation of leadership than the preceding models. Leadership is *attributed* by a representative group. The leader is the spokesperson for the group, but exercises no real independent authority. The leader's individual freedom and innate abilities are not really at issue, although the leader might possess some personal traits that enhance the leadership role. Possessing such traits would be convenient, but not necessary to the role. The group attribution model might be called the democratic socialist interpretation of leadership.

The Model of Institutional Legitimation. In this model the position of leadership is *structurally* important to an institution, rather than functionally important to a group that associates voluntarily. Leadership validates the institution, but the leader can accomplish nothing at all by virtue of individual freedom or innate ability. In fact, the entire group served by the leader operates with a restricted scope of freedom. In this model, the leader's authority derives from, and—via the misperceptions of those who are led—contributes to the power of the larger institution. This model might be interpreted as a totalitarian view of leadership.

account of leadership. Part of its problem for education is that it does not provide a familiar setting in which to imagine the actions of a leader. In fact, we no longer create the kind of heroes described by the theory. The great man theory also fails to provide a set of definable skills that might be taught to potential leaders.

The model of small group dynamics is both easier to conceive and easier to implement than a model of training based on the great man theory. For example, we know that there is a plausible connection between some gifted students and professional assignments of committee work. There is also a large literature on the topic. These features seem to make this model the natural choice for most gifted programs (Foster, 1981).

Contemporary research, however, suggests that it is very difficult to improve the functioning of committees (Woodman & Sherwood, 1980) and that improvement may even produce *undesirable* institutional effects (Boss & McConkie, 1981). A program to train gifted leaders in the dynamics of small groups could be premature or even misguided. Leadership training would certainly be misguided if views of leadership, other than the small group dynamics view, were accepted as correct.

Identification.   Not surprisingly, little has been done to develop adequate methods for identifying leadership ability as a specific talent. In addition to the unresolved questions about the nature of leadership, a major problem is the fact that leadership is a *performance skill*. Like good teaching, leadership is difficult to train and cumbersome to measure. Moreover, adult leadership is different from the school leadership roles filled by students. Leadership training might best be provided by professional schools, where students' roles more closely approximate their work roles.

Because methods of finding leadership potential are so primitive, the consensus of the field has been to provide leadership training to *all* students identified as gifted (Kitano & Kirby, 1986). Selection for such programs is, however, typically made on the basis of academic aptitude (Cox et al., 1985). Longitudinal studies suggest that these students are likely to enter occupations of higher status than unselected students. Whether or not they become leaders in their chosen fields, however, *cannot* be predicted from their academic aptitude (Baird, 1985). Leadership, however it is defined, seems to bear little relationship to intellectual ability (Bass, 1981).

Eminence

The first use of this term in English, in 1420, corresponds closely to modern usage. "Eminent" denoted a quality "remarkable in degree" (Oxford English Dictionary, 1971, Vol. 1). As used in the following discussion, *adult success* is the quality remarkable in degree.

Galton (1869/1962) investigated eminence and developed a scale that measured degree of remarkable attainment among adults. Eminence in Galton's study represented *extreme* rarity of success. He rated the degree of rarity of the success of his subjects upward to 1 in 1 million.

Though Simonton (1984) has used similar techniques in his studies of historical figures, such ratings remain quite subjective. Part of the problem lies in the nature of statistics. As a phenomenon becomes increasingly more rare, its description becomes increasingly more prone to error. Thus, the confidence band around a degree of rarity of 1 in 4 is small, but around a judgment of 1 in 1 million it is quite large. Studies require impossibly large human samples to confirm the statistical reliability of a judgment as extreme in degree as 1 in 1 million. Galton's judgments of eminence were therefore quite unreliable by modern standards of statistical reliability.

Nonetheless, for all its statistical shortcomings, the idea of eminence is still intriguing. Why do some figures seem to exert extraordinary influence on the thought and practice of their times? These figures are our cultural heroes; their contributions to understanding and to the quality of life are believed to be great; and their universal celebration provides de facto support for the great man theory.

The prediction of eminence is also a motive, oddly enough, behind the identification of gifted students (Bull, 1985; Howley et al., 1986). It would be pleasant to learn that our cultural heroes were shaped in legitimate and meaningful ways by their experiences in school. But because eminence is so rare, and because even our tests of academic aptitude and achievement cannot make reliable judgments as fine as 1 in 1 million, the accurate prediction of eminence from early promise is *necessarily* impossible.

A continuum of talent.   One way to view such qualities as academic talent, career success, leadership, eminence, and genius is as a continuum from uncommon to extraordinarily rare. School "giftedness" is the *lower end* of this hypothetical continuum of talent. This degree of rarity—about 1 in 50—is a comparative rarity only among schoolchildren. Such rarity is in fact quite common among holders of ordinary occupations. Fewer than 1 person in 50 holds any *particular* job. By this standard, for example, clerks, retail merchants, and educators are rare among the general population.

If, however, one measures success as the initial qualification for a *highly selective career*—for example, graduating from medical school—the rarity is somewhat more extreme, about 1 in 300 adults (Taylor, 1975). (The rarity of some occupations, of course, is not the result of selection on academic talent, nor are all those who complete the training for a highly selective career uncommonly talented in academics.)

Career accomplishment as a physician is another matter still. Success might be measured by income, size of practice, or by contributions to research or medical technique. Successful physicians will necessarily be even more rare than physicians.

Among all physicians, whether successful or not, may be a number of physicians who are widely known regionally, nationally, or internationally for their work. They would constitute a group of *renowned physicians*. Among internationally renowned (or eminent) physicians might be a few recognized for *medical genius*. This small final group would constitute physicians who had made revolutionary contributions to medical knowledge and practice.

Studying the Relationships among Rare Phenomena

It should be apparent that, as the degree of rarity increases, it becomes more and more difficult to judge the quality by which accomplishment can be deemed successful, eminent, or of genius ("truly gifted") status. Only a few observers could even claim the right to judge the accomplishments of a hypothetical "medical genius." Such a judgment might be sound, but it might not be. Even eminent contemporaries often misjudge their "truly gifted" colleagues (Simonton, 1984).

Although it may be impossible to determine the relative status of successful adults, we can nonetheless make some distinctions by analyzing the use of the terms "academic talent", "career success," "eminence," and "genius." The rest of the chapter will consider these distinctions in detail. It is, however, important to keep two facts in mind during the subsequent discussion:

1. Gifted adult accomplishment is much more rare than the phenomenon of exceptional academic potential.
2. The study of the relationship between the two phenomena is made difficult by their rarity and by the inadequacy of the statistical tools used to study rare phenomena.

Unwarranted claims characterize the development of programs for exceptionally talented students. The distinctions that follow should help teachers of the gifted distinguish between what special programs are *likely* to influence and what they are *unlikely* to influence in the subsequent adulthoods of their students.

EMINENCE AND GIFTEDNESS

Gifted programs do not, of course, aim to make *all* uncommonly bright students eminent. Gifted education, however, has always valued the attempt to find and work with children who will eventually become eminent

(Gallagher, 1985; Terman, 1925). Most of us believe that—if we could locate them—we ought to provide such children with a special program.

One of the criticisms of traditional IQ tests is that they have failed to locate children who eventually become eminent (Feldman, 1984; Jenkins-Friedman, 1982). The critical question—describing precisely the relationship between eminence and childhood giftedness—has not yet been addressed by much research, however. Part of the problem, of course, is that eminence is so rare, much more rare, in fact, than childhood giftedness. Nonetheless, commitment to the search for children who are prospectively eminent adults has contributed to recent experiments with new identification techniques, such as multiple selection measures and biographical inventories.

The relationship between childhood talents and eminence is an interesting topic for study, but to predict extremely rare adult accomplishment from *any* measure of childhood performance is probably premature. It may even be an unwise goal altogether (cf. Hersey, 1960). In any case, a great deal happens to people between the promise of childhood and their actual accomplishments as adults.

If it is a problem to *find* children who will subsequently become eminent, the problem of defining eminence in a way that educators can *use* is more striking still. The definition varies not only from society to society but from era to era within societies (Bull, 1985). Of particular concern for educators of the gifted is the degree to which, at a given time in history, what is popularly termed "eminence" is related to intellectual pursuits. Can we create a definition that accounts for the fact that good luck (e.g., being the right color, coming from the right background, and being in the right place at the right time) plays a role in who becomes eminent? If not, then we are sure to repeat the same abuses that have so often characterized the application of IQ tests.

Intellect and Eminence

This chapter has already considered the fact that intelligence does not *predict* eminence, defined as extreme adult accomplishment. The brightest youngsters *do not* become the most eminent adults, even though above-average intelligence probably is required for eminence in most fields (Baird, 1985; Walberg, Rasher, & Parkerson, 1979). Conventional wisdom explains the inability of IQ tests to predict adult eminence as a weakness of the tests (see e.g., Alvino & Weiler, 1979). The previous discussion showed how the conventional wisdom really reflects difficulties associated with measuring extremely rare phenomena. This analysis was based on an appreciation of *quantitative* concepts.

The following discussion is *qualitative*. It explains the lack of relationship between intelligence and eminence as a question of cultural values. It examines the way our values shape how we interpret the role of reason in society. The discussion explains two phenomena: (1) the frequent misinterpretation of the observed low correlation between academic success and life success and (2) the failure of academic measures to correspond with measures of life success.

Eminent persons embody our cultural values. Some of these values come from a cultural tradition of many centuries; others form the basis for new cultural legacies. For example, talented classical violinists become eminent because they help translate a long-standing cultural tradition of serious Western music. They perpetuate a heritage that is valued by an intellectual elite. Because works of serious music, art, and literature are valued solely by an intellectual elite, they represent "high culture." The key question here is whether or not the values of the intellectual elite determine the boundaries of our cultural tradition.

Can individuals who excel in fields other than those validated by the high culture be considered eminent? These questions suggest the need to define such terms in a way that will enable us to make some useful distinctions.

Eminence, renown, and fame. Although the literature on gifted education does not qualify the term "eminence," it is enlightening to restrict the use of the term. In particular, one can distinguish among "eminence," "renown," and "fame." Although they are often used as synonyms, these three terms actually reflect relationships that exist between different groups of individuals and society as a whole.

In common parlance, for example, one does not usually speak of an eminent football player. This sort of cultural hero is called "famous." So are rock stars, movie actors, popular singers, and certain corporate executives. Medical doctors who treat wealthy and famous clients are called neither eminent nor famous. They might better be called "renowned." Famous painters and theoretical physicists, may, however, be referred to as "eminent," especially if they are no longer living.

The distinctions concern different levels of participation in the high culture by each category of hero; we call "eminent" only those heroes who further that legacy. Moreover, since the high culture represents a long historical tradition, it admits new fields quite slowly. Although science, for instance, has occupied increasingly larger portions of the intellectual legacy over the last three centuries, we still do not accord eminence too readily to living scientists. Within the high culture, however, rock music does not hold anywhere near the same status as science. It has not been around nearly so long. Therefore, we *never* accord eminence to rock stars, even posthumously. Classical violinists, on the other hand, are clearly involved in the high culture. When they become famous, they achieve eminence automatically.

The real rewards of fame, renown, and eminence.   So far, this discussion might make it seem that the classical violinist is the most fortunate of the cultural heroes mentioned. At a higher level of abstraction, the discussion might also seem to indicate that the activities of the high culture were the activities most valued in the United States.

These conclusions, however, would be mistaken. For one thing, they misrepresent the way our society really works. Respect for the heroes of the high culture seldom involves the rewards that motivate most of us and that most accurately represent the things we really value: substantial material rewards and effective influence in the larger society. Hence, the heroes of the high culture—in spite of their eminence—contribute very little to the values we cherish most in our society.

In fact, our society, like most, has an ambivalent attitude toward both the high culture and the intellectuals who take an active part in it (Hofstadter, 1963; Perry, 1984; Shils, 1972). The intellectuals are by no means the ruling elite in our culture, nor do they promote the economic and political interests of the ruling elite (Gouldner, 1979; Hofstadter, 1963; A. Howley, 1986; Shils, 1972). Instead, most intellectuals reject or rebel against the ruling elite—a trend that holds for other ancient and modern societies, whatever their economic or political systems (Lipset & Dobson, 1972).

The ruling elite is not interested in giving *its* heroes the status of *eminence*, but it can provide them with ample rewards, including money, power, and renown. The group that warrants the status of cultural hero by the standards of the ruling elite is composed of technocrats—applied scientists, technicians, corporate executives, and university advisers to government and industry. Whereas some authors (e.g., Perry, 1984) classify technocrats as a subgroup of intellectuals, the failure to distinguish between the two groups obscures the important mechanisms by which power and intellect are separated in our society (Gouldner, 1979; Hofstadter, 1963, A. Howley, 1986; Mills, 1959).

The heroes of *popular* culture, though they are not rewarded overtly by the ruling elite are nevertheless controlled by that elite. Executives of the entertainment and communications industries have almost exclusive authority over their fate (Mills, 1959). Popular stars help make huge profits for corporations, and their constant presence on TV and radio actually manifests the stability of our culture. A few popular entertainment and sports stars may take unpopular positions on public policy, but their personal influence is necessarily limited by their economic usefulness.

Popular heroes also serve a useful role with respect to education: They provide support for the illusion that fame and the financial rewards of fame are accessible to *anyone* in our society. As a result, many students seek refuge in fantasies of fame in athletics and show business—fantasies that are as unattainable as they are self-deceptive.

The plight of the intellectual. Intellectual work in the United States is seldom valued for its own sake. It gets strong support, however, when it is used to further the goals of government, the military, and business. Hofstadter (1963, p. 25) distinguishes between intellect, which is "critical, creative, and contemplative" and intelligence, which is "manipulative, adjustive, [and] unfailingly practical." He characterizes America's reaction to intellect and intelligence (see p. 70).

Because of the low value placed on intellectual work, U.S. society often does not accommodate intellectual *vocations* (Hofstadter, 1963). Significant intellectual activity frequently takes place outside formal economic institutions. Learned individuals often use their *intelligence* to direct careers—as professors, lawyers, doctors, and executives. A small number of learned individuals use their *intellect* in activity that is best termed "avocational," since it is not profitable economically (Lopate, 1978). This intellectual activity may include scholarship, artistic production, and literary or political criticism. Even in universities, scholars have far less chance to do autonomous intellectual work than most people imagine.

Implications for the education of the gifted. Because there are very few avenues of employment that accommodate autonomous intellectual work, society, through the mechanism of the schools, guides intelligent youngsters away from scholarship for its own sake. Instead, it seeks to give them practice in the skills and, especially, the behaviors that characterize professional technocrats in our society. As a result, our schools *do* help to produce enough trained professionals and technical experts. However, they also teach the proposition that what is useful is of greater worth than what is beautiful or true.

Schools do not seem to be cultivating intellectuals or artists. In fact, there is evidence that schools actually try to suppress rather than nurture intellect (Coleman, 1961; Oakes, 1985; Torrance & Myers, 1971). Schools can actually function as an anti-intellectual force in society (Sawyer, 1988; Hofstadter, 1963). This may even be an important—if less than noble— aim of schools with respect to their gifted students (Coleman, 1961; Tannenbaum, 1962), who have been found to cherish aesthetic and theoretical interests (Tidwell, 1980).

Anti-intellectualism and eminence. Certainly eminent attainment in intellectual and artistic spheres requires a high level of intelligence (see e.g., McNemar, 1964). According to Baird's (1985) careful review, the empirical evidence *does* suggest a positive relationship between intelligence and success of various forms. As Baird (1985) notes, the relationship may be greater than correlation studies indicate. Most such studies have involved only academically talented—often gifted—subjects. The restricted range means that obtained correlations are probably underestimates. Despite the facts, popular opinion underestimates the relationship between academic ability and eminence. Why?

For one thing, such a view helps support the belief that anyone can become eminent, a sentiment that reflects the notion of fairness. Moreover, such a view justifies paying little attention to the development of existing academic ability, which may be the result of unfair advantage. Since the cultural institutions (e.g., symphony orchestras and universities) cannot make room for *more* eminent individuals than they already manage to accommodate, the cultivation of many more such individuals would just increase competition for the few places that do exist within these institutions.

In general, our society functions as though academic pursuits relate little to life success. Thus our social institutions (particularly schools) cultivate noncognitive behaviors that have a more practical connection to life success (Baird, 1985; Bowles & Gintis, 1976; Hofstadter, 1964; A. Howley, 1986). These social institutions condition behaviors that support the continued prosperity of business, industry, and government. In the process, however, they alienate those intellectuals who may provide access to an important past and future legacy.

Research on Eminent Individuals

There has been very little research on the characteristics of eminent individuals. In part, research has been limited by the extreme rarity of the kinds of accomplishments associated with eminent status in the high culture. Researchers find it difficult to identify a large sample of eminent individuals at any given time. Because of this difficulty, some researchers (e.g., Cox, 1926; Goertzel & Goertzel, 1962; Simonton, 1984) have analyzed historical reports of eminent persons from many eras. This research is based on a narrow definition of eminence, similar to the one that we have articulated. Other research (e.g., Segal, Busse, & Mansfield, 1980) is based on a broader definition of superior performance, and the results of this research will be considered subsequently, in the section of this chapter devoted to leadership.

Biographical research on eminence. Most of the studies about eminence are based on biographical records of men and women who have earned national or international reputations for accomplishment in scholarship, politics, or the arts. Some findings are based on studies of contemporary eminent subjects and include the results of interviews, aptitude tests, and personality measures. Most of the findings characterize the nature of eminent men and women and their families. A few studies have considered broader influences, such as geography and popular culture.

In general, the biographical research on eminence is more circular, more anecdotal, and more speculative than most contemporary research in psychology and sociology. Seldom do the biographical reports of eminent persons contain data that can be manipulated statistically. The few quantitative data that do exist vary among subjects. Moreover, since there is so much biographical detail to choose from, selection and interpretation are largely a function of the researcher's bias.

The empirical literature on eminence began with Galton's (1869/ 1962) *Hereditary Genius,* which reports his assumptions, methods, and conclusions about eminent men. His conclusions led him to prescribe eugenics as the means of improving human achievement, since he believed that heredity alone was sufficient to explain eminence. His conviction that heredity was virtually the only source of resemblance among members of the families of eminent persons was completely unwarranted. A distinctive family environment was as likely a source, and few researchers since his time have assumed a position so extreme. Some have taken the opposite view; most have taken an intermediate position.

Odin (1895), who studied eminent French literati, disagreed sharply with Galton's conclusion that no man of innate exceptional ability could be deterred from eminence by environmental circumstance. Ward (1906) presented the viewpoint that ascribed significant influence primarily to environmental forces. In *Applied Sociology,* Ward (1906) asserted that the working class is as capable as the upper classes of producing eminence and that the difference between the classes lies not in innate talent but in privilege.

Clarke (1916/1968), who was influenced by Odin and Ward, included demographic variables in his study of American men of letters and found that several geographic and economic variables were associated with literary eminence. Taking population size differences into account, he found that the greatest proportion of literary men and women in his sample of 1,000 came from the New England states. The southern and northwestern states contributed the fewest subjects. Thirty-two percent of the American literati were from relatively metropolitan areas even though these areas contained only 9 percent of the population at the time Clarke's subjects lived (none was born later than 1850). Seventy-eight percent came from families with at least average incomes. According to his statistics, a man or woman with some college education was several hundred times more likely to achieve literary distinction than someone without any college education.

Catherine Cox (1926) was concerned primarily with the psychological characteristics of eminent persons, particularly their degree of intellectual ability. She attempted to estimate childhood and adult IQ scores for 301 famous men and women based on juvenilia and biographical records; her subjects included some of the most famous figures in English, European, and American history. The group with the highest estimated childhood IQs, according to Cox's formula, was composed of the 12 philosophers among her subjects. Their average estimated IQ was not less than 175. Cox suggested that a "true" IQ (i.e., actually measured at the time the subjects were children) for the entire group would not have been lower than 155 to 165. Cox's estimated data, however, yielded an average IQ about 20 points lower. On the basis of her study, Cox characterized these subjects as having above-average heredity *and* superior advantages in early environment.

Davis (1929) studied the life histories of 163 leaders of the Russian revolution. On the basis of historical and biographical records, he concluded that the greatest influences on these eminent men were teachers, revolutionary literature, and the idealism of their father or mother. He also noted that the leaders had nearly all done university work and that most of them came from middle- and upper-class families.

In *Cradles of Eminence,* Goertzel and Goertzel (1962) described the emotional and intellectual climate in the homes of eminent persons. They included in their study 400 Americans and Europeans who lived into the twentieth century. They concluded that virtually every subject had at least one parent who showed a high degree of commitment, ability, or emotional intensity. As a result, *family life was neither pleasant nor comfortable;* it was often tumultuous. Their research led Goertzel and Goertzel to suspect that eminence develops in families that cultivate extreme levels of intellect, emotion, and commitment to principles.

Psychological research on eminence.   Research on eminent contemporaries has been conducted by psychologists interested in creative behavior (see Chapter 4 for research related to creativity per se.) Recent studies have focused on the effects of intellectual abilities, personality traits, life history, and family background on the emergence of exceptional talent. Like earlier studies, they found that eminent persons have exceptional ability. In most cases, although their talent in early childhood was evident to their families, it was not evident to their schools.

Recent studies of eminent individuals have therefore tried to identify personal and familial characteristics that condition eminence. Economic and social influences have been examined less closely, though they are equally important (cf. Jencks et al., 1979). Like earlier researchers, contemporary writers have also noted that eminent persons and their parents are committed to learning and to principled action. Bloom (1982), in particular, in his study of internationally recognized young mathematicians, athletes, and musicians, called attention to the extraordinary commitment of family time and resources necessary for superior achievement.

LEADERSHIP AND GIFTEDNESS

Akin to the notion of eminence, leadership implicates certain kinds of exceptional performance. Unlike eminence, however, leadership has been considered *extensively* from both philosophical and empirical perspectives.

This brief survey of the empirical literature on leadership first presents an analysis of the *idea* of leadership; then it presents research findings about leadership. Finally, it applies both theory and research to an analysis of the role of leadership training in the education of gifted students.

Who Are Leaders?

Political philosophy has considered, throughout history, the nature and role of leadership. Philosophers have articulated different views of leadership, based on their more general notions about the structure and function of government. In their consideration of leadership, some philosophers have also described the personal traits and types of behavior required of a leader in an ideal system of government.

Our discussion considers three philosophical views of leadership and characterizes each view by briefly examining the work of one representative philosopher. A meritocratic view is presented in Plato's description of the philosopher king in the *Republic.*. An autocratic view is expressed in *The Prince* by Machiavelli, and a democratic view is expounded by John Locke in *Two Treatises of Government.*

Philosopher kings. In order to understand Plato's political philosophy, it is important to know something about his metaphysics, the branch of philosophy that considers questions about the ultimate meaning of life. For Plato, ultimate meaning involved knowledge of *ideal* reality (i.e., the way things really are as opposed to the way things seem). The purpose of each individual's life and the collective life of individuals in society was to conform to the ideal and thereby to achieve goodness.

Because, for Plato, knowledge of the ideal was the essence of life, he saw as natural leaders those individuals who had the greatest access to this knowledge. He maintained that knowledge of the good was equivalent to goodness and that evil was merely ignorance of the good. Since government existed to rid society of evil, those who governed should be those most knowledgeable of the good. By this logic, Plato concluded that philosophers were the most capable rulers.

Plato compared the leadership of philosophers with that of politicians and intellectuals. He found politicians to be concerned with gaining and keeping political power, an activity that entailed evil actions. He found intellectuals to be totally unconcerned with action and therefore apolitical: Philosophers, according to Plato, were able to resist the allure of power while still being able to enact the good. This combination of virtues resulted from their inherent abilities and an appropriate education.

Plato maintained that leaders (whom he called guardians) needed to have physical strength, courage, and a philosophic temperament. These inherent capabilities were not sufficient, however, to produce philosophers capable of ruling. In addition to these innate capabilities, potential leaders needed extensive education. Their education involved additional studies beyond the primary and secondary education that Plato advocated for all citizens. Thus, philosophers needed to receive primary education that involved reading, writing, and physical education; secondary education that involved the study of literature and music; and higher education that involved the study of mathematics and pure philosophy.

Plato viewed government as rule by an intellectually and morally superior elite. He understood that such a form of government would be unpopular with the citizenry. The role of the leader, however, would be to provide the citizens with knowledge of the good. When citizens were aware of the good, they would be less likely to resent the rule of the philosopher kings.

"The Prince."   In contrast to Plato, Machiavelli was concerned with how leaders function in the real (as opposed to the ideal) world. He wrote:

> How we live is so far removed from how we ought to live, that he who abandons what is done for what ought to be done, will rather learn to bring about his own ruin than his preservation. (Machiavelli, reprinted in Harris, Morgenbesser, Rothschild, & Wishy, 1960, p. 469)

Although Machiavelli wished it were otherwise, he nonetheless viewed humankind as disorderly and evil. He believed that humans needed to be governed by powerful leaders whose rule would provide order and stability. Based on the premise that *any* government was better than chaos, Machiavelli set out to define the method by which rulers could get and maintain power.

Machiavelli's political philosophy was founded on the assumption that the goal of establishing order justified any means of getting and retaining power. He believed that fewer people would suffer as a result of a prince's rise to power than would suffer as a result of anarchy. Hence, Machiavelli believed that it was ethical to recommend that rulers seize and maintain power by force or deceit. He wrote:

> A man who wishes to make a profession of goodness in everything must necessarily come to grief among so many who are not good. Therefore it is necessary for a prince who wishes to maintain himself, to learn how not to be good, and to use this knowledge and not use it, according to the necessity of the case. (Machiavelli, reprinted in Harris et al., 1960, pp. 469–470)

According to Machiavelli, the prince should learn to make use of whatever virtues and vices would be required in order to maintain power. To learn how to govern in this way, the prince needed an education in the organization and discipline of war. This study entailed the practice of military maneuvers even during peacetime. Such practice was intended to accustom the prince to physical hardship and to acquaint him with the terrain of his principality. This knowledge was necessary to assure the prince's military success in the wars that would be an inevitable part of his maintenance of power. In addition to physical training, Machiavelli recommended that the prince study history so that he might understand the ways in which leaders from other eras gained and used power.

Like the rulers that Plato envisaged, Machiavelli's princes were not likely to be popular. In fact, Machiavelli suggested that it was better for them to be feared than to be loved. He warned, however, of the dangers of being a hated ruler. He believed that a prince should keep from being hated by refraining from stealing his subjects' property. He also suggested that a prince might improve his popularity by *promising* to bestow various benefits on his subjects. Machiavelli, however, did not require that the prince actually deliver promised benefits.

The social compact. The philosophy of John Locke implied that political leaders should be very different from the sorts of rulers put forward by Plato or Machiavelli. Locke's view of the social compact could be practiced only if leaders represented the interests of the public. Leaders, therefore, needed to be very much like the citizens whom they represented.

Locke's views were based on two premises: (1) that there are certain natural rights accruing to all people and (2) that groups of people can *willingly* give up some of their natural rights in order to be protected by constitutional rule. Government, according to Locke, should be based on the principles of equality and liberty. Each individual is equal because each has the same natural rights. Each individual is free to exchange some of these natural rights for the protection of government.

Such a government, however, would be legitimate only if it functioned to protect the interests of the majority of its citizens. Its legitimacy also would depend on the fact that it allowed people whose interests were not represented to withdraw from the compact and seek other, more favorable governments. In addition, such a government would be effective only insofar as its structure allowed for the separation of the law-making and the law-enforcing functions. Thus, the democratic government advocated by Locke needed to be composed of a legislative and an executive branch. Locke suggested that a third branch of government, the federative branch, should be responsible for international affairs.

Because the leaders of government were accountable to the majority of citizens, Locke did not concern himself with their characteristics or training. His approach to democratic leadership was based on the assumption that all citizens would be equally capable of serving as political leaders. This view of leadership strongly influenced the men who framed the U.S. Constitution, and it even lent support (a hundred years later) to those who advocated the compulsory education of all children.

Who Needs What Kind of Leaders?

It is clear from the discussion above that the nature and role of good political leaders depends on the qualities of the government that they serve. Common sense suggests that complex societies may need many sorts of leaders and that the characteristics of these different leaders may vary according to the nature of the enterprises they lead. Because of the diverse roles filled by different sorts of leaders, it may be hard for society to predict the characteristics of potential leaders (Bull, 1985). Nevertheless, the rationale for providing leadership training to gifted students is that such training will help them in whatever leadership positions they eventually find themselves (Foster, 1981).

The discussion that follows evaluates the nature of leadership in contemporary social institutions. It compares the types of roles assumed by corporate leaders, political leaders, and cultural leaders. It also tries to determine the degree to which particular personality characteristics or social behaviors assure the success of different kinds of leaders.

Corporate leaders. Although the prototypical American businessman is the entrepreneur or "self-made man", this type of businessman is neither the most powerful nor the most prevalent in modern U.S. society (Mills, 1959). The most influential corporate executives work for companies that are owned by wealthy individuals or families, some of whom have maintained wealth over many generations and others of whom have acquired vast sums of money more recently. The leadership role assumed by these owners varies greatly; such owners often assume no leadership role at all. In the most common case, corporate leadership comes from managers rather than the founders or owners of corporations.

According to Bass (1981), there are innumerable typologies of leadership. Many of these typologies are designed to characterize corporate managers. Bass (1981, p. 22) suggests that the following types of leaders are common to many leadership typologies:

authoritative	dominative	directive
autocratic	persuasive	arousing
charismatic	seductive	convincing
democratic	participative	group developing
considerate	intellectual	eminent
expert	executive	bureaucrat
administrator	head	representative
spokesperson	advocate	

He also notes that "most recent researchers have devoted comparatively little attention to three of these types: persuasive, intellectual, and representative" (Bass, 1981, p. 22).

There seems to be no consensus about what type of leadership is most appropriate for a particular management function. Bass (1981) suggests that to understand effective management one may need to analyze the system in which the leader is embedded. This analysis would include the study of "multiple inputs from the environment, the organization, the immediate work group supervised, the task, the leader's behavior, and relationships with subordinates, and outputs in terms of effective performance and satisfactions" (Bass, 1981, p. 613).

Clearly, no *one* style or method of management determines success as a corporate leader. Therefore, it would be difficult to identify potential corporate leaders on the basis of their personal characteristics or to base leadership training for corporate success on any *particular* set of behaviors.

Political leaders.   While many of the characteristics of political leaders are conditioned by the requirements of their roles, the media and the public relations industry also influence political leadership (see e.g., The Ripon Society, 1969). Training in particular leadership skills may play a part in political leaders' *exercise of power*, but it probably does not influence their ability *to govern wisely* or to represent the commonweal.

According to Mills (1959), there are two types of political leaders, those who assume executive functions and those who assume legislative functions. Of these two types, Mills finds the executive leaders to be more powerful because of their close connections with the corporate and military elites. The success of executive leaders depends on their ability to make use of connections with other powerful groups rather than on their ability to develop or exploit particular personal qualities.

Mills believes that legislative leaders *do not* have any real authority to represent the majority of citizens. First, he asserts that the majority of citizens do not constitute an informed public that guides the actions of its representatives. Second, Mills suggests that any legislative representative must secure and maintain the backing of the powerful constituents in his or her district. Thus, legislators are bound to develop and vote for laws that promote the interests of their most powerful supporters. According to Mills, legislators are the middlemen who promote the interests of the ruling elite.

Like Machiavelli's princes, political leaders may need to act in ways that serve to keep them in power. Although the methods of maintaining power need *not* entail virtue, they cannot be *too overtly* dominated by vice (Mills, 1959). Nonetheless, according to Mills, our society has traditionally tolerated a considerable amount of wrongdoing on the part of its political representatives.

Because of their close affiliation with the ruling elite, most political leaders are better educated than the average citizen. Many of them are lawyers or businessmen. In spite of their educational attainment, however, most political leaders disassociate themselves from intellectuals and denigrate scholarly pursuits (Hofstadter, 1963). The anti-intellectual posture assumed by political leaders serves to safeguard their existing popularity and to protect them from the appearance of elitism (Mills, 1959).

Cultural leaders.   The characteristics of and the roles assumed by the most notable cultural leaders were considered in the preceding section on eminence. In that discussion, eminent cultural leaders were viewed in terms of their ability to advance the high culture. The production of enlightening works of scholarship or beautiful works of art hardly ensures eminence, however.

Many cultural leaders are not, in fact, eminent. Some cultural leaders may remain unrecognized in their own eras but later achieve eminent status, but many more live and work in relative obscurity. To prepare anyone for a leadership role of such a speculative nature is clearly impossible (Bull, 1985). On the other hand, it may be possible to provide an education that acquaints many capable students with significant cultural traditions. By educating many students in these traditions, we can perhaps simultaneously nurture those few who will become cultural leaders (Howley et al., 1986).

Because cultural leaders are most often intellectuals or artists, their interests may be contrary to the interests of political and corporate leaders. Anti-intellectual forces in our society may make it difficult for many cultural leaders to gain popular support or economic reward (Hofstadter, 1963; Lipset & Dobson, 1972). Cultural leaders may actually exist in spite of our social institutions (including schools) rather than because of them (Hofstadter, 1963).

As a group, cultural leaders are probably even more diverse than the corporate or political leaders discussed above. It is very unlikely, therefore, that the sorts of leadership training that might provide some benefit to corporate or political leaders would have *any* bearing on the contributions made by cultural leaders.

Characteristics of Leaders

A great deal of research has aimed at identifying traits that characterize leaders. Some of this research investigates the characteristics and behaviors of capable managers, whereas other research explores the traits of charismatic politicians. It is possible to interpret the research only when it is organized around a theoretical premise. *Generalization,* however, is very difficult because the research is based on so many different definitions of leadership.

Transactional and transformational leaders.   Burns (1978) makes a theoretical distinction that allows for a meaningful synthesis of the research on leadership. He suggests that there are two distinct types of leaders, transactional leaders and transformational leaders. These types of leaders serve very different sorts of social functions and consequently behave quite differently.

According to Burns (1978, p. 19), "transactional leadership . . . occurs when one person takes the initiative in making contact with others for the purpose of an exchange of valued things." Transformational leadership occurs, on the other hand, "when one or more persons engage with others in such a way that leaders and followers raise one another to higher levels of motivation and morality" (Burns, 1978, p. 20). Burns classifies managers as transactional leaders and charismatic politicians as transformational leaders.

In the discussion that follows, we will use Burns' distinction to help explain some of the research findings on leadership. In particular, his distinction will help us evaluate the degree to which leadership can, or even should, be trained.

Children's personality traits and leadership. Researchers have attributed a wide variety of personality traits to leaders, including superior intelligence, motivation to excel, originality, judgment, sociability, aggressiveness, generosity, dependability, scholarship, and physical prowess (Stogdill, 1974). Various studies have also found personality differences in leaders on the basis of the sex, ethnic membership, socioeconomic status, and other characteristics of their constituencies. Sex-related differences associated with leadership have been found among children in sexually homogeneous and heterogeneous groups. In elementary school, boys' leadership seems to depend on verbal aggressiveness and girls' leadership seems to depend on success at school tasks (Zander & Van Egmond, 1958). Male leaders of boys' gangs and play groups are usually above average in athletic ability and physical prowess (Partridge, 1934). An extensive study of boys' gangs in Chicago found the salient trait of the leader of the group to be his gameness (Thrasher, 1927). In girls' dormitories leadership is correlated with generosity, enthusiasm, and affection; dorm leaders tend to be characterized as protective of the weak, dependable, tactful, considerate, confidence-inspiring, and able to establish rapport quickly (Jennings, 1943).

In general, leaders tend to epitomize the values of their followers (Litzinger & Schaefer, 1984). Superior socioeconomic status and scholastic standing, for example, differentiate campus leaders from other students (Sward, 1933). The most influential college campus members represent dominant values on the campus (Stogdill, 1974). These findings suggest that an acceptable leader must internalize a group's norms (Litzinger & Schafer, 1984).

Group values, however, are subject to change. For example, student leaders of the 1960s differed from student leaders of other periods. The unpopularity on college campuses of the Vietnam War contributed to the emergence of student leaders who repudiated established political and economic beliefs. Leadership, then, is not merely the possession of a combination of personality traits. An individual may be able to rise to the top with one group of peers but not with another; an individual who is a leader in one era may not be an acceptable leader in another era (Stogdill, 1974).

Identifying potential adult leaders. The identification of children who might become leaders as adults often proceeds from a view of leadership based on personality traits. This view also influences the content of leadership training programs. The validity of predicting children's future leadership from studies of the personality traits of adult leaders has not, however, been established. Moreover, it is not even clear that the general personality traits of some adults condition their performance as leaders.

Much of the research on leaders' personality traits is based on subjective accounts. In the first half of this century, authors biased their accounts of leaders' characteristics by seeking to identify predetermined qualities (Bavelas, 1984). More recent research efforts have been limited by the lack of an adequately standardized instrument to measure general personality traits that predict leadership capability. Recent research, therefore, has relied on experimental instruments for identifying leadership potential among specific groups and in specific situations.

The situational nature of leadership. According to Stogdill (1974), to understand leadership, one must analyze situations as well as leaders. Power is an important determinant of situational leadership. Sources of power include expertise, legitimation, coercion, reward, and reference (liking) (Stogdill, 1974). Since personality traits may help explain why individuals are liked, they may influence effective transactional leadership to some degree.

If not assigned by superiors, committee leaders are those who assume ad hoc responsibility for seeing that the committee accomplishes its task. They are not necessarily more competent or more popular than other committee members, although they seem to participate more in group discussion (Stogdill, 1974). Committees often cede leadership to their most active member. In these cases, committee members are willing to relinquish control of the task because they believe either that all committee members are equally competent to accomplish the task or that the committee's task is not very important.

Research simulations of committee work seem to reproduce the conditions under which some committees actually function. The committees to which these findings are applicable are those in which the stakes for performance are not high, committee members are not hostile to one another, and the task is imposed by a benign external authority. Cooperation with a particular group leader under such circumstances is more likely to depend on the leader's likeableness than on other sources of power. Effective transactional leaders in experimental groups—and in the actual groups they simulate—tend to be spontaneous, tolerant of a range of ideas, accepting of diverse personalities in the group, and solicitous of participation by all members. It is, however, clear that many real life committees function under circumstances quite different from these experimental conditions. For example, an employee who is not liked may be designated to chair a committee. In this case, the preceding discussion does not apply.

For transformational leadership, where the stakes are higher, personality traits probably carry far less weight than other sources of power, such as political or economic leverage. Many great transformational leaders were isolates; many were irascible, tactless, and overbearing. Interpersonal skills are relevant to effective leadership primarily when the leader's main source of power is likeableness. Personality traits *should not*, however, be expected to predict leadership in situations where significant cultural, political, or economic change is at issue.

The interaction between personalities and situations.

According to Bavelas (1984), a leader exhibits leadership in some situations, but not in others. The degree of structure, the cooperativeness of the group, the nature of the task, and many other variables determine the *personality traits* required for effective leadership. The individual who is at ease and capable of influencing a group under certain circumstances may not be effective under other circumstances. Authoritarian leaders, for example, are more likely to accomplish clearly defined, important goals; they are less likely to be effective in situations where goals are unclear or unimportant to the group's well-being (Korten, 1972).

On comparatively rare occasions, the effective leader's personality may affect the *context* in which transactional leadership occurs. Different leaders, for example, define and structure tasks in different ways, in part because of differences in personality. Such differences of style may, in certain situations, distinguish between merely competent and noticeably adroit leadership. When transactional leaders significantly affect the context in which their leadership occurs, however, they are behaving like *transformational* leaders.

This metamorphosis may be appropriate; on the other hand, it may exceed the requirements of the organization in which the committee exists. Success or failure to accomplish limited tasks depends, in part, on compatibility between the leader's personality, the nature of the task, and the composition of the group. Committees that become *too* effective can cause organizational problems (Boss & McConkie, 1981).

Leadership and IQ.   Leadership is included in the federal definition of giftedness in Marland's (1972) report to Congress on the status of gifted education in the United States and in the revised definition published in Section 902 of PL 95–561, The Gifted and Talented Children's Education Act of 1978. Of the five types of giftedness established by the definition, leadership is the least frequently addressed through identification efforts. As we have seen, research offers no good reason for labeling a particular group of children as uniquely gifted in leadership. Educators lack valid and reliable means of identifying the potential for leadership in young students. It is not possible to exclude any child from a leadership program on the grounds that the child lacks leadership potential.

Concern for leadership talent is therefore more commonly addressed through leadership training provided to intellectually gifted children. The justification for this approach is that the research consistently reports that leaders are above the average intelligence level of the group they lead. In addition, many educators cite the correspondence between some of the personality traits of leaders and some of the traits of high-IQ children.

Clark (1979), for example, believes that leadership entails skills that enable a group to maintain itself, reach its goals, adapt to environmental change, and permit self-fulfillment among group members. According to Clark (1979, p. 236), "leadership skills are mostly interpersonal and include flexibility, openness, and ability to organize. Leadership requires self-esteem, high values, and mature emotional development." Clark believes that these characteristics are compatible with traits typical of gifted children.

It is probably true that many high-ability students and few low-ability students possess the *cognitive* skills needed for leadership (Gallagher, 1985). "High ability" in this case does not mean exceptional ability, however. Research indicates that the leader is usually only slightly more able than the group of followers; the correlation between ability and leadership is not very strong. Zander and Van Egmond (1958) found a low positive correlation between intelligence and social power among second- and fifth-grade students. Their correlation is about the same as the average correlation of other studies, approximately 0.28.

Are gifted children destined to be leaders?   In general, leaders appear to be above the group average, but not too far above it. The individual with an IQ of 160 is *not* likely to be the leader of an average group. According to Hollingworth (1926), an IQ range from 115 to 130 is more typical of leaders of average-IQ groups. Children with IQs of 160 and above are not excluded from leadership of *gifted* groups, however (Hollingworth, 1926).

Subsequent studies have confirmed Hollingworth's assertions. A study of managers found that individuals with either low or very high scores were less likely to achieve success in management positions than those with scores at the intermediate level (Ghiselli, 1963). Other studies of businessmen report the same finding (Baird, 1985). In contrast to the expectation that gifted children would be natural leaders, it may be likely that many gifted children are *less* apt to be leaders than children with IQ scores only slightly above average.

This observation may be true not only of high-IQ children, but of children with superior divergent thinking ability as well. In a study of elementary children, Torrance (1963) found that the most highly divergent thinkers among the older children were often ignored and subdued by the other members of the group. Torrance (1963) was surprised to find that the older and more organized the group, the more it inhibited the member who had scored highest on a test of divergent thinking. He commented on this effect:

> Plainly, the tendency of organization to control the most creative tends to coerce some highly creative children and reduce their usefulness. There are, of course, the aggressive, irrepressible subjects . . . There are also diplomatic, creative persons who feel their way gradually and slowly win acceptance of their ideas . . . That creative people should be required to expend so much energy in "being nice" in order to obtain a hearing for their ideas is regrettable. (Torrance, 1963, p. 135)

Although 68 percent of the top scorers on divergent thinking tests initiated more ideas than any other members of the group, only one-fourth of these students were credited as making valuable contributions to the group's performance. Only the most persistent or most diplomatic of the top scorers were actually able to make a contribution; others withdrew from the process, disrupted it, or accepted minor tasks that denied them the opportunity to contribute.

If leaders tend to epitomize the values of the groups they lead, the interests and behavior of intellectually gifted persons may inhibit their effectiveness as leaders. Opportunities for leadership by the intellectually gifted are most likely to arise as a result of their expertise. They might, through professional influence, lead groups constituted of other capable persons in their fields. Gifted persons might also occupy leadership positions as a result of characteristics obscurely related to their giftedness, such as attractiveness or economic power.

Group dynamics and leadership training for gifted students. Research on group dynamics typically suggests the content for leadership training programs for gifted children. Such research investigates transactional leadership exclusively; programs based on research about group dynamics typically try to develop communication skills, decision-making skills, planning skills, and skills in values clarification (Karnes & Chauvin, 1986).

One such program described by Foster (1981) trains adolescents who have been identified as gifted in social ability. The program attempts to teach group communication skills, problem solving, and decision-making procedures. Students are matched with mentors who hold leadership positions in local political, business, and social organizations. Since intellectual giftedness is not a prerequisite for success in these programs, it is unwise and unfair to exclude average ability students who could benefit from them (Cox et al., 1985). Such programs include limited opportunities to improve academic skills, but they are unlikely to provide sufficient academic challenges to intellectually gifted students.

What is the program of study for transformational leaders?   When educators discuss the need for leaders who can solve important national and international problems (e.g., Cox et al., 1985; Torrance, 1984), they are clearly referring to transformational leaders. Transformational leaders assume responsibility for work that is both more dangerous and more important than the committee work of transactional leaders. In providing transactional leadership training to intellectually gifted children as a means of cultivating leadership potential, educators may be making two serious errors. First, they may be providing the wrong sort of training to a talented group. Second, by devaluing intellectual skills, they may discourage children of all ability levels from acquiring the knowledge and skills that will enable them to understand and participate in significant political, economic, and cultural changes (cf. Coleman, 1961; Katz, 1971; Scott, 1986).

In a comparison of charismatic and consensus leaders, Zaleznik (1984) proposes that major change is brought about primarily by leaders who do *not* conform to accepted values in the area in which they effect change. If leaders are to be creative, they may have to violate accepted standards of polite behavior (McCall, 1984). The social values and transactional skills taught to gifted students in leadership training programs may therefore actually *hinder* the development of transformational leaders.

The potential leaders of significant artistic, scientific, or political movements are better served by training that develops superior intellectual competence. Transformational leadership usually requires an understanding of the history of the pertinent discipline and the relationship of its principal concepts and methods to other disciplines (cf. Kitano & Kirby, 1986).

The power that legitimates transformational leaders, as noted previously, is not likely to be interpersonal skill. Programs for intellectually gifted students should cultivate cognitive skills; teaching noncognitive skills is unlikely to prepare intellectually gifted students to exercise the sorts of leadership roles for which they *do* seem to be best suited. On the contrary, it may well inhibit them in such roles.

OCCUPATIONS AND GIFTEDNESS

Virtually all men, and increasing numbers of women, take paid occupations after they finish school. The object of this portion of the chapter is to provide a background for understanding the characteristic relationships of giftedness (academic and intellectual talent) to the performance of gifted individuals in occupations and careers. Teachers of the gifted need to consider these matters because career preparation programming for their students is increasingly recommended (e.g., Feldhusen & Kolloff, 1979; Fleming, 1985; Van Tassel-Baska, 1981).

Two Views of Careers

In a broad sense, a "career" is an individual's occupational progress over an entire lifetime, and an occupation is the general activity to which an individual devotes the most time and effort at a given time. In one view, neither occupations nor careers need be paid employment (Fleming, 1985; Hoyt & Hebeler, 1974). For example, a person who raises five children, without ever receiving a salary or wages for the effort, can be said to have a career. The problem with this definition, however, is that it promotes a view of careers that is blind to gender, race, and class prejudices. It ignores factors that strongly influence the occupational fate of everyone (Wright, 1979). Perhaps this omission is necessary in career education in the interest of equality of opportunity, but it is not very helpful in clarifying the characteristic occupational progress of gifted individuals.

Ginzberg (1971) uses the term "career" differently in his survey of career guidance:

> Since most blue- and white-collar workers seldom move more than a few rungs up the skill and income ladder during the course of their working lives, their work experience, with its limited progression, cannot be called a career. (Ginzberg, 1971, p. 7)

Ginzberg's definition better approximates the common sense of "career." It also recognizes such influences as elevated social status, high income, and other labor market influences (such as gender, race, and social class).

For three important reasons, the subsequent discussion follows Ginzberg's sense of the term. First, the aim of this chapter is to understand what is known about the occupational fate of gifted individuals. It is less concerned with ways to help students make career choices. Second, gifted children are typically identified by academic tests, and we need to consider carefully the relationship of academic ability to conventional occupational success. Finally, American sociology has most commonly used occupational status and income to study the questions that concern us. It is an established fact that not all occupations and not all human beings are regarded with equal worth in our society. For some reason, much of what is written about career education ignores these facts. This discussion does not.

Reasonable but Unrealistic Occupational Preferences

The occupational preferences of schoolchildren have been studied for a long time. Surveys of adolescent occupational preferences have repeatedly yielded disquieting results. Unselected junior and senior high school students report an overwhelming preference for the professions (Roe, 1956). This phenomenon disturbs educators because the disparity between job preference and job availability is so great. At a time when 6 percent of the population was employed in professional work, 50 percent of all students elected the professions as a possible occupational choice. *None* elected manufacturing as a possible choice, although 50 percent of all workers were at the time employed in manufacturing (Roe, 1956, p. 256). Similar results have been reported before and since Roe's research.

These findings are disturbing because they suggest that the vast majority of young adults is unable to enact avowed preferences. Occupational dissatisfaction threatens the stability of both family life and political life. One spends at least one-third of one's time working; dissatisfaction with work is likely to affect the quality of relationships at home. Moreover, if the job dissatisfaction is shared among co-workers, it leads to labor unrest. Clearly, the satisfaction that we derive from work is important in many ways.

The finding is all the more distressing to educators because, according to Marland (1974), Americans still subscribe to the seven cardinal principles of secondary education developed by the National Education Association in 1918. The goals represented by these principles—which include worthy home membership, a productive vocation, good citizenship, and worthy use of leisure time—cannot be fulfilled if citizens remain dissatisfied and unfulfilled in their work. This problem has been dealt with in two ways.

Fantasy. First, adolescents' job preferences have been found to become increasingly more realistic as students near the end of their school experience (Griffin, Kalleberg, & Alexander, 1981; Roe, 1956). Researchers have often concluded, reasonably enough, that fantasy plays an important part in adolescent development and that normal adolescents adjust quickly to the demands of adult reality. This approach suggests that the problem is not so threatening as might be imagined.

This finding, however, merely reduces the magnitude of the problem; the approximation of job preference to job availability remains lopsided. Moreover, after age 18, job preferences change little (Roe, 1956), so that remaining dissatisfaction is likely to be a persistent problem. These facts suggest that it is very important to change students' attitudes about jobs while they are still in school.

Career education.   Therefore, a second approach has been to provide schoolchildren with information about the variety and nature of available jobs. One intention of this effort is to increase students' awareness of the employment options that are *potentially* available to all citizens. Another intention is to apprise students of their abilities, both cognitive and noncognitive, and the requirements of various occupations (e.g., Ginzberg, 1971; Marland, 1974; Winefordner, 1988). Educators hope such knowledge will help individual students choose occupations that are *actually* (rather than potentially) available to them.

These types of programs are carried on under the rubric of "career education." The term is misleading because it implies that professional occupations (i.e., careers) are potentially available to all students, a misconception that it seeks to dispell. In fact, the types of conventional success in which virtually all Americans are most interested (high pay and high status) *cannot* be supplied to all students. The conventional symbols of success are unfortunately in comparatively short supply. There are not enough such jobs for everyone, and everyone wants them.

Occupational satisfaction increases dramatically as security, pay, and status increase (Roe, 1956; cf. Terman & Oden, 1959). It is unlikely that the instrinsic worth of relatively tedious work can be substituted for the extrinsic rewards of security, high status, and high pay. Some intellectually talented individuals may find important qualities in jobs that seem tedious to others, but these individuals will be the exception. In general, satisfaction is a concomitant of security, high status, and high pay. In the current economy, however, the most tedious and lowest-paid jobs are experiencing the most rapid growth (Rumberger, 1984; Thurow, 1987).

Professional status-seeking and gifted children.   More than unselected students, gifted students prefer the professions. Tidwell (1980) reported that 91 percent of her sample of 1,593 gifted students expressed such a preference; virtually all planned to attend college, with half planning to acquire master's degrees and one-fourth planning to pursue doctorates. This combination of preferences and plans, when enacted, strongly conditions occupational status, *regardless of IQ* (Jencks et al., 1979). That is, students of average ability who carry out the same plans achieve occupational opportunities equal to those of their gifted peers. The gifted are more likely to carry out such plans than *unselected* students, but their professional prospects are not so auspicious as one might expect. For example, even in

Terman's sample, with a mean IQ of 151, many students did not become professionals (Terman & Oden, 1959).

This fact is important because it reflects the strong influence of some variable other than educational attainment. After the student's own level of educational attainment, his or her father's educational level is the sociological variable that most strongly influences adult attainment (Blau & Duncan, 1967; Jencks et al., 1979). Though most gifted children do come from middle-class families in which parents are highly educated, so do many other children. Children of above average ability (IQ 110–120) with advantaged family backgrounds doubtless outnumber children identified as exceptionally able, since 20 percent of all children fall in this IQ range.

The competition for professional positions, however, is not even restricted to such *above average* students. Most colleges are not very selective; many undistinguished students complete undergraduate and graduate programs. The potential for high occupational status among the gifted is further compromised by the fact that professional jobs are likely to become more scarce as the cybernetic revolution invades the professions (Rumberger, 1984; Leontief, 1982; Wiener, 1954).

The preceding discussion suggests three conclusions:

1. The occupational preferences of gifted students differ in degree rather than in kind from those of unselected students.
2. Most gifted students have "realistic" occupational and educational goals.
3. Professional jobs are scarce, and competition for them is intense.

Giftedness and Professional Status

The previous discussion also suggests two possibilities that need to be explored further. First, it is possible that most professionals are not gifted individuals. Second, it is possible that many gifted students will not become professionals. The discussion that follows considers, first, the IQs of professional groups, and second, the careers of the highly gifted Terman sample (Terman & Oden, 1959).

Examination of these possibilities is as important to an understanding of political, economic, and educational theory as to an understanding of the characteristics of gifted students. Differential education for gifted students is often justified by the claim that the gifted are future leaders (Terman, 1925) and that our economic system naturally favors the abilities of the gifted (Hollingworth, 1926; Herrnstein, 1973; Hoyt & Hebeler, 1974). The research presented below suggests the need for more plausible justifications (cf. Bull, 1985).

The IQs of professional groups. The IQs of various professional groups have been reported by several researchers in the past (Hollingworth, 1926; Herrnstein, 1973; Roe, 1956; Thorndike & Hagen, 1959; Jensen, 1973). In general the mean IQs of professional groups are found to exceed the national average. The more exclusive the profession, the higher the mean IQ of the group seems to be. Thus, the three most coveted and exclusive professional groups, doctors, lawyers, and engineers (cf. Katchadourian & Boli, 1985), are typically found to have mean IQs varying from one to two standard deviations above the national mean.

Of the researchers cited above, Roe (1956) provides the most thoughtful discussion. She notes that in examining the IQs of occupational groups, one needs to consider not only the means, but also the standard deviations and ranges as well. Roe notes that the IQ ranges of all occupations overlap substantially and that the IQ ceilings for all occupations are similar. It appears that gifted individuals not only follow all occupations, but also are represented in them. (see Box 5-2).

BOX 5-2   *Intellectual Talent in Occupational Groups: Means, Standard Deviations, and Ranges*

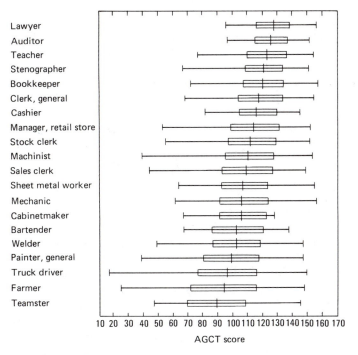

Source: Roe, A. (1956). *The psychology of occupations* (p. 72). New York: Wiley. Used by permission.

The mean ability of lawyers is about 125, the standard deviation 10, and the range from 95 to 160. The means for farmers and truck drivers, on the other hand, were much lower (about 95), but the standard deviations were about 25, and the ranges were about twice as large as for lawyers. The ceilings for the two lowest-status occupational groups were about 150. The distributions for both farmers and truck drivers were positively skewed, an indication that many subjects were marginally literate.

Roe's observations address the two possibilities raised at the beginning of this section. Although a large percentage of professionals score in the gifted range of general intellectual ability, most do not; moreover, many highly gifted students will not become professionals. Since relatively few persons are employed in the professions and since the vast majority of persons is employed in nonprofessional work, it is possible that more gifted individuals are employed in nonprofessional than in professional jobs. This possibility may be more likely if one includes women, who are still under-represented in the most coveted professions (cf. Fleming, 1985; Rumberger, 1984).

These conclusions are consistent with the findings of Jencks et al. (1979). Being gifted is not sufficient or necessary for achieving entry into any profession. Even being gifted *and* well-educated is not sufficient to ensure professional status. Competition for professional jobs is intense, and factors other than academic ability may be of strong interest to employers.

Careers among Terman's subjects.   Lewis Terman and Melita Oden published the 35-year follow-up of their very high IQ sample in 1959. At the time data were collected (1949–1954) the subjects were about 44 years old on average, and their occupational patterns were therefore considered to be well-established (Terman & Oden, 1959). Because most of the data considered in this section of the chapter are based on the occupations of men, discussion of women among Terman's sample is given less attention here. At the time of the study, women suffered great sex discrimination in employment, a condition that has improved only somewhat since 1959. Interested readers are urged to consult Sears and Barbee (1977) for a discussion addressed particularly to the fate of women in the Terman sample. In interpreting the following discussion, readers should recall that Terman and Oden's subjects were a highly gifted cohort.

Terman and Oden (1959, p. 74) report that 45.6 percent of their sample were employed in the professional category of the Minnesota Occupational Scale. This figure excluded business executives and others whose activities would now (because of the rise of postbaccalaureate business schools) be construed as professional. These figures can nonetheless be compared to Roe's (1956) data cited previously, and they suggest that the gifted are far more likely to achieve professional status than unselected persons.

Since most of the gifted sample completed college (70 percent of the men and 67 percent of the women), a more germane comparison involves *gifted* college graduates versus *unselected* college graduates. In order to compare the professional employment of their sample to the professional employment of unselected college graduates, Terman and Oden combined three categories from the Minnesota Occupational Scale. The resulting "professional" group, defined more loosely than on the Minnesota Occupational Scale, accounted for 94 percent of all gifted college graduates in the sample. The comparable figure for unselected U.S. college graduates was 84 percent, according to Terman and Oden (1959). The occupational advantage enjoyed by Terman's subjects was *slight* in comparison to all college graduates. The occupational attainment of all *gifted men* in the Terman sample about equaled the occupational attainment of *both male and female* college graduates, according to Terman and Oden's figures (1959, p. 80).

Terman and Oden's data make it apparent that, depending on the definition of "professional," many subjects *did not* become professionals. Sometimes these were students who did poorly in school or did not continue their education beyond high school. Sometimes they were college graduates who accepted lower-status jobs as a matter of choice (Terman & Oden, 1959).

Some observers have noted that most jobs, even professional jobs, may require more education and higher levels of skill than are called for by the demands of the job (Berg, 1972; Bowles & Gintis, 1976; Jencks et al., 1979). This observation may be particularly true in the case of gifted students; for them, even the most coveted occupations may prove somewhat limiting or unfulfilling (Gold, 1965; Willings, 1985). About half of Terman and Oden's (1959) male subjects reported "deep satisfaction" in their work; about 40 percent were "fairly contented"; the rest were not particularly satisfied or were discontented. Doctors, bankers, and college teachers were more satisfied than the average gifted subject; authors, engineers, clerks, and skilled tradesmen were less satisfied than average. Levels of satisfaction were lowest among authors (20 percent), skilled tradeworkers (18 percent), clerks (17 percent), and school teachers (10 percent).

Among Terman and Oden's sample, at all occupational levels, there appears a type of individual whose behavior attests to the existence of compelling intellectual interests not fulfilled by occupational activity. These individuals tended to find more meaning in their "avocational" pursuits than in their occupations. Anecdotes about these individuals—housewives, executives, teachers, housepainters, carpenters—report that in an attempt to accommodate their intellectual interests, they often made choices that could be judged economically unwise or impractical. The significance of this characteristic will be explored further in our discussion of intellectualism among college students.

It is not possible to conclude from Terman and Oden's (1959) data that giftedness is a substantial occupational advantage. Terman and Oden believed it was, of course, but more recent work (e.g., Baird, 1985; Jencks et al., 1979) documents only a slight positive overall association of IQ with occupational performance, once the effect of educational attainment is controlled. Jencks et al. (1979) found that although there is a 0.47 correlation between IQ and occupational status, 60 percent to 80 percent of this correlation is attributable to the amount of schooling. When amount of schooling is controlled, variations in intellectual ability account for only about 8 percent of the variance in occupational status. This finding is consistent with the reinterpretation of Terman and Oden's (1959) data.

Conclusions and cautions. Though many gifted students become professionals, perhaps an equal number do not; though many doctors and bankers are exceptionally talented intellectually, many are not. A one to one correspondence between exceptional intellectual ability and professional status does not exist. The IQs of professional groups and the professional status of highly gifted students illustrate the influence of factors other than academic ability on occupational status. Intellectual talent, though important, is only one kind of talent needed to achieve entry into a profession. Talents unrelated to intellectual ability are probably of equal or greater concern to prospective employers or colleagues (Baird, 1985; Jencks et al., 1979).

The free enterprise system determines the nature and distribution of jobs for aspiring students, and that fact is often overlooked by career education. Schools may function to legitimate the distribution of scarce and desirable jobs to advantaged students (Meyer, 1977); moreover, such a function seems to take surprisingly little note of exceptional talent (Howley et al., 1986). Nonetheless, to conclude that schools should cultivate noncognitive characteristics that would help more students acquire well-paid jobs of high status would be unwise. As the following discussion indicates, many gifted students possess intellectual abilities and interests that cause them to regard employment prospects skeptically (Katchadourian & Boli, 1985).

Intellectualism and Careerism

The job market for college graduates is considerably worse than it was in the 1960s (Rumberger, 1984). Professional positions are now more difficult to secure, and many college graduates take nonprofessional jobs. In a survey of job prospects for college graduates in the years 1960–1990, Rumberger (1984) notes that the employment prospect of college graduates no longer resembles that of college graduates during the 1960s but more closely approximates the prospects of college graduates during the 1950s. This survey confirms the impression of many observers.

Many observers are convinced that more college students than ever are anxious to acquire lucrative jobs after graduation. These observers fear that students often hold such career interests to the exclusion of cultivating intellectual interests and values. This possibility concerns liberal arts colleges particularly. Katchadourian and Boli (1985) studied careerism and intellectualism among a cohort of Stanford University undergraduates. Their findings about the characteristics of the Stanford cohort should be of considerable interest to teachers of the gifted.

The Stanford study.   Katchadourian and Boli (1985) were interested in discovering the extent to which careerism and intellectualism motivated their undergraduate students. From 1976 to 1983 they followed a 20 percent random sample of students (n = 320) in a single class (the class of 1981), collecting data on career choices, academic majors, grades, sociological background, and so forth. They also conducted structured interviews that are quoted extensively in their report, *Careerism and Intellectualism Among College Students* (see Box 5-3).

BOX 5-3   *Careerism and Intellectualism at Stanford*

Most students in the Stanford sample (72 percent) came from public high schools. Their mean Scholastic Aptitude Test (SAT) scores were SAT-Verbal, 600, and SAT-Mathematics, 654. (In 1976 the SAT national means were 429 and 470, respectively.) The parents of most students were well educated; family income was high compared to the national median (18 percent came from homes with an annual income above $100,000; 24 percent from homes with an annual income below $30,000.) The high cost of attending Stanford doubtless explains this skew. Though it is not a sample of gifted students, the gifted seem to be as well represented at Stanford as they are in the most coveted professions.

Some students scored high on both scales and some students scored low on both scales. As a result the researchers developed a four-part typology: *intellectuals* scored high on intellectualism and low on careerism; *careerists* scored low on intellectualism and high on careerism; *strivers* scored high on both scales; *unconnected* students scored low on both scales (see Figure 5-1).

FIGURE 5.1   Typology of College Students (from Katchadourian and Boli, 1985, p. 34)

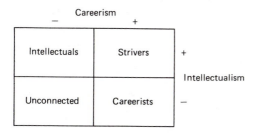

Using factor analysis, Katchadourian and Boli (1985) developed unrelated (r = 0.10) scales for intellectualism and careerism. The scales used items that addressed three basic concerns: reasons for attending college, characteristics desired in a major, and characteristics desired in a career. For example, students who scored high in careerism cited "acquisition of marketable skills," "future financial security," and "establishing professional contacts for the future" as the prime reasons for attending college. Students who scored high in intellectualism cited "learning to think critically," "[pursuing] general liberal education," and "developing artistic and esthetic taste and judgment" as prime reasons for attending college (Katchadourian & Boli, 1985, p. 31).

Careerists tended to be "mercenary" in their pursuit of a coveted career (Katchadourian & Boli, 1985, p. 102). Earning a lot of money quickly was a goal for many. Most careerists regarded their studies as unpleasant work necessary for achieving professional goals. They often expressed boredom with academic work, while acknowledging Stanford's usefulness as an "elite finishing school" (Katchadourian & Boli, 1985, p. 86). They were largely uninterested in social and political issues. Overall, careerists tended to have the highest educational aspirations of all four groups: 50 percent of each sex planned on earning doctorates (in spite of the fact that they regarded academic work as distasteful).

Intellectuals, on the other hand, regarded learning as an activity pleasurable in itself. Intellectuals were very interested in social issues, but tended to be political moderates rather than progressives. Their occupational ambitions were directed at securing work that was interesting rather than lucrative. They were much more likely than careerists to change plans after starting college. These changes resulted in movement *into* humanistic disciplines, whereas the net changes of other groups drew students *away* from humanistic disciplines.

Although strivers espoused strong intellectual interests, their educational aspirations, career choices, and college majors resembled those of the careerists. In general, their strong career interests seemed to take precedence over intellectual involvement.

When the researchers examined the data on unconnected students, however, they identified a subgroup who resembled the intellectuals. Members of this subgroup were interested in and active in pursuit of intellectual issues, but they failed to endorse Stanford's institutional perspective. Katchadourian and Boli (1985, p. 192) called these students the "academic dissenters"; the politics of many could be described as progressive rather than moderate. Of all groups, the unconnected were the least likely to choose business as a career; after the intellectuals, the unconnected were the group most likely to choose humanistic professions (writing and journalism) and teaching.

Implications. The Stanford study documents clear differences in values among a group of very talented undergraduates. The findings are consistent with findings about the career choices of gifted high school students (Marshall, 1985) and about gifted adults (Willings, 1985). Katchadourian and Boli's findings provide further evidence that the pursuit of theoretical and aesthetic interests motivates many gifted individuals, regardless of employment prospects. While it is probable that many gifted students will resemble the Stanford intellectuals and academic dissenters, it is also certain that many others will resemble the careerists. The careerists, however, seem *least* in need of career education, whereas the intellectuals are intent on making their own way.

Gifted Students, Intellect, and Occupational Life

As they mature, students with exceptional academic and intellectual talents begin to function as adults. Some of these students are fortunate enough to enact comparatively independent decisions about the use of their talents. For others, parental values and social conventions overtly determine their actions.

The difference in occupational outlook is perhaps inherent in the nature of intellectual talent, which may either develop itself or be applied to a practical task. The motivation for self-development is intrinsic interest, which seeks understanding rather than acquisition. By contrast, the motive of practical intelligence seems to be acquisition. "The dominant value orientation among hard-core careerists is to make money: a lot of it, and fast" (Katchadourian & Boli, 1985, p. 102). It is probable that the gifted high-school careerists observed by Marshall (1985) shared this motive.

The demands of occupational life obviously favor the application of intelligence to practical tasks. All adults must come to terms with this fact. For most students, whose intellectual values are less extreme than among the gifted, the reckoning is not so difficult. The findings cited above suggest that gifted students resolve the occupational dilemma in two fundamental ways.

Intellectualism and vocation. The difference between intellectuals and careerists is perhaps best illustrated by the term "vocation." A vocation is literally a "calling," and intellectuals seem to be engaged more in the process of *heeding a call,* that is, of discovering a vocation, than in *acquiring a career.*

The Stanford intellectuals and academic dissenters constitute a group whose primary intellectual activity is to construct meaning. Two characteristics of this group are of particular relevance. First, students of this type have intellectual interests that span several fields. They do not become specialists easily or happily (cf. Willings, 1985). Second, this type of student typically possesses strong verbal skills. Exercise of those skills may be what draws such students to the humanities. They are less interested than other students in math or science. These students hope that their intellectual interests will eventually lead them to discover occupations that are intrinsically rewarding. The conventional success represented by lots of money seems to be much less important to this type of student than to the careerists.

Careerism and anti-intellectualism. Treating the intellect solely as an instrument that is useful in securing entry to lucrative professions seems to entail denial of the intellect. Careerists do not even expect to enjoy their studies. Many careerists apparently ignore their own perceived need for intellectual self-development (cf. Katchadourian & Boli, 1985, p. 107). The Stanford researchers were most distressed with these students' failure to discover wider intellectual interests.

The most striking suggestion, however, in Katchadourian and Boli's account of the careerists is that their anti-intellectualism may be imposed from without. Careerists are strongly compelled by extrinsic influences. Parents often exert authority overtly by such manipulations as threatening to withhold financial support (Katchadourian & Boli, 1985, p. 96). Students are thus conditioned by their family values to make practical career decisions early and to stick with those decisions. Coleman (1961, p. 304) observed that a similar process pulled even average high-school students away from scholarship.

Occupational prospects for the gifted. A talented student can choose to ignore the call of the intellect for self-development and opt single-mindedly for the best-paid occupation. Alternatively, a talented student can ignore the issues of practicality and pursue intellectual interests single-mindedly.

It seems, however, that whatever route gifted students choose, they will inevitably feel misgivings. Some careerists regret that they dare not follow more compelling studies (Katchadourian & Boli, 1985); some intellectuals regret that their choices lead to less well-paid occupations. Many gifted students will share in both regrets. Teachers ought to recognize that only a fortunate few will find a comfortable existence doing well-paid, meaningful work.

Teachers of gifted students should understand that the characteristic of exceptional intellectual ability does have some practical value in the occupational world. They should also realize that the machinations of the economic system overwhelm the practical value of the intellect. It is not clear, for example, that *exceptional* ability is a greater practical occupational asset than *moderate* ability. A fortuitous combination of moderate ability, the right background, and occupationally relevant noncognitive characteristics is probably a more effective influence on occupational status than extreme ability alone.

It is questionable whether reliable diagnosis of such fortuitous combinations of characteristics will ever be possible. Considering the scarcity of desirable jobs, the changing nature of the job market, and the continuing restructuring of the economy, it is also questionable whether public elementary schools and high schools *should* be the institutions to identify and groom students for occupational success.

SUMMARY

This chapter examined the adulthoods of children identified as gifted by the schools. It began by developing the notion of a continuum of talent in which substantial adult success (leadership, eminence, or career success) was viewed as a phenomenon more rare than childhood giftedness. The relationships between giftedness and these three varieties of adult success were explored in depth. In general, the chapter noted that intelligence does not predict adult success very well. It examined the historical and cultural influences that may account for the weakness of the observed relationship.

The discussion of eminence and giftedness distinguished among fame, renown, and eminence. The relationship between eminence and intellectual traits was viewed critically through the work of C. Wright Mills and Richard Hofstadter. The discussion concluded with an historical review of research on eminence, contrasting the work of Galton with that of later researchers.

The chapter next examined the relationship between leadership and giftedness. The discussion reviewed significant historical models of leadership (in the works of Plato, Machiavelli, and Locke) and major contemporary leadership roles (corporate, political, and cultural). The importance of the typology of transactional and transformational leadership to gifted education was examined critically.

The chapter concluded with an investigation of careers among the gifted. Like average students, gifted high-school students express preference for professional careers. Nonetheless, studies indicate many gifted students do not become professionals. Two types of career interest were distinguished in the discussion: (1) strong professional commitment based on the desire to become affluent and (2) other career interests based more on a search for satisfying work.

6

Academically
Talented Children

    3. Penmanship as a confounding variable in composition
  D. Foreign Language Aptitude
      1. Verbal intelligence and foreign language achievement
      2. Other correlates of foreign language achievement
  E. School Responses to Verbal Precocity
      1. Identifying verbal precocity
      2. Placement
      3. Program characteristics
      4. Acceleration, enrichment, and instructional level
      5. Programming cautions
      6. Trends for the future
III. Mathematical Ability
  A. Mathematical Skills
      1. Calculation
      2. Concepts
      3. Logic
      4. Problem solving
  B. The Characteristics of Mathematical Ability
      1. Krutetskii's study
      2. Mathematical ability according to Krutetskii
      3. Quantitative traits not part of mathematical ability
      4. Gender and mathematical ability
  C. School Responses to Exceptional Mathematical Ability
      1. Identification
      2. Placement
      3. Enrichment
      4. Acceleration
      5. The dilemma of school responses to mathematical ability
IV. Summary

Focusing Questions

1. How is verbal precocity related to intellectual ability as measured by an IQ test?
2. How do language comprehension and language production differ, and how does each relate to IQ?
3. How should schools respond to the needs of verbally precocious students?
4. What are the characteristics of mathematically gifted students?
5. How do verbal ability and spatial ability relate to mathematics achievement?
6. How should schools respond to the needs of mathematically gifted students?

RELATIONSHIP BETWEEN IQ AND ACADEMIC TALENT

The moderately high, positive correlation between IQ and academic achievement is well established. The average correlation varies from about 0.50 to 0.80 depending on the measurements used (Vernon, 1979). Children's standardized achievement test scores usually correlate more highly with their IQ scores than their grades do.

The size of the correlation also depends on the range of scores. When a wide range of IQ scores and academic achievement levels is considered, IQ scores are "remarkably accurate" in predicting academic achievement (Messe, Crano, Messe, & Rice, 1979). When the range of IQ or achievement test scores is restricted to a small portion of the distribution of test

---

BOX 6-1 *Schematic Representation of IQ and Academic Abilities*

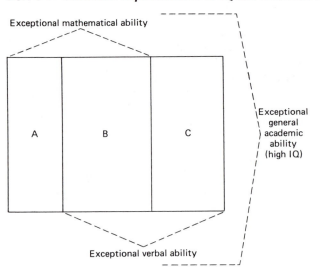

DESCRIPTION

A, B, and C are distinct sets of students: the three sets do not intersect.

> A + B + C = all students with significant academic abilities
> A + B = all students with exceptional mathematical ability
> B + C = all students with exceptional verbal ability
> A = students with exceptional mathematical ability *only*
> B = students with *both* exceptional mathematical *and* exceptional verbal ability
> C = students with exceptional verbal ability *only*

---

scores, as it is in studying gifted children, the correlation is lower. The purpose of this section of the chapter is to discuss likely reasons for these effects and to consider the relationship between high IQ and talent in specific academic areas.

In this section and throughout the book, the terms, "talent," "aptitude" and "achievement" are used nearly synonymously. Talent may be exhibited as academic achievement or as academic aptitude. When referring to the concept of genetically endowed ability, we use the phrase "innate ability." See Box 6-1 for a schematic representation.

High-IQ Children

High-IQ children are, by definition, academically apt in general (see Chapter 2). Their general aptitude strongly influences, but does not determine, their performance in the classroom and on standardized achievement tests. They usually do well in school, but some high-IQ children drop out of school, earn poor grades, achieve far below expectancy, or exhibit mediocre mathematical aptitude.

Academic achievement of high-IQ children.   Although high-IQ children usually earn above-average achievement scores in most academic areas, their achievement test scores are not as far above average as their IQ scores. As a group, they score highest in reading comprehension and language usage. They are also superior in spelling and mathematics, but their achievement in these areas is sometimes significantly lower than their IQ scores. High IQ scores show little or no correlation with achievement in school subjects that emphasize motor skills, and gifted children often make only average grades in penmanship or physical education, for example.

This achievement pattern was first reported by Terman (1925), whose gifted subjects' achievement on a standardized test was highest in language usage, next highest in reading, then spelling, and lowest, though still far above average, in arithmetic. The subjects' mean language quotient was 147, whereas their arithmetic quotient was 137. Their mean IQ of 151 was 25 percent higher than their mean academic achievement score. Most studies show similar results: *Gifted children's achievement scores are typically less extreme than their IQ scores.*

Gallagher and Crowder's (1957) study of high-IQ children in the regular classroom found most of them achieving above grade level. Like Terman's subjects, these children's scores in reading comprehension were highest; their scores in arithmetical computation lowest. Sixty-eight percent of this group of children, who had a median IQ of 150, scored more than three grade levels above their chronological age grade placement on paragraph meaning. Fifty-eight percent scored three or more grade levels above on science; but only 27 percent scored three or more grade levels

TABLE 6-1   Wide-Range Achievement Text Scores of Gifted Children in Grades 4, 5, and 6

	READING	ARITHMETIC	SPELLING
Grade 4	8.2	5.8	7.1
Grade 5	8.7	6.8	7.6
Grade 6	9.9	7.2	8.5

Source: Adapted from Whorton, Karnes, & Currie, 1985, p. 151.

above in arithmetical reasoning. Very few, only *3 percent* scored three or more grade levels above grade placement on arithmetic computation.

A study by Hollingworth and Cobb (1928) suggests a possible explanation for gifted students' relatively low scores on computation. The researchers speculate that the more *complex* the task, *the greater the advantage of high IQ.* In simple tasks, such as addition of whole numbers, for example, high-IQ students seem to enjoy little or no advantage in comparison to average students (Hollingworth & Cobb, 1928; cf. Krutetskii, 1976).

The achievement pattern of gifted children with IQ scores lower than 150 has also been established (Whorton, Karnes, & Currie, 1985). A group of gifted elementary-school children with a mean WISC-R IQ score of 131 was found to perform two to four grade levels above actual grade placement on different subtests of an achievement battery. The children scored as shown in Table 6-1 on the Wide Range Achievement Test.

All of these scores are above grade level, but nearly all are below the achievement levels that might be expected on the basis of IQ. Arithmetic scores are much farther below the expected level than are reading and spelling scores. This pattern of performance is similar to that of Terman's (1925) and Gallagher and Crowder's (1957) findings, despite a 20-point difference in the mean IQ scores of the samples.

Aptitudes of high-IQ children.   High-IQ children usually score above average on tests of special aptitudes, but their performance varies greatly depending on the test and the type of aptitude. On tests of verbal and quantitative aptitude, they score as high as students who are several years older (Martinson, 1972). On tests of other kinds of aptitude, for example, artistic, musical, or mechanical, their scores are closer to the norm.

Wilson's (1953) study of high-IQ children's performance on special aptitude tests found their mean scores to be above average on every test administered. On tests of art judgment, musical ability, science achievement, and mechanical aptitude, this group of children, whose mean IQ was 150, scored higher than the mean for children their age or a year or two older. The children scored highest on a test of music memory. They scored lowest (but still above average) on a test of musical accomplishment, apparently because superior performance on that test depended on rather extensive instruction in music (Wilson, 1953). The distribution of their scores on all of the tests, however, was closer to the norm than the distribution of their IQ scores; and the correlation between their aptitude test scores and their IQ scores was, for the most part, low to moderate (ranging from 0.16 to 0.57).

A study of science aptitude in six- and seven-year-old children with a mean IQ of 150 also found low correlations between IQ score and special aptitude (Lesser, Davis, & Nahemow, 1962). The children's Stanford-Binet IQ scores correlated 0.21 with a battery of seven criterion-referenced science achievement tests. It averaged about 0.10 with two forms of an experimental science aptitude test. The aptitude test was reported to be a better predictor of science achievement than the IQ test. The restricted range of the group's IQ-test scores may, however, account for the low correlation between IQ and science aptitude and science achievement in this study. On the other hand, the similarity between the content of the science aptitude and achievement tests (both were based on the school's third grade science curriculum) probably accounts for the high correlation between those two measures.

The studies discussed above suggest that, among gifted children, IQ is not a good predictor of narrowly defined aptitudes. This conclusion suggests that children with IQs of 130 are as likely to have high aptitude scores as children with IQs of 160. Similar findings, you may recall, characterize the relationship between IQ and divergent thinking.

Academically Talented Children

Academic *achievement* is usually categorized according to school subjects, whereas academic *aptitude* is typically construed more broadly. The two major varieties of academic aptitude are mathematical (or quantitative) and verbal (see Box 6-1). Occasionally, science aptitude is differentiated from mathematical and verbal aptitude.

Both mathematical and verbal skills are prerequisites to success in many academic fields, including science. Science aptitude is investigated primarily because it is perceived to be in the national interest, rather than because it reflects distinct cognitive skills. Success in science courses, however, like success in history courses, can largely be accounted for by quantitative and verbal abilities (Brandwein, 1955; Howley et al., 1986).

Although scores on verbal and mathematics tests are positively related, there are many talented students with a large discrepancy between their verbal and mathematical aptitude. Some verbally gifted students have only average mathematical aptitude; some mathematically gifted students have only above average verbal aptitude. The more extreme a student's verbal aptitude, the less likely it is that the student's mathematical aptitude will be equally extreme, and vice versa. Nonetheless, exceptional aptitude in one category (general, verbal, or mathematical ability) *usually* indicates above-average aptitude in the others (see Box 6-1).

Verbal aptitude is usually associated with advanced comprehension and facility in language usage. Verbally apt students are likely to perform better on IQ tests than on tests of mathematical aptitude, since IQ tests sample verbal material more heavily than quantitative material (Oller & Kyle, 1978).

Verbal aptitude.   Several distinctions are relevant to the examination of verbal aptitude. Language comprehension and language production implicate different levels of performance and different sorts of tasks. Learning foreign languages requires good skills of perception and auditory memory not associated with advanced comprehension or with most intelligence constructs.

Mathematical aptitude.   Tests of mathematical aptitude correlate moderately with *g*, Spearman's general intellectual factor, probably because they measure conceptual knowledge and reasoning skills. Excellent (as opposed to merely adequate) computation skills are not, however, related to high levels of mathematical ability (Hollingworth & Cobb, 1928; Gallagher & Crowder, 1957; Krutetskii, 1976). High-IQ students' mathematical achievement may also be less extreme than their IQs and their reading achievement because such students may depend on classroom instruction to learn arithmetic. There is no mathematical equivalent of reading difficult works independently, the experience that is probably responsible for the exceptional reading achievement characteristic of so many gifted students.

Science aptitude.   Different sciences—biology, chemistry, physics, psychology, sociology—make very different demands on the quantitative and verbal abilities of students. Whether or not a single construct ("science ability") underlies achievement in subjects so diverse is not clear. Though mechanical and spatial abilities (Roe, 1953) and analytic abilities (Guilford, 1950) are presumed to be important to achievement in some natural science courses, their predictive validity has not been demonstrated. It is not even clear that chemistry and physics, for example, make similar demands on these skills.

Investigations of science aptitude concern adult accomplishment more than school achievement (Holland & Astin, 1962; Holland & Richards, 1965; Taylor & Ellison, 1975). This focus is a direct result of the need to supply accomplished scientists in the national interest. In all cases the individuals who are the subjects of these studies are *all* very talented; thus, a very high level of academic achievement is a *prerequisite* to a high level of adult scientific accomplishment (Baird, 1985).

IQ scores of academically talented children.   Few studies have investigated the IQ scores of children identified as gifted on the basis of exceptional verbal or mathematical aptitude; however, these few studies have consistently found academically talented children to score at least above average on intelligence tests and other tests of cognitive development.

Stanley (1976b) reports that none of the children identified as mathematically talented by their high scores on the Scholastic Aptitude Test-Mathematics is of average or below-average intelligence. In a case study of seven junior-high students identified as academically talented by their performance in a science competition, Fox (1976a) found that the students scored far above average on two measures of intelligence, Terman's Concept Mastery Test (CMT) and the Raven's Progressive Matrices. Keating (1976c) assessed the performance of mathematically talented children on a Piagetian test of cognitive development and found that the talented fifth-grade students performed at a more advanced level than average seventh-grade students. Though Piagetian measures do not yield intelligence quotients, superior performance on Piagetian tasks is usually associated with high IQ scores (see Chapter 8).

Weaknesses in correlational studies.   There are several factors that must be taken into account when interpreting correlational studies of gifted students: (1) many studies of gifted children yield low correlations because the ceilings of the tests (IQ, aptitude, or achievement) are too low to represent accurately the gifted children's performance level; (2) even when test ceilings are sufficiently high, extreme test scores are associated with the greatest amount of error in measurement; and (3) the construct validity of some IQ, aptitude, and achievement tests is questionable. To an *unknown* extent all of these limitations confound the measured relationship between intelligence and academic talent.

Sources of individual differences.   Among children who have comparable IQ scores, differences in performance on measures of academic aptitude or achievement may stem from any of the three possibilities mentioned above; or they may reflect real performance differences caused by (1) differences in instruction, (2) differences in interest, or (3) differences in innate ability.

Instruction in school has a much greater effect on aptitude and achievement test scores than on IQ scores. High-IQ children who have been provided superior or additional instruction in mathematics, for example, acquire more advanced knowledge and so score higher on measures of mathematical aptitude or achievement (Keating & Stanley, 1972). By contrast, poor instruction or limited access to advanced instruction reduces the likelihood that gifted children's math performance will correlate highly with their IQ scores.

Although it is difficult to determine the direction of the causal relationship, it is apparent that children's interests and their achievement are related. Most likely, interest and achievement are interactive, with higher achievement promoting higher interest, and higher interest, in turn, effecting higher achievement. Even as children, internationally acclaimed mathematicians, musicians, and athletes spend much of their time engaged in the kind of activities in which they later excelled (Bloom, 1982; 1985). Adult scientists often report childhood interest in mechanical and scientific projects (Roe, 1953). Both scientifically and mathematically talented children express greater interest in theoretical ideas than average children (Haier & Denham, 1976; Krutetskii, 1976). Verbally gifted students are also highly interested in theoretical ideas, but they express more interest in aesthetic ideas than do mathematically or scientifically talented children (Fox, 1976c).

The existence of innate abilities has not yet been demonstrated convincingly. Instead, their existence has been inferred, principally from observed differences in the performance of schoolchildren on standardized tests. The inferences of numerous studies reinforce popular opinion; and many educators and lay persons attribute all sorts of individual differences to heredity (Gould, 1981). The work of Benjamin Bloom (1964, 1971, 1976, 1982, 1985), however, illustrates an alternative. His recent work, a study of 30 highly accomplished musicians, athletes, and mathematicians, suggests that *upbringing* most strongly influences the development of talent. (For a detailed discussion of nature and nurture, see Chapter 2.)

Special Talents

Some special talents seem to bear little relationship to the major varieties of academic talent discussed previously. These special talents seem to have limited value in predicting significant academic accomplishment. They relate to (1) prerequisite academic skills and (2) cognitive or perceptual processes.

Talent in prerequisite academic skills.   Students who are exceptional spellers and "lightning" calculators have served to entertain professional and lay audiences for centuries. The study of these special talents is pertinent to basic research in psychology, but is, however, largely unrelated to the cultivation of academic talent in schools. Excellence in some school subjects, such as spelling or arithmetical calculation, does not predict academic talent because a moderate level of success (i.e., competence or mastery) in these subjects is all that is required to achieve excellence in later academic work. These elementary skills make very limited demands on students' intellectual abilities.

Many high-IQ children exhibit only slightly above average or even average achievement in spelling, word attack, arithmetical computation, or penmanship. Gifted children have something of a reputation for poor penmanship, in fact (Freeman, 1979). *Some* high-IQ children are below average or deficient in some of these skills. It is even possible for students to exhibit below-average achievement in all these skills and still score in the gifted range on IQ tests. These skills are hardly sampled at all on IQ tests. Thus, the prominence of prerequisite skills in the elementary curriculum may explain the difficulty of identifying gifted elementary-school children on the basis of classroom performance or observation. Tasks that require comprehension, reasoning, and interpretation seem to be more closely associated with the major varieties of academic talent than skills that depend on motor coordination, visual perception, or rote memory.

Talent in traits thought to describe cognitive processes. Complex intellectual tasks obviously require the integration of a number of skills. There is a problem, however, in defining separate abilities for all such skills. A larger number of abilities necessarily results in the diminished predictive validity of each new ability (Krutetskii, 1976). Narrow cognitive traits—such as spatial scanning, perceptual speed, spatial orientation, and flexibility of closure (Carroll, 1976) or Guilford's (1959) 120 different intellectual abilities—are of very limited use in predicting overall academic talent (Carizio & Mehrens, 1985; McNemar, 1964). Testing for such skills is primarily of interest for basic research. Often research findings yield insights into puzzling encounters in the classroom, but a great many questions must be answered before educators can trust these findings to guide educational practice.

The practical status of some broad, nonverbal, cognitive skills (e.g., spatial and mechanical reasoning) is even more equivocal. Though spatial and mechanical reasoning skills seem relevant to a variety of fields (such as engineering, architecture, astronomy, geology, and fine arts), their function in predicting talent is questionable. Krutetskii (1976), for example, believes that spatial ability is not a necessary element of exceptional mathematical ability. No academic disciplines appear to be so heavily dependent on these skills that their assessment predicts talent more effectively than IQ, verbal, or quantitative measures.

Sometimes special abilities are commended as a vehicle with which to improve the fairness of identification efforts. It has been hypothesized, for example, that disadvantaged or handicapped children show superiority on nonverbal tests of cognitive processes but not on academic aptitude tests. Nonverbal reasoning ability, however, predicts achievement in an academic discipline less well than tests that sample skills that are more strongly represented in most academic disciplines. Children identified as talented by their scores on nonverbal reasoning tests, rather than on tests of academic achievement and aptitude, must be provided extraordinary instruction to upgrade their verbal and mathematical skills.

VERBAL PRECOCITY

Verbal precocity, or exceptional verbal ability, helps ensure high scores on IQ tests. Strong verbal-logical skills also characterize mathematical ability (see the following section). As we noted above, gifted children often exhibit both exceptional verbal aptitude and exceptional mathematical aptitude.

In fact, so few studies have investigated exceptional verbal ability *as distinct* from high IQ that it is difficult to discuss verbal precocity as a separate phenomenon. Our discussion of verbal precocity, therefore, focuses primarily on the performance of high-IQ children in reading, writing, speaking, and foreign language learning.

School-related Characteristics of Verbally Precocious Children

Tests of verbal ability and aptitude, such as the verbal portion of the Scholastic Aptitude Test (SAT-V) and the Stanford-Binet Intelligence Scale, are good predictors of school success. One of the most significant school characteristics of verbally precocious children is that they are usually successful students. Among middle-class students who score in the 97th percentile or higher on the Stanford-Binet Intelligence Scale, about 90 percent can be expected to have a grade point average of 3.0 ("B") or higher (Pegnato & Birch, 1959).

School success is partly a function of these children's superior comprehension of what they read. Many verbally precocious children excel in productive language skills, but the salient school-related characteristic of these children is their rapid and accurate *understanding* of verbal material. Children identified as gifted on the basis of their IQ scores are almost certain to be superior in their understanding of spoken and written language because IQ tests are heavily loaded with receptive language items (Oller & Kyle, 1978). More variability is found in gifted children's *production* of language since IQ tests usually do not measure the quality of children's speech or writing.

Receptive Language Skills and Giftedness

Ironically, most of the research on gifted children's listening comprehension relates only to bright students who are not performing well in the classroom. There appear to be no statistics comparing high-achieving gifted children's listening comprehension with their reading comprehension.

Barbe and Milone (1985), however, report that there is a discrepancy between gifted children's intellectual level and their reading comprehension. This discrepancy between intellectual ability and reading comprehension seems to decrease as children progress through elementary school (cf. Fox, 1983; Stanovitch, Cunningham, & Feeman, 1984; Whitmore, 1980). By the time they are in high school, most gifted students show only a small gap between intellectual ability and reading comprehension.

One reason that reading comprehension typically keeps pace with older children's intellectual development is that once children learn how to read (a phenomenon sometimes referred to as "breaking the code"), they can take control of their own reading achievement. Children can read in an erratic fashion, skipping from one topic to another, following their current interests, and still improve their vocabulary and reading comprehension.

However, the increase in the correlation of intelligence and reading comprehension may mean that among children with serious reading problems, a decline in IQ scores occurs. Reading achievement is itself an important source of intellectual growth for both gifted and nongifted students. Since IQ tests are normative comparisons, older students with reading difficulties may not fare well in the comparison.

Gifted students' reading achievement. Many gifted children are early readers, and they maintain consistent superiority in reading achievement (Durkin, 1966). This observation is true, in particular, of gifted children who are accelerated.

Durkin (1966) found a smaller discrepancy between IQ scores and reading achievement levels among early readers who were accelerated than among early readers who were maintained in a chronologically determined grade placement. By the end of the fifth grade, some accelerated early readers in Durkin's study were reading at the ninth-grade level.

Another sample of bright students with IQ scores of 120 or above presents a more representative picture. As seventh graders, half of these students scored two grade levels or more above their grade placement, and a little over a quarter of the group scored at the tenth- or eleventh-grade level on a test of paragraph comprehension (Tyler, 1962). Even gifted children who are referred for testing because of suspected learning problems tend to have above average reading achievement. A significant proportion (25 percent) of one sample of such children read two or more grades above their grade placement level (Fox, 1983).

Interest in reading: then and now. Early studies (e.g., Hollingworth, 1926; Stedman, 1924; Strang, 1963; Terman, 1925; Terman & Oden, 1947) found that gifted children were not only better readers than other children, but that they were more interested in reading, read more widely, and read more often than other children. Records of children's reading habits over a two-month period showed that gifted seven-year-olds read more books than unselected children up to the age of 15 (Terman & Oden, 1947). More than other children, gifted children tended to select classics, biographies, nature books, fairy tales, folk tales, and legends for pleasure reading (Terman & Oden, 1947). It seems likely that this selection is at least partly the result of family values.

One recent study of gifted children found reading to be the favorite pasttime of 75 percent of the group. The preferred reading material of this sample was science fiction (Van Tassel-Baska, 1983). These students could probably be considered to be highly gifted, since in the seventh grade they scored at or above the mean for college-bound seniors on the SAT-V.

Tidwell (1980), on the other hand, reported that TV, dancing, sports, and talking on the telephone were the preferred free-time recreational activities in her sample. She noted that the 1,600 gifted tenth-grade students (mean IQ = 137) in her sample spent an average of 11 hours per week watching television, slightly more than they spent studying. Since 1947, when Terman and Oden published the data reported above, TV has probably reduced the time gifted children spend reading. Nonetheless even Tidwell's sample read, on the average, 3.5 books per month, a figure that substantially exceeds the national mean.

Terman and Oden's (1947) observations may still accurately reflect the *comparative* amount of reading done by gifted students. Moreover, if Van Tassell-Baska's (1983) report is correct, more reading or greater interest in reading could be associated with the highest levels of academic aptitude. Highly gifted students may read more and profess greater interest in reading as a pasttime than other gifted students do.

Speech and Written Composition of Gifted Students

Despite the paucity of research to determine precisely how gifted children's spoken or written language differs from that of other children, many observers consider gifted children's speech and written language to be superior. For example, gifted children are credited with verbal behavior which is expressive, elaborate, and fluent (Renzulli & Hartman, 1971). They are also said to have superior facility in expression (Syphers, 1972). Gifted students' debating and speaking ability are reported to be the skills that most distinguish them from other students in the classroom (Terman, 1925). All of these are probably true at least to the extent that such characteristics make it more likely that these students will be referred for testing for possible placement in the gifted program.

Statements about the expressive language characteristics of this group are, however, based primarily on informal observation (e.g., anecdotal information and teachers' or parents' ratings) rather than on objective measurement. There has been little study to determine specific quantitative or qualitative differences in the expressive language performance of gifted students (Bruch, 1975). On the whole, the small number of studies correlating IQ and language production lend only weak support to the belief that high-IQ students demonstrate superior expressive language skills. A large usage vocabulary is one of the most common means of comparing the productive language of school-age children; but this and other characteristics generally associated with verbal precocity, such as complexity of sentence structure, do not necessarily correlate with higher quality language production (see, e.g., Labov, 1972).

Oral language of gifted students. Studies of school children's oral language have found that, compared with their classmates, children who score high on verbal tests show some difference from other children in the frequency of using tentative explanations, language mazes, and figurative language (Loban, 1967). They also show some differences from other children in the maturity of their syntax and in their frequency of making grammatical errors (J. Jensen, 1973).

In studying the language of elementary-school children, Loban (1967) found that children who were verbally proficient used language to express tentativeness more frequently than did other children. Tentative statements include suppositions, hypotheses, and conditional statements.

Children, and adults as well, exhibit many false starts, repetitions, and hesitations in their oral language. Loban studied these phenomena, called "language mazes," and found that elementary students who scored high on verbal aptitude tests exhibited fewer mazes in their oral language than did other children.

Loban (1967) also noted that very few elementary students used figurative language. In his study, the incidence of figurative statements was so low even among verbally proficient children that the difference between groups was not statistically significant. Of the few children who used figurative expressions, however, all were high scorers on verbal intelligence tests (Loban, 1967, p. 56). Later research by Paivio (1971) on the same topic suggests that within the group of verbally precocious children there is a subgroup whose language is characterized by frequent use of images, similes, and metaphors. This subgroup may represent those children who are interested or talented in writing poetry or fictional prose.

Written composition. If, as some researchers believe, written language reflects cognitive development more accurately than does oral language (Greenfield, 1972), then we could expect the written language of gifted children to be more mature than (1) their oral language and (2) the written language of other children. Neither this belief nor its implications have been verified. According to Fearn (1981, p. 26), the belief that "gifted learners are uniquely equipped for writing well is a widely disseminated generalization that enjoys not a shred of evidence."

It must be admitted that the evidence is slim. One study even reported the surprising result that the writing of an above-average group of students was more syntactically mature than that of a gifted group (Dupuis & Cartwright, 1979). Dupuis and Cartwright compared their gifted sample's scores on a measure of syntactic maturity (mean length of independent clauses) with those of Loban's (1967) above-average group, which had a mean IQ of 116 (on a group test). They were surprised to find that the above-average group outperformed the gifted group. Dupuis and Cartwright attributed these unexpected results to the rural environment of their gifted students.

One of the few factors found to distinguish the written composition of gifted from nongifted students is the gifted students' use of rare words and jargon (Pendarvis, 1983). Gifted seventh graders wrote science fiction stories that contained infrequently used words such as "disdainfully," "mage," "galumphing," "turbos," and "scanner." The average seventh graders did not use jargon so extensively, and their compositions contained fewer rare words.

Strang (1956), on the other hand, found gifted adolescents' compositions to be different in both content and form from those of average students. The essays of the gifted students she studied contained more frequent references to abstract concepts such as morality, peace, and freedom. In addition, their essays tended to be lengthier and more freely written than those of other adolescents.

Penmanship as a confounding variable in composition. In the preschool through primary years, one of the academic problems facing gifted children is the extreme discrepancy between what they can understand and what they can write. Even early readers typically write much less well than they read.

The compositions of young students are so affected by the physical demands of the handwriting task, that it is difficult to judge the quality of their ideas by reading their compositions. It is clear, however, that gifted children's skill in handwriting depends more on their chronological age than on their intellectual development (Terman & Oden, 1947). Five-year-olds who read like eight-year-olds, or comprehend verbal concepts like ten-year-olds, still print like other children in kindergarten or first-grade (Roedell, Jackson, & Robinson, 1980).

Foreign Language Aptitude

Gifted children seem to learn jargon (Pendarvis, 1983) and formal grammar (Durden, 1980) with relative ease. These characteristics suggest that gifted students are likely to succeed in foreign language studies. Research shows that in general, they do. The success of individual gifted students is not, however, insured. Characteristics other than high IQ are often associated with students' success in learning modern foreign languages (Stern & Cummins, 1981).

Verbal intelligence and foreign language achievement.   A review of the literature on intelligence test scores, verbal aptitude test scores, and measures of foreign language competence shows significant, though moderate, correlations among the variables. The correlations reported in Pimsleur, Mosberg, and Morrison's (1962) review of research on junior-high, high-school, and college-age students are typical of others in the literature. The correlations average about 0.45 (Pimsleur et al., 1962).

This magnitude of correlation means that IQ accounts for about 20 percent of the variance in foreign language achievement. Verbally loaded IQ tests such as the Stanford-Binet, for example, are more closely correlated with reading comprehension. They account for 40 percent to 50 percent of the variance in reading comprehension. Apparently, foreign language achievement requires some skills not measured by IQ tests.

Other correlates of foreign language achievement.   As noted previously, students with high verbal IQ scores are most likely to be precocious readers. We know less about their skills in listening, speaking, and writing. Some children whose foreign language performance is deficient have scores on tests of vocabulary and verbal reasoning that equal those of foreign language achievers. Such children often perform less well, however, than achievers on measures of auditory ability (Weeks, 1974). Success in foreign language may be based on speaking and listening comprehension rather than on other verbal abilities (Weeks, 1974).

The ability to decode, store, and encode phonetic material in an auditory mode may be a specialized skill that is relatively independent of intelligence as measured by IQ tests (Stern & Cummins, 1981). Carroll (1963) found the ability to encode phonetic material rapidly and accurately to be a better predictor of foreign language achievement than were IQ scores. A gifted student with auditory processing problems may experience difficulty in foreign language study. The difficulty may be compounded for such students by instruction in foreign languages that relies heavily on speaking and listening exercises. Children with serious expressive language weaknesses will probably experience difficulty with such instruction (Weeks, 1974). Although they may learn to read the foreign language, without special assistance they are unlikely to learn to converse fluently. Students with auditory processing problems are less handicapped in classical language courses or in modern foreign language programs that do not rely on a strongly conversational approach (Curtin, Avner, & Smith, 1983).

School Responses to Verbal Precocity

Assuming that schools should develop advanced achievement in students with exceptional potential, there are two groups who should be considered for placement in programs for verbally talented students:

- high-IQ gifted students, and
- students who score high on tests of verbal aptitude or achievement.

Both of these groups have, in general, demonstrated verbal precocity sufficient to justify exceptional programming in the verbal domain. The first group is typically regarded as verbally apt and in need of accelerated programming (Gaug, 1984). The second group is made up of apt students who may not score in the highest percentiles on an IQ test, but who do score in the highest percentiles on an aptitude or achievement measure of language comprehension or production. The same language arts program provided to high-IQ students will usually be suitable for these students as well. In fact, some of these verbally gifted students will demonstrate achievement that surpasses that of some students in the high-IQ group.

Identifying verbal precocity.   There are few tests specifically designed to identify the potential of verbally precocious school-age students. As the construct of intelligence evolves, however, such tests may evolve (cf. Gardner, 1983; Sternberg, 1977). For the time being *current* achievement can serve as a convenient proxy for specific aptitude tests to predict *future* achievement.

For younger gifted students, subtests of familiar individually-administered tests such as the Peabody Individual Achievement Test (PIAT; Dunn & Markwardt, 1970), the Woodcock Reading Mastery Tests (WRMT; Woodcock, 1973), and the Woodcock-Johnson Psychoeducational Battery: Tests of Achievement (Woodcock-Johnson, 1977) are suitable.

Horodezky and Labercane (1983) caution against using the criterion-referenced tests that accompany basal reading series to predict reading performance. These researchers suggest that an informal reading inventory (IRI) is a better predictor than the tests associated with basal reading series. The Test of Early Reading Ability (Reid, Hresko, & Hammill, 1983) might also be more appropriate. It is a norm-referenced test developed specifically to assess the early reading achievement of preschool or kindergarten children.

The tests listed above have few items difficult enough to assess the abilities of older students. For bright children older than 10 or 12, the ceilings of these tests are too low. One group achievement test battery that *can* test the upper limits of many older gifted students' achievement is the Sequential Tests of Educational Progress (STEP) of the Educational Testing Service, Cooperative Test Division, 1956–1972.

It is important, however, *not* to use grade-level achievement tests for the purpose of identifying academic precocity. Grade-level achievement tests, such as the California Test of Basic Skills (CTBS), measure student mastery of grade-level material. Such tests have relatively high floor and low ceiling effects. Unlike the STEP, they do not test a range of knowledge over many levels.

For older gifted students, off-level testing may also be a good alternative. In this case, identification of precocity will usually involve administering college entrance tests (e.g., the SAT). These tests are given to apt students who would not normally be considered old enough to take them (Stanley, 1981).

Placement. Educational policy needs to be formalized at the state and district levels to promote a consistent approach to identification and placement issues. Such policy should comprise the following broad features:

1. the use of valid and reliable assessment procedures,
2. a systematic means of considering and making placements,
3. the availability of program alternatives.

The educational placement of verbally gifted students in many states occurs in the context of special education procedures. Many of the states that have mandated gifted programs have included gifted education with other special education programs. In these states, changes in gifted children's programs are often subject to the state's regulations that derive from Public Law 94–142, The Education of All Handicapped Children's Act of 1975 (cf. Mitchell, 1981). Placement procedures for children identified by virtue of their high aptitude or achievement test scores (i.e., the second of the two groups listed previously) may not need to be as complex as those for high-IQ students, who may require special provisions to address precocious achievement in mathematics and other subjects as well. The multidisciplinary placement process is, however, one orderly way to handle complex placement issues (cf. Pfeiffer, 1980; Ysseldyke, Algozzine, & Mitchell, 1982).

Program characteristics. The keys to mounting a successful program seem to be the following:

1. identification procedures that relate reliably to program content,
2. program content at students' instructional levels, and
3. cognitive press.

Children must be identified with tests that reflect performance reliably. Unreliable scores guarantee poor decisions. Evaluators must have confidence in the scores used to make decisions.

The tests must also relate to the content of the program. Creativity tests, for example, would be inappropriate identification measures for accelerated reading programs, advanced grammar and composition courses, advanced literature courses, and probably for imaginative writing classes (cf. Hocevar, 1979, 1980).

Programs must approximate students' instructional levels, by definition, if they are to be considered appropriate. They must move gifted students into curriculum content they would not encounter until later in the regular program. Ideally, such instruction should also match the students' pace of learning.

"Cognitive press" is the instructional momentum of academic learning. Cognitive press in gifted programs implicates a comparatively rapid pace of learning. Even underachieving gifted children can proceed through the curriculum 50 percent to 100 percent faster than average children (Fearn, 1982; cf. Hollingworth, 1942).

Clearly, good programs for verbally precocious students cannot carry on acceleration and exclude enrichment in the process. Likewise, appropriate enrichment *cannot* be carried on without acceleration. Verbal materials (e.g., plays, poems, novels, histories, technical writings) that are appropriately advanced will, via the meaning of the text, challenge and enrich students' thinking and ways of viewing the world.

Many commentators have noted the need for both acceleration and enrichment in gifted programs (e.g., Clark, 1983; Gallagher, 1985; Hollingworth, 1942). A careful distinction needs to be made between these two approaches because the selection of one approach to the exclusion of the other will strongly influence the emergence of program options.

This task is difficult in the verbal domain, however, because of the way in which more advanced texts imply more complex thought. Accelerated or advanced content inevitably exposes students to a richer world of meaning and to the more complex, more adult issues of life.

Acceleration, enrichment, and instructional level.   Although some educators interpret enrichment to mean enhanced curriculum at a student's grade placement level, such enrichment is not appropriate for the verbally precocious student. First, the term "precocity" leaves no doubt of students' readiness for advanced instruction. Second, enrichment should imply provision of additional materials at the student's *instructional* level, rather than at the student's grade level.

These observations contrast somewhat with reports of regular classroom teachers about their own practices with respect to verbal precocity (Gaug, 1984). Gaug reports that the suburban teachers in her survey (n = 116) unanimously endorsed enrichment activities and that two-thirds endorsed the use of higher level reading texts. About half of the teachers reported that they were teaching high-ability reading groups. All teachers with high-ability groups claimed to use enrichment activities, but fewer than half of these teachers (or one-fifth of the total sample) actually used with their high-ability groups "a textbook designed for a later part of [the class's] grade level or a higher grade level" (Gaug, 1984, p. 373).

Grade-level enrichment was probably the only modification made for about half the high-ability reading groups. Gaug (1984) believes that this situation is typical, in spite of the fact that research substantiates the benefits of early reading instruction and acceleration for gifted students. Her report of the research is succinct (see Box 6-2).

BOX 6-2 *Reading Acceleration*

Earlier research (Adams & Ross, 1932; Dohan, 1948; McCracken, 1960; Wilkins, 1936) showed that gifted children who were accelerated had greater academic achievement than comparably gifted children who had not been accelerated. More recent programs, the Astor Program (Erlich, 1979), the Rapyht Project (Karnes, 1978), and the Program for Academically Talented Students (Barthe, 1980), have also shown the success of acceleration programs that include reading acceleration. Durr (1981) provides data in favor of reading acceleration. As reported by Trezise (1978) general learning characteristics of the gifted would indicate that gifted readers are ready for certain kinds and levels of instruction earlier and can move through material faster.

One important finding relates to the future reading achievement of students who begin reading in or before kindergarten. Durkin (1966) found that after six years of instruction, children who had read before entering first grade still maintained their lead over classmates who were of the same mental age but who did not begin to read until first grade. These children, however, were not specifically accelerated in elementary school. Research by Clark (1979) and Callaway (1970) also supported early reading experience as beneficial.

Source: (From Gaug, M. (1984). "Reading Acceleration and Enrichment in the Elementary Grades." *Reading Teacher, 37* (4), 372–373. Reprinted with permission of the International Reading Association.)

Programming cautions.   Teachers need to be aware of the sorts of difficulties that can interfere with effective programming for verbally precocious students. They can work to overcome difficulties with acceleration programs by planning carefully. Problems with enrichment programs may be less amenable to change, however. Teachers often do not have control over the structure and content of part-time enrichment (i.e., pull-out) programs (Cox et al., 1985); and seldom within the regular classroom can a consistent program of enrichment be provided. There are too many other demands on the teacher.

Acceleration has not been very widely practiced since the early 1950s. Gifted education seems to be in the process of changing educators' minds on the subject, however. Teachers should be aware of some issues they are likely to encounter in arranging accelerative options in the verbal domain (cf. Durden, 1980; Gaug, 1984):

1. Work in accelerated placements should carry credit.
2. Grade-level, skill-based mastery testing in reading will tend to restrict accelerative placements.
3. Teachers may be concerned about the fate of students who complete the prescribed reading series "too soon."
4. Teachers may perceive the need to protect younger students from advanced content in literature and the humanities.
5. Students younger than 12 or 13 may experience difficulty in *interpreting* literature; they will encounter this difficulty, however, with both advanced material and with grade-level material.

When acceleration is arranged, credit should be awarded for work completed, or requirements should be waived for competencies demonstrated. A third grader who completes the sixth-grade reading book should not be considered to need reading instruction much longer. To place such a child in the sixth reader of another series would be, in effect, to undo the previous acceleration.

Classroom teachers sometimes believe that gifted students must demonstrate full mastery of *grade-level skills* before acceleration can be considered to be appropriate (Gaug, 1984). If, however, reading is more than the sum of subskills (cf. May, 1982), then this practice may be unjustifiable. Apt readers are especially able to assimilate many skills by inference, even though they may be unable to complete criterion-referenced skill exercises according to the typical schedule of instruction (Clark, 1983; Gallagher, 1985).

Gaug (1984) notes that even teachers who endorse acceleration in reading are concerned about what to do with students who complete a textbook series early. The concern is legitimate, and it should be dealt with in a way that accommodates acceleration, not in a way that prevents it.

Part of the reluctance to accelerate the verbally gifted will come from a desire to protect children from the content of reading at a more advanced level. According to Gaug (1984, p. 372), the teachers in her sample claimed "that stories at a higher grade level would be inappropriate, involving situations beyond students' emotional and social level." Terman (1925, 1947), of course, reported that gifted children typically chose difficult works for independent reading.

A final caution concerns the type of work suitable for accelerates in verbal programs. Durden (1980, p. 36) notes that younger students do not function well in "the framework of interpretative thinking." In Piagetian terms, interpretative thinking is probably a function of the formal operations stage. Carter and Ormrod (1982) indicate that gifted children (IQ

130+) typically attain the formal operations stage about the age of 12 or 13. Gifted students older than 12 or 13 might, therefore, show increasing aptitude for interpretative thinking.

As indicated above, the term enrichment has often been used to indicate supplementary activities at grade level. Such supplementary activities are appropriate for all students in regular classrooms, when time or instructional method permit (cf. Guskey, 1984). For that very reason, however, these activities are not specifically appropriate for gifted children. Since the instruction most appropriate for gifted children matches their instructional level, appropriate enrichment for them must also match that instructional level.

Some enrichment techniques have not proven themselves capable of promoting student growth outside the context of an academic discipline (e.g., Gordon, 1961; Torrance, 1965; Williams, 1972). Indeed, such techniques were not intended to provide all essential instruction. When they are used to provide the only special programming for verbally precocious students, their value is limited.

Trends for the future.   Too little has been done to provide appropriate acceleration and enrichment in the verbal domain. Durden (1980) reports that many of the disciplines his program (PVGY) treats are lacking in the school curriculum, even at the secondary level. Foreign language instruction, which may be especially suitable for at least a subset of verbally precocious students, may be inadequate even in high school (Cox et al., 1985; cf. Sizer, 1984). Increased concern about gifted students over the last decade, however, indicates that perception of the need to provide programs is growing. The Program for Verbally Gifted Youth and the reading programs mentioned by Gaug (1984) have also demonstrated that not only is the need palpable, but that something can be done to meet it.

MATHEMATICAL ABILITY

Like verbal ability, mathematical ability accounts for a large part of general academic ability. Some experts, in fact, believe that mathematical ability is the chief component of intellectual ability because of mathematics' heavy reliance on logical methods; factor analysts have shown that mathematics tests are strongly related to g (Spearman's general ability factor).

Commentators in many countries have noted the military and industrial motive for discovering and educating mathematical ability. The pressing nature of this presumed need has periodically attracted strong support for the education of gifted students in the United States (Tannenbaum, 1981).

Mathematical Skills

Krutetskii (1976) distinguishes mathematical *skills* from mathematical *abilities*:

> By skills and habits we mean specific actions within an activity that a person does at a comparatively high level . . . Abilities are psychological traits on which depends an easy mastery of skills and habits in an activity (Krutetskii, 1976, p. 71).

According to this view, skills are characteristics of an activity. Their existence does not depend on a particular human subject. Goals and objectives, for example, describe skills. Abilities, on the other hand, are characteristics of a person. Abilities exist to varying degrees in the minds of students. Because academic abilities are developed in accord with existing knowledge, however, it makes most sense to define mathematical ability in the context of mathematical knowledge.

This knowledge can be described either functionally, in terms of the way it works (e.g., in particular mathematics courses), or structurally, in terms of how it is pieced together (e.g., in categories of skills). Structural descriptions represent mathematical knowledge in a way that is more pertinent to the definition of mathematical ability. (Box 6-5, however, provides a functional description of school mathematics courses.)

Calculation.   Skill in calculation consists of mastering basic number facts, such as simple sums, differences, products, and quotients, as well as the algorithms used to calculate more complex sums, differences, products, and quotients (Resnick & Ford, 1981). Calculation is necessary in most mathematical work, and in the United States it is the central skill taught in arithmetic. In higher mathematics (sometimes referred to as "abstract math") other skills are more important, but calculation may develop habits of attending to numerical relationships. Apprehension of numerical relationships is especially important in learning algebra, trigonometry, and calculus (Edge & Friedberg, 1984; Krutetskii, 1976).

Calculation, however, is not important to a conceptual understanding of mathematics. A major goal of the mathematics curriculum reforms of the early 1960s (i.e., "new math") was to impress this fact on educators in the elementary schools. The attempt was unsuccessful for a number of reasons, and in the United States today a disproportionate amount of time is still spent on drill and practice of calculation skills. Nevertheless, whatever reforms are instituted, a certain amount of class time will have to be devoted to assuring students' mastery of calculation skills (basic facts and algorithms). These skills are so necessary for success in higher math that the ability to compute should be a firmly established, nearly automatic habit (Resnick & Ford, 1981).

Concepts. As a result of the axiomatic method of mathematics, mathematical concepts seem to grow out of themselves. For example, the concept of a rational number (i.e., a fraction) is derived as the *ratio* of two integers. The concept of negative whole numbers can be seen to result from the redefinition of addition as subtraction, or to be the set of counting numbers and their opposites. This final example illustrates nicely the potential for complexity in mathematical concepts. The notion of integers (positive and negative whole numbers and zero) is derived from the basic facts and operations of arithmetic, but the ways it is derived (redefining addition as subtraction, or conceiving of opposites) are related to each other and to concepts in higher math. In this way mathematical conceptions form a complex web of meaning.

As students learn new concepts, they are expected to be able to relate them to previously learned concepts. Though some of these relationships can be noted during instruction, many cannot. In this sense it is correct to say that students "discover" mathematics for themselves (Bruner, 1960; Krutetskii, 1976). Box 6-3 is a brief annotated reading list of sources for learning more about mathematical skills and concepts.

BOX 6-3 *More about Mathematical Concepts*

To learn more about mathematical concepts, consult the following works:

BERLINGHOFF, W. (1968). *Mathematics: The art of reason.* Boston: D.C. Heath. This older liberal arts mathematics text treats mathematical concepts rather broadly. The text is accessible to anyone with a knowledge of elementary algebra.

DAVIS, P., & HERSH, R. (1981). *The mathematical experience.* Boston: Houghton Mifflin. A series of loosely connected essays that examine topics of philosophical importance. Its treatment is provocative.

KRUTETSKII, V. (1976). *The psychology of mathematical abilities in schoolchildren,* J. Teller (trans.). J. Kilpatrick & I. Wirszup (Eds.). Chicago: University of Chicago Press. (Original work published 1968.) The nature of mathematical concepts is forcefully illustrated in 23 series of 79 tests contained in Chapter 8. Wirszup commends the problems to mathematics teachers.

MILLER, C., & HEEREN, V. (1986). *Mathematical ideas* (5th ed.). Glenview, IL: Scott, Foresman. This more recent liberal arts mathematics text is more comprehensive than Berlinghoff, but it requires more algebra. It is, however, filled with interesting facts, illustrations, and problems. It would make an excellent source book for an elementary gifted program.

Logic. The logical method of mathematics typically involves a step-by-step deductive reasoning process in which the truth of an assertion is understood to be conclusively demonstrated. Mathematical logic links given facts to conclusions by reference to axioms, definitions, or previously proven assertions (theorems). Prospective mathematicians are expected to achieve consummate mastery of this sort of reasoning.

All students, however, are expected to follow such proofs and are presumed to profit intellectually from such activity (Krutetskii, 1976).

Textbooks typically present the concepts of each branch of mathematics principally through such logic. The deductive skills of mathematical logic, however, are not useful simply in proofs. They are essential in most mathematical schoolwork. For example, when students in trigonometry derive trigonometric identities (e.g., $\sin^2x = 1 - \cos^2x$), they apply such skills. The numerous techniques of integration (in calculus) also draw heavily on deductive skills. Application of mathematical logic is of course based on an understanding of mathematical concepts.

Problem solving.   The solution of word problems is often believed to require particular skills. Such skills are perhaps best conceived as skills of *translation* (Bloom et al., 1956). In the United States we often teach students to translate verbal statements into their mathematical equivalents in order to solve word problems. Skills of mathematical translation, however, are only part of mathematical problem solving conceived more broadly. In other parts of the world, "problem solving" is the term used to characterize *all* mathematical activity (cf. Krutetskii, 1976). Thus, problem-solving skills may also be viewed as the interaction of concepts, calculation, and logic.

The Characteristics of Mathematical Ability

Most research on mathematical ability has devoted greater effort to identifying it than to describing it. For almost 30 years, however, U.S. mathematicians interested in curriculum development have been aware of Soviet investigations into mathematical ability. Mathematicians and educators (e.g., Heid, 1983; Wirszup, 1981) note that this work is critically important to any discussion of the nature of mathematical ability. The following discussion is based on the comprehensive monograph by the Soviet psychologist Vadim Krutetskii (1976).

Krutetskii's study.   *The Psychology of Mathematical Abilities* by Krutetskii (1976) is particularly valuable for its close observation of the mathematical work of approximately 200 schoolchildren who were divided into four groups: very capable, capable, average, and incapable. The very capable and capable students were considered to represent paragons of mathematical talent.

Teaching experiments were constructed to allow observations of students during mathematical activity, and the observed differences were interpreted as reflecting differences in mathematical ability. The experiments, which resembled the teaching experiments of Hollingworth's era (cf. Hollingworth, 1926, 1942), investigated three stages in the solution of mathematical problems. These stages were (1) gathering mathematical information, (2) processing mathematical information, and (3) retaining mathematical information. Categories of problems were devised to investigate each of the three stages of mathematical activity; one category also investigated hypothetical types of mathematical ability. In all, approximately 500 items were used in the study. See Box 6-4 for examples of the problems used by Krutetskii.

BOX 6-4   *Examples of Krutetskii's Problems*

FROM SERIES I [PROBLEMS WITH AN UNSTATED QUESTION]:

Before the end of a day there remains four-fifths of what has elapsed since the day began. [Unstated question: "What time is it now?"]

FROM SERIES VI [SYSTEMS OF PROBLEMS OF DIFFERENT TYPES]:

There are some rabbits and some hutches. If one rabbit is put in each hutch, one rabbit will be left without a place. If two rabbits are put in each hutch, one hutch will remain empty. How many rabbits and how many hutches are there? [Classified as an *arithmetic* item; answer: three hutches, four rabbits.]

FROM SERIES IX [PROBLEMS ON PROOF]:

1.   Can it be said that $(-d)$ always expresses a negative number? [Easiest item in first seven items of the series.]

2.   Prove that for any a the expression $(a - 1)(a - 3)(a - 4)(a \doteq 6) + 10$ will be a positive number. [Most difficult item in first seven items of the series.]

3.   The diagonals of a trapezoid divide it into four triangles. Prove that the triangles adjacent to the lateral sides are equal in area. [Classified as a geometry item.]

FROM SERIES XXIII [PROBLEMS WITH VARYING DEGREES OF VISUALITY IN THEIR SOLUTIONS]:

1.   How much does a brick weigh if it weighs 1 kg plus half a brick? [Classified as an arithmetic item; see also "mathematical cast of mind," which follows.]

2.   In an isosceles triangle one of the medians divides its perimeter into two parts: 12 cm and 9 cm. Determine the sides of the triangle. [Classified as a geometry item.]

Mathematical ability according to Krutetskii.   The reported characteristics of mathematical ability are organized around the three stages of mathematical activity. Altogether there are eight such characteristics, six of which describe the processing of mathematical information by mathematically able students. All eight characteristics are described and illustrated below.

1.   *The ability for formalized perception of mathematical material, for grasping the formal structure of a problem.* This ability characterized the first stage of mathematical activity, gathering information about a problem. Krutetskii and his colleagues noted that capable and very capable mathematics students apprehended very rapidly what a problem was about. This included facility in distinguishing superfluous from essential information, being able to identify missing information, and sensing how to retrieve missing information from given information. For example, upon hearing a distance problem (two trains leaving from

two cities at different speeds) with missing information, a capable student asked immediately if the trains were traveling in the same direction or in different directions.

2. *The ability for logical thought in the sphere of quantitative and spatial relationships, using number and letter symbols; the ability to use mathematical symbols as a mode of thought.* This characteristic typifies the second stage of mathematical activity in general. The following characteristics are more specific.

3. *The ability for rapid and broad generalization of mathematical objects, relations, and operations.* The specifics of mathematical problems represent abstractions in various ways. Very capable and capable students find these abstractions easily during mathematical activity. For example, when learning about negative numbers, a capable student may easily understand subtraction as the addition of the opposite of a number.

4. *The ability to curtail the process of mathematical reasoning and the system of corresponding operations; the ability to think in curtailed structures.* With very capable and capable students, steps in the reasoning process seem to fall away. However, when asked, capable students are able to supply the complete sequence. Capable students need far fewer examples than average students to achieve mastery (Krutetskii, 1976, pp. 263–275; Stanley, Keating, & Fox, 1974; Stanley, 1981). This characteristic, which Krutetskii found striking, permits capable students to learn very efficiently.

5. *Flexibility of mental processes in mathematical activity.* Flexibility is the characteristic necessary to devise or investigate alternate routes to a solution. Capable students, for example, were able to elaborate multiple solutions of a problem, whereas average and incapable students had difficulty finding more than one (cf. Torrance, 1984). Flexibility is extremely helpful in overcoming obstacles in the solution of a problem; it permits students to shift from one strategy to another. With capable students, the discovery of one correct solution does not seem to suppress discovery of others.

6. *Striving for clarity, simplicity, economy, and rationality of solutions.* This characteristic addresses the goals of mathematical elegance and scientific parsimony. For example, upon finding one solution to a problem, capable and very capable students often spontaneously revise their work with a view to parsimony and elegance. ("Parsimony" and "elegance" refer to the related qualities of simplicity and clarity in a formal proof, solution, or scientific theory.)

7. *The ability for rapid and free reversal of the mental process in mathematical reasoning.* This characteristic allows capable students to reconstruct the process of solving problems and to see the patterns and connections of mathematical concepts. For example, a capable student who was studying complex numbers was asked to multiply $(a + bi)(a - bi)$. The student noted immediately that the result provided for the factorization of the sum of two squares because $(a + bi)(a - bi) = a^2 + b^2$, a factorization not accounted for in elementary algebra, but analogous to the convenient factorization of the difference of two squares. As noted in our discussion of skills, many mathematical concepts are related in this way.

8. *Generalized memory of mathematical relationships, type characteristics, schemes of arguments and proofs, methods of problem solving, and principles of approach.* This is ability for the third stage of mathematical activity. Capable students demonstrate both longer and better organized mathematical memory than other students. The generalized or abstract nature of this characteristic is its significant feature; it is not a memory for details. For example, although a very

capable student remembered the essential features of problems nine months after working on them, the student began to forget concrete details by the end of a lesson, and inessential details were rarely remembered at the end of a lesson. Incapable students, however, tried to remember everything about a problem.

Finally, the study describes one characteristic that was studied only in capable and very capable students. Krutetskii (1976, pp. 314–315) implies that only in capable students is the operation of this characteristic observable, because its observation requires the presence of very well developed skills. This characteristic, mathematical cast of mind, manifests itself in four ways. These four types of developed mathematical ability can be represented as a 2 × 2 cell. (See Figure 6-1.)

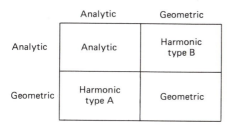

FIGURE 6.1 Types of Mathematical Ability among Capable Students (mathematical cast of mind)

According to Krutetskii, all mathematical ability is characterized by a verbal-logical (or "analytical") component, and therefore the type of mathematical ability "can only be a matter of the greater or lesser development of the visual-pictorial [or 'geometric'] component. Accordingly, one can speak of the predominance of the visual-pictorial component over the verbal-logical only in a relative sense" (Krutetskii, 1976, p. 316).

The capable student with an analytic type of ability demonstrates *very strong* verbal-logical performance combined with *weak* visual-pictorial performance. Such a student's spatial concepts are weak. The student does not feel the need to use visual supports and uses an analytic approach even in problems designed for visual-pictorial solution.

The capable student with a geometric type of ability demonstrates *above-average* verbal-logical performance combined with *very strong* visual-pictorial performance. Such a student's spatial concepts are very good. The student feels the need to use visual supports and uses a visual-pictorial approach even in problems designed for analytic solution.

Capable students of the harmonic types A and B possess both *strong* verbal-logical skills and *strong* visual-pictorial skills. Their spatial concepts are good. The harmonic type A student, though able to use visual supports in solving mathematical problems, does not benefit from their use! After solving a problem, usually in the analytic mode, such a student can, however, construct a visual representation. The harmonic type B, by contrast, benefits from the use of visual aids in solving mathematical problems.

Krutetskii (1976) reported that the "brick" problem cited in Box 6-4 distinguished reliably between analytic and geometric casts of mind. In solving this problem, students classified as geometers drew pictures and diagrams. Analysts reasoned or composed equations.

Quantitative traits not part of mathematical ability. Several traits associated with mathematical activity were excluded from Krutetskii's structure of mathematical ability. These included (1) rapid working tempo; (2) computational abilities; (3) memory for symbols, numbers, and formulae; (4) ability for spatial concepts; and (5) visualization ability.

The first excluded trait (rapid working tempo) *should not be confused* with a rapid ability to apprehend a problem (the first characteristic of mathematical ability), or with a rapid ability to generalize mathematical material (the third characteristic of mathematical ability). This observation implies that power tests may be more effective than speed tests in identifying mathematical ability.

The exclusion of computational abilities might surprise some teachers. Krutetskii does not intend that students remain ignorant of basic facts or algorithms. He notes, however, that very good calculation skills *are not* symptomatic of mathematical ability. This observation is extremely important to teachers of the gifted because of the emphasis placed on calculation in elementary classrooms in the United States.

The third excluded trait represents the influence of rote memory in mathematics. An average memory is adequate; even a poor rote memory need not diminish mathematical ability. This observation reinforces the notion that mathematical ability concerns abstractions more than particulars.

The fourth and fifth excluded traits derive from Krutetskii's observations of the mathematical cast of mind of capable and very capable students. Apparently, even geometry can be understood with weak visual-pictorial ability, whereas weak analytical ability severely limits mathematical ability, and these limits cannot be overcome even by strong visual-pictorial achievement. This observation also points up the abstract character of mathematical ability.

Gender and mathematical ability. A number of studies substantiate the better performance of 11-year-old males on the SAT-M (Benbow & Stanley, 1980; 1982; Stanley & Benbow, 1983). This difference is reflected in significant mean score differences (one-half to one-third standard deviation) between the scores of males and females, as well as in the greater numbers of males scoring at extremely high levels (Benbow & Stanley, 1980; Stanley & Benbow, 1983; Stanley et al., 1974). Krutetskii (1976) also noted the greater number of males in his small samples of very capable students (brilliant 7 to 10 year-olds).

For a time the cause was thought to be poor spatial skills among females, but this hypothesis has been shown to be weak (Boles, 1980; Krutetskii, 1976). Differences in achievement and course-taking are now being investigated (e.g., Eccles, 1985; Maines, 1985). The SAT, of course, explicitly confounds ability and achievement (i.e., aptitude is commonly understood to be a compound of achievement and ability).

One recent study of mathematically able students (Weiner & Robinson, 1986) found that males' SAT-M scores accounted for about twice as much variance in the mathematics course-taking as did females' SAT-M scores, whereas the males' SAT-V scores accounted for *none*. On the other hand, the researchers found that females' SAT-M and SAT-V scores accounted for equal amounts of variance in course-taking. This finding may be related to Krutetskii's notion of mathematical cast of mind.

School Responses to Exceptional Mathematical Ability

Krutetskii's study illustrates just how the characteristics of mathematically able students allow them to learn more rapidly than average students. These characteristics confirm the need to alter the curriculum for mathematically able students. School responses to exceptional mathematical ability can be categorized as identification efforts, eligibility determination and placement decisions, and instructional programs that involve acceleration and enrichment.

The general observations about the establishment of school programs that were noted in the verbal precocity section also apply to mathematical ability. They will not be repeated here.

Identification. Exceptional mathematical ability is a matter of degree, and it is determined most reliably by performance on norm-referenced tests. Unfortunately, reliable individually-administered comprehensive tests of mathematical ability do not exist. The mathematics portion of the Scholastic Aptitude Test (SAT-M), validated by the Study of Mathematically Precocious Youth for the identification of mathematical *brilliance,* is of limited use. The characteristic that suits it for the identification of brilliance, many difficult items, makes it unreliable for distinguishing average students from exceptional students (i.e., those whose performance in mathematics is approximately 2 standard deviations above the mean).

The lack of a comprehensive individually-administered test of mathematical ability makes it impossible to identify mathematical talent on the basis of mathematical *ability.* The best alternative is to base identification on mathematical *achievement.* Ideally, achievement tests for this purpose would sample the skills that most reflect the characteristics of mathematical ability: (1) apprehension, (2) logic, (3) generalization, (4) curtailment, (5) flexibility, (6) elegance, (7) reversibility of thought, and (8) retained insights. They *would not* be influenced strongly by (1) speed, (2) computation, (3) rote memory, or (4) spatial skills and concepts.

Available individually-administered tests approximate these requirements to different degrees. The mathematics cluster of The Woodcock-Johnson Psychoeducational Battery, Part II: Tests of Achievement (Woodcock & Johnson, 1977), is perhaps the best all-purpose choice. The mathematics subtest of the Peabody Individual Achievement Test (Dunn & Markwardt, 1970) might also be used, though it is shorter and probably less reliable than the Woodcock-Johnson mathematics subtest.

One test in particular should be avoided. The arithmetic subtest of the Wide Range Achievement Test–Revised (Jastak & Jastak, 1978) is *not suitable* because it samples computational skills exclusively; it is also timed. Exceptional mathematical ability cannot be inferred from a high level of computational skill (Krutetskii, 1976). Both the Woodcock-Johnson and PIAT subtests sample skills more pertinent to mathematical ability. Typical group achievement tests of grade-level performance should also be avoided for identification and placement purposes. They may be used as a source of referrals. (See Howley et al., 1986, pp. 26–32, 54–57 for more extensive discussion.)

Placement.   Eligibility criteria for gifted programs should include exceptional mathematical ability (operationalized for the time being as high achievement). Some school districts are apparently pursuing this option already; placement in most districts, however, is contingent on a high IQ score (Cox et al., 1985).

Teachers of the gifted therefore need to be alert for signs of exceptional mathematical ability among both high-IQ children and among other children as well. Almost always, exceptional ability in mathematics is associated with above-average, though not necessarily exceptional, IQ. The converse is also true: Gifted children almost always prove more capable in math than average students. Teachers of the gifted also need to be aware that a few gifted students will exhibit characteristics that indicate weak ability in mathematics.

Enrichment.   The need to alter the *content* of programs to accommodate capable mathematics students has long been recognized. The mathematics curriculum revisions of the 1960s effected permanent change at the secondary level. Many of the high-school textbooks now in use owe a large debt to the pioneering work of groups at Yale University and the University of Illinois. (See Box 6-5 for a description of secondary mathematics courses.) At the elementary level, however, many teachers were unable to implement the "new math." The elementary mathematics curriculum is therefore still based on computation, and mathematics instruction adheres slavishly to this outmoded curriculum (Kersh & Reisman, 1985).

The extreme literalness of elementary mathematics instruction represses the achievement of all children, but it is especially harmful to able students (Hersberger & Wheatley, 1980; Howley et al., 1986; Kersh & Reisman, 1985). In other countries more time is devoted to coaching students in manipulating concepts and in solving problems (Travers & McKnight, 1985). The tests on which Krutetskii (1976) based his observations, for example, contained "arithmetic" items that resembled word problems from elementary algebra texts in the United States. Krutetskii's subjects usually solved these problems without recourse to algebraic symbols and equations.

The complete revision of the mathematical curriculum ought to be an essential goal of curriculum development at the elementary level in the immediate future. Past experience indicates that elementary teachers, however, must be more mathematically able and more involved in active teaching. At present most elementary teachers do not feel competent in the subject (Kersh & Reisman, 1985). If such curriculum reform does not occur on behalf of all children, teachers of the gifted need to understand that curriculum reforms must be carried out in the gifted program for mathematically capable children.

BOX 6-5   *The Contents of High School Mathematics Courses*

Arithmetic, often taught as "general math" in high schools, is not construed as a high school level course (cf. Welch, Anderson, & Harris, 1982).

Algebra I and II are typically not taught sequentially, but with a year of geometry intervening (Travers & McKnight, 1985). Algebra I introduces the use and development of algebraic expressions, linear and quadratic equations, and solving word problems. Algebra II reviews these techniques, and typically introduces conic sections, logarithms, and the concept of functions.

Geometry is usually taught following Algebra I. In the United States these courses concern Euclidean geometry almost exclusively (Travers & McKnight, 1985). They aim to teach students to use the axiomatic method to reason logically and think visually.

Trigonometry introduces a family of functions different from algebraic functions, but derived from geometric notions: sine, cosine, tangent, and others. Various applications of these functions are usually taught as well. Trigonometry may follow Algebra II or be taught as part of it. Trigonometry, however, uses algebraic techniques.

Calculus course includes both differential and integral calculus. Differential calculus, taught usually in the first semester of the twelfth grade, develops the idea of limits and its application in finding derivatives for algebraic, logarithmic, and trigonometric functions. Derivatives are interpreted geometrically as the slope of a curve. Integral calculus is the process of finding the function of which a given function is the derivative. Integrals are interpreted geometrically as the area under a given curve or the volume described by the rotation of a given curve around an axis.

Acceleration. The work of the Study of Mathematically Precocious Youth (SMPY) over the last decade has established the validity of radical acceleration for mathematically brilliant youth (Stanley & Benbow, 1983). SMPY has also been influential in demonstrating the need for moderate acceleration among less extremely gifted students (Cox et al., 1985).

The work of SMPY establishes not only that acceleration is important, and even essential, but also that it can *take the place* of enrichment. Acceleration is able to accomplish this feat through strategies like early entry and grade skipping. Instead of suffering through unnecessary drill in computation, students who are prepared adequately can undertake a college algebra course instead of a pre-algebra course. For such students college algebra would be an enriched program.

The dilemma of school responses to mathematical ability.   The aim of both enrichment and acceleration is to promote achievement. Whereas enrichment is necessary for all students (especially at the elementary level where calculation is virtually synonymous with mathematics), the need for acceleration in mathematics is unique to students who are exceptionally able in mathematics. Cox and her colleagues (1985), however, found that even moderate acceleration (one to two years over the course of 12 years) was seldom practiced in gifted programs. Radical acceleration was rare. At the same time, the sort of enrichment practiced was not the sort described above. Instead, enrichment was practiced most often in resource programs that were uncoordinated, redundant, and ineffective in promoting achievement (Cox et al., 1985).

Given these facts, the most difficult option seems to be enrichment, which requires changes in curriculum structure, curriculum materials, and teacher preparation throughout a school system. Acceleration, on the other hand, requires the cooperative action of a few concerned individuals.

Whatever the school response, teachers should ensure that both high-IQ children and exceptionally able mathematics students take ample course work in mathematics. Learning mathematics requires the taking of courses (Howley et al., 1986). Bright students who avoid math classes are likely to remain ignorant of this very important subject. Student differences in the number of courses taken account for a *substantial* portion of the variance in mathematics achievement of high-school seniors (Welch, Anderson, & Harris, 1982). Research also indicates that arithmetic achievement affects performance in Algebra I (Bloland & Michael, 1984), and that mastery of algebraic skills (Algebra I and II) *strongly* influences performance in calculus (Edge & Friedberg, 1984).

SUMMARY

This chapter examined various kinds of academic talent. It related the characteristics of high-IQ children to the characteristics of verbally and mathematically apt students, and it distinguished between academically significant talents and talents that do not correlate very highly with academic achievement.

The discussion of verbal aptitude focused on the performance of gifted children in reading, writing, and learning foreign languages. It noted that early reading achievement did not predict general academic ability very well, though about one-third to one-half of gifted children read before starting school. It also noted that gifted students' writing differs little from the writing of average children, at least through junior high school, and that foreign language aptitude seems to incorporate some skills not strongly associated with general academic aptitude. The section on verbal ability concluded with a discussion of school responses to verbal precocity, including a section on optimal identification and placement practices pertinent to all varieties of academic talent.

The discussion of mathematical ability began by examining the function of mathematical knowledge of computation, concepts, logic, and problem solving. The important role of concepts and logic in mathematics was noted. Krutetskii's thoughtful study of the characteristics of mathematical ability was reviewed. The ability to generalize concepts and operate logically were among eight prominent characteristics noted. Discussion also included an explanation of five traits excluded from the structure of mathematical ability, but commonly ascribed to mathematical ability by other observers. A discussion of school responses to mathematical precocity followed. It considered the need to identify on the basis of achievement and the need to revise the mathematics curriculum, in order to improve mathematics instruction, especially at the elementary level. The discussion also considered the need to accelerate the progress of mathematically apt students.

7

Children with Talent in the Visual and Performing Arts

Focusing Questions

1. Why is it helpful—and why is it misleading—to compare the use of artistic media to the use of verbal language?
2. What is the relationship between the development of creativity and the development of arts talent?
3. Why is inadequate instruction in the arts an impediment to the identification of talent in the arts?
4. Is absolute pitch required for a high level of musical performance or musicianship?
5. What is the role of cognition in the development of arts talent?
6. Why is public school training in the arts so often delivered as enrichment rather than as a well-structured curriculum?

ARTS TALENT, CREATIVITY, AND ACADEMICS

The arts form a crucial part of the intellectual legacy of a culture. They provide media through which aesthetic interpretations of the world can be expressed and understood. Like verbal expression, arts media allow individuals to express and comprehend ideas. Unlike verbal expression, however, music, art, and dance do not allow for a one-to-one correspondence between a symbol and a clearly expressed meaning, as is possible in language or mathematics. The meaning of many works of art, therefore, is only partially accessible. That quality is part of what makes the arts so intriguing. In the Western world, arts media form the basis of personal statements that may become profoundly meaningful to contemporary or future audiences.

Because of the combination of personal and universal elements in artistic symbol systems, learning to understand art and to express oneself in an arts medium is more difficult than learning a language. Language learning entails exposure to and practice with an idiom whose usage—by comparison with expression in the media of art—depends almost *totally* on convention. One cannot say, "See the cat," and, in fact, mean "See the fish." On the other hand, one's use of a bold red line in a painting does not by itself mean anything in particular. The meaning depends on the context of the particular painting and on artists' previous uses of bold red lines. The line does not *denote* something specific; rather, it may *connote* a web of related associations within a context that depends on the painter's aesthetic sense, the history of painting, and the knowledge of the viewer.

Because arts production involves a highly personal use of a medium, many arts educators believe that instruction should involve freeing the creative impulse rather than channeling it. These educators (see e.g., Lowenfeld & Brittain, 1970) maintain that creativity in the arts occurs naturally in all children. They believe that arts talent will develop only if it is freed from the constraints of convention.

This view reinforces the idea that *creativity in general* is the goal of arts instruction. Creativity, however, cannot be the goal of arts instruction, because creativity does not function apart from a particular medium. Although it is essential to encourage creative vision so that individuals can produce art, the encouragement of creativity cannot guide the *development* of arts talent.

The creative impulse is a kind of motivation. Students need to be motivated to learn any academic subject. As they are successful in the subject, their motivation for further learning will, in theory, increase. The same is true of instruction in the arts. As students learn to control an arts medium and to understand its legacy, they will become more creative.

For these reasons this chapter views the development of arts talent as a legitimate academic issue. It suggests that arts talent is learned and that proficiency in the arts should be taught. Early exposure to or instruction in the arts often precedes later achievement in an art form. However, preschool instruction is not essential for talent development in the arts. As an important part of the intellectual tradition of Western civilization, arts understanding (or literacy) should be the minimum goal for all educated individuals. Mastery of expression in one or more art forms should be an instructional goal for those who show particular aptitude for the arts. Most of this chapter is devoted to a discussion of children who seem to exhibit exceptional talent in music, visual arts, dance, and drama. The beginnings of arts talent in children are examined and the kinds of instruction such children need are briefly indicated. Each section also reviews some of the basic concepts without which any discussion of these arts is impossible.

Arts Talent versus Creativity

In Chapter 4 we noted that creativity was initially defined in terms of arts talent. There we suggested that arts talent offered a more fertile and intellectually relevant field for instructional efforts than creativity training. Here we want to make sure that creativity is not mistaken for talent in the arts. This point needs to be made because creativity tests are, unfortunately, among the most frequently used methods of identifying artistically talented students (Clark & Zimmerman, 1984a).

Creativity is viewed as a global cognitive skill, like intelligence in its scope. It is unlike intelligence, however, in the way it works, in its measurement, and in its social implications. For instance, ample research shows that children's scores on creativity tests can be improved rapidly (Perkins, 1981; Rose & Lin, 1984). Whether this is due to the to ease with which creativity can be trained, to the efficiency of training programs, or to the inadequacy of creativity tests has not been settled.

Creativity in arts identification. Part of the desire to identify the arts talents of children comes from the perception that schools are doing little to nurture such talents. Many persons interested in this effort are, however, discovering that it is very difficult to identify arts talent. There is no consensus on the natural developmental sequence of skills in each art form, nor on the sorts of pedagogical methods that are best. Moreover, most schools do not have complete arts curricula; the arts are typically taught in enrichment programs. Considering the limitations of typical arts programs, even subjective assessment of arts talent would be difficult.

Under these circumstances, it may seem that *any* effort at identification is better than no effort. Hence, less than serviceable methods of identification come to be used. Because we still think quite naturally of artists as being creative, some school systems have adopted creativity tests to identify students talented in the arts (Clark & Zimmerman, 1984a).

As a primary selection mechanism, creativity tests have limitations so severe that they are useless for identifying specific talent in the arts. First, they were not designed to identify arts talent. Torrance's original intention was to account for academic achievement not predicted by IQ tests (Torrance, 1984).

Second, students selected by creativity tests are presumed to be creative individuals, but creativity tests do not specify the field in which their creative potential might express itself. As Perkins (1981) notes, almost any human activity under any circumstances can be considered creative. Because creativity has been so broadly defined, there is no way of inferring from creativity tests whether or not a student has *any* kind of arts talent. Third, identification of students using creativity tests implies that such students will be instructed in creativity training programs. Identifying and training creativity will not, by itself, develop arts talent. Development of arts talent depends on knowledge of technique in the arts. Creativity training programs are, unfortunately, more readily available than arts training programs.

Creativity in arts training. There is no reason why creativity (i.e., divergent thinking) exercises cannot form a part of instruction in the arts. As classroom calisthenics they make good instructional sense when they are relevant to the task at hand. Good arts teachers have used just such exercises for some time, in part because arts teachers are themselves divergent, nonconformist personalities (Perkins, 1981; Getzels, 1979). This observation illustrates the error inherent in applying creativity research to the development of arts talent. Divergence is characteristic of artistically talented students. As a trait separated from the exercise of craft, it is merely a personality trait, and it does not need to be *taught* to such students.

Kinds of Arts Talent

Important distinctions exist between understanding, performance, and creation. The distinctions apply in different ways to each art form.

Music. When people think of musical talent, they probably think most often of the ability to play a musical instrument. This is an example of talent for performance. It sometimes happens, however, that quite talented performers do not understand the music they can play so well (Shuter, 1968). Such performers are said to demonstrate poor musicianship. Moreover, even virtuoso performers (who by definition exhibit exceptional musicianship) do not usually compose music. Possibly, composition is another kind of musical talent.

Some training in performance is a prerequisite for a high level of musical understanding. Nonetheless, when a school identifies musical talent, someone needs to give thought to whether instruction will consist of training to play an instrument, to compose, or to understand music. Choosing to train *exceptionally talented* students in performance, in particular, may require extraordinary resources to locate and employ talented teachers. Training in composition will be a rare choice, since, as noted above, the sort of curriculum necessary to support this activity is lacking in many schools.

Visual arts.   Performance is not a substantial feature of the visual arts. Objects of art are viewed after the act of creation (with a few avant-garde exceptions). The visual arts involve making objects of art or understanding art objects made by others.

Understanding the visual arts may seem less technical and forbidding than understanding music. The literature of visual art is, however, both older and more extensive than that of written literature, and far older than the musical literature (which dates only from about 900 A.D.). Arts understanding implicates at least 5,000 years of history: The serious visual arts student is working in a tradition in which the technical possibilities of virtually every medium have been elaborately (if not completely) explored. As in the history of music, each new historical period changes artistic conventions in some way. Iconography (the symbol system used by works of art), composition, media, and technique may all be affected.

Dance.   Dance talent includes both performance and choreography (composition), although performance talent is most commonly identified. Virtually all instruction in dance consists of training to perform. Dance *creation* (choreography) is usually the work of retired dancers or of dancers who decide they would rather choreograph than perform.

Understanding dance requires some sort of physical training, just as understanding the visual arts requires some experience making works of art, and understanding music requires some experience in performance. The history of dance, however, is much less accessible than the history of the visual arts or music. Only recently has a system of "dance notation" been developed to record choreographic ideas. In choosing to identify and train students who are talented in dance, emphasizing performance skills over choreography and dance history seems justified.

Drama.   Talent in acting is a performance capability that depends on the effective delivery of words, gestures, and movements. It is closely associated with an understanding of the history of the theater and interpretation of the dramatic literature. Therefore, dramatic talent requires knowledge of and interest in literature as well as the ability to portray characters in a convincing manner.

The Study of Arts Talent

Arts talent has been studied by artists, who have described their own creative efforts. It has also been studied qualitatively and philosophically by aestheticians and critics. Psychologists and educators have studied the arts in a more descriptive and quantitative fashion.

The autobiographical reports of artists allow for insight into their methods of working and motives for creating (see e.g., Morgenstern, 1956). Biographies of artists also provide an understanding of the personal histories and theoretical viewpoints of individual artists.

Aestheticians and critics have also discussed the nature and results of artistic creation. Usually aestheticians have considered issues such as the nature of beauty, the uses of art, and the origin of the artistic impulse. Critics have evaluated the art products of particular artists in the context of the arts legacy.

Understanding the literature of criticism and the philosophy of art requires extensive knowledge of critical and philosophical discourse, as well as of the particular art works or types of art work under discussion. Such an approach to the study of art is quite scholarly. Artists, aestheticians, and critics have been writing about art for centuries.

Within our century, however, psychologists and educators have also begun to study and write about the artistic process. These social scientists have been concerned with a variety of issues related to arts production. Cognitive psychologists, for example, have been concerned with the processes of seeing (in the visual arts) and audiation (in music). Developmental psychologists have been interested in tracing the sequence of arts skills acquired by both normal and exceptional individuals.

Educators have studied arts talent in the school context. They have considered the value of arts instruction in general education as well as the rationale and methods for instructing talented young artists. Because this chapter is concerned with pedagogically relevant findings about arts production, it relies more heavily on studies by educators and psychologists than on biographical or critical works. In particular, the chapter emphasizes studies that relate to the identification, development, and training of artistically talented youngsters.

MUSIC AS A CONCERN OF SCHOOLING

Music now surrounds us almost without interruption. Americans love music, and they use it to improve retail sales, citizenship, and academic skills. They understand the power of music, but they do not understand its meaning (Barzun, 1965). According to Allen Britton, Dean of the University of Michigan's School of Music, "music [in the public schools] can never be just music, an art that is its own justification; it is always being asked to produce 'something more' such as better health or citizenship, improved reading or math skills" (Murphy, 1980, p. S-16).

The Pedagogical Dilemma of Musical Talent

Most children get a bit of music on a regular basis in the elementary schools. From middle school through senior high school most schools sponsor a band and a chorus, which typically serve only 10 percent of the high-school population (Petzold, 1978). Instruction on instruments that are not *band instruments* (e.g., string and keyboard instruments) is much more rare. The sort of music instruction provided in school does not favor the identification or cultivation of exceptional musical ability.

At the same time that more people hear more music than ever before, most of what most people hear is music that is *merely* serviceable. Such music exists *only* to influence trade. As a result, many people have difficulty distinguishing between musical trash and music that is good of its kind. Barzun (1965) characterizes as "fanatical zeal" the devotion with which people cling to the music they like. This devotion is enough to cause most adults (including teachers) to regard wide differences in knowledge as mere differences of taste.

The classical music literature, which contains much music that is good of its kind, remains a foreign language to most students (cf. Miller, 1979). Few high-school general music classes require students to listen to challenging music (Miller, 1979). Western "classical" music is perhaps not the *best* music in the world, but it is very complex, it is profoundly expressive and meaningful to our culture, and, like any great literature, its relevance endures.

In our culture it is imperative that very apt music students become fluent in the Western classics. In fact the Western classics are quickly becoming world classics, played in Delhi, Tokyo, and Nairobi, as well as in New York, London, and Vienna.

The Formal Musical Language

In order to understand what musical talent is, readers must understand a few things about the formal musical "language." It is helpful to make the analogy between the musical symbol system and verbal language in order to explain a realm of meaning with which some readers may be unfamiliar. The distinction between the cognitive and emotional import of music is difficult to grasp. It requires some sense of the way music works.

Like all analogies, the analogy of music and language is misleading. Music does not convey meaning in the same way as verbal language. Particular phrases and combinations of harmonies do not inevitably communicate specific emotional content in a universally understood dialect (Barzun,

1965). Psychologists of music (e.g., Jackendoff & Lerdahl, 1981) persist in misunderstanding this fact, perhaps because their primary musical activity is listening (Murphy, 1980).

Nonetheless, music has a kind of syntax, and it exists in varieties that are analogous to dialects (Sessions, 1979). Concerted intellectual effort is necessary to understand complex musical works. This effort is certainly pleasurable, but the artfulness of music *does not* consist in its presumed emotional content.

The syntax of music.   Music, like speech, depends for its effect on the passage of time. As with speech, extracting as much meaning from the passage of time as possible requires attention to several qualities simultaneously. The informed music listener understands that the music of a particular time or place is organized (much like verbal syntax) in conventions of rhythm, harmony, and melody that combine to produce a characteristic effect. Those who master the syntax of several such "dialects" manage to make accessible to themselves a large literature of meaning.

The basic qualities of musical syntax are melody, rhythm, and harmony. Melody, a sequence of pitches joined together, is in some ways the most basic quality of music. Perception of melody, however, depends on exposure to, if not training in, the musical conventions of one's culture. The lack of ability to hear more than one type of melody is, however, a major impediment to the musical growth of many people (Murphy, 1980).

Rhythm refers to the temporal pulse of music and, in its broadest sense, implicates *tempo*—the speed at which music is played. At a more specific level, *meter* establishes a fundamental pulse pattern (usually in groups of two or three beats) against which rhythmic elaboration can occur. At the most specific level, rhythm may refer to a specific *rhythmical motif*, a pattern that can be used in one or several meters to help structure a very elaborate piece (e.g., much of Beethoven's fifth symphony is structured on the opening four-note motif.)

Harmony is the most complete aspect of musical syntax. It is the interaction, according to prescribed conventions, of two or more pitches played simultaneously. In any harmonic pattern, there exist both horizontal pitch (melodic) and vertical pitch (chord) arrangements. Vertical arrangements may themselves proceed horizontally (i.e., in "chord progressions"). In its simplest form, harmonic perception refers to perceiving the interval between two notes, to identifying chords, and to anticipating chord progressions. This skill is among the last to emerge in children (Shuter, 1968).

There is a more difficult harmonic skill, however. In complex compositions the listener must simultaneously perceive both vertical and horizontal harmonic changes, each associated with characteristic rhythmical motifs and variations. Students, however, need to know that this complex skill is worth learning, and that it *can* be learned (Broudy, 1958). Unfortunately, most never do (Shuter, 1968).

Musical notation.   For the musical intellect, the invention of musical notation (about A.D. 900) equaled the significance for the verbal intellect of the earlier invention of the alphabet (about 1700 B.C.) The system of musical notation allows complex works to be brought into existence, interpreted carefully, studied, and reinterpreted with fresh insight.

Even most playing "by ear" (i.e., without training) is merely repetition of a melody with a suitable accompaniment. Complex music, however, cannot be played in this way. The accompaniment to a Bach fugue, for example, cannot be improvised—it has no accompaniment: it is *at once* (and this is the incredible beauty of the fugue) all melody and all harmony. There is a natural limit to the length, coherence, and complexity of a composition that can be improvised. Musical notation helps extend this natural limit.

Aptitude in the Musical Language

The preceding review clearly indicates the degree to which the musical "language" is a cultural product. Musical precocity, far from being the hereditary possession of exactly the right equipment, is tantamount to a coincidental opportunity to make fluent and original use of the cultural heritage (Feldman, 1979; Petzold, 1978; but cf. Gardner, 1973; Kwalwasser, 1955).

Nature versus nurture.   The nature-nurture debate has engaged musicians as well as psychologists. Do certain families tend to raise musically talented children, or are such children born to talented families? As we note elsewhere, the evidence in favor of the hereditarian hypothesis of intelligence is not firm. The genetic studies of musical talent (e.g., Feis, 1910; Friend, 1939; Galton, 1869/1962; Kwalwasser, 1955; Mjoen, 1926; Shuter, 1964) are even more flawed and therefore less conclusive than the studies of the heritability of intelligence.

Nonetheless, because musicians tend to come from "musical" families, the literature tends to confirm the hereditary origin of musical talent (e.g., Gardner, 1973). The consensus (by no means complete) illustrates the way in which inconclusive research results often support prevailing beliefs (Gould, 1981). Like Feldman (1979), Gordon (1980), and Walker (cited in Murphy, 1980, p. S-24), we believe that the quality of the child's musical environment is critically important, whatever the child's genetic endowment.

The musical environment.   In a musical environment, both parents usually play a musical instrument and actively encourage their children to do the same. Their children repeatedly hear music that engages the parents' interest, and they probably take part in musical discussions. The wider the range of the parents' musical activity, the wider the children's understanding is likely to be. The recent research of Bloom and his colleagues (Bloom, 1982, 1985; Bloom & Sosniak, 1981) documents the extraordinary instructional effort mounted by exceptionally musical parents. Very musical families seem always to have known what recent researchers (Gordon, 1980; Petzold, 1978; Shuter, 1968; Wooddell, 1984) have discovered: Musical aptitude can be increased if music instruction starts early (cf. Kwalwasser, 1955, pp. 61–73).

Signs of Musical Talent

Musical precocity is related to a number of special conditions and experiences. Shetler (1985) tentatively reports that consciously manipulated prenatal experiences make a marked difference in ability even among the children of musically talented parents.

Nonetheless, these conditions and experiences are in the nature of developmental *omens*, and caution is in order. Just as early speech is unrelated to IQ, so the emergence of a single musical omen does not usually imply great talent. A developmental pattern of early skills, in the context of musical activity, however, probably *does* indicate talent by the age of five to nine (cf. Gordon, 1980).

Absolute pitch.   Probably the most interesting of musical omens is "absolute pitch," the ability to identify accurately any note played. Absolute pitch is a specific talent that amazes those who do not possess it. Surely, this seems to be the case of a talent inborn. Research on absolute pitch, however, suggests this is unlikely.

One study reported by Shuter (1968) examined four groups of musicians (professors and students, n = 261) of moderate to high musical ability. Within ability groups, absolute pitch subjects began their lessons one to six years earlier than subjects without absolute pitch. The largest difference was in the highest ability group. In some cases, subjects were completely successful in naming notes played on the earliest studied instrument, and completely unsuccessful in naming notes played on the instrument studied subsequently (even when the instrument studied later had become their major instrument!).

Absolute pitch has been thought to be necessary for a high degree of musicianship. Shuter (1968) reported a study that compared highly talented professional musicians gifted with absolute pitch to equally talented colleagues who did not have absolute pitch. The researcher transposed the beginnings of standard repertoire pieces and asked subjects to identify which versions were not played at correct pitch. The subjects without absolute pitch scored better than those with absolute pitch. Shuter concluded that absolute pitch, though helpful to exceptional musical achievement, is not essential.

Rhythm. A number of music educators have proposed the idea that rhythm is the most fundamental aspect of the musical syntax (cf. Mark, 1978; Orff, 1955; Seashore, 1938/1967, p. 147–148; Sessions, 1950/1965, pp. 11–15). The proposal is not, however, substantiated by research. Jersild and Bienstock (1935, cited in Shuter, 1968) appear to have been among the few to use other than anecdotal records. They photographed children aged two, three, four, and five who were instructed to walk or to move their hands in time to music. A sample of seventeen adults served as a control group. The researchers observed that children's accuracy improved with chronological age, but concluded that subjective impressions of children's ability to keep accurate time were untrustworthy. Whether rhythmic skills develop before, after, or concurrently with melodic skills is still an unresolved issue (Horner, 1965; Shuter, 1968). In spite of this fact, rhythmic movement activities dominate early music instruction in schools (e.g., Aronoff, 1965; Mark, 1978; Nye & Nye, 1970).

Melody and pitch discrimination. Some music educators (e.g., Wing, 1954) continued all along to doubt the relevance of early rhythm and movement activities to musical training. They believed instead that a child's sense of melodic shape was the earliest musical skill to emerge.

According to Shuter (1968), a good ear for melody seems to develop in two stages. At first, children perceive only the direction of movement of the notes, but not the correct intervals between them. The second stage involves perception of correct intervals in a melody, and this stage is *not* attained by all children.

Shuter (1968) compiled observations made by musical parents on the emergence of the musical skills of their children. According to these reports, such children first recognized tunes and were able to reproduce individual notes between the ages of 9 months and 2.5 years. The earliest age reported by the parents for singing a complete tune correctly was 1.3 years, with the mean about 2 years. Gesell and Ilg (cited in Shuter, 1968, p. 69) report the following developmental norms for average children:

using phrases, not usually on pitch	2.0 yrs.
recognize several tunes	3.0 yrs.
a few sing entire songs correctly	4.0 yrs.

Nye and Nye (1970, pp. 540–543) narrate the following approximate norms for average children:

12–26 months	begin to imitate pitch
26–36 months	sing tunes within the interval of a third or fourth
36–60 months	individual differences emerge
60–72 months	sing tunes within the interval of a sixth

Kwalwasser (1955) observed that, even though it is possible to identify the average age at which particular skills are attained, the actual age of skill attainment by different children varies greatly. In fact, Kwalwasser (1955) found that the range of achievement differences within any particular grade exceeded the range of differences between all levels in the elementary school. This finding is more likely to reflect lack of instruction in school than hereditary differences in musical ability.

Sensitivity to harmony. Harmonic patterns (tonality, simultaneous melodies, chord progressions, the interaction of melodic theme and accompaniment) are accessible to perception only after a great deal of listening. This explanation may account for the fact that although average students begin to sing songs correctly by the age of six or so, average students do not begin to prefer concords (e.g., intervals of a major third or fifth) to discords (e.g., major or minor seconds) until the age of 11 to 13.

Musically apt children probably acquire this level of understanding much earlier (Horner, 1965; Kwalwasser, 1955; Shuter, 1968; Shetler, 1985). One musical child known to the authors, for example, showed a preference for thirds (demonstrated by producing them spontaneously at the keyboard) at the age of five. This same child could reproduce individual notes at nine months and sing complete songs on pitch at age two.

Musicality. Musicality is sensitivity to musical meaning (Mursell, 1958, p. 146; Shuter, 1968, pp. 222–226), and the development of such sensitivity implicates musical knowledge (cf. Broudy, 1958). Musically talented students are *receptive* to this sort of knowledge. Some examples of such knowledge follow.

The harmony of Mozart (and his contemporaries) is very much like that of our familiar homophonic music (i.e., music with a single, prominent line of melody). Nonetheless, homophonic tonality of the late eighteenth century is more rudimentary than ours. The late eighteenth century seldom used seventh chords, for example. As a result new listeners to this music find it "childlike" or "boring."

As another example, the music of Bach tends to be more dissonant than the music of Mozart. Bach's harmony is most frequently built on the vertical coincidence of simultaneously played melodies, a difference that implies differences in the elaboration of those melodies and in the tonality which shapes them. In the case of Bach, listeners who have not perceived the conventions of the early eighteenth century are apt to find this music "mechanical" or "cold and intellectual." The remarks noted in these examples reveal the predicament of listeners who have not perceived the conventions, much less understood the art, of the music to which they have listened.

School Response to Musical Talent

Though musicians and music educators have often claimed that schools do not take music seriously enough (Hollander, 1978; Murphy, 1980; Petzold, 1978), their observations seem to conflict with Barzun's (1965) characterization of Americans as a devotedly music-loving people. Perhaps the contradiction can be resolved by noting that Americans make too great a distinction between musical pleasure and musical knowledge (cf. Broudy, 1958; Marcuse, 1978). Whereas we love music a great deal, we do not necessarily insist on understanding it.

Identification. The schools' identification of musical talent is jeopardized by the lack of programs that implement a sequential music curriculum (Broudy, 1958; Howley et al., 1986; Murphy, 1980; Sessions, 1979). Still, some alternative methods of identification do exist. They are considered in more detail in our textbook about teaching gifted children (Howley et al., 1986).

One alternative is to use standardized tests to select musically talented students. Shuter (1968) probably still provides the most extensive review of music tests. She favors the Wing Tests of Musical Intelligence (Wing, 1948), whereas we recommend (Howley et al., 1986) the Gordon Music Aptitude Profile (Gordon, 1965). Gordon's (1979) Primary Measures of Music Audiation, for children aged five through eight, also merits scrutiny in the context of the present discussion, which stresses the importance of early training. There are other tests available as well. Although all probably measure musicality (see previous discussion) to some degree, none assesses a child's aptitude for music performance.

Performance ability can be identified by jury auditions similar to those that precede admission to special schools. In this case, the instrumental instruction provided must be excellent. The program must be controlled and taught by talented professional musicians.

The most typical way that schools identify some musical talent is through participation in such school music programs as do exist. In these programs (band and chorus) some students naturally emerge as more talented than others. Since so few students participate in these programs, this method is probably not effective or efficient.

Programs.   Three groups of musically capable students can be identified: (1) talented young performers, (2) students with general musical talent identified by standardized music tests, and (3) students with general academic talent. The third group has been identified as possessing strong interest in aesthetic issues (Tidwell, 1980). Many observers (Hollander, 1978; Kwalwasser, 1955; Seashore, 1938/1967, pp. 6–9; Shuter, 1968; Wing, 1955) note that musicality (if not performance ability) is strongly related to general intelligence (measured as IQ).

It is important to observe the above distinctions when programs are implemented. Of the three groups of students, public schools are probably in a position to serve in a single program both those academically gifted and those musically talented students that can be identified by standardized tests.

These students could be expected to benefit from group keyboard instruction or group string instruction, from *concurrent* instruction in music history and theory, and from *concurrent* attendance at required listening and discussion sessions. Substantial effort, however, will be required to provide a sequential curriculum of this sort for these children. With hard work, such a sequence could be carried out by a team of talented amateurs (*not* volunteers) working with a knowledgeable music teacher. (For sensible remarks about the talents needed to teach arts programs for gifted students see Alexander, 1981.)

Acceleration and enrichment.   Music serves a recreational role in our schools. Most music instruction that currently takes place in school should therefore be considered enrichment. Without school programs that teach a sequential curriculum, acceleration is clearly impossible (cf. Broudy, 1958). Even when students work with a good private teacher, few receive instruction in the history of music, or *any* listening experience. Talented young performers, however, may be lucky enough to be referred to the few specialized arts high schools, where acceleration is theoretically possible. As Shuter (1968) observes, young children should first experience music as fun. It is unfortunate that though we like music, we persist in teaching even our most musically apt students little about it (cf. Miller, 1979).

TALENT IN THE VISUAL ARTS: THE ARTS CONTEXT

This portion of the chapter looks at the characteristics of students who are talented in the visual arts. We review these characteristics in the context of certain assumptions. First, we assume that the definition of art determines those talented in art. If all representational activity is considered art, for example, then all students who engage in such activity are artists. Second, we assume that training uncovers talent. Only in an environment that nurtures talent can students with uncommon abilities be discovered. Finally, we assume that art is a cognitive activity embedded in an intellectual tradition (see also, Arnheim, 1966). Art depends on literacy in both the techniques of expression and the history of the tradition.

These three assumptions allow us to view the talent of artists as developmental. A developmental view of talent emphasizes the importance of nurture. It equates art talent with other intellectual talents and focuses on the interaction between ability and instruction.

The Visual Arts: A Definition

The question, "What is art?" has been answered in various ways by different artists, art critics, aestheticians, and art educators. Although it is not the purpose of this chapter to review all such definitions or to decide among them, we must clarify some issues surrounding the definition of art in order to consider the nature of individuals talented in art.

Definitions of art include the pre-Renaissance Christian belief that art is worship accomplished through the act of creation (Chiari, 1960) and the more contemporary belief that art is self-expression (Arnheim, 1972). The earlier view emphasizes the technical nature of the artistic process, whereas the modern view stresses the psychological import of the artistic process. In practice, neither view alone supports a complete aesthetic. Consequently, art education based exclusively on either view (technique or psychology) is unbalanced.

At one time art education consisted only of disciplined instruction in the crafts of drawing and painting (Duncum, 1985). Later, art education became the arena in which children expressed their feelings through creative activities (see e.g., Lowenfeld & Brittain, 1970). The former approach molded children's art in conformity with models of "good" art, and the latter approach validated children's art irrespective of judgments related to the quality of their art products. Both approaches, however, limited the range of children's artistic development (Taylor, 1966).

A more comprehensive approach to the development of artistic talent incorporates both the training of technical skills and the nurture of individual expression. According to Aso (1984), art is experience of the world realized through various media. This experience of the world, however, is shaped by historical and cultural forces (Korzenik, 1981). Art, then, is a mediation of experience that is both direct and itself mediated by history and culture. An important force guiding the work of any artist is the artistic language of previous generations. Art is defined in relationship to its antecedents. Good art both uses and transcends its heritage.

The artistic process is not the exact replication of the world; it is not the process of copying the works of others; and it is not an egocentric catharsis. It goes beyond both technique and individual self-expression.

Without technique and knowledge of the language of art, meaningful self-expression cannot take place. Without the expressive effort of the individual, art cannot come into existence. To make art, artists must know the history of their medium; they must know themselves; they must know how to express themselves through their medium; and they must be willing to do so.

Although the training of art talent cannot produce art, it can teach craft, make the artistic legacy accessible, and encourage effort (cf. Arnheim, 1966). Skilled artists are able to use their craft in a dialogue with the art of earlier times and thereby aim to produce art that is both novel and universal (see e.g., Aso, 1984).

The Media of the Visual Arts

According to Herbert Read (1959), "art" is:

> a means of conceiving the world visually . . . The artist is simply the man who has the ability and the desire to transform his visual perception into a material form. The first part of this action is *perceptive*, the second is *expressive*, but it is not possible in practice to separate these two processes: the artist expresses what he perceives; he perceives what he expresses. (Read, 1959, p. 12)

This definition can help us examine the ways in which visual perception can be realized in material forms. As artists seek to gain control over a medium (e.g., drawing, painting, textiles, photography), they learn the techniques and history particular to the medium. A certain amount of this learning, however, may influence their production in other media as well. For instance, skill in pencil drawing may influence an artist's ability to paint. In general, however, the most transferable skills in art are those involving perception. The artist learns to see in a characteristic way—perhaps conditioned by work in a particular medium. This characteristic vision may then manifest itself in works regardless of the medium in which it is realized.

In practice, many artists limit their attention to one or several media. Very few artists paint, sculpt, weave, and take photographs, for instance. The tendency of artists to use only a few media probably reflects some element of ability as well as an element of interest. The skills of a photographer differ considerably from those of a painter. Nevertheless, when we concern ourselves with the identification of children talented in the arts, we are most likely to look for and to develop talent in the most commonly used art techniques. These techniques include skills in drawing and painting, at least, and perhaps sculpture and printmaking as well. Drawing, however, is often viewed as the "executive skill" basic to all art forms (Stalker, 1981, p. 49).

Determination of Visual Arts Talent

Determining who is talented in the visual arts would be easy if all activities involving manufacture were thought of as art. Based on this view, the most prolific producers would be the most talented. At one time, art educators perpetuated this view of art. In the Fortieth Yearbook of the National Society for the Study of Education (Whipple, 1941), art educators presented their views on art in American life. Chapter titles from this yearbook provide examples of the concerns of this group of educators: "City Planning," "The Domestic Setting Today," "Landscape Design," "Flower Arrangement," "The Handcrafts," "Art in Industry," "Clothing and Personal Adornment," and "Art in Commerce."

The art educators who contributed to the yearbook failed to distinguish between the aesthetic (or visually pleasing) and the artistic. According to Best (1980, p. 78), an "art *form* must at least *allow for* the possibility of the expression of a conception of life issues such as moral, social, and political issues." Clothing, for instance, can be visually pleasing, but it is difficult to see how clothes can ever express anything *coherent* about the substantive issues of life.

A more limited definition of art leads to a more specific way to identify those talented in art. Stalker (1981, p. 50) maintains that successful artists demonstrate executive drawing skill, cognitive complexity, and a high level of perseverance. With such a definition art educators can distinguish arts talent from aesthetic awareness, a characteristic typical of gifted students in general (Tidwell, 1980).

Drawing skill.   Although most children draw, only some exhibit unusual talents in drawing. According to Clark and Zimmerman (1984a, p. 17), "all differences in drawing skills . . . of highly able and less able students are differences in degree and not in kind."

Precocity and sophistication in drawing skills may characterize children talented in the visual arts. At the same time, however, it is unclear how to define precocity or sophistication in drawing. Clark and Zimmerman (1984b) describe a model of evaluating children's drawings on a continuous scale ranging from naive to sophisticated. They write, "applications of the Naive-Sophisticated model are age/grade dependent; whether a child's art work can be judged naive or sophisticated is dependent upon reference to an age/grade norm" (Clark & Zimmerman, 1984b, p. 215). The determination of sophistication in this model depends on a number of elements including the organization of a drawing, an indication of linear perspective, the use of varied line widths, and the use of shading.

Another approach to the determination of precocity in drawing skill involves the evaluation of children's performance on tasks required for skilled drawing. Children with high levels of manipulative dexterity, speed, and control may be viewed as *potentially* talented in the arts even if they do not seem to be motivated to produce art works.

There is no consensus among art educators concerning the nature of talent in drawing. Some art educators, for example, regard early representational skills as an indicator of art talent. Others regard the bold use of line and color as an indicator of art talent. Whatever approach is used, however, some children possess skills in drawing that surpass those of other children. Although we can and should encourage the artistic development of all such children, we cannot determine in advance which of them will want to become artists. We are even less likely to determine which of them *will* become artists (cf. Getzels & Csikszentmihalyi, 1976).

Cognitive complexity. In general, artistically talented individuals have higher than average levels of intelligence. Clark and Zimmerman (1984a) review the literature on the relationship between art talent and intelligence. They conclude, "Though superior intelligence and superior art abilities are clearly interdependent, not all children with a high IQ possess art talent. All children with superior art talent, however, do possess a higher than average IQ" (Clark & Zimmerman, 1984, p. 14).

According to Stalker (1981, p. 50), "cognitive complexity [is] the most adequate equivalent of the kind of intelligence necessary for artistic performance." She views cognitive complexity as the ability to:

(a)   handle greater amounts of information,
(b)   handle more complex information environments,
(c)   assimilate conflicting or inconsistent information, and
(d)   make better judgements about complex information. (Stalker, 1981, p. 50)

Perseverance. Art educators seem to agree that, in general, achievement in the visual arts is associated with extensive practice (see e.g., Duncum, 1985). In most cases those who prove to be artistically talented as adults begin artistic production early in childhood (Meier, 1939/1966). Many children, however, who are prolific in early and middle childhood stop drawing in early adolescence (Gardner, 1973). It is not certain why this change occurs in some children, although levels of ability, interest, and encouragement by others may have some influence on adolescents' continued artistic production.

It is also not certain that the most artistically prolific children are actually the most talented. Nevertheless, children who are consistently making images should be encouraged to continue to do so. It would be wise to consider such children at least *potentially* gifted in the visual arts.

The Measurement of Artistic Potential

For the purpose of identifying those students most talented in art, it would be convenient if there were a reliable and valid norm-referenced test of art talent. Such a test would need to be based on norms of artistic performance at various ages (Clark & Zimmerman, 1984b). A test of this sort would also have to define and measure the subskills of art talent. Unfortunately, art educators do not agree on the skills that comprise art talent. Neither do they agree that early development of art skills necessarily relates to art talent (see e.g., Saunders, 1982).

The indicators of art talent.   Clark and Zimmerman (1984a) present a thorough review of the literature concerning the characteristics of students talented in art. Their review reveals a lack of consensus among those who have studied the development of talented students. For example, some researchers conclude that children talented in art specialize in drawing one subject matter, but others conclude that talented children draw a wide variety of things. It is beyond the scope of this text to examine these speculations, but we recommend that readers to whom this topic is critically important consult Clark and Zimmerman's (1984a) work.

Identification of the artistically talented.   Because of the many unresolved issues concerning the nature of art talent, it is unlikely that any standardized test would accurately predict art achievement. In practice, students presumed to be talented in art are identified using various selection procedures. According to Clark and Zimmerman (1983, p. 26), the most commonly used selection procedures (listed in the order of their popularity) are (1) self-nomination, (2) portfolio review, (3) classroom teacher nomination, (4) interview, (5) creativity test, (6) informal art test, (7) art teacher nomination, (8) achievement test scores, (9) structured nomination, (10) peer nomination, and (11) parent nomination. All of these approaches, however, have limitations and the authors suggest that "procedures currently in use and those recommended for use . . . be critically examined and evaluated before they are implemented" (Clark & Zimmerman, 1983, p. 28).

Since previous achievement often correlates with achievement later in life, schools should perhaps identify and train all students who are precocious in art development, all those who are prolific in artistic production, and all those who are cognitively advanced (see e.g., Salome, 1974). This approach would assure that the students most likely to be talented in art would have the opportunity to develop their abilities. Such an approach, however, would depend on a very high societal regard for art production. Finding and nurturing future artists would have to be a social priority.

Nature versus nurture.   In the absence of social validation for artistic production, the nurture of artistic talent is not widespread. Under such circumstances, it is convenient to assume that art talent is a genetic endowment that will mature without training and encouragement (Clark & Zimmerman, 1984b). This view provides a rationalization for neglecting the artistic training of children.

It is clear, however, that training of some sort, either self-training or tutelage, is necessary in order for even the most talented students to develop fully. Gardner writes:

> individual differences in genetic endowment are, at most, one contributing factor to the eventual level of artistic accomplishment. While a deficient hereditary history may preclude high achievement, only arduous training and development of skills can convert the potential for excellence into its realization. (Gardner, 1973, p. 231)

Because we cannot predict talent in the absence of training, we are not likely to find a test that identifies early in childhood the select few who will become the most talented artists. Only if we train everyone, can we be sure of missing no one. We also cannot be sure that talent coupled with the most extensive training will produce artists. According to Getzels and Csikszentmihalyi:

> One does not become an artist just by painting. To paint might be the only thing that matters subjectively. But to be able to earn a livelihood and to develop a self-concept as a bona fide artist distinct from a "sometime painter," artistic behavior is not sufficient. One must be legitimized by the appropriate social institutions. (Getzels & Csikszentmihalyi, 1976, p. 185)

Since this legitimation is governed by numerous social, political, and economic forces, we cannot assume that the most talented artists will be allowed to earn their livelihood through the practice of their art. Under such conditions, all of the identification and training efforts on behalf of students talented in art will be compromised.

School Responses to Art Talent

In elementary schools, "perhaps art is the least understood, the most difficult, and in many cases the poorest-taught subject" (Johnson, 1965, p. 55). Often what is called art instruction in elementary schools involves the completion of craft projects that are carried out almost as a manufacturing enterprise. Such projects usually conform to specifications that prohibit both the learning of technique *and* the exercise of imagination. Many elementary classrooms are decorated with children's attempts to imitate the teacher's Easter bunny, Santa Claus, or paper-cup Snoopy. While such projects may improve classroom climate, they do not succeed in teaching art to children.

Another approach to elementary school art instruction is to view it as a channel through which children can express their emotions (see e.g., Lowenfeld & Brittain, 1970). This approach stresses the affective import of art education and ignores the cognitive import. It discourages any attempt to provide structured lessons that might limit children's free expression.

In secondary schools, art education is beset by other problems. Generally, art classes are offered as electives. Often bright children are discouraged from taking art electives, and below-average children are scheduled into these classes. According to Silverman and Lanier (1965, p. 117), "the validity of art as a legitimate area of study for *all* students has been recognized in less than 10 percent of American senior high schools."

Enrichment and acceleration.   In some school districts art instruction is part of the enrichment program provided to children who are identified as gifted. In a very small number of other districts, art instruction is provided to children selected because of their talent in art (Alexander, 1981). In either case, the instruction provided is of such short duration and of such limited scope that it can only be considered enrichment.

Extensive, high-quality instruction in art necessarily provides both enrichment and acceleration. It requires a curriculum that includes art history, art technique, and art criticism. Although programs based on such a curriculum are rare, they do exist. Such programs are most often found in specialized high schools that offer programs for talented students (Cox & Daniel, 1983).

DANCING AND ACTING AS PERFORMING ARTS

Singing, playing musical instruments, dancing, and acting make up the performing arts. All have been intimately connected since ancient times (Sorrel, 1967). In our educational system, however, there is a hierarchy of respectability among the performing arts. Music, including both singing and playing, is typically considered the most academic of the performing arts, and most public schools make a feeble effort to teach basic music appreciation and performance skills. Of the other performing arts, acting and dancing, acting is usually considered the more academic. Most educators, at least grudgingly, accord to acting the status of an art, but many view dance as a form of sport (cf. Best, 1980).

These attitudes affect talent development in the performing arts. School priorities determine that children will have little opportunity to develop their musical ability in the public schools and even less opportunity to develop ability in drama or dance. Lack of support for drama and dance is partly due to the prevalent view that the arts are noncognitive and therapeutic, rather than academic. Drama and dance, however, are given even less support in the schools than the other arts, perhaps because they are more overtly seductive than music or the visual arts. Performers are often seen as instrumental, rather than essential, and as technicians, rather than artists.

Singers, musicians, actors, and dancers are, in a sense, media (Arnheim, 1972). Their bodies and behavior are components of the art work. Their appearance and behavior are the center of attention. In a successful performance, the appearance and behavior of the performing artist pleases the audience. In fact, the audience will be unable to distinguish between the person of the artist and the role assumed by the artist in a successful performance.

The difference between creative and interpretive skills is an issue in the performing arts. It is not in the literary or visual arts. Only a small proportion of artists in the performing arts originate works. Composers, choreographers, and playwrights, like painters, sculptors, and novelists, create their art with relative autonomy. In contrast, the public nature of the *performing artist's* work has implications for both the status of the performers and their talent development opportunities.

Dance and Dancers

Dance is the least academic of the arts because of the lack of an adequate system of notation with which to compose and record dances. Musical notation specifies in great detail the qualities of the music; lyrics and scripts give the content of songs and plays even though they do not specify interpretive vocal inflections, gestures, and facial expressions. Dance notation was, until this century, virtually nonexistent. Dances were passed down from one generation to another, like folk tales. No collected body of dance works is readily available for study, criticism, and stimulus to further development. There are no basic works that students master in order to learn the history of dance technique and content. This lack of a written record prevents dance from achieving the academic status that characterizes other artistic disciplines.

Dance is, in a sense, a form of acting; however, the discursive content of a dance is necessarily much more limited than that of a play. Because it employs words, drama makes much more specific statements than dance. Although dances often have narrative content, dance movements are primarily connotative. The more denotation demanded by the content, the more dance resembles pantomime.

The primary vehicles of expression in dance are position and movement. Usually dance employs stylized movement, but ordinary movements, such as walking, are not uncommon components, particularly in dances choreographed by contemporary minimalist artists (e.g., Yvonne Rainer). The main difference between movement in dance and movement in other activities is that all movement in dance is intended to achieve an aesthetic effect.

The varieties of dance (social, folk, theater, and concert) differ in their relative emphasis on aesthetics, recreation, and pantomime, however. Social dances are designed primarily for recreation rather than for performance. In contrast to choreographed dances (i.e., incidental dance in plays or musicals or classical concert dance), social dances are neither physically demanding nor complex. Folk dances usually combine elements of dancing for recreation and dancing for an audience. The steps in folk dances are prescribed by tradition and are descended from ritualistic dances that enacted community events and myths (Sorrel, 1967). Folk dancing is often more complex and more strenuous than social dancing.

Despite these differences, the basic psychomotor skills of dancing are present in all forms of dance; and identification of talented social or folk dancers would be a viable means of selecting students for formal training. Such selection would need to be accomplished fairly early in children's school careers, however, because professional dancing demands many years of training.

Characteristics of Dancers

Successful dancers have usually begun to study dance seriously by the time they are fifteen years old. Girls often begin training at a much younger age. According to some ballet critics, dance instruction for ballet must begin by the time the child is eight or nine years old (Kirstein, 1983). Like musicians, dancers make the decision to become professional artists early in life, usually between twelve and eighteen years of age (Ryser, 1964). By their high-school years, most female dancers are spending a large portion of their free time in dance classes, at least an hour and a half per day (Braunschweig, 1981). Outstanding achievement in dance, as in other artistic and academic disciplines, demands early and continuing commitment from both child and parents. Twyla Tharp's early dance education is typical of that of many successful dancers:

> Although Twyla Tharp grew up in a small town in California, her mother was determined that she should have a proper education in music and the arts. "She had the luck," Tharp says, "to find these teachers who came out of the Ballet Russe tradition . . . Later she drove hundreds of miles to take me to study with Beatrice [Beauchamp] Collenette (a student of Anna Pavlova)." (Vaughan, 1984, p. 54)

In addition to commitment, accomplished dancers share several personality traits, physical characteristics, and cognitive skills.

Personality traits of gifted dance students.   Personality traits of dance students resemble those of other artists and art students (Wilson, 1964). Good dance students value aesthetic and philosophical ideas; they also take pleasure in arts other than dancing (Ryser, 1964). They are perfectionistic and willing to devote considerable energy to dance (Alter, Denman, & Barron, 1972).

The emotional intensity common to creative artists is also found in dancers' self-descriptions. Both male and female dance students see themselves as highly emotional, but male dance students describe themselves as less confident and subject to more internal conflict. This conflict may be caused by sex-role stereotypes that proclaim dancing to be a feminine activity.

Dancers share the childhood isolation that seems to characterize the lives of many artists. Particularly during adolescence, they feel alienated from peers (Ryser, 1964). This feeling may arise from their different interests as well as from the need to spend much of their out-of-school time in dance classes.

As a group, dancers tend to reject many middle-class mores. Ryser (1964) views dance students' rejection of middle-class values as a result of their isolation during adolescence. Whatever the cause, a similar rejection is characteristic of most artistically creative groups. Nonconformity to middle-class standards of behavior is typical of artists. The comments of one of Ryser's subjects portray an attitude prevalent among creative subjects:

> I was always different from the people I met in high school . . . They were doing all the things that kept them from thinking. (Ryser, 1964, p. 112)

Feelings of superiority over the general population are also typical of artists (Maddi, 1975), and dancers are apparently no exception. It is interesting to note that dancers also disdain other dancers (Ryser, 1964). The dancers studied by Ryser saw other dancers as ill-informed, too specialized, and uninterested in other arts. Each saw him or herself as an exception to this generality, however. Ryser suggests that this degree of idiosyncrasy may also characterize other types of artists.

Physical characteristics of dancers.   Although modern and jazz dance have somewhat less stringent physical requirements than ballet, there are some physical characteristics common to dancers in all three major forms of concert dance. Dancers must be slender, well-proportioned, flexible, strong, and well-coordinated. The relative importance of some of the characteristics varies with the sex of the dancer. Strength is important for both, but more important for male dancers, at least in ballet. Flexibility is probably more important for female dancers whatever the form of concert dance. The following characteristics are commonly cited as standards for the most strictly defined body type, that of the female ballet dancer:

> *Balanced body proportions*—The length of legs and arms is important. Short legs cannot achieve' impressive extensions in arabesques and kicks. On the other hand, a disproportionately short torso sometimes lacks the strength to sustain high arabesques. Short arms are not so lyrical as long arms, but arms that are too long may look grotesque on stage.
>
> *Strong feet with a flexible arch*—This is important because so many female dance roles are performed en pointe. Even with support in toe shoes, this form of dancing is extremely difficult if the dancer's feet are weak or inflexible.
>
> *Pelvic structure that allows "turn out"*—Most ballet steps are based on dance positions that require the dancer's legs and feet to be turned out in a nearly 90 degree angle to the front of the body. Some women's pelvic bones angle in a way that limits their ability to attain good turn out.[1]
>
> *Sloping shoulders*—Square shoulders are usually less flexible and sloping shoulders give the appearance of a long neck. Following the influence of Balanchine, nearly all American ballerinas today have a slender, elongated appearance. (Jacob, 1981)

More important than these characteristics, even for female ballet dancers, are the psychomotor skills used in dance. Nonetheless, psychomotor skills are related to body structure, and postural anomalies or overweight disqualify even the most graceful dancer from a stage career in the United States.

Psychomotor and cognitive skills.   Among the psychomotor skills required for dancing are (1) ability to discern and imitate kinesthetic patterns in detail, (2) quick memorization of those patterns, and (3) superior retention of learned kinesthetic patterns. When choreographers are working out a dance, they may change the dance 20 or 30 times (McKayle, 1966). Dancers who cannot quickly learn new combinations are at a distinct disadvantage, and their chances for success are limited.

The ability to discern and imitate complicated body positions and movements is essential. If dancers had to have each element of a position or movement called to their attention separately, learning a new dance would be a slow, arduous process. The ability to see and imitate even the most subtle component of a dance step or combination of steps enables the talented dancer to progress rapidly. This skill is learned, but the skills of discriminating small differences in movement and of coordinating complex movement patterns in imitation of a model takes years of training and practice.

---

[1]Like all of these characteristics, this quality is a consideration, but not essential to success; Anna Pavlova was considered to have rather poor turn out [Fonteyn, 1979].

Interpretation requires understanding of the semantic content of the dance and of its emotional tone. Interpretation in dance requires some of the same skills as acting: sensitivity to gesture and its significance, sensitivity to facial expression, memory for both, and the ability to imitate them. Musical intelligence adds to the dancer's interpretive ability (Duncan, 1927).

Dancers' interpretive ability is closely related to their style, an important variable in dance. Although technical ability is necessary to achieving eminence in dance, the most acclaimed dancers are not always the most technically competent.

For example, Isadora Duncan's contribution to dance was not based on her technical competence so much as her style, which was so dramatically different from ballet that it constituted a new form of dance (Kraus, 1969). Style reflects both dancers' anatomical makeup and their personalities. The fluidity with which a dancer moves, the height of leaps, and the precision with which the dancer defines movements are among the elements of individual style. These are prescribed primarily by physical structures. Related qualities, such as the authority that a dancer projects, are probably linked to personality. Rudolf Nuryev's dancing was characterized by spectacular leaps, strength, and intensity (Fonteyn, 1979). Mikhail Baryishnikov's style is lighter, more androgynous, and more urbane. Different styles appeal to different audiences, but each audience is influenced by local and contemporary ideals of beauty.

The Schools' Response to Dance Talent

Even though several states include ability in the performing arts as part of their definition of giftedness, this part of the definition is virtually meaningless in all school systems except the few that have specialized schools in the arts, for example, North Carolina's School of the Arts or New York City's High School of Performing Arts. In most school systems there are no efforts to identify students who are gifted dancers, and there are no public school programs to develop talent in dancing. The development of dance in this country is almost exclusively left to private dance schools, a circumstance which has several disadvantages, not the least of which is that much of the instruction in private dance schools is of poor quality (Braunschweig, 1981).

Identification.   Gifted dancers are rarely identified through the public school system. Most pursue private lessons until they are out of high school and then compete for a place in musical theater, professional dance companies, or university dance programs. Their talent is evaluated through auditions. Dancers without formal training cannot compete successfully for a place in a professional ballet company, and would rarely be able to compete with dancers trained in jazz or modern dance. As with any discipline, students with a history of good instruction are most likely to be identified as talented. In the United States, the population with *any* history of formal dance instruction is primarily composed of middle-class and upper-class females.

Since most dance students train in private schools, the cost of instruction usually limits its accessibility to students from affluent families. Because of sex-role stereotypes, most dance students are girls. The chances of an economically disadvantaged boy's being identified as a talented dancer are very small. (See Box 7-1.)

BOX 7-1   Break Dancing

Break dancing, a popular form of dance that received widespread publicity during the late 1970s and early 1980s, aptly illustrates the circumstances of economically disadvantaged males with dance talent. Although this group would not usually be identified as gifted in dancing, some talented minority adolescents were spotlighted for a short time.

Break dancing belongs so completely to poor, urban, black youths that it is, in a sense, an ethnic dance. It originated in the predominantly black ghetto of the South Bronx, N.Y. (Rosenwald, 1984). Until it gained attention nationwide, it was performed almost exclusively by members of the population that developed the dance.

Break dancing embodies daring, physical prowess, and defiance. The dancers take turns executing difficult feats in an effort to out-do each other. The dance steps combine elements of acrobatics, the martial arts, and rock and roll dance movements. It is not a coincidence that break dancing was invented and performed by poor, black males, who, through the dance, set up and engaged in a competition that they had a chance of winning. (They also had a chance to pick up a little money from passersby who stopped to watch.)

Break dancing's spectacular acrobatics drew notice from the media; and break dancers appeared briefly in movies, on television, and on concert stages. Their popularity, however, was short-lived because the appeal of break dancing was primarily its novelty. Ironically, its domestication for the stage, television, and movies doomed break dancing to a short life on the streets as well. The middle-class's cooptation of a subculture's music, dress, or slang destroys its ethnic validity. The influence of cooptation is present throughout the history of black music, from early blues to modern jazz (Jones, 1971).

Although the break dancing fad is an interesting social phenomenon for many reasons, it is of special interest to educators of the gifted in that it is an example of the limited forms of expression available to talented but disadvantaged youngsters. There were many dancers among this population whose talent became evident even though they had no formal instruction whatsoever. The situation illustrates the point that talent alone cannot secure a dance career.

Programs.   Serious dance training is rigorous; it requires at least an hour and a half a day at the dance studio (Braunschweig, 1981). For most talented dance students this study is not a part of their school curriculum. Dance in the elementary schools, when it is offered at all, is offered in the form of folk or social dance in the physical education program. Even these programs do not often form a central part of the curriculum, but are taught only if the physical education teacher happens to view them as important. Although learning creative movement skills, performing structured dances, and developing individual dances are considered to be important elements of early dance education (Kraus, 1969), these skills are seldom taught.

In the secondary schools, dance is also neglected. Where dance courses exist, they are often sustained *only* by a particular teacher's knowledge and interest. One such program is the Marmaroneck (N.Y.) High School program, which has been in existence since the early 1970s. It offers four levels of dance classes and a planned curriculum (Barylick, 1983). The teacher of the program attributes its success to three circumstances: (1) availability of a dance studio (not a gymnasium to be shared with the physical education program); (2) a performing arts program including several teachers who act as advocates for each other; and (3) a curriculum that recognizes the value of dance as an end in itself, not as a means to developing spiritual values or staying fit (Barylick, 1983).

A small number of specialized arts schools offer programs in dance on both a public and tuition-paying basis, depending usually on the student's place of residence. Some examples of such schools are Houston's High School for Performing and Visual Arts (Grades 10–12), Cincinnati's Center for the Creative Arts (Grades 9–12); New York's High School of Performing Arts (Grades 9–12); the National Academy of Dance (Grades 7–13) at Champaign, Illinois; and the Philadelphia College of the Performing Arts (Grades 1–12) (Jacob, 1981). These schools usually select students on the basis of auditions and interviews and provide programs designed to meet both regular academic requirements and the needs of developing artists.

Aside from these specialized schools, publicly funded dance programs are available almost exclusively at the college level. This is too late to start the instruction of talented dancers. Moreover, most universities cannot provide the exposure to expert choreographers and dancers that association with a professional dance company can (Jacob, 1981). Choosing to purse a dance major in college is more common among and more relevant to modern—as opposed to classical or jazz—dancers (Jacob, 1981).

Acceleration and enrichment.   Because there are so few sequential programs in the elementary and secondary schools, there is little opportunity for any progress, much less acceleration. Even enrichment efforts are minimal in most schools. An annual performance of "The Nutcracker" constitutes the dance enrichment program for many public school students. The ambivalence the public feels toward all the arts is less evident in their attitude toward dance—they are, apparently, fairly certain that dance has no place in the schools.

Acting and Actors

Like dance, acting has a long history. In fact, it is only in the last 600 years that acting and dance have become two distinct theater arts (Sorrel, 1967). The combination of dance, mime, song, and speech to enact dramas has been chronicled as early as 2,000 B.C. in Egypt (Kraus, 1969). The early Greek playwrights, including Thespis, were called "dancers," and Aeschylus instructed his own choruses in dancing and choreographed figures for them (Lawler, 1964). The primary medium of expression in acting is not movement, however, but words. Although gesture and movement are quite important in acting, the basic skills in acting are substantially different from those required for dancing.

Personality characteristics of actors. There are few studies of talented young actors, but at least one (Barron & Denman, 1972) reports that student actors, like other artists, are highly interested in their art and committed to perfecting their talent.

These students also report that, since childhood, they have enjoyed doing imitations of other people's speech and mannerisms and have often impersonated others for the fun of it (Barron & Denman, 1972). Apparently many actors and comedians have entertained themselves through mimicry and the development of different personae long before they entertained others with their talent (Gardner, 1973; Lane, 1960). Imitating other people and enacting imaginary characters seem, in many cases, to be the potential actor's or comedian's way of coping with difficult situations. (Gardner [1973] specifically mentions school as one of the difficult situations that comedians have made more bearable for themselves by employing their talents.)

Cognitive skills in acting. According to the nineteenth century English actress, Ellen Terry, acting requires intelligence, industry, and, most of all, imagination (Albright, 1967). More specific skills have been mentioned by others: the ability to discern and to imitate speech patterns and gestural mannerisms (Gardner, 1973), superior ability at comprehending verbal material (Wolf, 1981), and the ability to recall and to recreate emotional states (Stanislavski, 1948).

The Schools' Response to Acting Talent

Its close association with literature, an unquestionably academic subject, assures drama some attention in the public schools. The study of plays in English classes and occasional oral interpretation of literary selections may afford some students very limited experience in acting even where there are no drama classes. Experiences in drama are more readily available in the public schools than experiences in dance. There *are* teachers who have had some training in speech and drama in most public school systems.

Identification of acting talent.   In most school systems, identification of acting talent is not undertaken on a systematic basis. Because they are allowed some opportunities to act in elementary and secondary school, however, a few children may be recognized as talented actors. Since most school systems offer no drama programs, talented young actors have to find private instruction to develop their talent. The young drama student is, however, at a much greater disadvantage than the talented young dance student, because dancing schools can be found even in small towns. Acting schools are, on the contrary, uncommon even in medium-sized cities. Children's theater is an option available outside of school in some communities, but it is only an introduction to theater.

In the few public school programs with established identification procedures, selection is usually based on the student's commitment and superior acting performance as demonstrated through audition. Preliminary auditions are sometimes submitted on video tapes and live auditions reserved for those students selected through review of the taped auditions.

Programs.   The acting programs that do exist usually take the form of minicourses in enrichment programs at the elementary school level and electives, such as drama or oral interpretation, in the secondary grades. A few gifted programs specialize in the theater arts. For example, one federally funded project for gifted disadvantaged students in a largely black and Hispanic urban school provided instruction in dance, music, drama, and graphic arts (Wolf, 1981). Most of the performing arts schools, such as those mentioned in the section on gifted dancers, also offer instruction in drama.

Acceleration and enrichment.   In most public schools, acting is not taught on a formal basis, and the activities provided are not sufficient to foster progress in talent development. Typically, acting is offered as enrichment: Perhaps a few students are involved in production of occasional plays for the student body, a class of students may attend a performance at a local theater, or a few students may participate in interpretive reading competitions. Like dance training, dramatic training is not available to most students until they enter college. Performing arts schools are the only public school programs in which the curriculum is comprehensive and sequential enough to allow acceleration.

SUMMARY

Artistic talent is distinct from creativity, and it cannot be assessed using the instruments developed to identify creativity. For a variety of reasons, artistic talent is better viewed as a number of separate talents. In most cases, the research reported here noted that above-average intelligence seemed necessary for a high level of talent development.

In arts other than the visual arts, performance ability differs in some ways from the ability to make works of art. In dance and music, however, the chapter reported that *interpretation* was closely related to the ability to make works. In music, particularly, excellent musical performance seems to have a great deal to do with the musical understanding necessary for composition.

Most artistically talented students share an uncommon degree of devotion to their work. Whether they study dance, acting, music, or visual arts, the intellectual interests of talented young arts students seem in all cases to extend to issues of aesthetics and philosophy. Research also confirms that arts students are critical nonconformists. During their school years they feel isolated and out of touch with their peers and with their experiences in school.

Though little support exists for public school education in the arts, the research discussed here strongly suggests a determining role for early nurture and training in the arts. Early, high-quality instruction seems to be crucially important for musicians and dancers, and it is apparently an influential experience for visual artists and for actors as well.

8

Typical Gifted Development

Focusing Questions

1. In what ways do Lombroso's and Terman's views of gifted individuals represent conventional stereotypes?
2. How does the early development of the oral language of gifted children compare with that of other children?
3. To what degree do intellectual skills, perceptual skills, and environmental support correlate with early reading ability?
4. What do Piagetian measures suggest about gifted children's concept development?
5. What factors contribute to the popular perception that gifted children are at risk for social and emotional problems?
6. How does most recent research characterize gifted children's social adjustment and emotional health?

TYPES AND STEREOTYPES

Considering the fact that gifted children are identified because of their *atypical* development, a discussion of the *typical* development of gifted children may seem problematic. A number of writers, however, have tried to describe characteristic patterns of development among gifted children. A review of the ideas presented by the most notable of these writers provides a basis for distinguishing between accurate representations and stereotypical views of gifted children's development.

Nineteenth Century Views

The ideas developed in Darwin's *The Origin of Species*, published in 1859, prompted a number of nineteenth-century thinkers to apply the notion of natural selection to the study of human characteristics. Intelligence (genius and feeble-mindedness) was among the characteristics most often explained in terms of Darwin's theory.

The reasoning behind this application of Darwin's theory was as follows:

1. The characteristics of all living things are hereditary.
2. The most successful characteristics are those that provide the individual with an adaptive advantage.
3. Those individuals who adapt better have a greater chance of producing offspring.
4. A greater amount of intelligence is an adaptive advantage.
5. Hence, intelligence is hereditary and the most intelligent members of society should be the breeders of offspring (and less intelligent members of society should be kept from breeding).

Based on these premises, the nineteenth-century hereditarians began to study the traits of individuals who were feeble-minded and those who were eminent. Galton (see Box 8-1), for example, studied eminent families in several occupational categories. He concluded from his study of these families that "genius" was an inherited trait of positive benefit to society (see Chapter 4).

Lombroso, by contrast, concluded from his study of eminent men that genius and degeneracy were closely connected. He characterized the genius as a sickly and unstable type who was likely to be antisocial and to die early. Lombroso saw normality as the characteristic of most unqualified benefit to society. He was suspicious of any form of abnormality, including abnormal brilliance. .

Although these nineteenth-century views of genius differed greatly, neither was derived from what we now consider to be a scientific sampling of highly intelligent or creative individuals. The work of these investigators raised the issue of extreme talent more extensively than ever before, but their work also tended to substantiate unfounded prejudices.

BOX 8-1   Sir Francis Galton as a Gifted Child

Sir Francis Galton, who is noted for his statistical study of eminence, was himself a highly gifted child. According to Terman, Galton probably had an IQ of 200 (Burt, 1975). The last of nine children, Francis received his early education at home with his sister Adele serving as his first teacher. Francis' precocious development and early tutelage resulted in highly advanced academic development. By the age of one year, Francis could recognize letters. By the age of three, he could read children's stories and by four could read adult literature. At six, Galton was able to read the classics in both Latin and Greek and had reportedly memorized the *Odyssey* and the *Iliad*.

When he was eight, Galton was sent to a private school where he was placed in a class with fourteen- and fifteen-year-old boys. Here, and in his later placement at King Edward's School in Birmingham, Galton found the pace of the curriculum slow and the content boring. His interests in science and mathematics were not satisfied by the classical education he received at these schools.

Considering his own experience as a highly precocious youngster, it is not difficult to understand why Galton spent a large part of his adult life speculating about genius. Although his views about the nature and transmission of intelligence have been disputed and discredited, Galton's statistical methods for studying human characteristics served as the basis for later studies in the nineteenth and twentieth centuries.

Terman's Findings

In 1921 Lewis Terman began a longitudinal study of 1,528 high-IQ children in California. He was interested in identifying characteristics common to gifted children and to trace the life histories of such children (Seagoe, 1975). As a result of this study, Terman and his associates concluded that gifted children were intellectually, physically, and emotionally superior to average children. These results tended to refute the beliefs of nineteenth century theorists like Lombroso.

Physical development. Although the physical differences between gifted children and average children were not dramatic, they were statistically significant. Terman found the gifted to be taller and heavier at birth, to walk and talk earlier, to start puberty earlier, and to be healthier than average children. Rather than being prone to physical weakness as was previously thought, gifted children appeared to be athletic, muscular, and well-nourished.

Emotional development. Terman found that gifted children surpassed average children in emotional and moral qualities. Although he acknowledged that the tests of character he used were not highly reliable, Terman nevertheless concluded that the gifted group was superior in character to the control group. He found gifted children to demonstrate creativity, aesthetic sensitivity, perseverance, self-confidence, cheerfulness, achievement motivation, a sense of humor, and leadership ability. He found them to be more emotionally stable and more adaptable socially than average children.

Intellectual development.   Children with IQs above 140 were selected for Terman's study. The average IQ of the group was 151, and the range of IQs was from 140 to 200 (Seagoe, 1975). Although the children in Terman's sample represented the top 1 percent on measures of intelligence, they were not quite so superior in academic achievement; their average achievement quotient was 144. Only half of the children in the sample had learned to read before entering school, and on average the gifted children tended to be performing school work at a level just two years above their chronological age expectancy levels (Burt, 1975). Terman was disturbed by the fact that children who were highly superior in intelligence and quite superior in academic achievement, were only slightly advanced in their grade placement in school (Laycock, 1979).

Problems with Terman's findings.   Bias in the selection of his subjects produced significant problems with Terman's findings. Because most of the children Terman tested were those whom teachers nominated, he failed to test—and thereby identify as gifted—many other equally bright children. Considering the usual biases in teacher referrals, these *unidentified* gifted children may have been underachievers or troublemakers. They were likely to have come from lower class or minority backgrounds.

Because children from middle-class and upper middle-class backgrounds were overrepresented in Terman's gifted group, some of the findings about gifted children might in truth have been findings about children from advantaged backgrounds. The greater-than-average birth weight of the gifted children in the study, for example, may have been a phenomenon more strongly associated with their socioeconomic status than with their IQ.

In considering the typical development of the gifted, we might be just as incorrect in accepting Terman's findings about their normality as we are in accepting Lombroso's speculations about their deviance. The obvious empirical advantage of Terman's methods over those used by Lombroso and Galton may still not have provided an accurate picture of the developmental history typical of gifted children.

Recent Studies of Preschool Gifted Children

Some researchers (e.g., Roedell et al., 1980) have taken a special interest in the very early development of gifted children. Usually, such researchers discuss the developmental histories of highly gifted children since these children appear unusual almost from birth. Young gifted children of less extraordinary capability are more difficult to identify: they may show some degree of precocity in one or more of the developmental domains, but their giftedness may not be apparent until they are older.

Developmental patterns.   Retrospective studies (Hollingworth, 1942; Terman, 1925) of children with very high IQs have noted their precocious verbal development. By the time they are two or three years old, these children demonstrate a speaking vocabulary that is larger than average and sentence production that is more advanced. With parental encouragement and assistance, they are often reading a little and doing some addition and subtraction before they start kindergarten. These high-IQ children also show early and rapid development of conceptual skills such as discriminating and labeling colors, drawing, identifying shapes, and working puzzles.

In the development of motor skills, preschool gifted children are most like other children. On tests of gross and fine motor skills, preschool gifted children may score slightly higher than average, but not nearly so high as they do on cognitive tests (Kitano & Kirby, 1986; Roedell et al., 1980).

Importance of early environment.   Recent studies of animal behavior suggest that learning can be greatly accelerated by early stimulation (Clark, 1988). In fact, we might reasonably speculate that, given appropriate early stimulation, most children could develop cognitive abilities in the gifted range. Even physical development, which seems most influenced by chronological age, can be accelerated considerably.

Stimulation of early learning seems to depend on a responsive environment. Simply to surround a baby with pictures, sounds, and objects may not be enough, however. The baby also needs to interact with the environment, and his or her actions must have some effect. Learning takes place when the baby's actions have predictable consequences. Parents who respond to their infant's crying, gurgles, and gestures give their baby an opportunity for this kind of learning. Such parents are more likely than less responsive parents to have high-achieving children. According to Clark (1988), every child needs to feel effective in order to learn at an optimal rate.

Prenatal and perinatal environment.   Although a poor prenatal environment is detrimental to babies, a good prenatal environment may not be exceptionally advantageous. It is difficult to demonstrate that excellent prenatal conditions contribute to the development of superior intellectual capacity. Since bad environments inhibit development, however, we might infer that good environments may stimulate it.

We can make the same sort of inference about the conditions of birth. If serious birth trauma, such as deprivation of oxygen, can impair intelligence, then unusually good circumstances at birth may enhance intelligence. Babies of unmedicated mothers are more alert immediately after they are born, although it is not certain that the effects are long lasting. Clark (1988) reports a study that suggests that increased oxygen to the brain can increase the intelligence of infants. She notes, however, that there is insufficient evidence to be certain of these findings.

Accelerated early learning.   Recently, some authors have suggested that children's development can be accelerated significantly by providing them with a program of highly stimulating experiences (see e.g., Prichard & Taylor, 1980). One of the most outspoken proponents of early stimulation is Glenn Doman, founder of the Institute for the Achievement of Human Potential and author of *How to Teach Your Baby to Read* (1964). His training program purports to teach children how to read at one year of age, how to do simple arithmetic at the same age, and how to speak a foreign language. Doman contends that, given an intensive program of enrichment, any normal child can learn skills at an accelerated rate. However, his claims are supported only by anecdotal evidence and not by controlled studies. The testimonies of parents who have participated in his program are mixed (Langway, 1983).

Some professionals feel that environments of the sort Doman advocates are too stressful for young children. These psychologists and educators believe that accelerated early learning causes children to have social or emotional problems, and perhaps even academic ones. There is, however, little evidence to support these assertions.

Problems of highly gifted young children.   One of the major problems of young gifted children is the disparity between their intellectual development and their physical development. As Roedell, Jackson, and Robinson (1980) point out, it is hard for teachers to accept that three-, four-, or five-year-olds whose writing is as laborious as that of their classmates can read and perform arithmetic at advanced levels.

Sometimes teachers are unable to recognize children's precocious cognitive development because they focus on the children's average motor performance. Kindergarten teachers, in particular, have trouble identifying the highly intelligent children in their classrooms; they may fail to recognize the ability of 90 percent of their gifted students (Jacobs, 1971). Even when they are identified, such children may not receive appropriate educational programming because it is difficult for schools to accommodate the disparity between young gifted children's skills in comprehension and their skills in written expression.

Young gifted children may also experience difficulty because of their advanced social development. Parents may not be able to find suitable playmates for gifted children whose interests and patterns of play are quite different from those of peers. Some authors (e.g., Freeman, 1979) point out that gifted children select older children as friends. Highly gifted children may also prefer the company of adults (Austin & Draper, 1981).

DEVELOPMENTAL DOMAINS: TYPES AND ANOMALIES

Now that we have considered several general perspectives on the development of gifted children, we can look more specifically at the empirical research. In the subsequent part of the chapter we will review the research on the development of gifted children in three domains: language acquisition, concept formation, and social and emotional development.

The findings discussed in these sections do not reflect a unified perspective on the development of gifted children, however. Unlike Galton, Lombroso, or Terman, we are not attempting to present a typology of giftedness. Nor are we attempting to characterize the early development of highly gifted children. Instead, we examine the development of particular skills in gifted children and contrast the rate and sequence of gifted children's development with that of average children.

It is important to remember that the empirical findings about gifted children's development merely reflect trends. These findings do not account for the individual variations in development that occur among the gifted. Many gifted children do not conform to the typical sequence of development; others conform in some domains but not in others.

To say, for example, that gifted children are emotionally more mature than average children is not to say that *every gifted child* is more mature emotionally than *every average child*. In particular, the findings about typical gifted children may not describe the actual experiences of underachieving children, disadvantaged children, or highly precocious children. The developmental patterns characteristic of these types of gifted children will be discussed in later chapters.

LANGUAGE ACQUISITION AND VERBAL PRECOCITY

Because language, written and oral, is the medium of formal instruction and of formal learning, its acquisition and early development seem—in some unclear way—to prefigure school learning. Are precocious talkers likely to become high-IQ schoolchildren? Do gifted children tend to be early readers?

Theories of Language Acquisition

Some quite plausible theories have been developed to explain the way in which language is acquired by young children. Recent research draws on these theories to help explain the typical development of gifted children.

The nativist theory.   Modern linguists have constructed the "nativist" or "innatist" view of language acquisition. Just as some theories of intelligence maintain that intellectual ability is an inborn trait (see Chapter 3), so the nativist theory of language acquisition maintains that language ability is an inherent trait of human beings.

There are, however, some major differences between nativist views of language acquisition and hereditarian views of intelligence. Whereas theories of innate intelligence tend to stress individual differences in intellectual ability, the nativist position on language acquisition tends to stress the commonalities of language ability in human beings. The ability to use language fluently is considered by theorists like Noam Chomsky to be the genetic heritage of all human beings.

The nativist theory credits *environmental* influences as the source of the vast cultural and individual differences evident in language performance. It credits genetic and *biological* influences as the source of a common competence.

The essence of the nativist view of language acquisition is the image of children as language rule makers. A child who says, "Mommy goed away" instead of "Mommy went away" demonstrates this rule-making ability. Although the child has probably heard the form "went" countless times, the internalized logic of grammar leads the child to say "goed". In a logical sense, the child's mistake is not a grammatical error.

The behavioral theory of language learning.   According to this view, language is learned through the mechanism of operant conditioning, and it is subsequently used by the learner to adapt the environment. Behaviorists view language as a set of stimuli and responses.

The internal mechanisms, the cognitive apparatus, and the developmental stages that may regulate language acquisition in young children are of little interest in the behavioral view. The practical interactions that condition specific language uses are, however, of immense interest to behaviorists.

Linguistic meaning and structure are of less interest in this view than the way in which verbal units condition behavior. The behavioral and practical content of language, not its phonology, morphology, or syntax, is of most interest to behaviorists.

Precocious Language Acquisition and IQ

Early speech is almost universally accepted as a token of a child's general aptitude for the important tasks of reading and writing. Fond parents are apt to look for signs of verbal precocity in their infants, and to find evidence for it in early speech.

Hollingworth (1942) reported the onset of speech in the case of 12 children with IQs above 180. Although the children are described as early talkers (Hollingworth, 1942), the data, supplied by parents, do not support that conclusion. The youngest age at which any of the children began talking is reported to be 9 months and the latest age is 24 months. The median was 14 months, approximately the same as for average children.

Recent research.   Recent studies that draw on both theories of language acquisition (often in the same study) may offer some insights into the language development of gifted children. Smolak (1982) studied cognitive precedents of receptive and expressive language in infants and beginning talkers (n = 48) tested at 9, 11, 12, and 15 months. Smolak reported that infants whose parents played verbal games with them performed better on comprehension tasks, and that children who performed better on comprehension tasks were more likely to talk. Evidently, being talked to is strongly related to talking, a finding that is not surprising.

Guilford, Scheuerle, and Shonburn (1981) studied language acquisition in a small sample (n = 11) of preschool children with Binet IQs above 140. These researchers concluded that their subjects *did not* have a better command of grammar than average children. They concluded, however, that their young subjects could apply more fully than normal subjects the rules that they knew. This study implies that it may be difficult to identify young gifted children on the evidence of their oral expressive language.

Gray, Saski, McEntire, and Larsen (1980) came to similar conclusions in their study of oral proficiency as a predictor of academic success. They reported that *when the effect of IQ was controlled,* "little relationship is evident between oral language proficiency and school readiness" (Gray et al., 1980, p. 266).

At present, research does not suggest that early language development, apart from IQ, is a very reliable predictor of later academic success. It is possible that this conclusion may be the result of the way in which early language is studied. Most studies involve small samples in a cross-sectional design.

This topic of research is sure to remain of interest, however, because of the apparent conflict between theories of language that stress the important influence of environment and theories of intelligence that stress the important influence of genetic inheritance.

Verbal Ability and IQ

For some time the literature on gifted children has suggested that these children possess advanced verbal abilities (cf. Terman & Oden, 1947). It is possible to specify the confirmed verbal skills that characterize gifted children. These major characteristics, which involve *receptive* verbal skills almost exclusively (cf. Gallagher, 1985), are as follows:

- They have vocabularies significantly larger than average children.
- They *tend* to read earlier, to read better, and to read more than average children.
- They comprehend difficult verbal material more easily than average children.

Receptive verbal tasks are, in fact, those most frequently sampled on IQ tests like the Stanford-Binet (Terman & Merrill, 1973), the Wechsler Verbal Scales (Wechsler, 1974, 1981), and other such tests. Since the development of receptive skills probably precedes the development of expressive skills, this method of assessing academic *potential* makes a good deal of sense.

Lack of instruction as a confounding variable.   When the expressive verbal performance of gifted children has been evaluated, as in the studies of language acquisition reported previously or in studies of the writing of older students (e.g., Fearn, 1981; Pendarvis, 1983), results have generally confirmed the *similarity* of gifted and average students. Why should such a discrepancy exist between receptive and expressive language performance in the case of gifted children?

The fault, according to William Durden, who directs the Program for Verbally Gifted Youth (PVGY) at Johns Hopkins University, seems to lie in students' instruction, not in their academic potential. He cites the neglect of the humanities and written expression in elementary and secondary schools as a probable cause for the difference between gifted students' receptive and expressive language skills (Durden, 1980).

Early Reading

Although it is uncommon for children to be taught to read before they enter first grade, a small minority do learn to read as preschoolers. Of these early readers, most start reading at four or five years of age; a few begin even earlier.

Early reading is an important issue for educators of the gifted because many, but by no means all, gifted children are also early readers. The following discussion reviews the research related to early reading by examining several pertinent questions:

1. Do early readers share cognitive characteristics?
2. Does early reading correlate with high IQ?
3. Do early readers come from homes that encourage early reading in particular ways?
4. Does early reading relate to perceptual skill development?

Characteristics of early readers.   Two general patterns emerge from studies of early readers: (1) these children have above-average intelligence and (2) they have been exposed to written language and other academically pertinent modes of expression at home. The parents of early readers support their children's efforts to read, even if they do not provide direct instruction. In addition, there are some specific interests and abilities common to many early readers and their families.

Evidence of the importance of intellectual precocity in learning to read early is found in many studies. One of the oldest (Davidson, 1931) is described in Durkin's (1966) *Early Readers*. Davidson selected 13 children ranging in chronological age from three to five years old, but having in common a mental age of four years. After receiving ten minutes of daily reading instruction for four and a half months, the children were tested. All of the children learned to read some words, but the bright three-year-old children learned more than the older children, a finding that suggests that even moderate intellectual precocity influences early reading achievement. Davidson's study also suggests that children can learn to read considerably earlier than the age at which they are typically instructed.

Estimates of the proportion of early readers among high-IQ children range from one-third to one-half. Terman (1925) surveyed the parents of 643 children with IQ scores of 140 or above to determine the incidence of early reading. He found that approximately 45 percent of the children were reported to have read before starting school. Another survey, based on self-reports by gifted junior high-school students, found that about half had learned to read before entering first grade (Strang, 1954).

Among *highly gifted* children, the incidence of early reading seems to be greater. All of the 12 children described by Hollingworth (1942) in *Children with Above 180 IQ* were early readers. Of 270 seventh and eighth graders who made composite scores of 1,100 or higher on the Scholastic Aptitude Test (Verbal and Math), 81 percent read before they were six years old (Van Tassel-Baska, 1983). Fifty-five percent of the group read before they were five years old.

Results of some studies of early reading, however, must be interpreted cautiously. Studies that rely on parent reporting or self-reporting may not be very accurate. Durkin (1966) avoided the methodological problem of self- or parent reporting. By testing 5,103 first graders in Oakland, California elementary schools during the first weeks of school before reading instruction had begun, Durkin and her co-workers were able to identify 49 (approximately 1 percent) who could read. Criteria for selection were (1) correct pronunciation of at least 18 of 37 vocabulary words and (2) a raw score of at least 1 on a standardized reading test. The children's reading grade levels ranged from 1.5 to 4.5. The IQ range in the Oakland study was 91 to 161, with a mean of 122. The correlation between reading achievement and IQ was 0.40

In a later study in New York City, employing similar identification methods, Durkin found 156 early readers among 4,465 children. Their reading grade levels ranged from 1.4 to 5.2. The IQ range was from 82 to 170, with a mean of 133. The correlation between reading achievement and intelligence in that study was only 0.24. From such findings it is clear that not all early readers are high-IQ children; neither are all high-IQ children early readers.

Durkin's low to moderate correlations might, however, reflect the effect of "restricted range." This concept refers to the fact that when the range of one of two correlated traits is "restricted" (i.e., reduced), their correlation will be reduced. Durkin's students exhibited *both* elevated IQ *and* elevated reading achievement. In the New York study, for example, 78.2 percent of the early readers had IQ scores of 120 or above. In the general population the correlation of early reading and IQ may well be higher than Durkin's reported statistics.

Correlations of early reading skill with various intellectual measures in the range of 0.30 to 0.64 are nonetheless typical for this age group (Hiebert, 1980; Stanovich et al., 1984). Correlations of this magnitude suggest the importance of identifying additional factors that contribute to precocious reading achievement.

Other abilities and interests of early readers.   Durkin described the early readers in her study as "paper and pencil kids" and as "scribblers." Their interest in reading, in fact, seemed often to derive from an interest in copying words and letters. An early interest in letters of the alphabet and in words is also reported in other studies of children who read early (e.g., Hollingworth, 1942; Salzer, 1984). Of course, not all gifted children share this important characteristic of early readers.

Another characteristic of early readers seems to be their interest in sedentary games and activities. The parents of early readers described their children as being adept at games and activities such as drawing (Durkin, 1966). Parents of equally bright children who were not early readers did not ascribe this characteristic to their children.

Other than an unusual interest in letters and words, little has been found to distinguish early readers except a difference in their families' tendency to encourage reading.

Families of early readers. Reading early is accompanied by some form of assistance. Even when the parents of early readers are unaware that their children are learning how to read, their reports suggest that they provide an environment that supports early learning efforts.

Compared with the mothers of equally bright children who do not read early, the mothers of early readers spend more time interacting with their children in educational games and in the daily routine of housework, meals, and recreation (Durkin, 1966). They read aloud more to their children, and spend more time providing assistance when their children show an interest in learning how to read. Parents of early readers are also more likely than other parents to describe themselves as avid readers.

At the time that Durkin's studies were conducted, many parents were reluctant to teach their children how to read because of educators' admonitions that to do so would be detrimental to the child's academic adjustment (Durkin, 1966). The parents of early readers tended to be unconvinced by these warnings (Durkin, 1966).

Hiebert (1980) found, however, that home experiences (including parental instruction) could not alone account for young children's print awareness. Parental teaching, in *combination* with high IQ and advanced Piagetian cognitive development *did* account for 59 percent of the variance (coefficient of multiple correlation = 0.77) in children's print awareness. (See a later section in this chapter for a discussion of Piagetian cognitive development.)

Perceptual skills in early reading. Learning how to read may make heavier demands on perceptual processes than on cognitive development. Abilities associated with perceptual development may therefore also help explain individual differences in young children's reading.

This view is supported by studies that have found a lower correlation between IQ and reading achievement in earlier grades than in later grades (Stanovich et al., 1984; cf. Carter & Kontos, 1982). After children master basic phonics rules in the early grades, they begin to encounter more semantically and syntactically complex material. Then the demands of the reading task seem to change dramatically (cf. Chall, 1967).

Reading achievement and decoding speed. Decoding speed is the speed with which readers can translate visual symbols into meaningful auditory signals. Research offers evidence for the importance of decoding speed in reading (e.g., Hunt, 1978; LaBerge & Samuels, 1974; Lesgold & Perfetti, 1978; Stanovich et al., 1984).

Taking issue with Arthur Jensen's (1980) assertion that reading achievement is largely a function of general intelligence, Stanovich, Cunningham, and Feeman (1984) studied the relationships between first graders' reading performance and their phonological awareness, decoding speed, listening comprehension, and general intelligence. The strongest correlation with reading achievement was decoding time (-0.52).

Stanovich and associates (1984) reported that the comparative importance of decoding speed versus IQ clearly emerged in multiple-regression analysis. Their analysis suggested that pseudoword naming (i.e., the speed of decoding nonsense words) made the most significant independent contribution to predicting reading achievement in first-grade children. When combined with measures of phonological awareness, the addition of decoding speed accounted for substantially more variance in reading achievement than did the addition of intelligence measures.

Most studies have shown a decrease in the importance of decoding skills at later grade levels (cf. Chall, 1967). It seems likely that as reading materials become more conceptually difficult and as readers become more fluent, then their perceptual skills (such as decoding speed) become less relevant to the task of reading.

Gifted children with reading problems.   Students identified as gifted by virtue of their high scores on IQ tests can usually read fluently by the end of the first grade; a significant proportion begin to be fluent readers somewhat later; and a small percentage experience much difficulty in learning how to read. A few high-IQ children have persistent reading problems in school.

Pringle (1970) found that about 25 percent of the underachieving gifted children in her study were reading below grade level. Whitmore (1980) also identified several primary-grade gifted students who read below grade level because of learning or behavior problems.

Fox (1983) studied children with scores of 125 IQ or higher on the Wechsler Intelligence Scale for Children-Revised (WISC-R) who had been referred for testing because of their poor school performance. The study found that 75 percent of these students were reading at or below grade placement level and 10 percent were reading two or more grade levels below grade placement as measured by a standardized instrument. At the same time, Fox found that 89 percent had listening comprehension levels two or more years higher than their reading level, as measured by an informal reading inventory.

It is clear that many preschool children with average or higher IQ scores are eager to read and have the ability to learn. The continued superior reading achievement of precocious readers (whether gifted or not) shows that to encourage and to support early reading does no harm to children's academic development (Durkin, 1966). For the relatively few gifted children who find early reading difficult, individualized instruction in reading has been shown to effect significant improvement.

CONCEPT DEVELOPMENT

The study of concept development is perhaps the most theoretical ped-agogical specialty. Its subject is how ideas emerge and mature during the growth of humans. Concept development is a field so broad that it neces-sarily impinges on every branch of psychology and pedagogy (Flavell, 1977). It draws on studies of perception, memory, motivation, and social competence. In order to focus discussion here, however, this section of the chapter will consider primarily the work of the Swiss scholar Jean Piaget. In the last 20 years Piagetian theory has guided the study of concept develop-ment in the United States and Britain.

Piaget's lifework was an investigation of the way in which certain concepts emerge in the human being. Piaget believed that the concepts he chose to investigate were important categories of human cognition. These concepts appear in Piaget's work as "pure" (i.e., nonverbal) concepts.

Piaget built his theory of learning on a profound understanding of epistemology (i.e., the philosophy of knowledge). This grounding sets Piaget apart from most U.S. and British researchers of cognitive develop-ment. Most research on cognitive development in the United States and Britain addresses the means by which individuals learn, not the interaction between the categories of knowledge and learning.

Because the gifted are seen to be facile abstract thinkers and to enjoy the consideration of theoretical issues, it is important to examine their development of concepts. Before we review the empirical literature on Piagetian concept development among the gifted, however, a brief review of several of Piaget's most important ideas is in order.

Piagetian Notions: Stages and Adaptation

Piaget maintained that individuals progress through discrete yet hier-archical stages of concept development. According to his theory, each stage involves characteristic modes of thinking. Children progress at their own rates from stage to stage by using the thinking modes of the preceding stage to propel them into the next higher stage. Piaget's concern is with the quality of thought at each stage, not with the rate at which individual children reach particular stages.

Piaget also described the process by which children come to make the transition from stage to stage or to incorporate new information into their existing structure of thought (called a *schema*). This process of *adaptation* involves two mechanisms, *assimilation* and *accommodation*.

Sensorimotor stage. The first stage takes infants from the level of thought that is totally constrained by immediate experience to a level of thought that transcends immediate experience. This ultimate mental accomplishment of the sensorimotor period is apparent in events such as babies' search for objects that are hidden and their crying for a parent who leaves the room. Even at the height of the sensorimotor stage, however, children's thinking is rooted in the concrete persons, things, and events of their immediate experience.

Preoperational stage.   In the preoperational stage, children begin to develop symbolic patterns of thinking that transcend immediate things and events. Children develop concepts of size and quantity, although these concepts seem to depend on particular perceptual conditions. For example, preoperational children can distinguish between more and less only on the basis of one variable. They can tell whether there is more water in one glass than in another based only on the height of the water line. They cannot conceive that the width of the glass is a second variable that affects the amount of water in the glass.

Concrete operations.   At this stage of development children are able to handle the abstract relationships among objects. They are able to understand that more than one variable can affect the properties of objects, and that objects can be manipulated without altering their essential properties. This latter process, often termed "conservation," allows children to understand, in concrete terms, mathematical concepts such as the commutative property of addition and multiplication, the principle of identity, and the reversibility of operations.

Although children at this level can manipulate *objects* abstractly, they cannot yet generate and manipulate *verbal ideas* that symbolize the relationships among objects and events. For instance, children at the stage of concrete operations can understand the principle of identity; however, they would be unable to use the principle of identity to manipulate variables in an algebraic equation.

Formal operations.   The greatest degree of abstraction of thought is possible at the formal operations stage. Children at this level of development are able to derive conclusions from hypotheses that are generated verbally. Their thinking is not constrained by the world of objects nor even by the rules that typically govern the relationships among objects in the real world. At this stage, children can speculate about *hypothetical* reality. They can generate logically consistent systems that need not be verified empirically.

Adaptation.   Piaget equates mental development to the biological process of adaptation. Just as all living things behave in ways that allow them to adapt to their surroundings, so thinking beings adjust their methods of thought in ways that allow them to adapt to the symbolic events that they encounter. Structural constraints limit biological adaptation, and the constraints of preexisting modes of thinking (schema) limit conceptual adaptation. According to Piaget, however, cognitive limits can be stretched through a process called "equilibration."

True equilibration can only occur when the mind changes its schema in response to new information. This process is termed, "accommodation." Children move from one stage to the next higher stage through this process. Another way that a child can handle new information is through the process of "assimilation." This process allows the child to fit new information into an existing mental structure.

A simplistic example can help illustrate these two processes. Let's assume that a young child (a girl in this example) has never seen a cat but has had plenty of experiences with dogs. When the child sees a cat for the first time, she is likely to call it a dog (that is, to think of it within the constraints of her existing mental schema). When the child calls the cat, "dog," she is assimilating the cat into her existing schema. If, however, the child distinguishes the cat from her experience of dogs, she may call the cat, "animal" or ask someone else what the strange animal is called. This latter process of accommodation allows the child to derive a new concept based on greater abstraction. In this case, the realization that the cat is not a dog has forced the child to derive the more abstract notion of animal. According to Piaget, such processes are not, however, dependent upon the language used to describe them. In this case, the child's language reveals the underlying mental process even though the mental process is not based on the linguistic act of naming the object.

Piaget and the Gifted

Because it has so often been claimed that gifted children are by nature better at understanding and using concepts and at thinking abstractly, the Piagetian studies that use gifted subjects are of particular interest. Gifted children (e.g., high-IQ children, precocious math and reading students) figure prominently in some of the empirical investigations based on Piaget's theories.

The work of Piaget seems to present theoretical clues for the empirical study of concepts (Carter & Kontos, 1982; Keating, 1980b). A critical task of researchers has been to translate Piaget's largely philosophical insights into a manageable empirical framework. Many of the early investigations of Piaget's hypotheses were flawed attempts at such translation, while others were more limited attempts to validate one or another of Piaget's untested hypotheses. More recently, better empirical studies (e.g., Carter & Ormrod, 1982; Keating, 1975) have begun to appear.

Gifted children and stage attainment. The central tenet of Piaget's view of concept development is the progression of human beings through an invariable sequence of four fundamental stages: sensorimotor, pre-operations, concrete operations, and formal operations. Children must, according to Piaget, progress through each stage in succession.

Given this premise, a question of concern to American researchers has been whether or not early attainment of stages is characteristic of gifted children. The results of the research are not clear, however. Some studies (e.g., Moore, Nelson-Piercy, Abel, & Frye, 1984; Norton, 1980; Smolak, 1982) have yielded weak or insignificant correlations between attainment of the *early* stages and measures of cognitive abilities such as IQ, language production, and reading achievement. By contrast, the association of high IQ with the early attainment of *formal operations* seems to be stronger (Carter & Kontos, 1982; Carter & Ormrod, 1982).

Why should this be the case? A logical answer lies in the approximation of high-level performance on IQ tests to formal operations, as opposed to other stages. Formal operations pertains clearly to many of the symbolic notions of conceptual mathematics (e.g., the properties of equality and of operations) and to facility in the formal study of language and literature. Precocious children acquire these skills early, and they are also likely to perform well on IQ tests. Carter and Kontos (1982) claim to have found that gifted children achieve the stage of formal operations about two years earlier than children with IQs in the average range.

Moot issues. One problem has stymied American researchers for some time. Unless carefully controlled distinctions can be made *within* Piagetian stages, then the association of IQ and stage attainment or acceleration of stage progress cannot be measured with very great accuracy. The inaccuracy results from the fact that children are expected to remain at a particular stage for quite a long period of time (e.g., approximately four years at the concrete operations stage). Piaget himself had begun to investigate the distinctions within each stage late in his life.

According to some critics (e.g., Sullivan, 1967), this sort of study was ill-advised. They claim that, like other philosophical credos, Piaget's doctrines are not subject to strict empirical confirmation. Critics maintain that Piaget should have remained consistent. Since he began his studies in the effort to describe an elusive phenomenon in a theoretical way, he should not have tried to predict the practical applications of his theories. Nevertheless, as his fame grew, Piaget did begin to advise teachers on the practical uses of his ideas.

There is substance to the charge made by critics. Piaget did not expound the details of his theory clearly enough so that they could be investigated empirically. Careful observers have found, for example, that the degree of stage attainment is difficult to measure. It is possible for a child to exhibit some of the characteristics of concrete operations (e.g., conservation of number) but not others (e.g., conservation of weight). Even in the stage of formal operations, some observers have noted that it is possible to have achieved formal operations in mathematics, but not in literature (Carter & Kontos, 1982; Sullivan, 1967). Carter and Ormrod (1982, p. 19) conclude that "available evidence . . . implies that an individual might be a formal thinker in one area but not in another."

How does one judge stage attainment in such a context? Unfortunately, many researchers have chosen to ignore the issue altogether. It is typical for researchers to evaluate stage attainment on the basis of the performance of just one task; and the task used to characterize a particular stage may be difficult (e.g., Brekke, Johnson, Williams, & Morrison, 1976), or it may be easy (e.g., Dimitrovsky & Almy, 1975).

The question of progress *through* a single stage has hardly been investigated because of the lack of definition within stages. A consensus is emerging, however, about the relative difficulty of various conservation skills at the concrete operations stage, but this consensus cannot yet be interpreted to indicate conclusively the existence of an invariable developmental sequence *within* the stage of concrete operations. The issue is even more obscure in the stage of formal operations.

Research also needs to determine whether or not progress in cognitive development is measurably continuous. It is possible that cognitive development occurs so covertly that qualitatively different stages emerge quite suddenly.

A good deal of research remains to be done before the relationship of IQ and Piagetian stage development can be clarified. For the time being, Carter and Ormrod's observation that "progression within the concrete and formal operational stages takes place more quickly for gifted children than for normal children" seems reasonable (Carter & Ormrod, 1982, p. 111). This tentative conclusion, however, is little different from the observation that gifted children learn faster than average children. Perhaps the question, though interesting, does not hold great *practical* significance for gifted education. Its relevance may be more critical to theory (Carter & Kontos, 1982).

Implications for concept development. It is difficult to draw inferences about concept development directly from the *empirical* research based on Piaget's theories. Even to follow the suggestions of proponents of Piaget may be unwise (cf. Sullivan, 1967).

For example, many observers have noted that mathematical logic infuses Piaget's sense of cognitive development. This observation suggests that, if attainment of formal operations can be measured reliably, it might be possible to decide if students should begin the study of algebra at an early age. Students who have not begun to acquire formal operations in the area of mathematics might be counseled to study algebra later. Carter and Ormrod (1982) have devised a test for formal operations in the social sciences. The relevance of this test (or similar tests) to success in algebra has not, however, been investigated.

Piaget and learning style.   There is one trend in gifted education to which Piagetian notions may nonetheless be relevant in a practical way. Roeper (1966, 1978) noted that children in different stages may be expected to think differently from children in other stages. More specifically, it might be possible to think of stage attainment as "learning style." If a teacher of the gifted needs to account for learning style (a requirement in some states), then perhaps the Piagetian scheme is the most instructionally relevant way to proceed.

For example, if a child does not conserve number (i.e., if the child has not attained the most rudimentary sign of concrete operations), there is *some* justification for proceeding to teach basic arithmetic facts using manipulatives rather than drilling with flashcards. The benefits of this kind of decision to children diagnosed as preoperational are, however, largely unknown. Despite these reservations, Piaget's work provides better justification for such an action than some other theories of learning style, and it is more academically germane than some alternatives.

Cautions.   One caution involves the relevance of Piaget's contributions to the study of particular educational practices. Such relevance has not been confirmed empirically. Glass (1983) suggests that an educational practice may be effective simply because a teacher believes it to be effective. (Glass does not, of course, mean that worthless educational practices can be effective.) Therefore, teachers who see a clear link between their methods of teaching, Piagetian notions, and their students' performance, may find it helpful to adopt strategies like those suggested above.

Another caution involves reliable and valid assessment of stage attainment. Most tests that purport to measure stage attainment include only a small number of items (one to five items), and the reliability of such very short tests cannot be determined. Very short tests are by nature more unreliable than longer tests. For longer tests, good reliability is possible to obtain. Carter and Ormrod (1982), for example, report reliabilities in the neighborhood of 0.80 for their 30-item test. Only a few tests of Piagetian stage attainment, however, make the attempt to establish reliability.

Because researchers believe it is possible, for example, to attain formal operations in one domain, but not in another, validity is an even more important unresolved issue than reliability. Reliable tests that are unrepresentative of the domain they intend to sample may yield deceptive results. With a good deal of work a very competent teacher could probably, over the course of several years, develop a reliable and representative test relevant to attainment of formal operations in a particular academic domain (arithmetic, algebra, history, literature). Such an effort would make a worthwhile research project and might be useful instructionally.

SOCIAL AND EMOTIONAL DEVELOPMENT OF GIFTED CHILDREN

Most lists of the social and emotional characteristics of gifted children could serve as compendia of middle-class virtues. Gifted children are typically characterized as friendly and outgoing, independent, self-confident, honest, trustworthy, and possessed of a good sense of humor.

In startling contrast to these ascribed traits are the grave concerns many educators and parents express regarding gifted children's social and emotional well-being. Among the problems predicted for the gifted are (1) difficulties in social interaction due to the differences between gifted children and their chronological age peers (Zaffran & Colangelo, 1979), (2) anxiety because of pressure to excel academically, (D'Heurle, Mellinger, & Haggard, 1959), (3) a tendency to drop out of school (Clark, 1983), (4) delinquency (Seeley, 1984), and (5) suicide (Delisle, 1986).

This section of the chapter presents a brief summary of research on the social and emotional adjustment of gifted children. It also considers possible explanations for educators' and parents' anxiety about gifted children's social and emotional adjustment in the face of the group's apparent normality.

Gifted Children as "Supernormal"

As we discussed earlier, Terman (1925) and his co-workers studied the social and emotional development of gifted children. One reason for this research was to discover how gifted children differ emotionally and socially from other children. Terman (1925) and his co-workers assessed the play and activity interests of gifted children and recorded their performance on tests of emotional stability, honesty, and trustworthiness. Terman's gifted group was described as normal (or better) on virtually every index of social and emotional development. Teachers and parents rated them as more sympathetic, generous, conscientious, and truthful than other children; and their performance on tests measuring emotional stability was above the norm. Far from displaying the physical, social, and emotional problems that might be predicted from Lombroso's (1891) observations and from popular stereotypes, most of the children were healthy, happy, and popular. Most were also high achievers.

Lewis Terman's longitudinal study is by far the most comprehensive study of the social and emotional development of gifted children, and other studies have tended to validate his findings (e.g., Boehm, 1962; Gallagher, 1958; Miller, 1956; Lehman and Erdwins, 1981). Nearly all studies have found that gifted children are, as a group, *at least* as healthy, both socially and emotionally, as other children.

Social interactions. Although the difference between the gifted and a group of nonselected children was small, Terman's subjects played alone somewhat more. They enjoyed activities that require comparatively little social interaction, such as reading, cards, puzzles, checkers, and chess. Because of these interests, about one-third to one-half of the sociability ratings of the gifted children were below the lower quartile of the control group. Nonetheless, the gifted were *more* interested in social activities than the norm, and 84 percent of the gifted *exceeded* the mean of unselected children in social *interest*. The children with whom the gifted preferred to interact socially were their older playmates (Terman, 1925).

Although gifted children are popularly believed to be socially inept, the basis of such beliefs may be a matter of gifted children's different values rather than their ignorance of social conventions. Based on a review of research on social cognition, Shantz (1975) concluded that advanced cognitive development is related to advanced social cognition. Scott and Bryant (1978) found that early readers in kindergarten showed greater social knowledge than did nonreaders. They also found a significant correlation between social knowledge and social behavior for these young readers. The early readers tended to have positive interactions with their peers, even though they interacted more with adults and less with their peers than did the nonreaders. Roedell (1978) also found a positive correlation between intelligence and social knowledge, but *not* between intelligence and social behavior. Apparently very young children, like adults and older children, may be aware of social conventions yet not act in accord with them.

There is no empirical evidence to support the belief that gifted children are socially incompetent. Rather, it seems that they are socially competent but that some gifted children, because of their preference for activities that engage their intellect, avoid social interaction with age-mates. They may prefer the company of older children or adults; or they may prefer solitary activities, such as reading. These preferences do not indicate emotional problems, nor do they appear to have a detrimental effect on gifted children's emotional well-being.

Emotional stability.   Contrary to the predictions of many educators, few empirical studies have found gifted children to be less emotionally healthy than other children. Most studies of gifted children's levels of anxiety, self-concept, and self-confidence indicate that they are, as a group, emotionally healthy (Galluci, 1988).

Feldhusen and Klausmeier (1962) found that the higher a child scored on the WISC, the lower the child's anxiety level. A more recent study, involving a sample of over 500 gifted children ranging in age from six to 19 years, demonstrated lower levels of anxiety among gifted children than other children their age (Scholwinski & Reynolds, 1985). These gifted students were among 5,000 children who completed the Revised Children's Manifest Anxiety Scale (Reynolds & Richmond, 1985), which yields three factors of anxiety: "physiological," "worry/oversensitivity," and "concentration." The high-IQ group scored significantly lower on all three scales.

According to most research, gifted children's concepts of themselves seem to be at least as positive as those of other children. In a study of the effects of aptitude and achievement on the self-perceptions of elementary schoolchildren, Davis and Connell (1985) found the gifted group to score significantly higher on self-evaluations of competence, feelings of mastery, and preference for independent decision making. Colangelo and Pfleger (1979) found that high-school-age students identified as gifted have a higher than average academic self-concept. Tidwell's (1980) study of 1,593 high-school students with a mean IQ score of 137 found these students to have high self-esteem, a positive self-concept, and an internal locus of control. A study comparing bright students' and slow students' willingness to trust their own judgment on an estimation task found that the bright students were less influenced by other children's estimates (Lucito, 1964).

As Davis and Connell (1985) point out, gifted children *ought to* perceive themselves as smart and capable: Most of them have a history of success in academic and extracurricular endeavors. The relatively few studies that have found gifted students to be more anxious (D'Heurle et al., 1959), to have poorer self-concepts (Freeman, 1979), or to be less well adjusted (Cornell, 1984) than other children, have been based on atypical samples. Most of these studies evaluated the self-concepts of bright underachievers or gifted students whose parents sought help because of their children's' behavioral or emotional problems. Considering their difficulties, it would be surprising if such students were found to be less troubled than average students.

From Terman's earliest studies through studies conducted more recently, gifted children have met or exceeded the norm on measures of emotional stability. These findings do not imply that gifted children are immune to emotional problems, but they do indicate that the gifted are no more at risk for serious emotional problems than are other children.

Gifted Children as Deviant

Because children are identified as gifted by virtue of their precocious intellectual development, they are by definition a deviant group. We have seen that this deviance seems to cause no serious damage to their social and emotional well-being; however, this does not mean that it has no effect at all.

Giftedness brings with it disadvantages as well as advantages that can be understood in terms of harmonies and conflicts between the values of society at large and those of gifted children and their families. Most identified gifted children are members of middle- and upper-class families that subscribe to the dominant beliefs of the larger society. However, the families of gifted students value intellectual activities more than most. There are more books in their homes, and the parents are more involved in the children's schooling (Terfertiller, 1986). Most high-achieving children come from families that are more cohesive and supportive than other families (Cornell, 1984). These characteristics contribute to gifted children's superior achievement and socioemotional health. However, they also contribute to conflicts between gifted students and their teachers or classmates.

Effects of deviance.   Many adults fail to recognize how deviant gifted children's abilities are. For example, a teacher may assert that the first grader who reads books written for fifth-grade children is reading with little comprehension (indulging in a profuse display of "word calling").

According to Cornell (1984), some adults idealize gifted children and credit them with every human virtue, whereas others resent them. Gifted children are sometimes accused of intellectual pretensions, and their parents are accused of pushing them too hard. The fact that some gifted children feel ambivalent about their deviance is not necessarily symptomatic of emotional difficulties. Their feelings may reflect society's ambivalence toward their talents. The active support of their families usually helps them to maintain their social and emotional stability in the face of others' fear and resentment.

Socialized to use their superiority to best advantage, gifted students nevertheless get into difficulty if they fail to behave diplomatically (Janos, Fung & Robinson, 1985; cf. Hollingworth, 1942, on "suffering fools gladly"). Gifted children are treated with hostility if they themselves acknowledge the difference between their abilities and those of other children. Generally, gifted children seem to heed the messages of others. In fact, Terman (1925) considered gifted children's tendency to *understate* their abilities as a sign of superior character.

The modesty demanded of gifted children is, in part, due to society's discomfort with the apparently unearned advantages of giftedness. The term "gifted" reflects the belief that superior ability is gratuitous (Cornell, 1984). Some teachers and classmates look for weaknesses in gifted children in an effort to satisfy a sense of justice. They may be offended by the notion that the gifted excel by dint of good fortune rather than hard work.

Thus, at the same time that they admire gifted children's abilities, teachers and classmates may resent the ease with which gifted children master material that is difficult for others. When enrichment programs are simply entertaining rather than academically challenging, as they sometimes are (Renzulli, 1977), they fuel this resentment. Such programs offer gifted students privileges rather than appropriate academic work (cf. Cox et al., 1985).

Emotional Problems, Real and Imagined

There are several reasons for the unusual concern over gifted children's emotional welfare. One is that adults who identify closely with gifted children attribute to the children some of their own fears and anxieties (Cornell, 1984). Another is the belief that though these children are not necessarily in greater jeopardy than others, society's *loss* is greater if they are emotionally or socially aberrant (Gallagher, 1985). Another reason for unusual concern is the belief that gifted individuals match the stereotype of the oversensitive, unbalanced genius. Though contradicted by Terman's research, the stereotype persists because of anecdotes and case studies of famous persons who have experienced severe emotional problems.

These perceptions result in unwarranted support for counseling and affective education programs for a group that is comparatively healthy. Nonetheless, there are few serious problems peculiar to gifted students and few gifted students with severe social or emotional problems. Teachers need to distinguish between real and imagined emotional and social problems of gifted students.

Real Problems of Gifted Children

The problems of gifted children, as we pointed out earlier, often result from differences in values. In a society whose priorities inhibit gifted children's intellectual development, such problems are inevitable. Unfortunately, these problems are ascribed too often to the child's "oversensitivity" or to the child's "poor interpersonal relationships."

Some of these problems are created by parents who, while demanding superior achievement, do not offer the support needed to help their children meet high standards. Other problems are created by teachers who assign busywork to gifted children. Conflicts among peers may occur when gifted students realize that many of their classmates value sports and fashion more highly than intellectual activities (cf. Coleman, 1961; Tannenbaum, 1962).

Peer relationships. Many gifted children feel different from other children, and some find it hard to establish friendships (Janos, Marwood, & Robinson, 1985). This is particularly true, as it is for most children, during adolescence. Society's ambivalence toward intellectual ability is reflected in the ambivalent statements gifted children make about their relationships with others. These statements can be angry and self-congratulatory at the same time:

> It makes you feel like a real outsider when people turn against you just because they find out you're gifted. It makes you feel like a freak.

> Just when you think you may be finding someone who understands what you're all about, you get a teacher who seems to be your worst enemy, just because you know too much! (Erlich, 1982, p.41)

Parents and teachers of gifted students often observe that these students make themselves unpopular by being argumentative or opinionated. Gifted children are probably not oblivious to the effect of their pronouncements, but many of them choose to express their opinions anyway. Although many of Tidwell's (1980) highly gifted secondary school students saw themselves as unpopular, they still described themselves as happy.

Young gifted children may focus on their similarities to other children rather than their differences. Among a group of gifted students ranging in age from five to ten years old, only a little over one-third saw themselves as different (Janos et al., 1985). There was an inverse correlation between feelings of differentness from peers and positive self-concept scores among these gifted children. The authors assumed that the children's giftedness caused the feelings of differentness; but they had no evidence of this relationship: There was no control group to determine the extent to which nongifted children saw themselves as different from others. *All* of the gifted students scored above the mean on a measure of self-concept, however, regardless of whether or not they thought of themselves as different.

Nevertheless, some gifted children may have difficulty finding friends because, though they prefer older playmates, older children do not always welcome their advances. The higher the IQ, the greater the difficulty may be. *Highly gifted* children are unlikely to find age-mate friends with similar interests (Hollingworth, 1942; Roedell et al., 1980).

The problem of finding friends is an important one, but it is a problem of the type that all children face in one form or another. The problem is usually resolved, often with support from the family, and is seldom associated with serious emotional maladjustment.

Oversensitiveness. The belief that gifted children are more sensitive than other children—even oversensitive—probably stems from both anecdotal reports and research on gifted *adults*. There is some evidence that highly intelligent, creative adults are more sensitive than other adults. MacKinnon (1962/1981), for example, found some authors to be unusually aware of their own feelings. These exceptionally creative authors (who were also highly intelligent—IQ 140 and above) seemed to be more aware of or more susceptible to feelings of despair, more excited by abstract ideas, and more subject to bad dreams than other authors in the study.

Freeman (1983) notes that oversensitiveness informs the work of creative adults, but that it makes life difficult for gifted children. There is, however, little research on *children's* sensitiveness as it correlates with intelligence and none sufficient to substantiate the claim that gifted children are oversensitive. In fact, as mentioned earlier, at least one study has found gifted children *less* likely to be oversensitive than others (Scholwinski & Reynolds, 1985).

Incidence of Severe Social and Emotional Problems

In general, there is a lower incidence of severe social and emotional problems among the gifted than among the nongifted population. This lower incidence is not necessarily a correlate of high intelligence. It is more likely to be a correlate of the higher socioeconomic status enjoyed by the majority of individuals *identified* as gifted.

Delinquency. According to Ehrlich (1982, p. 41), "When we speak about problems related to giftedness, we must realize that the gifted are generally a law-abiding, conforming group that contributes comparatively few offenders to the social order." When a high IQ score is the criterion for giftedness, the incidence of delinquency among gifted adolescents is very low (less than 5 percent). Those gifted children who *are* delinquent are usually from very poor homes. According to Seeley (1984), bright delinquents are even more likely than other delinquents to come from single-parent families, and they are more likely to be runaways. By comparison with other delinquent girls, those with IQ scores between 114 and 149 are more likely to be illegitimate, adopted, or separated from their mothers (Seeley, 1984).

According to Seeley (1984), many kinds of ability are represented in the delinquent population: academic ability, psychomotor ability, and artistic ability. However, delinquent students' abilities are usually unrecognized by the school system. Gifted delinquents are often severe underachievers who are more highly able in nonverbal than in verbal skills. Anolik (1979) found that gifted male delinquents were underachievers and likely to be classified as mildly disturbed. Nevertheless, they were slightly less neurotic and psychopathic than other male delinquents.

Mental disturbance. Most studies of mildly and moderately disturbed children have found their average IQ score to be in the low normal range. However, the range of scores extends from retarded to gifted with *relatively few* disturbed children in the upper IQ ranges (Kauffman, 1985). In the severely and profoundly disturbed population, there appear to be even fewer children with high IQ scores, theories linking genius and schizophrenia notwithstanding. "The highly intelligent, academically competent schizophrenic child is a rarity. . ." (Kauffman, 1977, p. 122). When compared with other adults, a smaller proportion of Terman's gifted group was hospitalized for mental disturbance (Terman & Oden, 1947).

Suicide.   It is popularly believed that gifted children are more likely to commit suicide than other children. There is, however, no empirical support for this belief. Studies of Terman's gifted sample found the incidence of suicide among them to be virtually the same as among the general population: For men the incidence was slightly lower, for women slightly higher (Terman & Oden, 1947). By the time *The Gifted Child Grows Up* (Terman & Oden, 1947) was written, five male and two female subjects had committed suicide. By 1970, twenty-eight of Terman's gifted adults had killed themselves (Shneidman, 1981).

Shneidman's (1981) analysis of Terman's data on a group of men who had committed suicide found some characteristics typical of this group. These men were more likely than other gifted men to have been rejected by their fathers, to have been disturbed as adolescents, to have been married several times, and to have been alcoholic. These men were more likely to have been disappointed in themselves, unstable, lonely, perturbed, and impulsive. There was, in some cases, a wide disparity between these men's aspirations and their accomplishments. A comment included in the file of one of these men is illustrative: "My gifts, if there were any, seem to have been a flash in the pan" (p. 261). This disparity is not always the case, however. At least three of the 20 men who committed suicide were considered outstandingly successful.

Other studies of suicide among intellectually superior males (Blachly, Disher, & Roduner, 1968; Paffenbarger & Asnes, 1966) have also found some common themes: early rejection by or death of the father, impaired health, depression, and moodiness. Characteristics such as these may, however, be typical of all individuals who commit suicide (see e.g., Kauffman, 1985).

SUMMARY

This chapter reviewed the literature on the typical development of gifted children. It contrasted popular views of the gifted with empirical findings in an effort to distinguish realistic perspectives of gifted individuals from stereotypes.

In its review of research on the language development of gifted children, the chapter showed that talking early bears little *predictive* relationship to verbal talent. Nonetheless, there is evidence that children who have been continually engaged verbally by their parents perform better on cognitive tests. Early reading was found to be more common among the gifted than among other students, though by no means universal. In particular it seems that precocious reading ability may depend more on excellent decoding skills than on high IQ.

The chapter found the issue of concept development among the gifted to be somewhat problematic due to methodological problems. The most prominent investigator of concept development, Piaget, did not use methods inherently compatible with the study of gifted children. Nonetheless, other researchers have used Piaget's theories to study gifted children. Often, but not always, these researchers have found gifted children to perform somewhat better than average students on measures of stage attainment. Caution in applying the principles of Piaget was advised.

The chapter concluded with a look at recent work on the social and emotional development of gifted children. Although gifted children may have some different problems from other children (for example, problems finding peers with similar interests), these problems are usually counteracted by the influence or intervention of supportive homes. When serious problems do occur among the gifted, the causes appear to be similar to those associated with maladjustment in other children. The presence of exceptional intelligence does not seem to contribute to these severe problems. The intellectual superiority of gifted children may, in fact, relieve them of some of the anxieties faced by other children.

Precocious Development

Focusing Questions

1.   Why must researchers rely primarily on case studies to examine the characteristics of extremely precocious children?
2.   In what ways have the parents of prodigies, such as John Stuart Mill, Michael Grost, and Terence Tao, been influential in guiding their children's education?
3.   What cognitive and affective characteristics are associated with extreme mathematical precocity?
4.   How do the families of musical, athletic, and literary prodigies support the development of their children's talents?
5.   What relationships appear to exist between intelligence and specialized skills such as eidetic imagery, rapid arithmetic calculation, and expert chess playing?

EXTREME PRECOCITY

Extremely precocious children are as different from typical gifted children as typical gifted children are from the average. Sometimes that difference intellectual giftedness is usually associated with IQ scores that are at least four standard deviations above the mean. The incidence of such high scores is about 3 in 100,000.

Nevertheless, extreme precocity is quite rare. For example, extreme intellectual giftedness is usually associated with IQ scores that are at four standard deviations above the mean. The incidence of such high scores is about 3 in 100,000.

Influences of Precocity

In the popular imagination, child prodigies are freaks of nature, children whose innate abilities set them apart from others. Prodigious development, however, may not relate to innate factors. Some authorities attribute prodigious development to social factors, others to the demands of different disciplines. The fact that more child prodigies have been identified in certain disciplines can be interpreted in either of these ways. Some writers, however, attribute prodigious development to a complex interaction of personal and social influences (see e.g., Feldman, 1979).

Social influences.   The role that society plays in children's prodigious development is not easily determined, and several different views have been put forth. The same social variables that affect the achievement of other individuals seem to influence prodigious development: social class, race, sex-roles, ethnicity, and birth order. The majority of prodigies are boys, usually the first-born or only sons in middle-class families (MacLeish, 1984). Even geographic location can affect the development of precocious talents. Fifty percent of the chess prodigies in the United States come from three metropolitan areas that contain about 10 percent of the U.S. population: New York, San Francisco, and Los Angeles (Gardner, 1982).

Pressey (1955) relates the different numbers of prodigies to the values society places on different disciplines. According to Pressey (1955), financially rewarding disciplines, such as professional athletics, are more likely to produce prodigies than less rewarding ones, such as painting.

Simonton (1984) suggests, however, that social rewards may actually inhibit the later productivity of child prodigies. Once an individual has reached a goal, his or her motivation may lessen; and acclaim may bring social obligations that are time-consuming.

The nature of various disciplines.   More prodigies have been identified in music and mathematics than in other academic or artistic fields (MacLeish, 1984). Some theorists see this difference as a function of the discipline. According to Page (1976), certain disciplines depend more on manipulation of symbols than on access to a large amount of knowledge; these disciplines are the ones in which prodigies can infer much from a relatively small set of examples. Disciplines, like history, that depend on accumulation and analysis of a great deal of knowledge may require years of study. This reasoning suggests that the more a work depends on the use of factual information, the longer it takes to accomplish.

In general, the peak period of the careers of eminent persons seems to be between the ages of 30 and 40 (Simonton, 1984). This early peak may depend on prodigious development in childhood (Gardner, 1982). Different disciplines have slightly different curves. In history and some other scholarly fields, the peak productive age is late, in the sixties. For poetry, music, and drama, the peak is in the thirties or forties. The peak period of scientists is earlier still. According to Simonton (1984, p. 99), "Scientific geniuses of the highest historical order tend to begin their careers at unusually early ages."

Problems of Description and Research

There are very few studies of highly gifted children or prodigies because there are very few prodigies. Finding a large number of prodigies for study is difficult, and using parametric statistics in research with small sample sizes is inconclusive. Therefore, educators should be cautious in applying evidence from the studies that are available. Foster (1986) supports certain uses of single-subject research, however. This type of research is descriptive and is useful to illustrate some similarities and differences among the highly gifted.

Unfortunately, much of the literature about precocious children is inaccurate and reflects common stereotypes of giftedness. Some of the literature claims that such children have serious failings that counterbalance their exceptional intellectual or artistic development. Usually, this literature claims that extremely precocious children are eccentric, unbalanced, or overly specialized. A comment about William Sidis exemplifies this type of reasoning. "He was brilliant at mathematics, but in all other subjects he was childishly ignorant. . ." (Huxley as quoted in Wallace, 1986, p. 118). This statement conflicts with biographical information about Sidis. According to Wallace (1986), for example, Sidis was so intelligent *in all areas* that he qualified to enter Harvard at nine years of age.

Study of mathematically precocious youth. Since the early 1970s, researchers at the Johns Hopkins University have been identifying and studying brilliant young mathematicians (Stanley, 1976a). Because this project entails an extensive talent search, it is able to locate relatively large numbers of such students. Consequently, the findings from the SMPY research are more broadly applicable than findings from case studies.

CHILDREN WITH VERY HIGH IQS

A number of researchers have investigated the characteristics of children with extremely high IQs. Hollingworth (1942) assembled case studies of children with IQ's of 180 and above. Terman compared a group of very high IQ children with the other gifted children in his sample (Terman & Oden, 1947), and Jenkins (1943) collected biographical information about black children with IQs above 160. Hollingworth's (1942) investigation of highly intelligent children is the most comprehensive of these studies.

Hollingworth's Research

Hollingworth (1942) followed the progress of twelve highly gifted children from early childhood through young adulthood. The following examples of behavior characterize the children in this study.

Child A.   This precocious child began to talk at 10 months of age. He could say the alphabet forward at age 12 months and could say the alphabet backwards at age 16 months. Child A began to read at three years of age and was reading fluently by the time he entered school. He was also talented in music and in rapid arithmetic calculation. When he was six years old, Child A scored a mental age of 12 years 2 months on the Stanford-Binet Intelligence Scale. In spite of his high ability, he did not earn exceptionally good grades, and his teachers were not very impressed by his talents.

Child D.   Like child A, this child also learned to read long before school age. In his preschool years, Child D amused himself by constructing a language, history, and literature for an imaginary culture. Throughout early childhood, he enjoyed composing music and was talented at playing the piano. By the age of 12 years, Child D had completed college entrance requirements in algebra, geometry, and trigonometry. He was admitted to college at the age of 12 years 6 months; he graduated with Phi Beta Kappa honors at the age of 16 years.

Child E.   By the time he was 8 years old, Child E was able to speak and understand simple sentences in four or five languages. At this age, his knowledge of English vocabulary was equal to that of an average adult. When he was 10, Child E began to do original historical research in the classics. He continued this activity throughout the remainder of his years in school.

Common characteristics.   The children that Hollingworth studied had a lot in common. They read before they entered school; and with few exceptions they achieved well in school. Most attended college early and many graduated with honors. These children had intellectual and artistic interests that persisted throughout their school careers.

Other biographical and autobiographical records confirm these generalizations (see Box 9-1). Many eminent individuals, however, lived before IQ tests were used. Biographers sometimes estimated their IQs from information about their developmental histories (see e.g., Cox, 1926). The validity of this practice is questionable. Nevertheless, biographies of children whose high-IQs are known (see e.g., Grost, 1970) also confirm Hollingworth's findings.

BOX 9-1   Prodigies and Their Education

JOHN STUART MILL

The degree to which Mill's exceptional achievement resulted from innate talents or from the extraordinary education he received from his father is unknown. Nevertheless, Mill accomplished prodigious feats at extremely early ages. By the age of eight, for example, he had read, in the original Greek, all of Herodotus, part of Lucian, and several of Plato's dialogs.

James Mill's educational methods, though apparently highly effective, were controversial during his time. They continue to be a subject of controversy today. Kelly (1985), for example, alternately lauds James Mill for effectively developing his son's intellect and blames him for harming his son's social and emotional development. At one point, she goes so far as to suggest that, had he been living in our times, James Mill might have been jailed for child abuse.

The principal characteristics of John Stuart Mill's schooling were as follows:

- one-to-one instruction at home under his father's tuition,
- early schooling in the classics,
- extensive reading and discussion,
- emphasis on critical thinking in the context of academic disciplines,
- exceptionally high standards for intellectual achievement.

MICHAEL GROST

Michael Grost is among the more recently acclaimed prodigies. His IQ score has been estimated to be over 200. Audrey Grost's *Genius In Residence* describes her son's schooling. After many efforts to obtain an appropriate education for Michael in the public schools, his parents took him out of elementary school and enrolled him in college. He was ten years old. This measure was not so drastic as it seems. It was preceded by his having taken several college courses on a part-time basis and earning an "A" average ("Where Are They Now?" 1969). During his years as an undergraduate, Grost won several awards and fellowships despite being much younger than the other competitors. By the time he was 16 he was enrolled in a doctoral program at a major Ivy League university.

TERENCE TAO

Terence Tao received his education in Australia. His exceptional mathematical giftedness was recognized at a very early age: He was the first eight-year-old to score 760 on the SAT-M. This score placed him in the 99th percentile for high-school juniors and seniors. Although Terence entered school at the usual age, his father soon saw the need for him to receive special instructional provisions. At the age of 6 and a half, Terry was receiving instruction in the third, fourth, sixth, and seventh grades. When he was 8 and a half, Terry began high school full time. There, too, he was placed in different grade levels for different subjects: Grade 12 for physics, Grade 11 for chemistry, Grade 10 for geography, and Grade 8 for general studies and homeroom. At the age of 9, Terry began taking some university courses in physics and mathematics. His father plans for him to continue in a dual placement until he is at least in his early teens. (For more information, see Tao, 1986.)

EXTREME MATHEMATICAL PRECOCITY

Since 1971, researchers at the Johns Hopkins University have been studying mathematically precocious youth. Their research considers the cognitive and affective characteristics of these highly talented students, and it traces their longterm progress. In addition, by testing tens of thousands of able students every year, SMPY is able to locate relatively large numbers of very talented young mathematicians.

Study of Mathematically Precocious Youth

The researchers at Johns Hopkins have been interested in studying *mathematically precocious* students, in contrast to students with *aptitude* for mathematics who do not manifest their talents at early ages. According to Keating (1976b, p. 24), "Precocity . . . means arriving at some stage of development earlier than expected, such that the individual's current state of development is more like that of someone much older." Quantitative aptitude, on the other hand, may entail sophisticated abstract reasoning without rapid learning (Stanley, 1976b). Precocity in mathematics involves *early* aptitude and interest in mathematics, but it does not *necessarily* predict later prodigious achievement in mathematics or science (Keating, 1974). On the other hand, some creative mathematicians and scientists do not demonstrate precocious achievement early in life.

Cognitive characteristics. The most significant cognitive characteristic of mathematically precocious youth is their rate of learning. According to Stanley (1976b), this characteristic is related to verbal aptitude. Hence, most students who demonstrate mathematical precocity also have superior scores on tests of verbal intelligence. High abstract reasoning scores on nonverbal intelligence tests, such as Raven's Progressive Matrices, are not as successful in predicting learning rate.

In general, results from SMPY suggest that precocity in mathematics is associated with superior academic achievement. Students who show early talent in mathematics seem to maintain their advantage over other students. Even among the group of talented young mathematicians, the trend seems to hold: The most talented maintain their advantage over the less talented.

A number of studies have compared the academic performance of mathematically precocious students with average and above-average peers. In a follow-up study of talent search winners, Benbow (1983) found that these students did significantly better than other college-bound students on measures of academic achievement: Their eleventh- and twelfth-grade SAT scores were higher, they took more science and mathematics classes, their grades were better, they entered college earlier, and they attended more academically challenging colleges.

A study comparing the most talented with the less talented SMPY students (Benbow, Perkins, & Stanley, 1983) showed that the most talented group outperformed the less talented on a high-school administration of the SAT. The most talented students in the SMPY group also took more science and mathematics courses than their less talented counterparts; they performed better on the CEEB mathematics achievement tests; they scored higher on the National Merit Scholarship Exam (the PSAT); they participated in more mathematics and science contests; they chose accelerative options more frequently; and they were more likely to choose a college major in a mathematics or science field.

Affective characteristics.   Haier and Denham (1976) evaluated the nonintellectual characteristics of 71 mathematically precocious students. Their research confirmed the findings of an earlier study (Weiss, Haier, & Keating, 1974). By administering several standardized tests of affective performance to the students, the researchers were able to compare the mathematically gifted students to average peers and to adults. The tests administered were the California Psychological Inventory, the Eysenck Personality Inventory, the Study of Values, Holland's Vocational Preference Inventory, and the Adjective Checklist. The results of the study enabled the researchers to conclude, "As a group these mathematically precocious youth are interpersonally effective and socially mature . . . Both boys and girls are confident and well-adjusted . . ." (Haier & Denham, 1976, p. 239).

The California Psychological Inventory (CPI) provided a measure of the interpersonal effectiveness of the mathematically gifted students. These students were compared with age-mates, both gifted and nongifted, and with high-school students, both gifted and nongifted. Their scores were most similar to the other groups of gifted students and least similar to the group of nongifted age-mates. The findings suggest that the mathematically precocious students were capable of mature social interactions. This research also found that the mathematically gifted students used their intelligence in innovative ways to improve their adaptation to environmental conditions.

In spite of their demonstrated social ability, the mathematically gifted students were classified as introverted on the Eysenck Personality Inventory (EPI). The following adjectives characterize introversion on the EPI: "introspective, serious, planning, fond of books, and reserved except with friends" (Haier & Denhan, 1976, p. 234). It seems that although these gifted students were able to interact with others, they preferred solitary intellectual pursuits. Results from the Study of Values support this finding. The mathematically gifted students demonstrated a strong orientation toward theoretical values. Their high regard for knowledge and truth fit in with their preference for independent, scholarly activities.

Similar responses were recorded on Holland's Vocational Preference Inventory. More than half of the mathematically gifted students favored investigative occupations over artistic, realistic, enterprising, conventional, or social occupations. According to Holland (1973), vocational preferences reflect personality types. The mathematically gifted students most resembled the investigative personality type, which is characterized by scholarship, intellect, self-confidence, independence, caution, precision, introversion, reservation, and rationality.

On the Adjective Checklist, the mathematically gifted students selected adjectives to describe themselves. Their selections tended to include more unfavorable adjectives than favorable ones, a finding that might indicate that the students had inadequate images of themselves. An analysis of the specific adjectives that were most often selected, however, suggests that the students may have been realistic in their self-appraisal. They most often selected the following positive adjectives to describe themselves: intelligent, capable, adaptable, logical, honest, and clear-thinking. They tended to choose the following negative adjectives: argumentative, sarcastic, impatient, opinionated, and cynical. These negative adjectives are relatively mild in comparison to some of the others that the students might have selected, and they tend to reflect the frustrations that are associated with giftedness. According to Haier and Denham (1976, pp. 238–239), the selection of these negative adjectives "may indicate the degree to which [the students] are bored or dissatisfied with conventional school curricula."

Sex differences.   In Chapter 6 we discussed the fact that boys get higher scores than girls on tests of mathematical aptitude. Among highly gifted young mathematicians, the trend is even more obvious (Fox, 1976b). When they used a criterion score of 600 on the SAT-M to identify mathematically precocious students in junior high schools, researchers found that many more boys than girls qualified. In a sample of 396 students who took the SAT-M, 22 percent of the boys and only 2 percent of the girls obtained scores of at least 600. According to Astin (1974), none of the girls scored above 600. Nineteen percent of the boys, however, scored above 600, and one scored as high as 790. Weiner and Robinson (1986) obtained similar results. They reported the ratio of boys to girls scoring at or above 600 on the SAT-M as 2.8 to 1. In the 1980 to 1983 study of junior high-school students with scores between 700 and 800, 269 (92 percent) boys were identified as compared with 23 (8 percent) girls (Stanley, 1985).

The discrepancies between the performance of boys and girls also become more pronounced as the students get older. In a test-retest study of scores on the SAT-M in seventh and eighth grade administrations, boys gained an average of 66 points and girls gained an average of 56 points (Astin, 1974). Similar differences occurred in the mathematics achievement test scores of boys and girls.

Weiner and Robinson (1986) reported that the mathematics achievement of the students in their study was predicted better by the SAT-M for boys and by the SAT-V for girls. This finding suggests that talented boys and girls may use different cognitive strategies to learn math.

These researchers found similarities in the affective characteristics of mathematically talented boys and girls. Astin's (1974) study, however, revealed some differences in their career interests, their liking for school, the ages at which they first became interested in mathematics, and their position in the family. She also noted similarities in the students' socioeconomic background, their mothers' level of achievement motivation, and their personality characteristics (Astin, 1974).

Fox (1976b) discussed the significant differences between boys' and girls' early involvement with mathematics. Even among precocious young mathematicians, boys reported more often than girls that they engaged in mathematics activities outside of school. According to Fox (1976b, p. 185), "very few girls study mathematics independently in a systematic way, nor do many girls frequently read mathematical books or play with mathematical puzzles and games in their leisure time."

Creative behavior. Studies of the creative potential and behavior of mathematically precocious students are inconclusive (see e.g., Keating, 1976a; Michael, 1983). According to Michael (1983), the results of these studies are confounded by theoretical and methodological difficulties. He noted the following problems with the SMPY research on the creativity of precocious young mathematicians: (1) inability to conceptualize relevant subconstructs of creativity, (2) failure of creativity tests to predict later accomplishment, (3) use of follow-up questions that did not elicit relevant information, (4) unreliability of measures of creativity, (5) comparison of subjects in a restricted range, and (6) violation of statistical assumptions in data analyses.

Values. Using the Allport-Vernon-Lindzey Study of Values (SV), Fox and Denham (1974) assessed the value orientation of 35 of the highest scoring males in the talent search. They measured values on the six scales of the SV: (1) theoretical—valuing intellectual, scientific, and philosophical pursuits; (2) economic—valuing practical and money-making pursuits; (3) aesthetic—valuing grace, symmetry, and artistic pursuits; (4) social—valuing people; (5) political—valuing power; and (6) religious—valuing mystical experiences.

The researchers found that the students scored highest on the theoretical and aesthetic scales. Their scores on the economic, social, and political scales were similar to average scores for high-school males. Their scores on the religious scale were rated as "outstandingly low" (Fox & Denham, 1974, p. 163).

Later research with a larger and less highly talented sample (Fox, 1976c) reported somewhat different results. Boys in this group scored highest on the theoretical and political scales, whereas girls scored highest on the social and political scales. According to Fox (1976c), girls' mean scores on the social, aesthetic, and religious scales were significantly higher than the means for the boys. The boys' mean scores on the theoretical, political, and economic scales were significantly higher than the means for the girls.

Conclusions from this research are tentative. It appears, however, that differences in value orientations may relate to gender and degree of talent (Fox, 1976c).

Vocational interests.   Fox and Denham (1974) studied the occupational interests of seventh- through ninth-grade participants in the talent search. Using the Vocational Preference Inventory, they found that more than half of the boys and more than a third of the girls preferred investigative occupations such as engineer, doctor, and scientist. Girls most often listed "mathematics teacher" as their first choice, whereas boys most often listed "scientist."

When the data were analyzed by age, the researchers found that seventh-grade girls rated artistic vocations most highly. They also rated social occupations more highly than the boys did. This trend was evident in the data for the eighth- and ninth-grade girls as well.

Even though more than 20 percent of the girls chose social occupations, almost none of them selected "homemaker." Instead, they favored careers in teaching and other social service professions. Among the most highly talented girls, however, investigative careers were ranked highest much more often.

A later study using the Strong-Campbell Interest Inventory (Fox, Pasternak, & Peiser, 1976) yielded similar results. The scores of both boys and girls were higher than those of average ability students on the scales that measure interest in investigative careers. Many of the girls in this study also tended to choose artistic and social careers. According to the researchers, "girls scored significantly higher than boys on the following interest scales: domestic arts, art, social service, music/dramatics, teaching, writing, nature, office practice, religious activities, and medical service" (Fox et al., 1976, pp. 247–248). Boys, on the other hand, scored higher than girls on the scales measuring interest in mechanical activities and science (Fox et al., 1976).

Follow-up studies.   The longitudinal studies that have been conducted thus far report the college achievements of the mathematically gifted students. According to Benbow (1983), over 90 percent of the SMPY students were attending college at the time of the first follow-up study. In general they were attending selective four-year colleges. Their majors were most often in the areas of science, mathematics, and engineering. Sixty-one percent of the males and 50 percent of the females were planning to major in these fields.

These students also had high expectations for their future performance. More than 96 percent planned to get at least a bachelor's degree; 37 percent planned to complete a doctorate. These figures should be compared to those for average high-school students, only 51 percent of whom aspire to a bachelor's degree (Benbow, 1983).

Stanley and Benbow (1983) reported the college attainment of some of the students who had the highest SAT-M scores. These students entered college very early and were successful there. One of the students completed a bachelor's of science degree in mathematics at Boise State University one month after he turned 12. Another was pursuing, at 13 years of age, a double major in mathematics and computer science at UCLA.

Other Research

Some agencies have initiated programs similar to those offered through SMPY. The state of Illinois, for example, began a pilot program in 1977 and expanded its identification and special classes in subsequent years (Van Tassel-Baska, 1983). Because these programs are more recent, however, they have not yet accumulated and analyzed sufficient data for comparison with SMPY findings. Other research, more similar to that conducted by Krutetskii (see Chapter 6), has attempted to describe the problem-solving strategies used by highly talented young mathematicians.

Problem-solving strategies.   According to Wagner and Zimmerman (1986, p. 246), highly talented math students use more sophisticated strategies to solve problems than do their less talented peers. Gifted math students seem to be both flexible and competent when attempting complex math tasks. The researchers found that mathematically talented students were adept at the following problem-solving tasks:

1. organizing material,
2. recognizing patterns or rules,
3. changing the representation of the problem and recognizing patterns and rules in the new representation,
4. comprehending very complex structures and working within these structures,
5. reversing processes, and
6. finding (constructing) related problems.

MUSICAL PRECOCITY

The most famous musical prodigies are those who have continued to produce extraordinary music as adults: singers, such as Jenny Lind; jazz musicians, such as Louis Armstrong; and violinists, such as Yehudi Menuhin. Most child prodigies do *not* become eminent composers or performers, however. They are, nonetheless, interesting because of their early manifestation of ability.

Characteristics of Famous Musical Prodigies

Mozart is the most famous of the many composers who were recognized as child prodigies. His abilities exemplify those of other children who became eminent composers. Beethoven, for example began to play original compositions at the age of 12; Mendelssohn, by the time he was 12 years old, had composed a piano sonata, a violin sonata, fugues, motets, and operettas; Paganini wrote his first sonata when he was eight.

Mozart's general musical virtuosity, at seven years old, would have been remarkable in a grown man (Brockway & Weinstock, 1958). His manner of composing suggests that he had an exceptional memory for music: He apparently worked out his compositions mentally before writing them. It is reported that he could write down, note for note, a long piece of music on first hearing (Schonberg, 1970). He also had absolute pitch, which he demonstrated at appearances arranged by his father.

Like Mozart, child composers seem to subscribe to a strong work ethic and possess an unusual love of music. Unlike Mozart, however, most contemporary musical prodigies do not compose. Technical proficiency in music tends to precede creative expression (Bloom & Sosniak, 1981). In the eighteenth and nineteenth centuries, however, the public *expected* that virtuoso performers would also compose. Today, many precocious classical musicians never develop the interest or the capacity to create excellent musical compositions. The modern public expects to hear excellent performances of classical works, and training emphasizes execution rather than composition.

Early identification and instruction.   Parents of prodigies often recognize their childrens' talents and provide special instruction for them. Artur Rubinstein began studying with a master teacher by the age of three; Jascha Heifetz by the age of five (Sward, 1933a). The instruction of prodigies is usually expert and reflects students' rapid rate of learning. It presses them toward increasingly difficult accomplishments (Bloom, 1982; Pressey, 1955). The teachers of musical prodigies are, almost without exception, master teachers who provide models of exceptional skill and dedication (Bloom, 1982).

Practice in the field must begin early and become increasingly intensive in order for outstanding talent to emerge (Bloom, 1982; Bloom & Sosniak, 1981; Sward, 1933a). Studies of prodigies indicate that instruction, practice, and performance take up increasingly more of the prodigies' time, until eventually most of their waking hours are spent in activities related to practice or performance (Bloom, 1982). Students show a marked commitment to the field of their interest (cf. Hollander, 1978). Willingness to work and enjoyment of work are evident (Feldman, 1979).

Another important condition of achievement in music is the premium placed on accomplishment by the children's families. Often the families value music so much that they are willing to make large expenditures of time, energy, and money to further the students' education (Bloom, 1982). Usually such families enjoy and participate actively in the field in which the children excel. Pressey (1955) remarks on the increasing recognition and social stimulation given prodigies by family, friends, and others who share the children's enthusiasm for music. Attention and praise from people who are significant in a person's life are powerful reinforcers for any human behavior; it seems unlikely that attention and praise are without effect on a prodigy's behavior.

Whether because of social rewards, innate qualities, or internalization of family values, prodigies show an amazing willingness to work for long hours, and they take much pleasure in their work. By the time they are adolescents, they spend more time being instructed, practicing, performing, and attending performances than in any other aspects of their lives (Bloom, 1982). At least ten years of devotion to the study of music preceded eminent status in all of the musically talented adults studied by Bloom. According to Tannenbaum (1983), this willingness to direct energy and effort toward accomplishment in an area is a highly significant variable in determining outstanding achievement.

Precocity and eminence.   According to Sward (1933a), many people who attain eminence in music were recognized as talented before their teenage years: Of over 400 adults identified as exceptionally talented in music, 83 percent of the males and 92 percent of the females were identified before they were ten years old. Almost half the group were recognized as talented before they were five years old. Sosniak (1985), however, notes that in the cases she studied, children's exceptional musical talent was not at first evident. Only as the children's talent was nurtured and as it matured, did their parents recognize it as significant.

It is not clear, however, why some child prodigies become excellent adult musicians and others do not. No doubt there are both intra-individual and educational factors involved. In many cases, prodigies do not receive the musical education they need to realize their potential. An extreme instance of this is reported in the historical case of a slave called "Blind Tom," who, when he was five years old, played from memory the musical pieces his slaveowner's daughters were learning. The child could reproduce immediately upon a single hearing, pieces played on the piano. Without any formal training, he also composed music. His owner began exhibiting Tom when he was eight years old. Despite his talent, Tom was denied an education that might have enabled him to integrate this ability with other skills and to become a mature composer (Fisher, 1973).

Sosniak (1985) believes that children who become successful professional pianists receive a great deal of assistance from their families. In her view, musical prodigies and their parents develop together—learning about the musical world together and reinforcing each others' expectations and actions.

Bamberger (1986) has studied the cognitive development of musically gifted children to try to discover individual differences that might explain why some go on to become noted adult performers and others do not. She investigated the possibility that changes in cognition, rather than changes in affect or lack of appropriate education, play a causal role. She contrasts young children's performance with that of adolescents. Young children demonstrate:

> . . . an ability to move their attention freely among the complexity of intersecting musical dimensions [such as pitch, durations, melodic and harmonic functions] that together give unique coherence to even a single moment in a composition . . . But in adolescence, multiple dimensions and their internal representations . . . come apart. . . . In practicing, focus shifts among these now differentiated dimensions. . . . As a result, the functional reciprocity within the network of representations that so characterizes younger performers—and the easy, all-at-once imitation it made possible—no longer works. (Bamberger, 1986, pp. 388–389)

Bamberger (1986) speculates that some children are unable ever to return to a more integrated approach to performance. More research is necessary to confirm her speculations.

Even if children's abilities keep pace with the requirements of musical performance, talented children may nonetheless fail to achieve at the highest levels. Achievement of eminence apparently requires years of continuous effort. Competing interests may encroach on practice time and may diminish the child's interest in music as a career. Some children may find that they are not temperamentally suited to performing even though they love music. In other cases, lack of financial resources may prohibit entry to the competitions and summer camps that contribute to the pursuit of music as a career. Many elements must combine in order for eminence to follow precocity (Albert & Runco, 1986).

Development of virtuosi. Sosniak (1985) conducted a study of 21 prodigious concert pianists under 40 years of age. Each of these musicians had been a finalist in a major international piano competition. Sosniak's study identified similar characteristics in the subjects' homes and training.

The importance of the parents' role is evident. All of the pianists' parents arranged for them to start music lessons early: as young as three, and no later than nine years old. During these first years, the social rewards for their musical performance increased. As the children improved, they were given attention not only from their parents, but from their music teachers, and as they began to give recitals and school performances, from their classmates and others.

About half of the pianists' parents had at least some formal training in music, and most of them valued music and listened to it frequently in the home before their children began lessons. Four sets of parents earned their living as professional symphony orchestra members and by giving music lessons. Five sets of parents were amateur musicians. The subjects reported that music was often played in their homes; some mentioned going to sleep or waking up to music. However, the percentage of musically oriented families among these highly gifted musicians is not necessarily much higher than average. According to Sosniak (1985), a market survey in 1974 found that almost 44 percent of the households polled included an amateur musician; and about 79 percent reported that they listened to records often. Possibly, musicians' families were more involved with the classical tradition.

In most cases, the parents insisted on lessons as part of the child's education; and they insisted on regular practice. They also paid attention to the suitability of the teacher for their child and were quick to change teachers if they felt the teacher did not have a positive influence on the child's musical development.

When the children first started taking lessons, they were required to practice about 45 to 90 minutes a day, on the average, six days a week. Practice time increased to about two to four hours per day. This increased involvement was sometimes required by a new teacher; but sometimes it reflected a student's growing commitment to music, and caused the parents to seek a new teacher. Later, when the children began to study under master teachers, practice time ranged from four to seven hours a day. Practice became a part of these musicians' routine very early in their lives; other activities were organized around their practice sessions. As this practice time increased, the young music students were excused from some household chores because their practice was considered crucial. They were considered "special" in a significant way and, at times, enjoyed privileges and attention that balanced the rigor of their daily routine.

Study with a demanding master teacher was an essential element of the training of each of these pianists. By the time the student began lessons with the master teacher, who was, in all cases, among the best practicing or retired concert pianists, the student was thoroughly committed to music as a career. The master teachers exerted an enormous influence on the students, who were in awe of them. They pushed themselves harder than ever to meet these teachers' high standards. After several years of lessons, the master teacher's role became more and more that of a coach, giving advice and making suggestions rather than giving direct instruction.

The importance of societal influences on these aspiring concert pianists was not studied by Sosniak (1985); however, she notes that there were relatively few female pianists and no blacks in the group. Thirty-five percent of the subjects came from professional families, 45 percent from white-collar families, and 20 percent from blue-collar families.

LITERARY PRECOCITY

Although few writers have been recognized as child prodigies, many wrote brilliantly in their early years. This finding seems to be particularly true of poets; there are, however, some novelists who published in their teens. Nevertheless, many children who write well and are prolific do not continue to produce in later life.

Juvenilia of Famous Authors

Burks, Jensen, and Terman (1930) studied the juvenile works of ten famous authors. They developed a scale for comparing these works to the literature produced by adult authors. According to their ratings, poems written by Byron at the age of 15 were slightly better than the average work appearing in literary magazines such as *Poetry* and *Atlantic Monthly*. A poem written by Coleridge when he was 15 was considered as good as the average work in popular magazines such as *Saturday Evening Post* and *Good Housekeeping*. The methodology of this study is quite naive, and the results should be treated cautiously. The researchers were not literary critics, and the superiority of selected juvenilia does not ensure the superiority of all the juvenilia of a given author. In general, the results of this study do suggest that the childhood work of eminent authors is a lot better than that of average children and adults.

Some authors produced extraordinary works in their teens. Most of Arthur Rimbaud's work was written before he was out of his teens. Percy Bysshe Shelley's "Queen Mab" was published when he was 18, and Mary Shelley started to write *Frankenstein* when she was 18. Other writers who produced significant works at very young ages include Blake, Boccaccio, Byron, Chaucer, Milton, Pope, and Robert Louis Stevenson.

Developmental History of Precocious Authors

The study by Burks, Jensen, and Terman (1930) also reported what was known about the development of the ten famous authors whose juvenilia they evaluated. It described their family backgrounds, their early interests, and their youthful accomplishments.

According to this research, most of the writers came from middle- or upper-class backgrounds. Their parents tended to be well educated and supportive of their children's literary efforts. Robert Browning's father, for example, was reported to have been a collector of books and a strong supporter of his son's literary interests.

Most of the authors displayed early interest in reading and writing. They were well-read at early ages, often in more than one language. They also engaged in other creative endeavors such as drawing and playing musical instruments. Keats, for example, demonstrated an early interest in poetry and nature, and he translated the *Aeneid* into prose during his fifteenth and sixteenth years.

Some of the authors achieved recognition when they were quite young. Keats received many prizes and medals during his school years for academic work and for literary productions. Sometimes the writers' early accomplishments defied social convention. Shelley, for example, was expelled from Eton because he wrote and published an essay on the necessity of atheism.

Child Authors

Another focus of the 1930 study of Burks and his associates was an assessment of the development and work of talented young writers in Terman's (1925) sample of high-IQ students. The investigators rated many of these students' poems as highly as those written by the famous authors at comparable ages. It seems unfortunate that even the best writers in the study typically did not develop their talents in writing. Except for one, they tended to enter other fields and to write only for their own pleasure. One subject, however, did become a published writer of fiction (Terman & Oden, 1947).

Terman and Oden (1947) were distressed by the fact that the girls who demonstrated exceptional literary talent failed to produce significant works in adulthood. Another well-known example of this phenomenon is recorded in stories about Daisy Ashford, a child who wrote a best-selling novel at the age of nine. Her novel, *The Visiters*, sold hundreds of thousands of copies over several decades, yet its young author stopped writing during her teens (MacLeish, 1984).

Although the young writers studied by Burk and his associates (1930) did not become famous in most instances, their backgrounds were very similar to those of the famous writers. Their parents were well educated and affluent, but perhaps they did not have so strong an interest in literary work as the parents of the famous authors. The children showed an early interest in reading, writing, and the arts. They won competitions for their writing and had work published in children's magazines. For example, one of the girls, by the age of 16, had written many lyric poems, a novel, and several short stories and plays.

ATHLETIC PRECOCITY

Since athletic precocity depends on physical, rather than intellectual, development, it seems unlikely that children could surpass adults. However, by the time they are 12 years old, a few children can outperform even professional athletes in some sports, such as gymnastics and tennis. In such sports, where coordination, flexibility, and balance are most important, the differences in size and strength between children and adults do not decide the outcome.

Extreme precocity in athletics seems to require the same devotion to practice as it does in scholarly or artistic disciplines. Children who excel at very young ages have already spent years developing their skill. World-class tennis players whose extreme talent was *not* demonstrated in childhood began to take lessons in the sport sometime between the ages of six and nine (Monsaas, 1985). In contrast, those who *were* nationally recognized by the age of 12 or 13 began lessons even earlier. Some of these young athletes, such as Chris Evert Lloyd, started lessons as early as three years old.

Development of World-Class Tennis Players

Monsaas' (1985) report of a study of 18 world-class tennis players, all under 40 years of age, provides a fairly detailed account of the development of their interest and ability in tennis. Most of the subjects were from middle-class to upper middle-class families. Few of the mothers worked outside the home. Three of these tennis players' fathers were tennis professionals. In about 80 percent of the families, at least one parent played tennis avidly. Nearly all of the subjects spent a large part of their time, even before they began to play tennis, at tennis or country clubs, where they swam and played active games with other children.

Two qualities of the family lives of these subjects struck the researcher as unusual: the closeness of the family and the intensity with which they worked. Part of the intensity seemed to derive from a spirit of competitiveness. Just doing well was often not considered good enough; being the best at what they did seemed to be important. The tennis players reported that they considered themselves and were considered by others to be highly tenacious and competitive.

As they became more skilled in tennis, these young athletes devoted more of their time and energy to practice. Their competitiveness and determination was not so pronounced in their other endeavors as it was in tennis, however. By the time they were ten to 12 years old, they were identified, at least locally, as talented tennis players. Their practice and playing time had increased, and they were on the tennis courts about 20 hours a week or more when weather permitted. At about this time, they typically changed from their beginning coach to a coach who could help them develop their own particular strengths.

The decision to make tennis a career was not usually made until their college years. Most played tennis on college tennis teams and had tennis scholarships. The women players, however, reported that they had difficulty getting scholarships because women's sports were valued less highly than men's sports.

All of the world-class tennis players who were interviewed said that they felt pleased with their careers. They felt that the satisfaction of doing something well was the greatest career benefit; but the tennis players also reported that they liked the chance to travel and to earn money doing something that was satisfying.

Development of Olympic Swimmers

Kalinowski (1985) studied 21 Olympic swimmers. In many ways, these athletes were similar to the tennis players discussed above. They too showed increasing levels of commitment to their sport as they got older. The swimmers first started their involvement with the sport as a recreational activity; later their training became more intense. Like the families of tennis players, the swimmers' families were close-knit and subscribed to a strong work ethic. The swimmers' families, by contrast to those of the tennis players, usually did *not* have an exceptionally strong commitment to their children's chosen sport.

The swimmers' initial experiences with their sport were unstructured, another difference between them and the tennis players. Often their first structured involvement was with a team; of those swimmers interviewed, about half had joined a team by the age of seven. The teams practiced about four hours per week, and often the students did not have individual lessons or coaching during that time. Usually swimmers received formal coaching only after they had demonstrated outstanding ability on a team.

OTHER PRECOCITY

Some early talents are very specialized. These talents are so rare and so specific that their relationship to more generalized abilities has not been determined. Talent in three specialized processes has been well documented: eidetic imagery, rapid mental calculation, and chess playing.

Eidetic Imagery (Photographic Memory)

Many prodigies are reported to have had photographic memories. Poincaré, a famous mathematician of the nineteenth century, could repeat from memory the exact page and line of a quotation from a book after reading it once (Bell, 1965). William Sidis, a highly intelligent prodigy, is said to have had a photographic memory as well as rapid calculating ability.

"Photographic memory," or "eidetic imagery," is defined as vivid visual imagery of things previously seen. Vividness and complexity of detail distinguish eidetic images from other images of remembered visual phenomenon (Stromeyer, 1970). Eidetic imagery reportedly occurs with greater frequency among prodigies and brain-damaged children (Paivio, 1971). Sipola and Hayden (1965), however, found no systematic differences in the intelligence of eidetic and non-eidetic children.

Paivio (1971) proposed that eidetic imagery might be a functional development encouraged by any factor that restricts development of verbal representation; but, as he cautioned, any theoretical interpretation is highly speculative. Although eidetic imagery is often said to disappear with the attainment of literacy, this is not always the case (see e.g., Stromeyer, 1970). The degree to which eidetic imagery contributes to outstanding scholarly or artistic performance is also unclear. Much more research is needed before the relationship between this ability and academic accomplishment can be determined.

Rapid Arithmetic Calculation

Smith's (1983) *The Great Mental Calculators* counters some of the popular claims about this type of prodigy. One such claim is that the ability to do lengthy arithmetic operations very rapidly, without pencil and paper, is as often a characteristic of retarded or brain-damaged children as of gifted children. Another is that this ability usually disappears when the child grows up. Although, like other types of prodigiousness, rapid mental calculation is usually attributed to innate ability, Smith contends that this extraordinary skill is the result of exceptional interest and continual practice.

The difference between the development of this skill among males and females seems to confirm his hypothesis. Far fewer females than males develop skills as rapid mental calculators. Smith sees this difference as a function of social values that fail to provide as much encouragement for those girls whose calculating potential is similar to that of boys.

According to Smith (1983), there is a distinction between auditory and visual calculators. The former are usually precocious. They begin calculating before they begin to read or write. The mathematician, Gauss, began calculating at three; and Ampere between three and five. Visual calculators, on the other hand, usually begin in their teens.

Like most researchers, Smith contends that mental calculating ability does not imply mathematical ability; and there is no reason to think that it is a necessary component of mathematical precocity. However, such an ability is probably useful for creative work in mathematics. Gauss, for example, said that his work was advanced by a memory that allowed him to work with many numbers at the same time (Bell, 1965). Poincaré's mathematics were done in his head and committed to paper only when a problem had been thought through (Bell, 1965). Galois's "peculiar gift of being able to carry on the most difficult mathematical investigations almost entirely in his head" is described in biographies of the mathematician (Bell, 1965, p. 365).

Others who are noted only for their rapid mental calculation might have become extraordinary mathematicians if they had had appropriate educational experiences. Zerah Colburn (see Box 9-2), for example, never was able to use his ability in the context of the disciplined learning of mathematics.

BOX 9-2 Zerah Colburn: Case Study

Zerah Colburn was born in 1804; he was the fifth son of a Vermont farmer. When Zerah was five years old, his father overheard him repeating multiplication tables to himself. When asked to multiply a two-digit number by a two-digit number, Zerah could respond immediately with the correct answer. His father started exhibiting Zerah and continued to do so for ten years. However, Zerah was not given a very good education during that period of time. Zerah was in school for only two or three years, and there is no evidence that he was educated at home.

At eight, Zerah could factor numbers as large as 171,395 and give the possible combinations of numbers that could be multiplied together to get that product. He could multiply five-digit by five-digit numbers, but six-digit by six-digit problems seemed to be out of his range.

Although Scripture's (1891) *Arithmetical Prodigies* describes Colburn as unable to learn much of anything and lacking in ordinary intelligence, Smith (1983) points out that Colburn was, in fact, self-educated and capable in many academic areas. Colburn made calculations related to astronomy, taught modern and classical languages and literature and wrote an autobiography in which he attempted to describe his arithmetic processing. Smith attributes Scripture's claim to snobbery, since Colburn had no scientific and little literary education, Scripture considered him presumptuous in writing about his psychology. Binet also misrepresented Colburn's level of ability. Using only secondary sources, Binet described him as being of mediocre intelligence. Another writer, Jacoby, reported Colburn's first and last names incorrectly and yet said authoritatively that " 'Zerald' did nothing in college, except calculations from memory; he either did not want to, or could not, learn anything" (p. 209).

Colburn's supposed ineptitude may be associated with his family background and social status. His father exploited his abilities, whether for his own aggrandizement or out of ambition for his son. An uneducated man himself, he lacked the means to provide his son with a high quality education. Zerah spent an inordinate amount of time practicing and improving his calculating skill, but no commensurate effort toward the development of more critical academic skills. (abstracted from Smith, 1983)

Chess Playing

According to de Groot (1978), himself a famous chess player, expert chess playing does not primarily depend on rapid thinking. Nor does it depend solely on the knowledge of different kinds of chess moves. Rather it is based primarily on knowledge of and experience with heuristic techniques. This experience is derived from an early devotion to the game.

Although there have been a number of chess prodigies, Bobby Fischer was the youngest of these to become international grand master of chess (Brady, 1973). He learned how to play chess when he was six and was invited to play with members of the Brooklyn (N.Y.) Chess Club when he was about eight years old. Throughout his childhood, Fischer practiced chess incessantly and studied from whatever master chess players he could find. At 14 he won the U.S. chess championship for the first time.

Fischer came from a middle-class family. His father was a biophysicist, and his mother was a schoolteacher and nurse. Both Fischer's mother and his sister provided him with a sense of emotional security and supported his interest in chess. Although Fischer was extremely intelligent, he was not willing to devote time or energy to school subjects. His IQ of over 180 and his temperament reportedly made it hard for him to relate to either his teachers or his peers (Brady, 1973). He was highly competitive in sports as well as in chess; and his determination to win was considered one of the reasons for his success. In order to pay more attention to chess, Fischer dropped out of high school at the age of 16. Nevertheless, he was obviously quite literate. He read widely about chess and eventually wrote articles and a book about the game (see Brady, 1973).

SUMMARY

This chapter examined the development of child prodigies. These highly gifted children, whether identified by virtue of their extremely high IQ scores or their remarkable talent, are able to perform like *gifted* adults. Because there are so few prodigies, there are few research studies that consider their characteristics. This chapter reviewed the research that is available and also presented supporting evidence from biographical sources.

The discussion considered several kinds of prodigies. It examined their childhood characteristics as well as their adult achievements. The chapter looked at case studies and empirical research on (1) children with extremely high IQ scores, (2) mathematical prodigies, (3) musical prodigies, (4) literary prodigies, and (5) world-class athletes. The chapter also considered some types of precocity about which little is known. It reviewed research about the precocious development of specialized skills, such as eidetic imagery, rapid mental calculation, and extraordinary chess playing.

10

Inhibited Development: Underachievement

IV. Handicapped Gifted Children
  A. Measurement Problems
  B. Adult Expectations for the Achievement of Handicapped Children
  C. Gifted Students with Visual Impairments
    1. Visual impairments and intelligence
    2. Giftedness and visual impairments
  D. Gifted Students with Hearing Impairments
    1. Hearing impairments and intelligence
    2. Giftedness and hearing impairments
  E. Gifted Students with Physical Handicaps
    1. Orthopedic impairments and giftedness
    2. Health impairments and giftedness
  F. Gifted Students with Learning Disabilities
    1. Definitions: brief history and research
    2. Discrepancy: brief history and research
    3. Characteristics of gifted children with learning disabilities
  G. Gifted Children with Emotional Problems
    1. Deviance as a measure of emotional imbalance
    2. Characteristics of gifted children with emotional problems
V. Summary

Focusing Questions

1. What characteristics of schools might account for the underachievement of some gifted students?
2. How do the personalities of gifted underachievers differ from the personalities of gifted achievers? In what ways are these personality factors conditioned by children's home environments?
3. In what ways do adult expectations limit the goals and achievements of gifted students with handicaps?
4. What characteristics of gifted underachievers predispose them to being incorrectly classified as learning disabled?
5. What factors limit researchers' efforts to conduct systematic studies of gifted children with serious emotional problems?
6. How do the minor adjustment problems that gifted students sometimes experience differ from serious emotional disturbance?

ETIOLOGY OF UNDERACHIEVEMENT

Sometimes gifted children's achievement falls short of their potential. The level of achievement of such children does not match their high level of ability as measured on IQ tests. Often, this underachievement is reflected in low grades. This type of underachievement, while frustrating for teachers, parents, and the children themselves, does not necessarily indicate a *lack* of achievement. Some bright children who make poor grades may actually score quite high on standardized tests of achievement. Another, more serious, type of underachievement occurs when a gifted child scores significantly below potential on a reliable test of achievement. This type of underachievement sometimes results from a handicapping condition that inhibits the child's development, but, at other times, the reasons for this sort of underachievement are more difficult to determine.

About 20 percent of the students identified as gifted earn grade point averages of 3.0 or lower on grade-level work. This fact is surprising when one considers that gifted students usually score at least two grade levels above grade placement on standardized tests: Gifted kindergarteners score at about the second-grade level, junior high-school students score at the high school and college level, and high-school seniors score at the level of the average college senior (Marland, 1972). A smaller, but still sizable, number of gifted students also score much lower than might be expected on standardized tests of achievement.

There are quite a few hypotheses that attempt to explain the under-achievement of some gifted students. Many of these hypotheses account for the school failure of such students, and others address students' discrepant performances on tests of ability and achievement. The literature on underachievement is often difficult to interpret because researchers define achievement—and hence, underachievement—in various ways.

Many studies, for example, use grades as a measure of achievement (e.g., Dowdall & Colangelo, 1982). Others equate it with performance on group achievement tests. The most rigorous studies tend to characterize it as performance on individually-administered, standardized tests of achievement (e.g., Mather & Udall, 1985). In addition to these measures of achievement, accomplishments (cf. Rimm & Davis, 1980) and vocational attainment have sometimes been used to study the achievement of gifted adults.

Psychological Explanations

Much of the research on underachievement has sought behavioral or attitudinal correlates that distinguish gifted underachievers from gifted achievers. Because gifted underachievers make high scores on tests of intellectual ability, many authors assume that the underachievement of such students has to result from emotional—as opposed to cognitive or school—problems. Psychoanalytic theorists hypothesize that unhealthy interactions between parents and children are the most likely cause. Other psychologists attribute the problem to students' personality problems or to an external locus of control.

The psychoanalytic hypothesis. Psychoanalytic explanations of underachievement view it as a syndrome of conflict within the student that results from unproductive patterns of family interaction. From this perspective, underachievement is often interpreted as a form of rebellion against parental authority by a child who is afraid to show overt hostility.

Psychoanalytic theorists, however, do not seem to agree about the *particular* types of family interaction that result in children's underachievement. Many writers believe that an unhealthy relationship between the mother and child is associated with underachievement, but authorities disagree about the particular nature of this unproductive relationship. Some studies have found mothers of female underachievers to be dominant (Fine, 1967); others have found them to be permissive (Raph, Goldberg, & Passow, 1966). Some theorists believe that underachievers (particularly boys) use poor school performance to enact their hostility toward overprotective mothers, but others interpret overprotective maternal behavior as an indication of the mother's hostility toward the child (e.g., Bricklin & Bricklin, 1967). To make the issue even more complicated, some studies suggest that the problem does not involve the relationship between mother and child at all, but rather involves the relationship between father and child (e.g., Kimball, 1953).

Personality problems.   Psychologists—who do not necessarily accept psychoanalytic explanations of underachievement—have found that underachievement is associated with certain personality traits. Terman and Oden (1947), for example, conducted follow-up studies to find out about the school and work success of their gifted sample. They reported that the men who failed to reach their potential in school or in their careers exhibited similar personality traits. Parents, teachers, and wives who rated the performance of these men noted that the men (1) lacked the ability to persevere, (2) failed to integrate goals, (3) tended to drift rather than take action, and (4) lacked self-confidence. Parents and teachers had made similar observations about the childhood personalities of these individuals, a finding that led the researchers to conclude that the underachieving men had *chronic* personality problems (Terman & Oden, 1947). See Chapter 5 for additional analysis of this research.

Bricklin and Bricklin (1967) identified the following personality traits of underachievers:

- passive aggressiveness—behaviors motivated by the fear of outward displays of anger,
- identification of self-worth with the ability to achieve,
- dislike of being considered "ordinary,"
- fear of success,
- low tolerance for frustration, and the tendency to deal with stress in infantile ways. (pp. 15–16)

External locus of control.   According to some researchers, high and low achievers attribute their success or failure to different factors (Kanoy, Johnson, & Kanoy, 1980). High achievers tend to attribute success to internal factors: ability or effort. They tend to attribute failure to an internal, unstable factor over which they have some control, that is, lack of effort (Bar-Tal, 1978). Because of this way of viewing their own achievement, these students are said to have an *internal* locus of control.

Low achievers, however, tend to attribute success to external factors such as luck or an easy task, but even highly intelligent underachievers often attribute failure to their own lack of ability. These students seem to have an *external* locus of control. As a result, these students deny their competence: They take no credit for their successes and blame their failures on lack of ability. High achievers work more intently and persevere longer at intellectual tasks. They believe that effort makes a difference. Underachievers apparently do not.

Sociological Explanations

Conditions in society may influence gifted children's patterns of achievement and underachievement. Among the most significant of these sociological influences are race, gender, ethnicity, and social class. These factors relate to children's achievement indirectly. They are mediated by factors in the home—parents' education, mother's aspirations, family income and wealth, housing characteristics, and parents' occupation—that have a more direct influence on children's school achievement.

Some cases of underachievement may be accounted for by severe hardship, and a number of studies of underachievement evaluate the effects of such meager environmental support. In such environments, a high degree of economic and emotional insecurity precludes the involvement of parents in their children's educational efforts. This etiology, however, does not account for the underachievement of children from affluent homes in which education appears to be valued.

Sociological variables are such powerful influences on students' achievement that they need to be considered in some detail. Therefore, the discussion of the effects of race, gender, ethnicity, geography, and social class on gifted children's achievement will be reserved for Chapter 11.

Educational Explanations

Except for the family, the school may be the most powerful social institution in modern society. In part, the influence of the school relates to its role as "culture-bearer," a role that empowers the school to convey the most important values of our culture. Teachers often present these values overtly when they state expectations for behavior, but they also teach some values through their covert actions. Teachers' differential treatment of children may convey the degree to which they endorse particular characteristics or behaviors. Although individual teachers may vary in their values, some values appear to be very common among teachers. In addition to conveying these values, the school also perpetuates the values of the peer-group culture that it houses.

Three perspectives on education explain the school's influence on the achievement and underachievement of students: (1) explanations that relate to schools' socializing function, (2) explanations that relate to teachers' expectations, both overt and covert, and (3) explanations that relate to the expectations of the peer group.

Socializing function of school.   Holt (Dulee, 1983) has summarized the socialization functions of schools quite well. He notes three basic socializing functions: (1) custody, (2) ranking, especially as an internalized sense of success or failure, and (3) compliance. These functions have been touched on in various contexts by many educational writers (e.g., Baer & Bushell, 1981; Bloom, 1977; Coleman, 1961; Cremin, 1961; Cuban, 1982; Jencks et al., 1979; Katz, 1971; Kohl, 1967; Raskin, 1972). Through these three functions, schools convey the fundamental values of society. These functions also enable schools to socialize children to adult work roles.

Schools' emphasis on conformity reflects the priority that our society places on affective as opposed to cognitive performance. It also reflects the prevalent anti-intellectualism in our culture. Many classrooms are unstimulating and confining. A study reported by Marland (1972) found that in over half the regular classrooms, students were not just neutral, but were negative and uninterested. Emphasis in most regular classes is on neatness, recall of factual information, and compliance. There is little room for reflection or for divergent thinking and behavior.

Even very young gifted children are dissatisfied with school because of pressures to conform, unfairness of teachers, and an irrelevant, unstimulating curriculum (French & Cardon, 1968). Gifted underachievers from the first, second, and third grades give the following reasons for their discontent: resentment or hostility from teachers and peers, social penalties for nonconformity, lack of opportunities to pursue individual interests, teacher criticism, teacher control, and an unrewarding curriculum (Whitmore, 1980, pp. 192–193). Of these variables, the unrewarding curriculum is the most damaging to gifted children as a group. These children are constrained by educators' expectations of what children of a certain age can learn.

All of the classroom variables listed by these young underachievers are related, however. They are manifestations of the essential problem facing such children: pressure to conform. Personality and attitudinal traits common among gifted underachievers actually make them *more vulnerable* than other bright children to pressures for conformity (Whitmore, 1980). Achievers appear to have the ability to protect themselves from such pressures; they may appear to conform, but nevertheless base their choices on personal values. Underachievers seem less able to tolerate such ambiguity.

Teachers' expectations.   Teachers verbalize many of their expectations for children's behavior. Most often these expectations relate to children's affective rather than cognitive behaviors. According to Baer and Bushell (1981, p. 264):

> . . . recent observational research suggests that teachers invest most of their behavior not in teaching academics but in maintaining order . . . and that teachers prize and acknowledge conformity with these rules more often and more vigorously than they do correct academic problem solutions. . . . The same research suggests that students learn exactly that emphasis from teachers and believe that it is much more important *to follow the rules and be good citizens* than to solve problems correctly. [Baer and Bushell's emphasis]

Nonetheless, teachers' expectations are not always overt. Recent research shows that expectations are conveyed through teachers' actions in the classroom. Usually, these actions reflect social stereotypes. Teachers favor children who are attractive, neatly dressed, middle class, high achieving, and conforming. They respond less positively to children who are culturally different, economically disadvantaged, low achieving, and unattractive. Curiously, teachers also respond negatively to divergent and highly intelligent children. In the classroom, teachers' biases are evident in their reactions to certain children. They call more often on the students whom they like; they give more positive feedback to these students; they seat them in more accessible locations in the classroom; and they provide them with more appropriate work. (See Good & Brophy, 1987, for an excellent summary of the research on teachers' expectations.)

It is clear that stereotypes affect teachers' behavior toward different sorts of students. An example is provided in a study that compares teachers' directives in a working-class school, in a middle-class school, in an affluent school, and in a highly elite school (Anyon, 1980/1987). Similar results are reported in a study by Wilcox (1982).

The teachers in the affluent and highly elite schools encouraged students to internalize academic discipline. The following examples of their verbal messages to students reveal their expectations:

> Decide what you think the best way is.
>
> Don't be afraid to disagree. In the last [math] class, somebody disagreed, and they were right.
>
> Even if you don't know [the answers], if you think logically about it, you can figure it out.
>
> I'm asking you these questions to help you think it through. (Anyon, 1980/1987, pp. 220–223)

These teachers explained the reasons for their actions and required the students to be responsible for their own academic progress.

The teacher in the working-class school, on the other hand, emphasized external control. Her instructions for students' academic work and behavior included the following statements:

> Remember when you do this, it's the same steps over and over again —and that's the way division always is.
>
> Throw your gum away—if you want to rot your teeth, do it on your own time.
>
> Do it this way, or it's wrong. (Anyon, 1980/1987, pp. 214–215)

The differences in teacher directives in Anyon's study reflect differences in the types of adult roles the children are expected to fill. Upper middle-class children are more likely to assume professional roles that entail self-direction. Roles that the working-class children are likely to fill involve much closer supervision. According to Anyon (1980/1987):

> School experience . . . differed qualitatively by social class. Differing curricular, pedagogical, and pupil evaluation practices emphasize different cognitive and behavioral skills in each social setting and thus contribute to the development in the children of certain potential relationships to physical and symbolic capital, to authority, and to the process of work. (p. 225)

Directives to students are one way that teachers convey expectations based on social stereotypes, but grades also reflect teachers' prejudices. Often they are assigned on the basis of students' conformity to behavioral expectations rather than on the basis of academic achievement (Baer & Bushell, 1981; Bloom, 1977; Glidewell Kantor, Smith, & Stringer, 1966; Kubiszyn & Borich, 1984).

Gifted students, who see themselves as disorderly, opinionated, and fault-finding (Pyryt, 1979), are at risk with respect to the expectations held by schools. Some—regardless of their aptitude—will refuse to comply with these expectations and will, therefore, fail to earn good grades. Others will avoid academic work to such a degree that their achievement (on standardized tests) suffers; and still others may never identify with intellectual values at all.

Peer pressures.   In schools, the peer group establishes expectations for behavior. These expectations are as limiting as teachers' expectations. The peer group often includes a number of cliques, the most prestigious of which base membership on the class background, race, and personal characteristics of students. Poor children, minority children, low achievers, and extremely high achievers are often excluded from membership.

Coleman's (1961) study, *Adolescent Society*, characterized the values of high-school peer groups. In his study Coleman identified three status categories—best scholar, best athlete, and most attractive student. Information from Coleman's study allows us to compare the position of attractive individuals, top athletes, and top scholars within the peer-group culture.

Top athletes were generally members of a top clique; top scholars were more frequently not clique members at all. Of the 32 top scholars identified in the study, half the girls and about three-fourths of the boys were not identified as members of any clique. Those who did belong to cliques were found at the fringes of low-status cliques. There were four isolates (i.e., students who had no mutual friends) among the 96 top-status students in the study. Three of the isolates were top scholar girls. Seldom were the top scholar and the top athlete of a class the same person. The combination was equally rare for both sexes. No top scholar, of either sex, was also selected as most attractive, but many top athletes were selected as most attractive.

Considering Coleman's findings, it seems likely that adolescent peer groups actually discourage the scholarly pursuits of some students. Capable students who are not willing to give up their academic interests risk rejection by their classmates. Such powerful influences probably contribute to some gifted students' underachievement, though the nature and degree of their influence might be difficult to discern.

Biophysical Explanations

Sometimes, underachievement results from students' physical, neurological, or emotional problems. Bright children who are handicapped often perform like other gifted underachievers: They may have difficulty getting good grades in regular classrooms. However, unlike some other underachievers, handicapped gifted students may also demonstrate discrepant test performance. Their IQ scores may far exceed their achievement test scores. The low achievement or distorted behavior of these students may bring them to the attention of their teachers.

In some cases, gifted children's handicaps may alter achievement or behavior only enough to mask students' giftedness. Some gifted children use their exceptional ability to compensate for their disabilities. Because their compensation strategies are reasonably successful, such children may appear normal to their teachers. When students compensate for their disabilities in this way, schools are likely to overlook both their giftedness and their handicaps.

There are many blind, deaf, and physically handicapped children who are also gifted. Fortunately, such students are not always underachievers. Sometimes they make successful adaptations that allow them to minimize the disabling effects of their impairments. Special educational services often help them achieve at levels commensurate with their abilities. Nevertheless, in many instances these children do not achieve as well as their intelligence test scores suggest that they should.

Other handicapped children, those referred to as specific learning disabled (SLD) and emotionally disturbed (ED), are characterized by their underachievement. Part of the process of identifying students with these handicaps involves the documentation of their academic underachievement (Cartwright, Cartwright & Ward, 1981; Lewis & Doorlag, 1983). These students, like other handicapped gifted students, often encounter serious difficulties in school. Whitmore (1981, pp. 109–110) considers several of these difficulties, including: expectations based on preconceptions about the handicapping condition, developmental delays that obscure superior performance, and lack of opportunities to demonstrate exceptional mental abilities.

Some writers consider specific learning disabilities and emotional disturbance to be biophysical causes of underachievement (see e.g., Johnson & Myklebust, 1967; Ritvo, 1977). These theorists believe that biochemical and neurological abnormalities account for the learning and behavior problems of such students. Studies of the brain chemistry of schizophrenics and research into the neurological basis of attentional deficits are examples of this approach.

Some theorists, however, do not characterize specific learning disabilities and emotional disturbance among the biophysical causes of underachievement. These writers emphasize the role that school and society play in causing children's learning disabilities and emotional problems (see e.g., Carrier, 1983). According to one authority (Whitmore, 1982), the emotional problems and learning disabilities of gifted children may be caused by social limitations on their ability to progress academically, express emotions, or pursue interests.

CHARACTERISTICS OF GIFTED UNDERACHIEVERS

This section of the chapter reviews the empirical research on the characteristics of gifted underachievers whose difficulties result from a cause that is not biophysical. As indicated in the previous section, different theories attempt to explain this kind of underachievement. Since none of these theories is conclusive, however, our discussion is not based on any single theory. Instead, it examines this kind of underachievement topically, discussing school behavior, personality characteristics, and families.

School Behavior of Underachievers

A number of researchers have assessed the school behaviors of underachieving students. This research suggests that, in general, underachievers dislike school and do not comply with teachers' or parents' expectations for their performance. According to some research, students' patterns of underachievement begin early and get worse as they progress through the grades.

How early does underachievement begin?   Convinced that underachievement results from students' maladaptive responses to problems, Shaw and McCuen (1960) tried to discover when underachievement begins. They selected a sample of students whose IQs placed them in the upper quartile of the population. Based on the students' grade point averages (GPAs) in the ninth, tenth, and eleventh grades, the researchers divided the sample into four groups: male and female achievers and male and female underachievers. Then the researchers reviewed these students' school records to find out how they performed at each grade level.

As a result of their research, Shaw and McCuen (1960) identified distinct patterns in the performance of underachieving males and females. Beginning in the third grade, the grade point averages of the male underachievers were significantly lower than the GPAs of the male achievers. The female underachievers, however, showed a different pattern of performance in the early grades. From the first through the fifth grades, these students actually made *better* grades than the female achievers. When they were in the sixth grade, the achieving females received higher GPAs than the underachieving females for the first time. From the sixth until tenth grade, this difference increased, although it was not statistically significant until the ninth grade.

In spite of the suprising findings for female underachievers, the authors of this study concluded that underachievement was a chronic problem for both sexes. They suggested that both the males and the females entered school with predispositions that kept them from succeeding.

Whitmore's research.   Whitmore (1980, p. 79) described three behavioral syndromes of underachievement: (1) the aggressive, (2) the withdrawn, and (3) the erratic. She compared the students in her group to find out the characteristics most commonly associated with these types of underachievement. She also identified characteristics that were common to all of the gifted underachievers in her sample.

Whitmore (1980) reported that all of the underachievers that she studied had the following characteristics:

- very high IQs—140 or above on either the Stanford-Binet or the WISC-R,
- tendency not to complete assigned school work,
- vast difference in the quality of oral and written work,
- school and test phobia,

- strong interest in one specialty area,
- very low self-esteem,
- sincere belief that they are not liked by others,
- autonomous spirit,
- inability to work well in a group of any size,
- tendency to set goals that are too high,
- dislike of repetitive tasks, and
- failure to respond to typical classroom motivators (e.g., praise or awards).

Less common, but still found frequently, were characteristics such as distractibility, hyperactivity, immaturity, psychomotor inefficiency, lack of academic initiative, chronic inattentiveness, and hypochondria.

According to Whitmore (1980), approximately 75 percent of the underachievers that she studied were of the aggressive type. These students often refused to comply with rules. They were disruptive in the classroom and sought attention in inappropriate ways. These students seemed to lack self-direction and self-control. They attempted to find any opportunity for avoiding assignments. They also had difficulty getting along with peers and tended to be either physically or verbally abusive toward them. Whitmore noted that most of the aggressive underachievers in her group were boys. She related this phenomenon to cultural expectations for boys' behavior.

A smaller proportion of underachievers were withdrawn. They rarely communicated with peers or with the teacher, and they tended to daydream. These students did not work well either in groups or individually. Often, they ignored assignments. When attacked by more aggressive children, the withdrawn underachievers failed to defend themselves.

A few of the students in Whitmore's study vacillated between aggressive and withdrawn behaviors. She labeled these children "erratic." According to Whitmore, students who were classified as erratic were more likely than the other students to have some identifiable biophysical basis for their underachievement.

Underachievement in high school. Identifying underachievement among high-school students is more problematic than identifying underachievement among elementary students. Some high-school students who make adequate grades are actually achieving considerably below their potential. Such discrepancies are difficult to measure, in part because the popular individual achievement tests (e.g., PIAT, Woodcock-Johnson) do not have sufficiently high ceilings for older gifted children.

Another group of high-school students make poor grades in spite of high achievement test scores. These students fail to comply with the noncognitive expectations of school. Their behavior is understandable in light of the fact that the high-school curriculum may be inadequate for them, assignments may be trivial or unchallenging, and teachers may be unresponsive to their needs. Unfortunately, such students suffer in the long run from their lack of attention to school assignments.

Although some of these students can do well as undergraduates, many of them lack the necessary habits of scholarship to succeed in (or enjoy) college classes. Students who behave as if scholarship were not a serious matter, or as if effort were irrelevant to learning, are at risk academically, even if their high-school achievement test scores are not bad.

Personality Characteristics of Underachievers

Much of the research about underachievers considers the personality characteristics of such students. This research should be interpreted cautiously, however. Because of the nature of their school problems, most underachievers experience a great deal of frustration. The behaviors and attitudes that are presumed to characterize underachievers may, in fact, reflect underachievers' high levels of frustration. In more supportive environments, underachievers might show quite different aspects of their personalities.

Passive aggression. The conclusion that underachievement is a means of expressing hostility toward an overly demanding parent recurs throughout the literature on underachievement. An early study of the personality development of underachieving college students described these students' explanations for their academic failure as "unrealistic, superficial, and largely implausible" (Kirk, 1952, p. 214). Kirk viewed underachievers' excuses as an effort to control their hostility; she believed that the academic failure of such students might be an unconscious manifestation of their hostility.

Similar conclusions seem to have been supported by a study of underachievers in high school. Shaw and Grubb (1958) reported that, on three of four personality scales, underachieving males had hostility scores that were significantly higher than those of achieving males. However, the study found no significant difference between the scores of underachieving and achieving females. Because the scale did not relate to hostility toward school, the researchers concluded that the genesis of the problem had to be elsewhere. They determined that the problem was likely to be caused by dynamics in the family.

Another study of high-school students used sentence completion items as a projective test of personality characteristics (Kimball, 1952). This study found that underachievers were less likely than achievers to complete the sentences in ways that suggested the outward display of aggression. Even in situations where aggressive action *would* be appropriate, many of these students failed to give aggressive responses. By contrast, many more of the achievers gave aggressive responses to such items.

Roth and Puri (1967) also used projective techniques to assess the degree of outward aggressiveness exhibited by underachievers. Their study, like the others reported here, concluded that underachievers either turn their hostility inward or repress it rather than expressing it openly. These researchers asked students to respond to a picture of a scene in which aggressive action was required in order to solve a problem. Rather than suggest aggressive action, however, the underachieving students tended to verbalize intrapunitive (inwardly aggressive) action. Their responses were contrasted to those of achievers whose responses favored extrapunitive (outwardly aggressive) action. The responses of some underachievers involved no punitive action at all.

Low self-esteem. Quite a few studies have explored the relationship between self-esteem and achievement. In general, achievers have more positive self-concepts and higher self-esteem than underachievers (Whitmore, 1980). However, it is difficult to tell whether low self-esteem is a cause *or* a result of poor achievement.

A study by Fink (1962) compared psychologists' ratings of achievers with their ratings of underachievers. This study showed that among the boys low achievement was associated with low self-esteem, but this finding did not hold true for the girls. In other studies (e.g., Mitchell, 1959), however, underachieving girls seemed to be more like the boys in Fink's study: They were more self-rejecting than achieving girls.

Although many studies yield similar results, Raph and associates (1966) caution against uncritical acceptance of this research. Studies of self-concept are limited because of confusion in both theory and practice. Theorists conceive of self-concept in different ways; and researchers do not agree on what tests to use in order measure students' self-esteem or self-concept. Related characteristics, such as self-image, self-perception, self-acceptance, and self-confidence are sometimes equated with self-concept. Until there is agreement about the nature of self-concept and its quantification, research results that link underachievement to a negative self-concept should be viewed quite circumspectly.

Attribution of success and failure. Many underachievers attribute their failure to poor teachers, bad luck, lack of ability, or an unstimulating curriculum (Gallagher, 1985). Bright students who do poorly in school seem to feel that they cannot improve their performance because they lack control over the factors that influence academic success.

According to Bar-Tal (1978), high and low achievers differ in the reasons that they give for their successes and failures. This research grouped the reasons that students gave for their success or failure on an academic task into four categories: ability, effort, luck, and task difficulty (Bar-Tal, 1978). High achievers usually attributed their failure to lack of effort, whereas low achievers attributed their failure to lack of ability. Low achievers attributed their *success,* however, to good luck or an easy task. These students denied their own competence and refused any credit for success. Discounting their own agency, they seemed to see themselves as powerless victims of chance.

Davis and Connell (1985) reported different results. These researchers discovered that the underachievers in their sample of 122 gifted and average students ascribed failure to lack of effort, *not* to bad luck or a difficult task. They also reported that the underachieving children were *less* likely than achieving students to credit the influence of teachers on their academic performance. That is, in this study, the underachieving children demonstrated a *greater* internal locus of control than the achieving students.

This is a surprising result. It contradicts the findings of other studies about underachieving students. Perhaps Davis and Connell's results stem from the design of the study, which examined the comparative influence of achievement on a wide variety of self-related constructs. On the other hand, the unexpected results might also be explained by the nature of the sample studied. All the students apparently came from middle-class homes. As noted previously in this chapter, schools cultivate an internal locus of control among middle-class children. It is possible that attribution of success and failure varies by social class, though this hypothesis has not been investigated among gifted students.

Families of Underachieving Gifted Students

Pringle (1970) blamed the home environment for the school difficulties of most underachievers. She noted that in the families of underachievers at least one parent tended to be either too indulgent or too strict (Pringle, 1970). A number of other researchers have reported similar results.

Parental expectations. Too little parental demand for achievement may leave children without incentive to persevere on arduous tasks (Fine, 1967; Pringle, 1970). Too great a demand may bring resistance. The underachievers' negative response to authority is often regarded as rebellion against overly demanding parents. Afraid to express their anger openly, they simply fail to perform, often attributing their poor performance to factors beyond their control, for example, that they are not very bright (Raph et al., 1966).

Some studies suggest that the parents of underachievers set overly high standards for the performance of their children. Similar findings, however, have been reported about the parents of *achievers.* For example, one longitudinal study of bright children claimed that the parents of high achievers were too pressuring (Haggard, 1957). In fact, the high achievers in this study exhibited more resentment toward their parents and other adults than did the underachievers.

Is pressure to achieve harmful to gifted children? The answer depends to a large degree on the sort of support that such children get. In order to live up to their potential, gifted children *must* be expected to perform at advanced levels; but they must also have the instruction and support necessary to accomplish difficult tasks. Children can respond to expectations for high-level performance only if they have the inherent capabilities *and* the environmental support required for high achievement. If they do not, they may become frustrated.

Other family variables. The discipline styles in families of achievers and underachievers do not appear to differ in any predictable way. Although many underachievers report that their fathers are unsupportive (Pringle, 1970), many achieving males also make similar assertions about their fathers (McClelland et al., 1953). Results that link underachievement to maternal overprotectiveness are also inconclusive (Bricklin & Bricklin, 1967).

Raph and associates (1966) identified no differences in the marital harmony, protectiveness, regularity of home routine, or pressure for achievement among parents of male achievers and underachievers. However, they did find differences in the degree to which parents shared activities and ideas with their children. The parents of achievers appeared to be more involved with their children's development. They were more likely than the parents of underachievers to provide their children with the resources and encouragement necessary for academic success. Pringle (1970) also found that despite above-average socioeconomic and educational levels, parents of bright underachievers failed to provide their children with stimulating cultural and social opportunities.

HANDICAPPED GIFTED CHILDREN

The incidence of giftedness among handicapped children and adults is not known. There may be as great an incidence in this population as in the nonhandicapped population generally. However, given the concurrence of mental impairment and severe handicaps, the incidence of giftedness among the handicapped may be less than it is among the nonhandicapped. Regardless of the exact degree of incidence, there is evidence of a large population of *unidentified* gifted children among those identified as handicapped. The purpose of this section is to discuss the relationship between various handicapping conditions and giftedness.

Measurement Problems

Sometimes educators have a difficult time measuring the giftedness of handicapped children. In the case of children with visual, auditory, and physical impairments, the usual tests and test administration procedures may not be appropriate. For example, evaluating the IQ of a child who cannot hear on a test like the WISC-R, which was normed on a population of children who can hear, is both unfair and misleading. Such children should be compared to other hearing impaired students or should be evaluated with tests designed specifically for the hearing impaired.

Less obvious, though perhaps as troublesome, are the problems encountered when attempting to measure the intelligence of learning disabled and emotionally disturbed children. Certain learning disabilities, for example, are known to interfere with verbal processing. When intelligence is equated with verbal reasoning, the abilities of such children will probably be underestimated. This difficulty is compounded because there are *no* IQ tests normed on a population of learning disabled or emotionally disturbed children. When the nature of the child's problems is known, however, evaluators can choose an IQ test that includes more items that will allow the student to demonstrate abilities, and fewer items that will reflect the student's disabilities.

Adult Expectations for the Achievement of Handicapped Children

Both teachers and parents often have lower expectations for handicapped than for nonhandicapped children. These expectations can have two detrimental effects: (1) they limit the goals and achievements of handicapped children and (2) they narrow the curriculum made available to such children.

Adults who hold low expectations for the performance of handicapped children often fail to provide them with learning experiences that are sufficiently challenging. Examples of the damage caused by lowered expectations were reported in a retrospective study of handicapped scientists (Maker, Redden, Tonelson, & Howell, 1978). This study identified some of the problems that the scientists experienced during their years in school.

Whitmore and Maker (1985, pp. 244–245) provide a list of the behaviors that reflect adults' lowered expectations for the performance of handicapped children. Low expectations are indicated by the following adult responses:

- directing conversation or giving instructions to others rather than to the disabled person;
- accepting one failure as proof that a task cannot be accomplished;

- giving higher grades relative to others;
- accepting or giving excessive praise for inferior work;
- using simple words and sentences with individuals who have cerebral palsy or a hearing impairment because their speech is difficult to understand;
- attempting to put a disabled person into a vocational program, despite the person's eligibility and interest in a college preparatory program;
- excluding a student with cerebral palsy from the chalkboard because the student has difficulty walking.

The ill-effects of such insidious discrimination are frightening. They may limit the achievement of bright handicapped children, and they often limit such students' access to appropriate programs and services.

Gifted Students with Visual Impairments

Visual impairments are usually defined in terms of acuity (i.e., sharpness of focus) or field of vision. A visual acuity score of 20/70 or less, with correction, is considered to represent a visual impairment; 20/200 or less, with correction, is considered legal blindness. Extremely limited field of vision, typically a visual arc of 20 degrees or less in the best eye, is also considered a visual impairment. These arbitrary cutoffs are used to determine which students are eligible for special instruction, special materials, and vision aids. Many visually impaired students have enough vision to use large print books and other visual materials, and even students who are legally blind may have enough functional vision to use such materials. For educational purposes, those students categorized as functionally blind (as opposed to "legally blind") are those who must rely primarily on braille and other nonvisual materials.

Visual impairments and intelligence.   Visual impairments are caused by disease, accident, and congenital conditions, both hereditary and acquired. Usually visual impairment is not directly associated with mental deficiency. In some cases, however, prenatal viral infections cause both visual and mental impairment. The factors that cause cerebral palsy may also affect both vision and intelligence. Visual impairment itself may influence learning and, consequently, affect intelligence and achievement test scores.

Some studies have found the average IQ score of blind and visually impaired children to be slightly lower than that of other children. Caton (1985), however, interprets these findings cautiously. She explains the slight difference as a function of testing difficulties. She concludes that, "the intellectual development of children is not directly affected by visual loss" (Caton, 1985, p. 255).

On the other hand, the academic achievement level of visually impaired children is significantly lower than that of other children. Often it is nearly two years behind that of other children (Birch, Tisdall, Peabody, & Sterret, 1966; Caton & Rankin, 1980). The effect seems to depend primarily on the degree of the impairment and the age of its onset. However, it is difficult to estimate the effect because of several confounding variables: (1) testing procedures are often inappropriate, (2) many blind children enter school at a later age than other children, and (3) most blind children are educated in separate schools. Special schools may affect achievement test scores because they have a slightly different curriculum than regular schools and a somewhat slower pace of instruction. Additionally, blind children do not have the opportunities for visual experiences, including reading, that promote the rapid acquisition of concepts.

Visual impairments have been shown to have a more noticeable effect on specific types of intellectual performance than on general intellectual ability. For example, visual impairment seems to affect children's ability to associate ideas with objects (Kephart, Kephart, & Schwartz, 1974). Concepts pertaining to spatial relationships also pose particular difficulties for visually impaired children.

Giftedness and visual impairments. Some subjects, such as mathematics and music, seem to give visually impaired children less trouble. In these subjects, visually impaired students may demonstrate their ability by rapid mastery of the curriculum. Such children are not, by virtue of their impairment, predisposed to perform more competently in these fields, however.

According to Whitmore and Maker (1985, pp. 83–84), indicators of giftedness are the same for children with visual impairments and those with normal vision. These indicators include "exceptional memory, advanced problem-solving skills, superior verbal communication, and creative production. . . ." However, educators will probably have difficulty recognizing these indicators if visually impaired children's achievement and intelligence tests scores are depressed.

Gifted Students with Hearing Impairments

As with visual impairments, hearing impairments can be classified on the basis of their severity. Hearing acuity is usually measured with reference to decibels, or the loudness of sounds, and pitch, or frequency levels of particular sounds. Persons who show a 20 to 40 decibel hearing loss are usually considered mildly impaired. Those whose loss is from 40 to 60 decibels are considered to be moderately impaired. Losses greater than 60 decibels are classified as either severe or profound depending on their degree.

Because of sensorineural damage, some persons experience a selective loss of hearing. These individuals can hear sounds in some frequencies but not in others. The most common selective loss affects hearing of high-frequency sounds. This type of loss often affects individuals' ability to hear consonants, the speech sounds which have the highest frequencies. If undetected, this type of hearing loss can prove to be particularly troublesome. Hearing impaired persons may misunderstand words, because of the inability to hear plural or past tense endings. They may respond inappropriately and appear unintelligent. In fact, it is not uncommon for persons with undetected hearing losses to be classified as retarded (Whitmore & Maker, 1985).

Hearing impairments and intelligence. Verbal intelligence is so closely associated with language that it is nearly impossible to separate the two. For this reason, children with hearing impairments tend to score lower than other children on verbal tests of intelligence (Green, 1985). Such tests can be administered using an interpreter to sign the questions and directions, of course. Nevertheless, the language basis of most verbal tests is considerable, and sign language interpretation may not be sufficient compensation for hearing impaired childrens' lack of exposure to oral language. Therefore, children who have had a severe hearing impairment since they were very young can almost never perform so well as children with normal hearing on verbal intelligence tests. Those studies that have used nonverbal tests, however, have found little difference between the average intelligence of hearing impaired children and that of children with normal hearing (McConnell, 1973).

Children with severe and profound hearing impairments sometimes have serious language problems. Even when their lip-reading skills are good enough to allow comprehension, they have difficulty responding to what is said. Because they cannot hear the way words are articulated, their speech is often labored or distorted (Green, 1985). Their speech problems sometimes cause them to be judged, by uninformed listeners, as unintelligent.

The academic skill most affected by a severe hearing loss is reading. Since reading is used in so much of school learning, the reading deficits of hearing impaired children help to account for achievement levels that are several years below those of other children their age (Whitmore & Maker, 1985). The reading difficulties of hearing impaired students also contribute to others' misperceptions of their intelligence. Since their written language is also likely to be affected by their limited language experience, hearing impaired students may also fail to express ideas clearly in writing. This, too, has a negative impact on others' perceptions of their abilities.

The lack of experience with oral language limits the vocabulary and grammar of many hearing impaired children. Its effect on concept development also seems to be considerable, although research studies have not determined the nature and degree of this influence. We know, however, that to learn most verbal concepts, children need to understand other, more rudimentary verbal concepts. Lacking these fundamental verbal concepts, hearing impaired children often cannot form more complex ones. It is not surprising that, as hearing impaired children get older, their achievement lags further and further behind that of children with normal hearing (Whitmore & Maker, 1985).

Giftedness and hearing impairments. Hearing impaired children who are identified as gifted are likely to be either extraordinarily intelligent or only mildly hearing impaired. Some hearing impaired children's aptitude may be apparent only in their performance of nonverbal tasks and in those academic disciplines—such as mathematics or chemistry—that are not highly dependent on language.

One case study describes the characteristics of an exceptional individual who had been hearing impaired since his infancy or early childhood (Whitmore & Maker, 1985). In spite of his impairment, he managed to function so well that his profound hearing loss was not detected until he was in the second grade. This child apparently learned how to lip-read without formal instruction. He also learned to read on his own, and, like most gifted children, he read well and enjoyed reading. His achievement in school was high, and he earned a "B" average in both college and medical school.

Gifted Students with Physical Handicaps

There are two major categories of physical handicaps: orthopedic impairments and health impairments. Orthopedic impairments include muscular and skeletal problems caused by accident, disease, heredity, and prenatal or perinatal complications. Cerebral palsy, spina bifida, muscular dystrophy, juvenile rheumatoid arthritis, paralysis, and the absence of limbs are types of orthopedic impairments. Health impairments include diseases, allergies, and other debilitating physical conditions that do not affect the musculoskeletal system. Diabetes, asthma, heart defects, and epilepsy are among the most common severe health impairments in children.

Orthopedic impairments and giftedness. Some orthopedic impairments are associated with mental impairments. Cerebral palsy, for example, which may affect only motor control, can also affect mental development. Approximately 70 percent of the people who have cerebral palsy also have a speech disorder of at least a mild degree; and approximately 50 percent have IQs below 70 (Cross, 1985). It should be recognized that IQ scores for these individuals are often inaccurate representations of their abilities. Spina bifida, too, is sometimes accompanied by mental retardation. In some instances, however, spina bifida is associated with precocious verbal development (Cartwright et al., 1981). In general, the incidence of giftedness among the orthopedically impaired is the same as in the non-handicapped population.

Health impairments and giftedness.   Very few health impairments affect intellectual development. However, such impairments may obscure children's abilities. For example, frequent absences due to illness may lower the academic achievement of health-impaired children. In some instances, the medication prescribed for these children may cause them to respond more slowly and to comprehend less well. Parents and teachers may fail to recognize such children's true abilities.

Gifted Students with Learning Disabilities

In order to understand the characteristics of gifted children who are learning disabled (LD), it is important to know something about this handicapping condition. Unfortunately, research about learning disabilities is difficult to interpret. No consensus has been reached concerning the definition of LD or the cause of this disability. According to Kirk and Gallagher (1983, p. 366), "the label 'learning disability' includes the heterogeneous group of children who do not fit neatly into the traditional categories of handicapped children."

Because there is no accepted definition of LD, educators cannot agree on the best way to identify LD children. Many presume that learning disabilities originate in perceptual or conceptual deficiencies, but such causes cannot be measured *directly* with much accuracy. The cause of a student's learning disability thus remains an untestable hypothesis. As a result, the diagnosis of the learning disability is most often made on the basis of *inference* from a severe discrepancy between the student's intelligence test score and achievement test scores.

The discussion below provides a brief review of the history and research about two crucial issues related to learning disabilities: definition and discrepancy determination. It provides a basis for understanding the next section, which considers the characteristics of gifted children with learning disabilities.

Definitions: brief history and research.   The definition of learning disabilities guides educators' efforts to identify LD children. When there is no consensus about the definition, however, certain problems arise. First is the problem of identifying too many students as learning disabled. During the decade between 1970 and 1980, more and more students were identified as LD: The proportion of all students labeled LD grew from 1.3 percent in 1970 to 3.4 percent in 1982 (Smith, 1983). By the 1985–1986 school year 42.8 percent of all *handicapped* students were classified as LD (Hume, 1987). This magnitude of increase had not been anticipated. Mac-Intosh and Dunn (1973), for example, indicated that among all students a prevalence of 1 percent to 2 percent was to be expected. Though writers like MacIntosh and Dunn attempted to draw distinctions that were sufficiently careful to prevent overidentification, their efforts were not universally effective.

The issue of *definition* is problematic also because too many *different kinds* of students have been said to be LD (Algozzine, Ysseldyke, & Shinn, 1982). The present confusion derives in part from the influence of a variety of historical constructs, for example "dyslexia" (Orton, 1937); "minimal brain injury" (Strauss & Lehtinen, 1947); and "psychoneurological learning disorders" (Myklebust & Boshes, 1960). Bryan and Bryan (1978) conclude that there is little agreement about what constitutes a learning disability. In a review of different definitions, Sutaria (1985) suggests that no one definition is satisfactory. Kavale and Forness (1985) attribute the problem to the exploratory nature of past and contemporary work in the field.

Although experts disagree about the definition of learning disabilities, school districts must nevertheless provide special education to *all* students who are said to be learning disabled. The 1977 Federal Register provides an operational definition: It equates a learning disability with the severe discrepancy between a student's ability and achievement. But the 1977 federal regulations neither specify the size of a "severe" discrepancy, nor do they indicate the method by which such a discrepancy should be determined.

The 1977 definition also lists conditions that exclude students from services in LD programs. Although some of these conditions can be measured quite easily and with great reliability (e.g., visual impairment), others are very difficult to measure reliably (e.g., cultural disadvantage). Even when the condition itself can be measured, however, educators *cannot* measure the degree to which the condition does or does not influence the discrepancy between a particular student's ability and achievement test scores (Smith, 1983). The difficulty of making this judgment also contributes to the heterogeneity of the population of students said to be LD.

Discrepancy: brief history and research.   The consensus of research does not endorse any definition of LD, including that in the federal regulations. Nevertheless, most *operational definitions* rely on some measure of the severe discrepancy between a student's ability and achievement. This method of identifying LD students is the most objective available measure of the failure of a normally intelligent child to learn. A *severe* discrepancy is interpreted as strong evidence that a learning disability may exist, although Carrier (1983) notes that it is fallacious to assume that *all* cases of severe discrepancy indicate the presence of neurological defects. Nonetheless, since the objective measurement of subclinical neurological defects is not possible, a discrepancy in criterion performance is perhaps a reasonable alternative.

Bateman (1965) first introduced the notion of discrepancy to definitions of LD. The notion of discrepancy is implicit in the definition of "minimal brain dysfunction" that was developed by a 1966 task force: ". . . children of . . . average . . . intelligence with . . . disabilities ranging from mild to severe . . ." (Clements, 1966, p. 9). According to Reynolds (1985), the discrepancy clause was included in PL 94–142 regulations because it was the only point on which a majority of experts could agree.

The notion of discrepancy is almost as old as norm-referenced IQ and achievement tests; and there are many different discrepancy formulas. Unfortunately, however, researchers (e.g., Forness, Sinclair, & Guthrie, 1983) have found that different formulas declare different numbers and kinds of students eligible. A perhaps more fundamental issue, however, is that some of the formulas are *mathematically improper.*

Reynolds (1985) provides the most cogent discussion of this issue to date. He reports that the *only* mathematically acceptable formula is the model called the "frequency of regression prediction discrepancy" (p. 461). According to Reynolds (1985, p. 464), the model "answers the question of whether there is a severe discrepancy between the achievement level of the student in question and all other children with the same IQ."

Characteristics of gifted children with learning disabilities.   Although in theory gifted underachievers should not necessarily be considered learning disabled, in practice their depressed performance on measures of achievement may make them eligible for placement in LD programs (cf. Wolf & Gygi, 1981). According to Senf (1983), most gifted students' achievement is significantly below their expected level of performance. Compounding the difficulty for gifted underachievers is the school's typical insistence that these children master basic skills before they proceed to more advanced content (Whitmore, 1982). Remedial programs designed to improve LD students' basic skills are not necessarily effective (Frauenheim, 1978; Haskell, Barrett, & Taylor, 1977), and placement in a remedial program may further restrict the gifted child's access to learning experiences that are advanced, content-specific, or interesting.

Gifted students, whose measured intelligence is two or more standard deviations above the mean, are more likely than average students to demonstrate severe discrepancies. For example, a six-and-a-half-year-old child with an IQ of 145 may achieve a 3.3 grade equivalency score on an individual achievement test. This score might correspond to a standard score of 122. The discrepancy between this child's IQ and achievement in reading is, therefore, 23 points (approximately 1.5 standard deviations). In many school districts, this degree of discrepancy would be considered severe. Yet, common sense suggests that this young child's reading achievement is adequate. The child's performance is actually 1.5 to 2.0 years above his or her grade placement level. The apparent discrepancy may result entirely from lack of preschool instruction in reading or from average perceptual-motor development, or it might in fact be the expected achievement level for most children of this age and IQ (cf. Reynolds, 1985).

Unfortunately, some teachers might refer such a child to be evaluated for placement in an LD program. If the child is divergent, disruptive in class, noncompliant, or has poor handwriting, the teacher may make such a referral. According to Bull (1987, p. 6), gifted children with learning disabilities "are usually only referred when they exhibit some signs of social, emotional, or personality disorder." Academic skill deficiency is rarely the reason for such referrals.

If a teacher chooses to make a referral, subsequent placement in the LD program is likely. According to Ysseldyke and Algozzine (1982), special education classification decisions are influenced more by background information provided by the referring teacher than by evaluation data— even when evaluation data clearly contradict the background information. These researchers (p. 228) suggest that "examiners hold and seek to confirm (with or without appropriate evidence) preconceived notions about the assessment outcomes based upon the child's *characteristics*" [Ysseldyke and Algozzine's emphasis]. The characteristics of some gifted children (e.g., divergence, nonconformity) may, therefore, increase their likelihood of being identified as learning disabled.

Another, though perhaps less common, situation involves neurologically impaired (i.e., organically brain-damaged) gifted students who use conceptual strengths to compensate for perceptual deficiencies. These students may disguise their difficulties but may also not reveal their giftedness (Whitmore, 1982). Hence, the underachievement of such students may be chronic because they may never be provided a stimulating curriculum. This problem is compounded by the tendency of "teachers . . . to be easily satisfied with work of a good standard" (Pirozzo, 1982, p. 19). Because such students do produce work of a good standard and seem to expend considerable effort in doing so, their teachers may overlook their other characteristics. A teacher is not likely to investigate whether or not such a student's large vocabulary and elaborate oral stories are associated, for example, with exceptionally high IQ.

According to Bull (1987), gifted students who are learning disabled typically exhibit certain characteristics. Frequently they have sloppy handwriting, difficulty in following directions, and poor spelling. They often make reversals in reading and writing letters and sometimes also make numeric transpositions. Bull (1987) emphasizes the emotional problems that such students are likely to suffer: They are told that they are gifted, yet in school subjects they fail to perform. This disparity may produce a high level of frustration which further impedes such students' learning.

Gifted Children with Emotional Problems

Although teachers and administrators continue to concern themselves with the presumed emotional imbalance of gifted children, researchers have tended increasingly to substantiate the normal emotional adjustment of the gifted (see e.g., Galluci, 1988). Gifted children are no more likely than average children to have emotional problems; nevertheless, a small percentage of gifted children *do* have serious emotional or behavioral difficulties. The discussion that follows briefly considers the nature of emotional disturbance, particularly when it is viewed as deviance. A review of the characteristics of those gifted children who are emotionally disturbed also follows.

Deviance as a measure of emotional imbalance.   Since gifted children are identified because of their deviant scholastic performance or potential, schools may be particularly anxious to ensure that these students do not behave in socially or emotionally deviant ways. This concern is demonstrated in spite of the general trend of recent research, which substantiates that the gifted *are not at risk emotionally.*

Children who have serious emotional problems have a difficult time adjusting to social expectations. They may have a great deal of difficulty getting along with others. Their self-concepts may be poor, and their interpersonal relationships strained. Students who truly have deviant patterns of behavior (1) display behaviors that are inappropriate for their chronological and mental age, (2) exhibit such difficulties over an extended period of time, and (3) fail to respond to parents' or teachers' attempts to modify their behavior. According to Nelson (1985), such children display disturbed behavior, not just disturbing behavior.

Unfortunately, some teachers are unable to distinguish between disturbed and disturbing patterns of behavior. One study found that classroom teachers perceived 20.4 percent of their students as exhibiting behavior disorders (Kelly, Bullock, & Dykes, 1977). In this study, teachers also identified boys and blacks more frequently than girls and whites (twice as often, in each case). Apparently, these teachers had a very low tolerance for deviance.

The behavior of gifted children *is* abnormal in some ways. Their responses to questions may be divergent, and they may challenge authority more often than average children do (Torrance, 1963). When gifted children demonstrate these atypical patterns of behavior, they may be at risk for classification as emotionally disturbed.

Characteristics of gifted children with emotional problems.   Most studies link low IQ with emotional disturbance and delinquency (e.g., White,

1966); nonetheless some studies have investigated the relationship of social and emotional disorders with high IQ (e.g., King, 1981; Morse, Cutler, & Fink, 1964). In fact, many studies (of both types) *do* include subjects with IQs in the superior range (Kauffman, 1981).

There seem to be no systematic studies of the characteristics of gifted children who are also emotionally disturbed. Such studies would, in fact, be very difficult to conduct, because locating a sample of disturbed gifted children would be a great challenge. Identification of emotional disturbance entails quite a bit more than the administration and interpretation of a test or battery of tests. Often, the diagnosis is based on the clinical expertise of a psychologist or psychiatrist, and the judgment of one clinician may differ considerably from that of another. Even if clinicians were to agree on all of the diagnoses, different children would still manifest their disturbance in a variety of ways. Hence, any group of children who were classified as emotionally disturbed would probably differ from any other such group, and individuals within any one group would also differ greatly from one another.

Compounding the problem is the difficulty in identifying the giftedness of seriously disturbed children. In many cases, these childrens' talents are hidden. Even situational anxiety can depress children's scores on tests of intelligence and achievement. The serious emotional disturbances of some children will obviously interfere with their ability to demonstrate talents. Unfortunately, if severe emotional disturbance lasts for many years during the developmental period, the child's cognitive development may be seriously impeded. Such children may suffer permanent loss of abilities that they might otherwise have developed more fully.

Although there is no research about gifted children who are emotionally disturbed, there is much speculation about the topic. Many educators and psychologists express concern about the stress that gifted students are likely to encounter. Foster (1985, pp. 142–144) presents the following list of adjustment problems that gifted students often must deal with:

1. inherent tension between the unusual expectations and needs of the gifted child and the normative standards of the larger society,
2. the child's awareness of issues prior to having the resources with which to resolve them, and
3. intellectual independence from parents and immediate family that precedes emotional and social independence.

According to Foster (1985), these difficulties can be handled through school counseling and guidance programs for gifted students. But this recommendation suggests that Foster is discussing only the minor adjustment problems that gifted students sometimes encounter. These problems are transitory and often disappear as children mature. Khatena (1978), on the other hand, expresses concern that the situational stress that some gifted children experience will lead to serious disturbance:

> . . . [P]rolonged enforced repression of the creative child's needs may lead to emotional problems and neurosis, and even psychosis. Neurosis . . . is a condition generated by acute and prolonged anxiety states. . . . Neurosis hinders rather than facilitates the functioning of the creative process. . . . The creative individual who has his productivity blocked may develop behavior traits similar to those of psychotics . . . his behavior might become withdrawn or schizophrenic. (Khatena, 1978, pp. 89–90)

Khatena'a conclusions should be viewed cautiously, however, since they are based on speculation rather than on empirical study. Considering the evidence that shows the relative emotional health of gifted students, it seems reasonable to assume that gifted children will weather situational stress at least as well as average children.

The more serious emotional problems that some gifted children—like some children of average ability—will face appear to be a different matter. These types of disturbance are likely to have the following manifestions:

1. They may involve inadequate ego development.
2. They may involve bizarre or self-destructive behaviors.
3. They may reflect serious problems of family interaction.
4. They may be resistant to change.
5. They may interfere with the child's interaction with *either* chronological—or mental-age peers.
6. They may limit the child's ability to interact with adults.

These are the sorts of problems that may require therapy with a psychiatrist, clinical social worker, or psychologist. Some critics question the value of therapy in treating acute or chronic emotional problems. Such critics cite institutional recidivism, the difficulty of working with schizophrenic patients, and organic deficiencies as evidence that explains why therapy is ineffective.

Nonetheless, gifted students, who so typically possess advanced verbal skills, may actually be more likely than other individuals to benefit from forms of therapy based on "insight." Such students may be in a good position to articulate their conflicts, to analyze their past patterns of behavior, and to plan better courses of action for the future. Readers should note that acute psychological problems (i.e., those associated with a crisis in an otherwise functional life) are more amenable to "insightful" therapeutic intervention than chronic problems (i.e., those associated with an ongoing problem that hinders a person's ability to function). Very bright students with chronic, disabling emotional problems may benefit from a combination of insight therapy and the kind of behavior modification recommended for many other students—often with average IQs or below-average IQs—who have behavior disorders. In the case of both acute and chronic problems, it is critical that students be placed in the hands of expert therapists. Poor therapy can contribute significantly to students' problems.

SUMMARY

This chapter presented theories and research about the underachievement of gifted children. By examining various hypotheses that attempt to explain underachievement, it provided a framework for evaluating the different empirical studies. Two kinds of underachievement were considered: (1) underachievement represented by low grades and (2) underachievement represented by low scores on standardized achievement tests. This latter type was associated with certain handicapping conditions that impede the performance of bright students.

In reviewing the literature on the characteristics of gifted students who get poor grades, the chapter considered school behaviors, personality traits, and family dynamics that might contribute to such students' underachievement. It reported the inconclusive, and often conflicting, evidence provided by such research.

The discussion of gifted students with handicaps suggested that stereotypes of handicapped children might limit parents' and teachers' expectations for such children's performance. Cautions were given about the effects of lowered expectations on such students' achievement.

This chapter concentrated on the underachievement of *individuals*— underachievement that often can be explained in terms of psychoanalytic, psychological, or biophysical etiologies. In most instances, the underachievement of such individuals can be attributed either to their handicaps, to peoples' responses to their handicaps, or to complex interactions between home, school, and personality factors. The more systematic underachievement of *groups of individuals*—underachievement that more strongly reflects social and economic influences—is considered in the next chapter.

11

Unfair Discrimination, Poverty, and Minority Gifted Children

Focusing Questions

1. How are students from different social classes treated by their classroom teachers? In what ways does this treatment relate to the future work roles that the students are expected to assume?
2. Why are so few minority-group children identified as gifted? Is it possible—using standardized tests—to identify more minority gifted children?
3. What differences in children's cognitive styles can be attributed to their ethnic backgrounds?
4. Why are boys at greater risk than girls of being categorized as learning disabled?
5. How does performance in mathematics reflect differences in the ways that boys and girls are socialized in their homes and at school?
6. What characteristics of rural families, communities, and schools contribute to the underachievement of bright children from rural areas?

FACT: DISCRIMINATION EXISTS

Unfair discrimination in educational practice exists. It exists despite the fact that most citizens look to the schools to provide a way for students to improve their social and economic standing. In fact, unfair discrimination exists in schools in spite of many educators' efforts to disable its effects.

We use the term "unfair discrimination" throughout this chapter to highlight pedagogical concern for justice. Some discrimination is *fair*, as when gifted students are discriminated from other students for the purpose of providing them with a challenging program. In general, "discrimination" means "making distinctions." Some distinctions are contrary to justice. This chapter investigates such distinctions as they affect gifted students. We refer to such distinctions as "unfair discrimination".

Evidence of unfair discrimination in educational practice abounds. Given such well-documented facts, it is no wonder that students in poor neighborhoods perform so badly. Three categories of evidence about discrimination in schools are indicated as follows:

• *First, schools are segregated by race and class.*
   Schools located in regions or neighborhoods where income or wealth is low

(e.g., in ethnic or racial ghettos) receive much weaker support than schools in affluent regions or neighborhoods (Jencks et al., 1979; Mosteller & Moynihan, 1972).

- *Second, some schools do not teach thinking and reasoning.*
  Students in segregated schools that serve the working class and underclasses experience a kind of learning different from their peers who attend more affluent schools. In working-class schools, students experience a regimen of rote learning and training in submission to arbitrary authority (Anyon, 1980; Bowles & Gintis, 1976; Wilcox & Moriarity, 1977).

- *Third, most of these schools are not effective.*
  In these schools, for example, the expectation for student achievement is low, use of instructional time is poor, and school climate is hostile (often dominated by violence and vandalism). Finally, students in these schools learn less than students who attend more affluent schools (Coleman et al., 1966; Oakes, 1985; Sizer, 1984).

Are educators to blame for such practices and such results? Only in part, for the source of such practices and results lies in how society is structured in general. Nonetheless, when the educational system—and when individual educators—know what needs to be done to promote learning, but fail to take the necessary steps, unfair discrimination is *enabled*.

Schools necessarily reflect the predominant values and social structures that characterize the societies of which they are a part. Schools, after all, exist to perpetuate the cultural heritage. They may, however, also *shape* the cultural heritage as they transmit it to students. Some of this shaping occurs by chance, some by choice.

For example, some schools in impoverished neighborhoods are "effective." Considering their social and economic circumstances, these schools produce higher levels of student achievement than would be expected. In addition, some teachers in less effective schools *do* succeed in teaching their students to learn and to value learning. Such schools and such teachers are rare, however, because fighting unfair discrimination requires positive action. It does not happen spontaneously in our culture, which endorses *many* kinds of unfair discrimination.

Fortunately, we *do* know a good deal about the targets of unfair discrimination in school, and we know a little about the measures that can be used to limit the effects of discrimination. For the most part, the targets of discrimination in gifted education are not surprising. Gifted black, Hispanic, and working-class students are most at risk. But various cultural stereotypes place many girls and some boys (of all class and ethnic groups) at different sorts of risk. Geography can also be used to identify the targets of discrimination; the distinction between town and country (urban and rural) is, for example, notable. Since Counts (1932) wrote on the topic, this distinction has been largely ignored in gifted education. It is, however, receiving more attention today.

Finally, educators should remember that the effects of discrimination are cumulative. Unfair discrimination is carried out insistently, and the effects of discrimination accrue steadily. In practical terms, this observation means that the effects of discrimination are themselves sources of further discrimination. For example, impoverished students start school with achievement levels not so very different from their more advantaged peers. But as they progress through school, they fall further and further behind. Those who fail to become marginally literate will, as adults, suffer additional discrimination on that account.

EFFECTS OF DISCRIMINATION

Unfair discrimination contributes to the division of members of society into different socioeconomic classes. The influence of this division is so significant that socioeconomic class is one of the most common control variables used in educational research. It is identified nearly as frequently as age and gender as an important source of variability in students' academic achievement. Efforts to understand and control the effects of social class are vitiated, however, by limitations in the terminology by which it is described. The terminology used to make comparisons between socioeconomic classes is often vague and misleading.

Social Class

Williams (1976) describes the history of the word "class" as a term for social groups. He notes that the term became widespread during the Industrial Revolution. During this time, "middle class" was coined to describe a position between the aristocracy and laborers. At about the same time, the terms, "productive classes" and "privileged classes," were used to distinguish between people who earned a living and the aristocracy. By the 1830s the term "working class" was used to distinguish between laborers and other economic groups.

These uses of the word "class" are based on two different perspectives. The upper-, middle-, and lower-class division of society is hierarchical and assumes a continuum. Upper-class families have more money and more prestige than middle- and lower-class families. But, the term "working class" distinguishes on the basis of production and does not imply an ordinal scale.

Most research is based on arbitrary assignment of students to upper-, middle-, or lower-class status. Lack of precision in these terms means that research that claims to control for social class does not always do so. The term "middle class," for example, covers a broad range of lifestyles. In an analysis of the income of the U.S. population, Rose (1986, p. 9) profiles two "middle-class" families:

> In one the husband works as a forklift operator at an assembly plant while the wife stays at home with the two children; total family income equals $18,000. In the other, a suburban couple with a $150,000 house, the husband is a dentist, the wife a psychologist; total family income is $90,000, and one child is in college and the other attends a local private school. Both of these families might describe themselves as being "strapped" for money and as having little left over for frills. Both would probably consider themselves part of the "middle class," the first family perhaps adding the adjective "lower" and the second adding "upper."

Rose contends that the category "middle class" is so broad that its use obscures important political and economic distinctions. The different resources of families such as those described previously lead them to approach educational issues differently as well. The prospects of the children from the first family are dependent on the quality of the local schools, but those of the children from the second family are not. Even when they attend public schools, the children of higher income parents have access to private lessons, artistic performances, travel, and other experiences that are unavailable to many "middle-class" children.

For educational research and practice, social structure is perhaps better defined in terms of discrete structural segments that relate to the economy. Social class interpolated from rank on a single dimension is flawed for several reasons: (1) classes must be defined by relative (and arbitrary) distinctions between low, middle, and high ranks; and (2) a continuous socioeconomic scale does not account for the conflicting interests of different classes (Poulantzas, 1974; Wright, 1979).

In discussing the need for more precise terminology, Labov (1972) had the following comments:

> . . . the term "lower class" is frequently used as opposed to "middle class" . . . it is useful to distinguish a "lower class" group from working class. Lower-class families are typically female-based . . . with no father present to provide steady economic support, whereas for the working class there is typically an intact nuclear family with the father holding a semi-skilled or unskilled job." (p. 181)

Although it should be recognized that many working-class families are female-based, the distinction that concerns Labov is an important one. There are major differences in the kinds of environments of children usually categorized simply as "lower class." Recently, the term "underclass" has been used to describe that portion of the population that has no wealth, no income, and no prospects of either (e.g., Lehman, 1986; Mann, 1986). Twenty-two percent of children in the U.S. live in households with incomes below the poverty level of $11,000 established by the Social Security Administration (Rose, 1986). Descriptions of the living conditions of children who belong to this class have been given some attention in the popular media, but, since the 1960s, severely economically deprived children have been virtually ignored in the education literature. Nonetheless, the number of children who belong to this class has been growing at a rate that alarms even the representatives of business and industry (e.g., Committee for Economic Development, 1985).

The bright children of the underclass have almost no chance of being identified as gifted except through the use of quotas or special methods of assessment, such as Mercer's (1981) System of Multicultural and Pluralistic Assessment (SOMPA), that take into account debilitating social and economic circumstances. No study has been conducted to determine how many children from this group have been identified as gifted. However, using Terman's data, we can calculate the chances that a child from this group has of being so identified: 1 chance out of 150. Of the 1500 gifted subjects, fewer than 10 came from families of laborers (Terman, 1925).

Social Mobility and the Culture of Schooling

Given an average IQ, the child from a middle-class family is 25 times more likely to end up with a well-paying, high status job than is the child from a working-class family (Bowles & Gintis, 1976). Among the factors that make it so difficult for working-class children to improve their socioeconomic status are (1) a limited education and (2) the inhibiting attitudes that result from their economic circumstances. These attitudes are originally imposed externally (e.g., at school and home), but most older children and adults have internalized them.

Advocacy of equal educational opportunity is based on the belief that education enhances social mobility. It is true that more schooling offers minorities enhanced status and a closer approximation of economic equality. The economic return for schooling, however, is much less for children from low-income families and for blacks than it is for children from middle- and high-income families (Bowles & Gintis, 1976; Wright, 1979).

Expectations.   Even under conditions of apparently equal educational opportunity, social forces undermine the academic efforts of poor children. As Good and Brophy (1987) report, children from lower socioeconomic status families are not always treated equitably in the classroom. Important, too, is recognition that membership in a lower socioeconomic group, whether underclass or working class, works against cultivation of the attitudes that are associated with success in school. According to Kohn (1977, p. 189), "The essence of higher class position is the expectation that one's decisions and actions can be consequential; the essence of lower class position is the belief that one is at the mercy of forces and people beyond one's control, often, beyond one's understanding."

Parents' expectations for their children are in fact influenced by their class background. Working-class parents report that they value obedience, manners, and cleanliness. They want their children to be "good" students. Middle-class parents, on the other hand, report that they value qualities such as critical thinking and curiosity. The former qualities represent obedience and external motivation; the latter imply independence and self-direction.

It is no accident that the high expectations of teachers appear as a significant influence on the achievement of children. It is also no accident that to promote high expectations in working-class or underclass schools is very difficult. There is much in the structure of society that undermines high expectations for such children: Cultural, economic, and familial practices can determine what typically happens in schools. Schools that do promote high expectations for these children, however, provide the essential counterexamples that demonstrate that it *is* possible for such children to be successful learners. As Edmonds (1979) notes, we can assure that these children learn well; the question is, do we want it to happen?

Internalizing status expectations. The conditions of occupational life at higher social class levels also foster the belief that the attainment of individual goals is possible. Professionals and managers learn to expect intrinsic as well as extrinsic rewards from their jobs. The conditions of occupational life at lower social class levels, on the other hand, limit the worker's view of a job to the extrinsic benefits it provides. Unskilled and semiskilled jobs foster a narrowly circumscribed conception of self and society and promote the positive valuation of conformity to authority (Kohn, 1977).

The same conception of self and society is taught, via the "hidden curriculum," in working-class and underclass schools (Anyon, 1980). The type of education that working-class and underclass students receive also seems to contribute to the development of attitudes that inhibit their self-direction. Schooling prepares them for roles as compliant participants in the labor force.

The differences between instruction in the schools attended by working class children and those attended by the children of parents who earn a high income have been documented in many studies (e.g., Wilcox, 1982). Upper class children are schooled for self-direction, and lower-class children are treated in ways that cause them to rely on external reinforcement for learning.

Identification with the middle class is an integral element of the teacher's role. By their expectations, attitudes, and behaviors, many teachers, unknowingly, contribute to the rigidity of the class structure. One study, for example, found that teachers' placement of students into reading groups was more highly correlated with the children's social class membership than it would have been if they had been placed strictly on the basis of achievement test scores (Haller & Davis, 1980). Placement in a low or high reading group is not only a response to social class differences, it also perpetuates them.

Discipline problems and the life of the mind.   Children who suffer unfair discrimination may seem to be hopelessly caught in a social structure and a culture that is bound to cripple their access to the life of the mind. Giroux (1983) points out, however, that rebellion and resistance to authority exist as latent reactions to submission to authority in these circumstances—among both adult workers and students. The discipline problems so common in working-class and underclass schools attest to this fact.

Giroux asserts that the resistance that these students practice is a token of their submission. He advises teachers to find ways to show students how the form of their resistance (e.g., acting out, discipline problems) puts them further under the sway of discrimination and oppression, and how it actually makes oppressed students more likely targets for exploitation. Giroux believes that through opening up this topic for ongoing dialogue among teachers and students, students can begin to understand where society has placed them and what their responses might be. Giroux (1983) clearly believes that it is the role of teachers to reveal to students in these circumstances the liberating power of knowledge, language, and reflection.

MINORITY GIFTED CHILDREN

From a biological viewpoint, there is every reason to expect the same incidence of high ability in children from racial and ethnic minorities as in racial and ethnic majorities (Gould, 1981; Lewontin et al., 1984); but the chances of minority group children being identified as gifted are extremely low. With the exception of children from Jewish or Oriental families, children from minority groups are grossly underrepresented in programs for the gifted. The fact that so few minority students are identified as gifted is usually attributed to (1) biases in the content and procedures of IQ and achievement tests and (2) cognitive differences between the minorities and the white, middle-class majority.

Despite the belief that minority gifted children can and should be identified, methods of identifying gifted students have changed very little in the past 60 years. The problem of identifying bright minority students persists. Teacher referral remains the first step in entry to the gifted program. An IQ cutoff in the 97th percentile or higher still serves as the primary criterion for placement in a gifted program, just as it did in the first large-scale effort (Terman, 1925) to identify gifted students in the United States.

Many of the provisions intended to overcome the effects of discriminatory tests and identification procedures make use of subjective measures. The subjective nature of such measures (e.g., teacher checklists) means that their predictive validity is questionable. The most *promising* methods for identifying gifted minority students, that is, those methods that take into consideration students' lack of educational opportunity and yet incorporate measures that are good predictors of academic success, are (1) quota systems and (2) the establishment of local norms.

Group Differences and Intelligence

Using socioeconomic status as a proxy for social class, studies have found that social class and intelligence correlate moderately, about a 0.50 Pearson product-moment correlation coefficient (Howley, 1982). Some researchers (e.g., Gardner, 1961) have argued that this degree of correlation is evidence of the efficiency of our social system in sorting individuals on the basis of aptitude. Other authors argue that this degree of correlation demonstrates the effects of a social system that attempts to strengthen the relationship between social class and cognitive performance (e.g., Lewontin et al., 1984).

Verbal ability and minorities.   The close association between superior verbal ability and high IQ test scores has implications for the identification of bright minority children. According to Davidson and Balducci (1956), gifted children from families of high income usually have a more advanced vocabulary than gifted children from families of low income. These researchers found this difference, even though the low income children had a slightly *higher* average IQ.

In order to score in the highest percentiles on most IQ tests, a child usually needs to have a large vocabulary. Working-class and underclass children are at a disadvantage; their vocabularies may not be as large as those of middle- and upper-class children. Sometimes their vocabularies—though large—include many words and expressions that are not standard English. Differences in the language used at home and in the community may account for limitations in the standard English vocabulary of some minority students. Others may fail to absorb or use the vocabulary of the classroom because they perceive the hostility of that environment.

In an ethnographic study of classroom behavior, Heath (1982) observed the response of a kindergarten-age black child to activities in the classroom. Although there are a number of possible explanations for this child's behavior, the behavior itself may adversely influence the child's vocabulary development:

During those school activities which focused on giving labels to things and naming items and discussing their attributes, Lem did not participate. He listened and often tried to escape these structured sessions to play with trucks, puzzles, and so forth. He had no interest in looking at books and being asked questions about them. . . . (p. 121).

Heath's explanation of this child's behavior is based on differences between the linguistic style of working-class black families and the linguistic style of the middle-class white teacher. The differences, she believes, makes the black children uncomfortable and uncertain about the proper responses to questions their teachers ask.

Labov (1972) addresses an issue that Heath's explanation ignores: Black children confronting white teachers or psychologists are, on some level, confronting an enemy. Labov acknowledges that most observations of the language behavior of black children have found relatively barren language. However, he sees this monosyllabic behavior as defensive; it is produced by placing the child in a situation in which "anything he says can literally be held against him" (p. 185).

Under the circumstances, the minority children's efforts to second-guess the questioners and their reluctance to speak spontaneously are understandable. This view offers a possible reason why, as the teachers in Heath's study report, the children just stare at them even when it seems that they could answer the question. The teachers' impression is consonant with Labov's opinion that minority children's defensive responses to threatening situations sometimes causes them to seem "inept" (p. 191).

Because of the circumstances under which observations are made, however, many samples of black and working-class children's language are of questionable validity. The inferences based on samples of such language are even more problematic.

Bernstein (1961), for example, attributes poor academic performance of economically deprived school children to their deviant language, which because of certain traits, results in deficits in their capacity for complex reasoning. He describes the language of uneducated persons, regardless of race, as inadequate for discussing abstract ideas. Among his generalizations about the language of working-class and underclass individuals are the following:

Language Characteristic	**Resultant "Deficit"**
repeated use of a small number of conjunctions (and, because, so, then)	logical qualifications cannot be expressed exactly
heavy reliance on implicit meaning	cognitive and affective differentiation reduced
frequent use of implied questions (i.e., tag questions) at the end of statements (e.g., "isn't it?")	further analysis and search for reasons discouraged

The inferences that Bernstein draws from these language characteristics are untenable. Logic systems usually rely on only a few conjunctions. In addition, many authors would disagree with the assertion that heavy reliance on implicit meaning *reduces* cognitive and affective differentiation. Also, one of the characteristics typical of middle-class mothers' speech to their children is the use of *many* tag questions. This characteristic does not seem to damage middle-class children's analytic thinking.

Labov (1972) counters claims such as Bernstein's by demonstrating that nonstandard English is as logical as standard English. In contrast to the deficit theory of *lower-class* language, Labov points out that much *middle-class* language is dysfunctional. Richard Mitchell (1979) in *Less Than Words Can Say* provides many telling examples to support this claim.

Blacks and scholastic achievement.   Economic deprivation is the major issue to consider in efforts to identify minority children with superior academic ability. Measures of intelligence correlate more with economic status than with skin color. The majority of economically deprived children are, of course, white (Martinson, 1972). Nonetheless, among blacks, a far greater *proportion* of children are poor. In 1982 less than 66 percent of blacks were employed (Shiels, Weathers, Howard, & Givens, 1982).

Black, female-headed families represent a growing proportion of poor people in America: from 7.3 percent in 1959 to 19.3 percent in 1984 (Lehman, 1986, p. 33). While the median income for two-parent households is $28,300, the median income for households headed by a woman (i.e., either white or black) is $13,500; and almost half of the black children in the United States live in single-parent households headed by a woman.

It is common knowledge that black children, as a group, have a relatively low mean score on IQ tests. In the United States, however, it is less well known that the mean IQ score of *poor* children, regardless of race is below the mean (Gould, 1981). When middle-class black students are compared to the norm on IQ tests, their mean IQ is average (Jenkins, 1950).

The disproportionately large number of poor black children is sufficient to explain the lower mean IQ score of black children. As mentioned earlier, however, controlling for social class is not always an effective means of insuring the comparability of students' backgrounds, and the results of studies with "matched" samples are mixed.

According to Jenkins (1950), educators' preoccupation with black children's low mean IQ score has diverted attention from the within-group variability of IQ. He points out that among middle-class black children, the incidence of recognized giftedness is as high as among middle-class white children. Referring to his study of highly gifted black students from several major cities, he also points out that the upper limits of intelligence tests are not the exclusive domain of white children. The black students in his study had IQ scores ranging from 160 to 200 (Jenkins, 1943).

Jenkins located no highly gifted black children from rural areas. Studies from the 1940s found that rural blacks from the South had even lower IQ scores than blacks raised in the North (Jensen, 1973). This effect seems to persist among recent black migrants from the rural South. On the basis of a study of blacks in Chicago, Lehman (1986) reports that the blacks who make up the underclass there are those whose parents immigrated from the poorest and the most rural areas in the South. In these rural southern areas, throughout the 1950s a system of segregation and share-cropping prevailed. Most blacks were denied the right to vote by a poll tax and a literacy test. Even a junior high-school education was rare among rural blacks. Black rural school systems in the South still face much more serious problems than face other rural districts (Nachtigal, 1982).

Simply moving out of the South to a northern urban area was enough to improve some black children's IQ scores (Lee, 1951). Lee's study of southern black children who moved to Philadelphia found that the IQ scores of the southern-born children who entered the school system improved as they progressed through the urban system. Those who entered the school system in the first grade showed a greater gain, apparently because they had been in the urban schools longer; but the rate of gain matched that of children who moved to Philadelphia later in their school careers. After several years in the Philadelphia school district, these children's IQ scores were equal to the IQ scores of Philadelphia-born black children.

Black children who score in the gifted range on IQ tests often come from middle-class families and attend better equipped schools than those available to most black children (Martinson, 1972). However, black achievers also come from families whose occupational level could be categorized as upper lower-class (Schultz, 1958). Their parents tend to be clerical, skilled, or semiskilled workers with relatively low incomes.

Regardless of social class, the parents of high-achieving black students apparently support their children's achievement in a number of ways. According to Shade (1978), the parents establish close family ties, use control mechanisms that include moderate amounts of praise and blame, give assistance in schoolwork, establish goals for performance, express interest in their children and encourage them.

Black achievers score high on traditional measures of intelligence, especially in verbal ability and analytical ability. The personality characteristics of black achievers suggest that they have positive views of authority figures, that they are self-confident and goal-oriented. They seem to be willing to conform to adult demands, and they are cautious and controlled (Shade, 1981).

Ability patterns across ethnic groups.   Some researchers have found differences in the ability patterns characteristic of various ethnic groups.

Lesser, Fifer, and Clark (1965), for example, found ethnic differences in both overall level of ability and pattern of performance on various tests. The Jewish and black groups scored highest in verbal ability; Chinese Americans and Puerto Rican children scored highest in spatial ability. Social class had marked effects on the level of performance but did not seem to influence the pattern of abilities.

A study by Backman (1972) found Jewish subjects to be relatively superior in verbal knowledge and mathematics; non-Jewish white subjects displayed a relatively flat profile; the black subjects scored highest on items measuring perceptual speed, accuracy, and memory, and the Oriental-American subjects scored highest in mathematics. However, in this study, sex was a better predictor of ability scores than ethnicity or social class. The relative superiority of Jewish children's verbal and numerical ability in comparison to their spatial ability was also found in a Canadian study (Marjoribanks, 1972).

Some researchers attribute the different ability patterns to differences in the cognitive styles of individuals from ethnic minorities (e.g., Buenning & Tollefson, 1987; De Leon, 1983). In discussing the abilities of Mexican-American children, these researchers suggested that culturally determined cognitive styles distinguished between minority and mainstream children. They found that gifted children from Mexican-American homes often used a field-dependent method of problem solving, whereas mainstream children often used a field-independent method. These researchers asserted that field-independent responses would result in higher scores on IQ tests. Hence, even the brightest Mexican-American children would score lower on IQ tests than their mainstream counterparts. Because they learn to give answers that take account of the social context, Mexican-American children seem to be penalized on tests requiring independent, abstract reasoning (De Leon, 1983).

According to Tonemah (1987), gifted children from American Indian homes also differ from mainstream gifted children. He believes that American Indian children are often excluded from gifted programs for the following reasons:

1. assessment procedures fail to account for tribal cultural influences;
2. standardized tests are biased in favor of children from the larger society;
3. some Indian students are unprepared to respond to the types of items that appear on standardized tests;
4. some Indian students have a negative attitude toward test-taking;
5. indian students are not included in the norming sample for most standardized tests; and
6. standardized tests do not accurately reflect the entire spectrum of intelligence or achievement. (Tonemah, 1987, p. 183)

Although research on the topic is not extensive, it does seem that ethnicity can influence patterns of cognitive performance to some unspecified degree. The types of behavior that are most valued by a particular subculture seem to be reflected in minority children's patterns of performance. Subcultures that value artistic performance, for example, cultivate the artistic abilities of children (Tonemah, 1987). Those that emphasize group rather than individual performance condition behaviors that may preclude high-level performance on tests of individual intelligence (Buenning & Tollefson, 1987).

Even though cultural differences undoubtedly influence IQ and achievement test performance to some degree, they may have a much less powerful influence than other factors, such as income, wealth, status, and expectations. Historically, ethnic minorities have suffered discrimination that has limited their attainment of income, wealth, and status. Hence, the effects of ethnicity are difficult to distinguish from the effects of poverty or of limited educational opportunity.

THE RELATIONSHIP OF GENDER TO PATTERNS OF UNDERACHIEVEMENT

Oddly enough, both boys and girls are subject to a variety of influences that make them differentially at risk for underachievement. In the case of boys, the influences that lead to underachievement might be viewed as "interaction effects." That is, in the case of at-risk males, a combination of gender *and* other characteristics produces an interaction that is associated with underachievement. Perhaps the most notable of these interaction effects is the interaction between gender and race; and as noted above, black males are at greater risk in schools even than black females.

Among the population of gifted students, however, girls are presumed to be more educationally disadvantaged than boys. This presumption is based on the understanding that performance expectations for girls are not universally high. Homemaking is, for example, still an acceptable vocation for a young woman. At the same time, homemaking is not a valued work. Both child care and housecleaning are tasks that are poorly paid when not performed for free by a homemaker. Men who undertake homemaking are apt to be regarded as very peculiar, if not dysfunctional.

Despite the influence of sexism, attitudes toward the accomplishments of women—and—their right to be as assertive, ambitious, and self-motivating as men, are steadily changing. Educators who work with bright students have a role to play in helping students achieve better by overcoming the constraints of sexism and sex-role stereotyping.

Risk Factors for Boys

A number of studies have found that more boys than girls are identified as underachievers (Pringle, 1970). In her study, Pringle (1970) found that the ratio of underachieving boys to girls was 3 to 1. Among those underachievers who are identified as learning disabled, the overrepresentation of boys may be even more striking. Harness, Epstein, and Gordon (1984) estimate that the ratio of LD boys to LD girls is 4 to 1. Phipps (1982) reports that in some LD samples 85 percent of the students are boys.

Although there are several hypotheses that attempt to explain why more boys than girls are identified as underachievers, there is no consensus. Some researchers in the 1940s, 1950s, and 1960s speculated that biological differences between boys and girls accounted for the phenomenon; others blamed cultural expectations and environmental conditioning (Pringle, 1970). More recently, educators have speculated about the overrepresentation of boys in LD programs. In her review of the research, Smith (1983) cites hypotheses based on medical factors, maturational factors, sociological factors, and brain organizational factors. According to Miles (1986), three variables might explain the phenomenon: (1) teacher bias, (2) achievement differences, and (3) gender differences in brain function.

Not much research has been conducted to support any of these hypotheses, however. Findings from many of the correlational studies tend to be contradictory, and current research on brain functioning is of questionable value. Research techniques for studying hemispheric differences in brain functioning are primitive, at best. At worst, they are based on unsound theories that are derived from the study of small samples of neurologically impaired subjects (Springer & Deutsch, 1981). The fact that LD students are identified in many different ways also makes study of this question extremely difficult.

Biological factors. Some researchers relate biological differences between boys and girls to the gender disparity in LD identification. Several studies suggest that boys are at greater risk for birth trauma than girls because newborn boys have higher birth weights and larger heads than girls (e.g., Silver, 1971). The birth difficulties that occur in the labor and delivery of some boys may result in their subsequent learning problems.

Other studies report that boys lag behind girls in all areas of maturation (Ames, 1968). According to these studies, boys are often unready for the school tasks that confront them in early childhood. Their frustration and poor performance in the early school years condition later patterns of underachievement.

According to some research (e.g., Gaddes, 1980; Olson, 1984; Restak, 1979), differences in the achievement patterns of boys and girls can be explained on the basis of innate differences in brain functioning. This research suggests that girls perform better in reading and boys in mathematics because of differences in their modes of cerebral functioning (see Harness et al., 1984). Since reading problems cause teachers the most concern, boys are referred more often. The mathematical difficulties that girls encounter may be of less concern to teachers and may not result in referral or identification.

Environmental factors.   According to Good and Brophy (1987), however, differential patterns of achievement cannot be explained on the basis of innate biological differences. "Performance differences between the sexes are for the most part learned behaviors (induced by societal expectations and the behaviors of adults)," according to Good and Brophy (1987, p. 32). Their synthesis of the literature suggests the importance of looking at environmental factors to explain differences in the academic performance of girls and boys.

The typical behavior of boys and girls in school is conditioned by society. Teachers' expectations tend to mirror more general societal stereotypes: Boys are, and should be, more aggressive; girls are, and should be, more compliant (Blaubergs, 1978; Good & Brophy, 1987).

Teachers' expectations and students' behaviors interact in complicated ways that influence both students' actual achievement and teachers' perceptions about their achievement. According to Carrier (1983, p. 963), "docile, industrious, polite, and conforming students . . . often get grades higher than their objective performance and aptitude merit." Conversely, aggressive students are perceived more often to be low achievers, and low-achieving students are at risk in school (Miles, 1986). They receive less positive attention from teachers; their grades, achievement test scores, and even their IQ scores tend to deteriorate over time (Good & Brophy, 1987; Rosenbaum, 1975).

These school factors affect special education referral and placement decisions, many of which are made on the basis of students' misbehavior. In one study (Phipps, 1982), 82 percent of the boys were referred primarily because of their behavior. Because aggressive behavior influences teachers' treatment of boys in the classroom, however, such students may, in fact, become underachievers. By the time they are referred, their patterns of underachievement may be entrenched.

This reasoning helps explain Clarizio and Phillips' (1986) apparently contradictory finding that gender bias *did not* influence teachers' referral and placement decisions. Both the boys and the girls who were placed in LD programs had similar discrepancy scores. Because Clarizio and Phillips did not compare a group of students who were referred with a sample of students who were not referred, however, they could not report the extent to which girls' underachievement was overlooked. They might have found, as others have (see e.g., Owen, 1978), that underachieving girls are less often referred for testing.

The underachievement of girls may go unnoticed because of their compliant behavior in the classroom. Because they get their work done and please their teachers, girls may be given higher grades than they deserve (Sexton, 1969). Teachers, who typically equate achievement with grades, may not notice the underachievement of girls. Teachers' perceptions and expectations may also reflect society's more pronounced interest in the achievement of males. Since boys are expected to be achievers, their academic difficulties may cause greater worry than similar difficulties experienced by girls (Schlosser & Algozzine, 1980; Smith, 1983).

Gifted Girls and Women

Although women's economic status has improved in recent years, women in the United States still earn less money than men. Part of the difference in salaries is due to the history of discrimination against women. Like blacks, their access to administrative positions, even their access to the professions and to business, is more recent than that of white males.

Although more women now have positions equal in status to men's, they lack the years of tenure that their male counterparts have. A study of salaries by West Virginia's Department of Education is illustrative. The study found that men hold 66 percent of the highest paying jobs in the state's educational system in spite of the fact that women outnumber men two to one ("More Women in Education," 1987). The women who *do* hold high-paying positions earn less than men in comparable positions.

Women's relative lack of economic resources becomes apparent when they are divorced from their husbands. In the economic changes that accompany divorce, women's standard of living declines by 73 percent; the husband's rises by 42 percent (Rose, 1986). The fact that the children of divorced parents typically stay with the mother may help explain divorced women's relative poverty.

The effects of racial discrimination are combined with those of sex in the case of black women; and their economic resources are even more limited than those of white women. More than half of the black women who are heads of household earn less than $10,000 per year (Rose, 1986).

Scholastic achievement.   Girls tend to earn better grades in elementary school than do boys; but some studies find that by the time girls are in high school, their grades are no longer higher than boys' (Gage & Berliner, 1975). Boys' poorer elementary school classwork may be a function of social pressures to behave in ways that are incompatible with high performance. The negative effects of discrimination against girls, on the other hand, are seen in their low mathematics achievement and in the comparatively limited forms their adult achievement takes.

Low math achievement.   The most consistent sex-linked difference researchers have found is in spatial ability (Maccoby & Jacklin, 1974), but differences have also been found in mathematics achievement. Although the differences at most levels are trivial, at the higher levels of ability they are dramatic. In the mathematics competitions sponsored by Johns Hopkins University's Study of Mathematically Precocious Youth, girls scored in the highest ranges with much less frequency than boys (Benbow & Stanley, 1981). Twenty-seven percent of the seventh- and eighth-grade boys scored higher than 600 on the SAT-Math; not one of the girls scored higher than 600 (Benbow & Stanley, 1980). The Johns Hopkins findings are mixed, however. It is, for example, interesting that the highest group of girls scored higher on a spatial measure than did the highest group of boys (Astin, 1974).

The difference in boys' and girls' math achievement seems to increase with age. Astin (1974) found that between the seventh and eighth grades, gifted boys' SAT-Math scores increased by more points than the girls' means.

Benbow and Stanley (1981) ascribe the differences they have observed to differences in biologically influenced intellectual factors. Nonetheless, other findings make it difficult to interpret the interaction of gender-related biological differences and the environment. For example, the fact that economically disadvantaged females score higher than economically disadvantaged males on both mathematics and verbal tests (Maccoby & Jacklin, 1972) suggests that socialization can strongly influence the character of achievement differences between males and females. It seems quite likely that the differences in the mathematics achievement of males and females can, with equal justice, be attributed to differences in how boys and girls experience mathematics.

Girls and boys experience mathematics unequally. Sells (1976) reports a study in which only 15 percent of the white females and 10 percent of the black females had the math prerequisites necessary for a math or science major in college. Casserly (1979) found that girls take fewer Advanced Placement courses than boys in math and science, and she found that counselors sometimes discourage girls from taking advanced math classes.

Fewer women than men pursue careers in mathematics or science. Women who do succeed in math may tend to identify with their fathers (Helson, 1971). Several studies report that girls who achieve at high levels in mathematics score high on masculine personality traits (e.g., Fox & Cohn, 1980). It should be recognized, however, that to refer to certain personality traits (like aggressiveness and independence) as masculine may be to conform to outdated stereotypes.

Girls' attitudes toward mathematics are most likely conditioned by complex family interactions; however, clear trends do not appear in the research. Helson (1971), for example, found that creative female mathematicians tended to be oldest daughters. Astin (1974), on the other hand, found that mathematically talented girls tended to be youngest daughters from large families. As Astin points out, the differences in boys and girls' achievement may, in part, be a difference in educational level of the parents. The girls' parents in Astin's study were not quite so well educated as the boys' parents.

According to Astin (1974) other factors in the family may also play a role in promoting children's interest and achievement in mathematics. During childhood, boys are given toys that are more likely to develop spatial ability than the toys given girls. Boys' parents are also more likely to purchase books, puzzles, science kits, microscopes, and other scientific toys for them. The parents of boys are more likely to provide them with tutoring and other instructional activities. Although the parents of all mathematically talented children indicate exceptionally high interest in mathematics and science, the parents of mathematically talented girls are much less apt to show their interest by holding high aspirations for their daughters' accomplishment in these fields.

Achievement and compliance.   Much of the antagonism gifted girls elicit from others may result from their failure to conform to social expectations for their behavior. Girls who are bright are sometimes viewed less favorably than their male counterparts. In one study, other children used the following negative adjectives to describe gifted girls: "aggressive," "aloof," "bossy," "careless," "conceited," and "dull" (Solano, 1977). Girls who score high on divergent thinking tests may also have greater difficulty winning acceptance from other children than do boys who score equally high (Kurtzman, 1967). Fox (1978) found gifted girls more fearful of peer rejection than gifted boys. If, as research seems to indicate, gifted girls *are* more likely to be rejected, girls' fears may be warranted (Solano, 1977).

Adult achievement of gifted women.   Among Terman's gifted subjects there was a dramatic difference between the scholarly accomplishments of males and those of females. Despite equal IQ scores and considerable literary talent among the gifted women, the men in the study published hundreds of times more books and articles than the women.

Sears and Barbee (1977) studied 430 of Terman's female subjects. In response to inquiries about their employment patterns and perceived success, the women who were working outside the home reported greater satisfaction with their lives than other women in the sample. Gifted women who were heads of household expressed particular satisfaction. The results of this study may not be representative, however. As with any self-report study, the accuracy of the subjects' responses influences the study's conclusions. In this study the respondents had some compelling reasons to be less than candid. These unmarried women may have been defensive about their status and, therefore, may have exaggerated their reported levels of satisfaction. Other studies suggest that, in general, more women than men are disappointed with their lives (Maccoby & Jacklin, 1974). According to Maccoby and Jacklin (1974, p. 153), women "tend to look back with some regret on what they now see as missed opportunities."

GIFTED STUDENTS IN RURAL SCHOOLS

Recently, educators have been concerned about the quality of schooling in rural and small school districts. The following discussion needs to be interpreted in light of the consistent finding that rural schools—and small schools in general—provide a better-integrated educational experience for students of all backgrounds and achievement levels than do large urban or suburban schools (Barker & Gump, 1964; Stockard & Mayberry, 1986; Tyack, 1974). In fact, some evidence suggests that once socioeconomic status is controlled, small schools also produce better achievement among students (Stockard & Mayberry, 1986).

This same literature nonetheless suggests that *very bright* students are at an academic disadvantage in small rural schools. Educators are particularly concerned about the difficulty that such districts have in providing adequate academic programs for their most academically able students.

Rural, Small, and Isolated Schools: Definitions

Recent interest in the problems of rural education has sparked some discussion about the distinction between rural and urban environments (DeYoung, 1987). One difficulty in making this distinction is the variety of geographies, economies, political realities, and cultures that characterize rural districts. Some rural citizens are poor, some affluent; some are white, some black; some speak English, some Spanish.

Focusing on the range of this variation, however, serves to obscure the long-standing disparities that have always existed between urban and rural districts. For example, wherever they live and whatever pursuits they follow, rural residents *do* tend to be poorer than metropolitan residents; they *are* close to nature because they work as miners, farmers, and fishermen; and they *are* more apt to know all about their neighbors' lives.

In order to study common phenomena, then, some definition of ruralness is needed. The National Rural Development Institute (NRDI, 1986) defined a rural area as having fewer than 150 inhabitants per square mile or as being located in a county in which 60 percent or more of the population lives in communities of 5,000 people or less. They defined "small school district" as one with an enrollment of 2,000 or less. According to NRDI, an isolated district or school was located at least 100 miles from a district that was not small.

Some organizations base their definitions of rural counties on the definition of "urban" used by the Federal Office of Management and Budget (OMB). In such cases, everything that is not considered urban is classified as rural. The OMB definition of "urban area" is based on a variety of demographic and economic characteristics. Basically, an urban area is associated with a population center of 50,000 or more. It has a population density of at least 1,000 persons per square mile and is bound together by an effective infrastructure (i.e., highways, railroads, and communications facilities).

Characteristics of Rural Gifted Students

In studying rural gifted children, some cautions should be kept in mind. First, rural children are a diverse group. There may be more differences between some groups of rural children than between rural and urban children in general. Low-income rural children, for example, are different from rural children whose families' incomes are average or above. Rural children who are isolated and who belong to cultural minorities are probably different from rural children whose families belong to the cultural mainstream.

In addition, it is probable that the majority of rural children who have been identified as gifted according to commonly used standards (e.g., achievement or IQ scores in the 95th percentile or above on national norms) are more like middle-class urban and suburban children than like most rural children. Consequently, the characteristics of identified gifted children may not be very helpful in identifying bright rural children whose academic achievement has been inhibited by lack of support for their education.

One significant characteristic of rural students in general is that they spend less time in school than urban children. They spend fewer days in school during the school year; and about 65 percent of rural, low-income children drop out of high school (Kuvlesky, 1973; Riddel, 1971). These findings suggest that the problem of underachievement among rural gifted students is related to conditions in rural schools. Rural communities may not have the resources to provide stimulating and varied academic programs, and they may not have funds to offer any special opportunities for their brightest students (Birnbaum, n.d.).

Identification problems.   Educators often fail to identify as gifted the brightest students from poor rural districts. Such students are probably excluded because of the effects of their poverty rather than the effects of their rural upbringing. Because they are not identified as gifted, however, these bright students may be deprived of the educational experiences necessary for their optimal cognitive development.

Procedures used to identify bright students do not typically result in the identification of many poor, rural children. Even the brightest students in poor rural schools may have IQ or achievement scores that are below the cut-off level for admission to gifted programs.

Educators sometimes adopt subjective identification methods because they believe that such methods will serve to identify gifted students from poor, rural backgrounds. Such methods, however, may be less culturally fair than they seem. Teacher nominations based on checklists of characteristics of gifted children may locate those children whose behavior is most like that of middle-class children; they may fail to identify those rural children who have the highest level of academic achievement within their peer group.

Characteristics of Rural Families and Communities

Cultural values in rural areas may contribute to the underachievement of the *identified* gifted students in those areas. In addition, they may create conditions that make it unlikely for many rural students to make high scores on standardized tests of ability and achievement. Finally, they may condition postsecondary school and career decisions that limit the adult attainment of the brightest students from rural areas.

Because the family is a crucial social unit in rural communities, it tends to be the most influential agency for promoting the cultural values of the community. Church and neighborhood groups also serve a socializing function. Though some characteristics of rural families tend to promote achievement, others tend to limit it. The following discussion considers some generalizations about the character of rural families and relates these characteristics to the achievement motivation of bright students in rural areas.

Characteristics of rural families. Rural families tend to be less accepting of diversity of belief and behavior than urban families (Willits, Bealer, & Crider, 1973). Because rural communities are more insulated than urban communities, their character is influenced by fewer agents of change. Families in such communities often preserve the traditions of previous generations and resist diverse ideas (Birnbaum, n.d.; Photiadis, 1983). Gifted children, however, are often divergent, and their patterns of development may differ considerably from the norm. Families of such children may attempt to suppress the children's divergent behaviors and deemphasize their developmental precocity.

Because they are concerned with preserving tradition, rural families tend to conform more rigidly to sex-role stereotypes than do urban families (Kleinsasser, 1986). Hence, they are quite likely to distinguish the kinds of activities and studies that are appropriate for boys from those that are appropriate for girls. Rural families may also be more concerned with the achievements of boys. Whereas boys are expected to choose a career as well as to have a family, girls are often expected to be homemakers only. These values limit opportunities for both boys and girls. Rural boys may be less likely to study subjects such as art and literature, which are considered to be "feminine." Girls may avoid "masculine" subjects like math and science. Additionally, bright girls may choose to marry early rather than to pursue a college degree.

Rural families are often ambivalent in their attitude toward education (see Box 11-1). Many rural families perceive the school as an *unwelcome* influence on their children. In rural communities where religious values are well defined, the school may be viewed as an agent of suspicious secular influence (Cummings, Briggs, & Mercy, 1977). Even when religion is not an issue, parents may consider the school curriculum to be irrelevant, or even hostile to their values.

Finally, some families may view education as a way for the larger society to lure their children away from the rural community (Nachtigal, 1982; Sher, 1977). Families may fear that when students learn new skills, they will develop higher aspirations. They believe that such aspirations will ultimately cause their children to leave the community. Unfortunately, such fears are based on real conditions. Rural economies often cannot support too many professional, managerial, or scholarly jobs (Nachtigal, 1982; Sher, 1977). Those rural students who get advanced training may *need* to leave the community in order to find suitable work.

Characteristics of rural communities. The ethos of the rural community is more egalitarian than meritocratic (Counts, 1930). In such an ethic, it may be considered uncouth to claim special privileges or services, even if some special provisions, like gifted education, seem to make pedagogical sense. This factor may explain both why it is difficult to establish *any* program for apt learners in a rural district, and why, when established, such programs tend to enroll disproportionate numbers of the children of the local elite (cf. Mills, 1959, pp. 39–42).

This dual observation makes it necessary to distinguish between gifted programs that serve genuinely rural populations and those that do not. Even in rural areas, gifted programs seem to be most strongly established in the largest towns, an observation that appears to be consistent with the findings of Cox and associates (1985). In many ways gifted children in programs located in these towns *do* resemble typical gifted students. Nonetheless, even in large rural towns, the egalitarian ethos may be stronger than in affluent suburban or urban districts.

BOX 11-1   Case Study of a Gifted Child from Southern Appalachia

In 1967, a residential high school, the Lincoln School, was established in central Kentucky to provide a program for gifted, but low-income and culturally different students. The students were nominated by local school district superintendents, who based their nominations on the students' socioeconomic status, ethnic or racial status, and potential for achievement. This report is about one of the 240 students who attended the school during the few years of its operation. It is taken from "Junior—Gifted and Disadvantaged," a chapter in Hauck and Freehill's (1972) *The Gifted—Case Studies.*

Junior's hometown is an isolated rural community in western Kentucky. The community, an approximately 800 acre area, has five Protestant churches and one grocery store, which is also the post office. The population is about 200. The nearest elementary school is fifteen miles away and the high school slightly farther. Most of the men in the town, including Junior's father, earn a living through unskilled or semiskilled labor and farming. Most of the women are housewives. Families in the area hold traditional, conservative views on politics and religion. They rarely leave the community. Going to town on Saturday, going to church, and visiting with relatives make up most of their social life.

According to Lincoln School personnel, Junior's family is strongly interdependent, valuing each other's affection and company, but also frequently in conflict. [Although the authors of the chapter assert that Junior's family members are extremely interdependent and hostile, it is possible that stereotypes about rural Appalachian families influenced their perception. They offer no examples that clearly support their view.]

Junior's grandmother appears to be a major influence in his life. He is her favorite grandchild, and she has taken special interest in his development, reading to him and encouraging his interest in books and in religion. Her attention to his intellectual development contrasts with his parents' lack of commitment to the education of Junior and his siblings.

The teachers and counselor at Lincoln School believe that the impact of Junior's community and home is seen in his alienation from his peer group at the school. His strong commitment to religion, his conservative politics, and his ambivalence toward racial integration set him apart from many of the other students. Junior likes the other students, however, and reportedly has become more tolerant of beliefs that differ from his. His teachers report: "He is torn between 'old time religion' and a kind of hedonism; between being close to nature with little responsibility and few worries and the satisfaction of intellectual encounter. . . . Rigid and conservative ways of religion, politics, social relationships, and race have given way to questioning since he came to Lincoln School."

Although, with an IQ score of 140 on the WISC, his fears seemed unwarranted, Junior is anxious about his ability to succeed academically at the school. He fears that he is neither smart enough nor self-disciplined enough to compete with the other bright students there. He is particularly worried about math, the subject in which his achievement is lowest. He needs frequent reassurance about his ability to do the work. The teachers find that he is more comfortable when math and science assignments are explained in detail so that he knows precisely what is expected of him. They think that Junior probably misses the easy success he enjoyed in elementary and junior high school. His exceptional intellectual ability allowed him to excel in his rural school district without much effort; and, not surprisingly, he enjoyed his success. His teachers believe that his easy success in the past left him unprepared for difficult academic work. They are confident that he has the intellectual ability to master the material they present.

Junior's IQ and achievement scores on different tests vary (as they do with most children); but, with the exception of one math subtest, they are consistently above average. His group IQ test scores range from 106 IQ in the first grade to 127 IQ in the eighth. Although this *may* represent real differences in his ability at those age levels, the limitations of group tests often result in gifted children's making lower scores than they do on more comprehensive, individually-administered tests. The apparent increase may simply reflect differences in the tests at different grade levels. In the eighth grade, Junior's grade equivalence scores on the California Achievement Test were in the eleventh grade in reading comprehension, in the twelfth grade in grammar, and in the tenth grade in arithmetic. His total score was in the 95th percentile on national norms. On an achievement test given in the ninth grade, Junior's highest scores were in social studies and literature (both in the 99th percentile); his lowest score was in quantitative thinking (math), in which he scored in the 40th percentile.

Junior's anxiety about schoolwork is manifest in his fear of evaluation and in his sharp self-criticism. His classsroom performance fluctuates from day to day; however, he excels in English and social studies. His compositions for these classes are particularly well written and creative. In math and science, he succeeds sporadically. In spite of his fear of math, he scored above average (in the 75th percentile) on a standardized algebra test. Teachers attribute his low grades to his poor study habits and ambivalent attitude toward school.

Source: Adapted from Tisdall, W., Brown, D., Bynum, C., & Robinson, S. (1972). "Junior—Gifted and Disadvantaged." In B. B. Hauck & M. F. Freehill (Eds.), *The gifted—Case studies* (pp. 86–104). Dubuque, IA: Brown.) Used by permission.

Characteristics of rural schools.   Although the underachievement of bright students in rural areas may relate to family and community characteristics, it may also relate to conditions in rural schools. Rural schools are often located in low-income areas. Therefore they may be unable to afford the cost of high-quality academic programs or of special teachers for gifted students. The effects of historically underfunded schools are felt by all the students, but they are as academically damaging to able students as they are to impoverished students.

Lack of appropriate programs may significantly harm the cognitive development of bright students in rural schools (Birnbaum, n.d.). According to Plowman (n.d., p. 73), gifted children in rural areas are likely to be "(1) isolated from intellectual stimulation and from learning resources; (2) unsophisticated—uniformed, lacking in social and learning skills; and (3) deprived culturally and educationally."

Why do rural schools have such a difficult time providing academic programs for the brightest students? The following list presents some of the constraints that rural schools encounter.

1. Rural schools in some areas may not have sufficient space to house special programs for gifted students.
2. Small rural schools may not have sufficient numbers of gifted students to justify the implementation of special programs for these students.
3. The distances between rural schools within one district may be so great that the cost and time of transportation to centralized gifted programs may be prohibitive.
4. Parents of rural gifted students may oppose programs that require their children to ride buses to gifted programs located at schools other than their local school.
5. Rural high schools may have very few elective options (e.g., science courses, foreign language courses, and music courses).
6. Rural high schools may be unable to provide advanced-level courses in required subjects such as English and mathematics.

The family, community, and school factors described previously help determine the nature of rural children's schooling in that they affect children's and parents' attitudes toward school and what is taught there. In addition, as Riddel (1971) suggests, the same factors affected many of the children's *teachers* when they were in school. Although these teachers may be as conscientious and hard-working as urban or suburban teachers, their education often suffered from the same lack of community resources and commitment to intellectual concerns as that of their students. Because they were not exposed to an excellent education system with ample resources and a public committed to high educational standards, rural teachers' expectations regarding student achievement are sometimes far too low. Consequently, bright children in rural school districts are seldom challenged to achieve their potential. They are in a "disadvantaged" school system. In some rural states and regions, the longer rural students are in school, the further their performance falls below that of the national norm.

SUMMARY

This chapter reviewed the effects of unfair discrimination on very bright students. The discussion reminded readers that discrimination is an established fact and then proceeded to examine the quality of that discrimination, in particular the nature of its impact on different groups. Among these groups, low-income students figured prominently because poverty is a condition associated with distinctions of social class. The discussion evaluated the underachievement of bright students from minority groups and from rural areas in light of evidence about the effects of discrimination.

Discrimination associated with gender was also examined. It was noted that under certain circumstances, males may be the object of unfair discrimination, as in the case of their disproportionate representation in programs intended for learning disabled students. In other cases, females are the object of discrimination. Their achievement in particular subjects such as science and mathematics is often adversely affected, and their career attainment may also be inhibited.

In general, discussion suggested that among groups who suffer the effects of unfair discrimination, the most crippling educational effect is diminished expectations. Low expectations—and internalized responses to those expectations—contribute not only to the underachievement of some students but also to their decreased social mobility and limited economic competiveness.

12

Methods of Talent Development

Focusing Questions

1. How should a school district's identification process relate to its definition of giftedness? Are some definitions easier to operationalize than others?
2. In what way can the special education "continuum of services" be adapted so that it provides suitable placement options for gifted students?
3. Why are accelerative options essential to the education of gifted students? In what way do these options enable gifted students to develop higher-order thinking skills?
4. What is the distinction between a broad notion of curriculum

enrichment and a narrow one? Which conception supports more appropriate programs for gifted students?
5. Why should academics form the basis of a curriculum for gifted students?
6. What contributions do inductive, as opposed to expository, formats make to the development of academic concepts and skills?

IDENTIFICATION PROCEDURES

Before it is possible to provide special educational services to gifted students, schools must identify such students. Identification methods depend, in large part, on the definition of giftedness that a school or district adopts. If, for example, a school considers giftedness to be high intelligence and high creativity, the school will need to use measures of intelligence and creativity to locate the most gifted students. If, on the other hand, a school defines giftedness as artistic talent, it will need to develop techniques to identify those students whose artistic performance is the most exceptional.

Although this precept seems so obvious that it hardly needs to be mentioned, it is violated nearly as often as it is followed (Howley et al., 1986). Part of the reason is that not all definitions of giftedness are equally operational. Although it is fairly easy to measure academic potential, for instance, it is much more difficult to measure leadership potential. Districts that attempt to identify gifted leaders will, therefore, find it difficult to locate technically adequate measures of this characteristic. Similarly, districts that include creativity or social intelligence in their definitions of giftedness will have a hard time finding appropriate measurement instruments.

Regardless of their definition of giftedness, however, most districts use a similar sequence of identification procedures: referral, assessment, eligibility determination, and placement.

Referral

Student referral is the first step in the identification process. A teacher or parent may be the one to make the school aware that a particular student demonstrates exceptional abilities. Often, schools solicit referrals from teachers. Less often, they refer all students who score at a certain high level on the group ability or achievement tests that are administered routinely. In order for the referral process to work well, however, teachers or parents must refer those students who are most likely to be eligible for placement in the gifted program. Sometimes this is a difficult determination to make. The patterns of performance that students demonstrate in classrooms may not reflect their true levels of achievement. On the other hand, students' performance on group aptitude or achievement tests may be more predictive of their performance on the individually administered assessment instruments most commonly used to determine eligibility.

Effectiveness and efficiency of referral procedures.   The goal of an identification effort is to locate all of the students who are eligible for placement in a program. The *effectiveness* of an identification procedure represents the degree to which the procedure is able to select all of the eligible students. For example, a referral procedure that locates 95 percent of the eligible children in a school is said to be 95 percent effective. At the referral stage, it is desirable to identify a sufficient percentage of potentially eligible students so that no eligible students are overlooked.

Many school districts will also be concerned that they avoid referring too many students who turn out *not* to be eligible for placement in the program. Students who do not qualify are often disappointed and, erroneously, consider themselves to have failed. The *efficiency* of a referral process represents the extent to which the process includes students who are eligible for placement and at the same time excludes students who are not eligible. In order for an identification procedure to be optimally effective, it will necessarily be less than optimally efficient. Referral procedures that are 100 percent effective tend to be about 50 percent efficient. Schools that make the commitment to find all of the students who will qualify have to test quite a few students who do not qualify. Schools that prefer to avoid excessive or unproductive testing have to accept the fact that they will overlook some of their gifted students.

Referral sources.   According to Marland (1972), classroom teachers are the most common source of referrals. Nevertheless, classroom teachers may not be the best source of referrals. Teachers may mistakenly assume that the most compliant students in their classes, or the ones with the highest grades, have the highest levels of ability.

A much more *effective* referral method involves the use of group ability or achievement tests. Pegnato and Birch (1959) compared several methods of referral and concluded that group tests were much more effective than teacher nomination. The most effective referral method they found involved a dual criterion: a group IQ score of at least 115 (mean = 100, sd = 15) *or* achievement scores in reading and math that were three years above level. Using this referral method, the authors were able to identify 96.7 percent of the gifted children in their sample. This high degree of effectiveness contrasted sharply with the effectiveness of teacher referral: 45.1 percent.

Assessment

The second step in the identification process involves the assessment of those students who are referred. Assessment usually includes testing. It may also include the evaluation of students' creative products or performances or the observation of students' behavior.

The accuracy of the assessment process is increased when educators follow certain guidelines. First, they should always choose assessment techniques that correspond to the districts' definition of giftedness. If the district defines giftedness as superior academic ability, educators should choose the best techniques for measuring academic ability. Considering the imprecision of grades as a measure of academic performance, their use to identify academically able students is questionable. Using individual intelligence tests or achievement tests is much more appropriate.

Second, educators should select assessment techniques that have been shown to be both reliable and valid. *Reliable* measures give the same results in repeated administrations. This characteristic of an assessment instrument is important because it assures that a score obtained on one administration of the instrument is likely to resemble a score obtained on a subsequent administration of the same instrument. The more reliable a test, the less error is reflected in a given score. The *validity* of an assessment instrument, on the other hand, shows the degree to which the instrument measures what it purports to measure. This characteristic of assessment instruments is determined in a number of different ways depending on whether the content of the instrument, its conceptual basis, or its predictive ability is being scrutinized.

Finally, educators should be cautious in their interpretations of assessment results. Because assessment instruments provide *samples* of behavior, they reveal only limited information about students' performance (Salvia & Ysseldyke, 1987). In addition, a score on any assessment instrument necessarily reflects a certain degree of error. Cautious interpretation of test results includes consideration of the error involved in the administration of the instrument.

Intelligence testing.   Because most definitions of giftedness implicate superior intelligence, IQ tests are among the most common tests given as part of school districts' assessment procedures (Alvino, McDonnel, & Richert, 1981). Many different IQ tests are available, and districts vary widely in their choice of tests.

Group intelligence tests are popular in some school districts because they are easy and inexpensive to administer and score. Such tests, however, have a fairly broad range of error. Scores obtained on these tests may actually reflect characteristics other than academic potential. Because of their format, such tests may really measure achievement in reading comprehension rather than academic potential. Some very intelligent children who are not good readers or who process information slowly will be penalized by group tests.

Individually administered screening tests are also used by some schools. These tests measure very limited samples of behavior; they are neither sufficiently reliable nor sufficiently valid to use as the basis for decisions about students' eligibility.

The best intelligence tests available are individually administered evaluation instruments such as the Stanford-Binet Intelligence Scale and the Wechsler Intelligence Scale for Children-Revised (WISC-R). Such tests take approximately two hours to give and can be administered and interpreted only by a psychologist or psychometrist. Nevertheless, using this type of test is warranted. These instruments are more adequate technically than other measures of intelligence, they sample a wider variety of behaviors, and they are better able to predict students' academic performance.

Achievement testing.   Definitions of giftedness that include academic talent require that students' achievement be evaluated to determine eligibility for placement in the gifted program. Students' academic achievement may also be measured as a way of determining their levels of intelligence. Since superior intelligence represents the potential for advanced academic work, high academic achievement implies high intelligence. Students whose academic achievement is in the superior range *do* have the intelligence necessary to achieve at such high levels, regardless of their actual scores on tests that purport to measure intelligence.

As with intelligence tests, there are three kinds of achievement tests: group tests, individual screening tests, and individual evaluation tests. Again, the individual evaluation instruments are the ones most useful for guiding placement decisions. This observation relates particularly to the measurement of elementary school children's achievement. To evaluate the achievement of older students, educators may need to rely on the use of off-level group achievement tests (Stanley, 1976b). This testing practice, while not optimal, is necessary nonetheless: There are no individual evaluation tests that adequately measure the achievement of older gifted students.

Measuring creativity and talent in the arts.   Some districts include creativity in their definitions of giftedness. Hence, educators must use instruments that intend to measure creativity. Such tests are of limited value, however. The relationship between high scores on such tests and superior creative performance is speculative. Many tests of creativity actually measure characteristics such as ideational fluency or intelligence (Hocevar, 1980). In addition, creativity tests have such poor reliability and validity that their use to guide placement decisions is unwise.

A better approach is for districts to measure creative *performance* in the arts rather than to attempt to evaluate general creative *potential.* To determine arts talent, however, is both difficult and costly. Districts with well developed programs for the artistically gifted usually rely on panels of experts to judge the artistic talents of those students referred for assessment (see e.g., Chetelat, 1981).

Unmeasureable characteristics. Some definitions of giftedness include characteristics that cannot be measured. Leadership potential and social intelligence are among such characteristics. When districts include these characteristics in their definitions, they most often rely on the judgment of teachers to identify those students who are eligible for placement. Basing program eligibility on such subjective assessments is troublesome. Teachers are not the best judges of students' academic aptitude. Can we assume that they are better judges of leadership potential or social intelligence?

The relevance of such characteristics is also questionable. Not much evidence supports the claim that leadership in the classroom predicts political or intellectual leadership in adulthood. Districts can probably strengthen their operational definitions of giftedness by eliminating such categories.

PLACEMENT OPTIONS AND PROCEDURES

Developing placement options and procedures is less "technical" than determining reasonable identification methods, but it is not necessarily easier. In the case of placement, educators and parents must understand why gifted students, as opposed to other students, can benefit more from certain instructional environments than from others. They also need to know that many people—including some educators—do not share this understanding. Therefore, it is important for those who advocate gifted education to define clearly the options and procedures that entitle gifted students to special programs.

Why Do Gifted Students Need Placement Options?

Very bright children encounter academic difficulties in the unmodified regular classroom (Lewis & Kanes, 1980). This is not surprising. According to the assumptions behind the high-IQ definition of giftedness, gifted children in a typical classroom are more advanced than all of the other children. They are more rare than 1 in 30 students. Because there are so few high-IQ students in the regular classroom, teachers cannot afford to spend too much time cultivating the academic talents of such children. It would not be efficient for them to do so. Therefore, in most cases, the regular classroom is not an environment of particular benefit to gifted students.

Before turning to a discussion of environments that better accommodate the needs of gifted students, it might be wise to consider a popular argument that has been advanced in *defense* of regular class placement for gifted students. This argument (e.g., Henson, 1976, p. 110) runs as follows:

> Gifted children will need to interact with average people all their lives. Gifted children, after all, are destined to become our national leaders. If they do not associate with ordinary people, they will become socially isolated. As a result, they will not be able to lead. They will have lost touch with the concerns of average people.

This argument has a compelling emotional appeal. At the same time, however, it is based on some shaky assumptions. Of these shaky assumptions, one is, ironically, elitist.

First of all, gifted children are not "supernormal." In many respects they are average. They are, for example, hard to distinguish from average students on the basis of social adjustment, social distance, or social attractiveness (Maddux, Scheiber, & Bass, 1982). They tend, perhaps, to be a bit more well adjusted than average students when they are put in accelerated placements (Braga, 1971; Robinson & Janos, 1986; Kulik & Kulik, 1984) but the social differences are never very great in either negative or positive directions.

Second, though many people are fond of saying so, there is little evidence to suggest that gifted students are any more likely to become leaders than other students of the same social class. Terman's work supports this finding (Terman & Oden, 1959). In Hollingworth's (1942) view, the highly gifted were *less* attractive as leaders than were students of only moderate ability.

Third, to promote the gifted as "natural" leaders is elitist (Weiler, 1978). It is odd that such undemocratic principles and values are espoused so openly by some educators (and some parents). After all, leadership demands a variety of abilities, and academic ability is only a small part of what is required for leadership (Bass, 1981). Many gifted students will demonstrate only average interest in and ability to lead. In fact, leadership within a profession—which is where we might expect it to be demonstrated in most cases—is *not* strongly related to academic ability or achievement (Baird, 1985).

What Sorts of Placement Options Are There?

There are enough gifted children in any school or any school district to provide a pool of students for a gifted program. It is clear that these children do not do nearly so well as they might because of the limits imposed by their placement in the regular classroom. It is equally clear that something of benefit ought to be arranged for these students.

The discussion above, however, suggests that the regular classroom is not an environment that provides appropriate academic expectations for gifted students. One way to get an overview of more suitable placement options is through the notion of "continuum of services," a concept that is familiar to special education teachers.

Howley and associates (1986) adapted this notion to include gifted students. The organizing principle of the original continuum for handicapped students was *social involvement.* The organizing principle of the adaptation for gifted students is *academic advancement.* Academic advancement, of course, reflects the uncommon academic talent and rapid learning rate characteristic of gifted children. The continuum of services in this interpretation can also accommodate the academic delay of some handicapped students.

A continuum of service. In this adaptation, the regular class represents the mid-point of the continuum of services. Here is the continuum for gifted students:

special school—advanced program	*(most advanced)*
special class—advanced program	
resource program—advanced program	
regular class—developmental placement	
regular class—enriched program	
regular class—regular program	*(least advanced)*

The basic point of using such a continuum is to illustrate the fact that a *variety* of placement options is necessary in order to accommodate the various needs and talents of the gifted students within any district. A district's program may, of necessity, emphasize one option or another.

Usually, developmental placement, resource program, and special class placements need to be the most commonly offered options. But *all* options should be potentially available, to serve students whose educational needs cannot be met in placement options that are actually available.

Among the options that fall within the above continuum are the following (ordered from least advanced to most advanced):

Regular Class—Regular Program

A gifted student may be left full time in the regular classroom. This placement should be made only if a gifted student exhibits a serious discrepancy between IQ and achievement in all areas; that is, if the gifted student's achievement is normal. It may also be the wisest placement if the gifted program is disorganized, is not academically based, or offers no better alternative.

Regular Class—Enriched Program

A gifted student may be left full time in the regular classroom with the regular teacher (or visiting teacher of the gifted) providing grade-level activities on topics related to, but not included in, the regular program. The goal here is to interest the child, not actually to provide advanced instruction. Enriched programs in resource rooms espouse the same goal and differ little from this placement.

Regular Class—Developmental Placement

A gifted student may be given instruction in a higher grade or in a more advanced class in a high-school sequence. This placement may be full time or part time. This sort of placement is a very economical way to implement acceleration.

Resource Class—Advanced Placement

A gifted student may attend classes with the teacher of the gifted to receive advanced instruction. Resource rooms, however, typically provide other sorts of services besides advanced placement, and many resource teachers travel between several schools. These limitations can cause problems that undermine consistent instruction.

Special Class—Advanced Program

A gifted student may attend a special class. At the elementary level, the teacher of the gifted might offer regularly scheduled accelerated reading and math classes. At the high-school level, a school might develop honors sections, or accelerated curricula (e.g., three years of mathematics in two). This option might also involve students in taking advanced courses at the college level.

Special School—Advanced Program

A gifted student might be sent to a special school that offers advanced and rapidly paced classes. A number of such schools exist, especially for advanced high-school and junior high-school students. In addition, a number of early-entry college programs seek specifically to accommodate gifted junior and senior high-school students. Such programs, too, fall in this category.

How Do We Determine Placements?

The need to keep placements potentially available challenges educators' problem-solving skills. In order to organize the placement of students in particular options, some set of procedures is necessary. In previous times, placement was much simpler—as was identification. An educator selected a test, gave the test to whomever was thought appropriate, and placed students in programs. In fact, students in regular classrooms are often assigned to particular teachers, programs, or sections in just this way.

Gifted children, however, are in many states considered to be "exceptional students." In fact, the Council for Exceptional Children (CEC) has included gifted students, together with handicapped students, in this category since 1922. Studies suggest that gifted education programs are stronger in states that include gifted students under the rubric of "exceptional students" (C. Howley, 1986). There is a big difference, however, between having somewhat stronger programs at the state level and having good placement options and procedures at the local level. Strong state leadership is a good sign, but whether or not it leads to good placements is unclear.

Hence, local districts—whether they have strong state leadership or not—are wise to develop placement procedures for gifted students. The authors' bias favors administration of gifted education within special education. When gifted education is administered in this way, special regulations and due process rights protect the interests of gifted students, just as they do those of handicapped students. These procedures and rights will not be discussed in detail below; however, one important procedural point must be made. That point concerns the basis on which placement is made.

Determining gifted students' needs. The preceding discussion focused on placement options. Placement, however, is the outcome of a process of deliberation and reflection that begins with referral. Actually deciding where to place a student is the *final* event in this process. This point cannot be stressed too much. It is critically important not to place a student until *after* the student's "educational needs" have been determined.

Important distinctions exist between the diagnostic information contained in an evaluation, a student's needs, "prescriptions" to meet those needs, and placement. The purpose of evaluation is to provide information that can help educators and parents make those distinctions.

If, for example, a student's IQ is above the 99th percentile, but the same student's written language is at the 34th percentile, then, most likely, there exists a need. The nature of the need, however, is a matter of opinion. In this case, the student's need might be expressed in any one of the following ways, depending on circumstance (e.g., judgment of participants, negotiations of the placement committee, and other information about the student):

"Susan needs to improve her performance on the Woodcock-Johnson Written Language Cluster by 0.5 standard deviations."

or

"Susan needs to improve her written language skills substantially."

or

"Susan needs to improve her skill in distinguishing written misspellings from correct spellings."

Once a need is determined—and probably no more than 3 or 4 needs should be defined for a particular student—educators and parents should consider what *instruction* (not what placement!) can meet those needs. Perhaps, in the above case, Susan should work twice a week with a peer tutor who will help her write and edit short essays. Perhaps she should participate in a remedial spelling program (not actually a prescription the authors would commend to anyone). Perhaps Susan should work on a word processing program to achieve successively better drafts of regularly assigned work. All of the above are examples of prescriptions. We have so far said nothing of placement.

Once the prescriptions are ready, then placement can be determined. Are the prescriptions best accommodated by the resource teacher? In an available special class? Are they so unusual that "potentially available" placements must be brought to bear?

The reason for waiting to decide placement last is that students' needs ought to come before the convenience of the educational bureaucracy. It is too easy for educators to say, "Here's our gifted program; let's put this kid there," without ever *reflecting* about what the student is like. Yet, this scenario is not at all unusual.

If placement occurs within the special education process, then the above sequence of events will help make better placement meetings. That sequence of events provides an agenda for the meeting (interpreting diagnostic information, defining needs, specifying prescriptions, and making the placement); and it involves everyone in the outcome. When everyone has participated in this way, parents, teachers, and administrators are more likely to support the placement and implement it diligently. Subsequent interactions among them are more likely to be positive and productive.

Is It Really Necessary to Be So Careful?

Teachers of the gifted are dealing—or ought to be dealing—with the most able students in our schools. The education of these students needs to be taken seriously. If placement is only a way to enhance students' status and a source of pride for their parents, and programs do not result in more rapid learning and better thinking and reasoning skills among gifted students, then we have done an injustice to the students identified as gifted. Moreover, we have done an injustice to those students who were labeled "non-gifted"; these students could have been as well served by the program as the gifted students. One of the things we can do to help avoid these results is to be more careful about how we place students.

ACCELERATION

Because of the way in which giftedness is usually identified (i.e., high IQ), one of the most notable characteristics of gifted children is the accelerated rate at which they learn. They learn rapidly even when they remain in unmodified regular classrooms. Even underachieving gifted students served in an enrichment program can make two years of academic progress in one year (Fearn, 1982).

Accelerated learning is a characteristic of gifted students. It is also a strategy for accommodating their progress through school. The discussion above noted that instruction should relate logically to evaluation. How and what should be taught to certain types of students ought to be determined on the basis of the students' characteristics. Acceleration is the strategy of choice when students are identified as gifted on the basis of uncommonly high scores on IQ or achievement tests.

Disputes about Acceleration

Not everyone thinks that acceleration is a good idea for gifted students. Many educators involved with gifted students believe that a "qualitatively different" curriculum, not a faster pace, best meets the needs of gifted students in general (e.g., Castiglione, 1984; Renzulli, 1977; Sisk & Bierly, 1979). Several critical issues are involved in this dispute. Identification, socialization needs of gifted students, and higher-order thinking skills all play a role in the ongoing controversy.

Identification. We know that the use of standardized tests discriminates against students from impoverished backgrounds. Some policy options can combat this abuse, but they have not been implemented widely (Council of State Directors of Gifted Programs, 1985; Howley, 1987a). Many educators seem to feel that a different approach is wiser, perhaps because it seems to offer totally new possibilities for equality. These educators feel that in identifying different sorts of talent, gifted education will become more accessible to students from the oppressed classes of society.

There is, however, little evidence to support this sentiment. In fact, many observers find that programs based on the premises of this approach to identification are not appropriate for academically able students (e.g., Copley, 1961; C. Howley, 1986; Stanley, 1976a; Weiler, 1978). Some find such programs to be elitist and anti-intellectual (Bull, 1985; A. Howley, 1986; Weiler, 1978).

Socialization needs of gifted students. The development of accelerated programs—as opposed to the characteristic of accelerated learning within students—fills some educators and parents with fear. Most children encounter social problems in school, just as most students encounter academic problems. All educators and parents know that social pecking orders dominate school life. Those who are fearful of acceleration worry that accelerated placements will jeopardize students' happiness.

This point is important because our culture values happiness very strongly, more strongly, in fact, than learnedness, beauty, or meaning

(Arendt, 1981; Hofstadter, 1963). We value achievement, not because it enacts beauty or meaning, but because it promotes happiness.

Acceleration appears to be an *immediate* threat to students' happiness. Hence, many educators and parents oppose it. They fear that gifted students will become social outcasts or, worse, intellectual introverts incapable of sustaining happy relationships with others.

These parents and educators need to be reassured. When accelerated and nonaccelerated groups are compared, only minor differences in social and emotional characteristics are found. On the other hand, there are significant differences in the achievement of accelerated and nonaccelerated groups of gifted students. We know that accelerated college students tend to win more honors, earn higher grades, and participate more in extracurricular activities than equally bright students who are not accelerated (cf. Fund for the Advancement of Education, 1957; Robinson & Janos, 1986; Pressey, 1967; Stanley, 1985, 1986). Results with elementary and high-school students are equally positive (Alexander & Skinner, 1980; Braga, 1971; Daurio, 1979; Kulik & Kulik, 1984). A highly readable presentation (see Box 12-1) of the issue that can help parents and educators

---

BOX 12-1   Accelerated Emotional Development?

Studies indicate . . . that while accelerated students are making rapid academic progress, their maturity is speeding up in other ways as well. According to research by Julian Stanley . . . accelerated students tend to date earlier, insist on greater freedom, and accept more responsibility than is customary for students in their age groups.

The earlier social and emotional development is to be expected. What's more, it's natural, normal, and healthy. After all, these students not only learn to behave like the older students they spend most of their time with, but they also develop a clearer sense that others appreciate their special skills and abilities. Adults shouldn't expect these accelerated students to behave like the children of the same ages who are in lower grades. Research . . . suggests that most of the accelerated students need no special protection and, in fact, cannot be protected from the influences of their more mature environment.

At the same time it is *foolish* to maintain that concern about accelerated students' social and emotional development is never justified. If an acceleration program is not implemented with great care, it could be harmful even for students whose placement in the program is most appropriate.

In addition, parents and teachers should remember that, even in carefully run programs, some accelerated placements will not work out. Recent work by Nancy Robinson demonstrates that a small proportion of accelerated students fail to thrive in an accelerated placement. At the same time, it is not clear that these unsuccessfully accelerated students were harmed, or that they would have been better off left alone. (adapted from Howley, 1987b, p. 33).

Source: Reprinted with permission from *American School Board Journal,* June. Copyright (1987), the National School Boards Association. All rights reserved.

consider all sides of the issue reasonably can be found in the June, 1987, issue of *The American School Board Journal* (Howley, 1987b, pp. 31–33, 40).

Higher-order thinking skills.   Most educators and parents are concerned that our schools are not teaching higher-order thinking skills very well (e.g., Arends & Kirkpatrick, 1987). Some educators believe that gifted students should receive special instruction in higher-order thinking (e.g., Clark, 1986; Maker, 1982). This line of reasoning sometimes leads to the proposal that gifted students take a course in higher-order thinking.

Since many educators and parents are worried about possible (or imaginary) threats to a child's happiness that might result from acceleration, the proposal to teach an important skill to gifted students without acceleration looks appealing on the surface. Educators and parents should, however, be aware that such proposals work against the real needs of gifted students. Most educators concerned with gifted children now agree that good thinking and reasoning skills comprise part of academic instruction (Gallagher, 1985; Howley et al., 1986; Swassing, 1985; Van Tassel-Baska, 1985). It is probable that good instruction at advanced levels cultivates advanced habits of thinking and reasoning.

Types of Acceleration

Grade skipping is the form of acceleration that comes most readily to mind. Though it is still not practiced as frequently as is warranted, it is probably used more than it was in the period 1950–1980.

Yet there are at least a dozen forms of acceleration. Educators concerned with gifted students need to be very familiar with all of these forms. They are the tools with which the "lock step curriculum" can be adjusted to the learning rate of gifted students. Some of these forms are introduced subsequently.

Accelerated regular class placement.   In this form of acceleration, a gifted student should be allowed to progress through instructional materials in the self-contained elementary classroom at approximately twice the rate of average students. This option requires a well-motivated student, because the regular teacher will not have much time to supervise the progress of the student. However, this form of acceleration is really a stopgap measure to use when other forms are not available or not appropriate. Gains made under this arrangement are hard to document and to maintain as students progress through the grades.

Special accelerated classes.   In this form of acceleration, a student can attend rapid-paced courses in academic subjects. Such courses are *designed* for students who can make rapid progress. (Of course, not all students who attend the class need be identified as gifted; students can be selected on the basis of advanced achievement in the subject.) Accelerated classes—as opposed to regular classes—maintain very high expectations for student progress. This difference has been identified as a critical influence in such courses.

Early entry. In this form of acceleration, a student begins elementary school, middle school, junior high school, senior high school, or college a year or more early. This form of acceleration is really a special form of grade skipping. The advantage of this form of acceleration is that it exploits the disjunctions of the educational system to the advantage of gifted students. Research on this form of acceleration is extensive and positive.

Dual attendance. In this form of acceleration, a student attends two institutions at once. In the ideal case, a student will receive dual credit for work done at the higher of the two levels. For example, successful completion of a one-semester college English course should count also as successful completion of a one-year high school English course. This can be useful to students, whose financial aid status in college may depend on receiving a high school diploma.

Other forms of acceleration. Other options that can be used to accomplish acceleration include combined grades, ungraded elementary schools, private schooling, and home schooling. An overlooked strategy involves transfer to a different school. Sometimes, when one school has a policy that prohibits acceleration or is very restrictive in its use of acceleration, a nearby school may better accommodate the academic needs of gifted students. (See Box 12-2 for a personal account of the use of acceleration.)

BOX 12-2   *The Experience of Acceleration: A Personal Report*

Between the three of us, we have five children. We have used some form of acceleration with each of them. Our five children are very different from one another, and not all of them have received "gifted services." Yet, acceleration has helped meet their educational needs. In each case, we think the acceleration was beneficial.

Two of us reported in some detail about our three children's experiences up through 1984 (Howley & Howley, 1985). Since that time, our eldest child has progressed rapidly through school. As a result of her earlier experiences with acceleration and with a variety of social settings, she seemed to develop her own educational time clock and a sense of her own academic values, needs, and expectations.

We were a bit surprised, however, when toward the end of the ninth grade she told us she wanted to enter college in the fall. We both worked at the college where she would enroll, and perhaps that made arrangements easier than they would have been for other students. However, the college had enrolled junior high-school students as fully matriculated students before. Some staff members there *were* aware that it could be done, and other parents have made similar arrangements with the college since that time.

At the age of 15, our daughter has now completed degree requirements in math and science (her "weak" areas), and she is majoring in psychology. She will shortly transfer to a larger school, where she will live in the dorms. She is mature for her age in every way. She conforms to the composite image of successful early entrants. Her grades are very good; she has an active social life; she participates in music and drama at the college and in the community.

She is not at all a perfect student, and—it may surprise readers—she is *not* highly gifted. She does possess the family commitment to reading and music, and to reflecting on social issues. Her success, if that's what it can be called, is a result of active parenting, her own temperament and proclivities, and hard work. There *have* been tears, anxious moments, and unpleasant surprises—as there are between any child and parent.

Can we be certain our daughter will lead a well-adjusted, productive life? No, we can't. We've taken some unusual risks, and we hope for the best. Matters are pretty much in *her* hands, however, as she really is more a young adult than a teenager. That's fine with her. (We're fairly certain she knows that she still has a lot to learn.)

ENRICHMENT

In contrast to acceleration, enrichment is an option for gifted students that is not often considered to be controversial. Nonetheless, enrichment programs vary greatly, and some of the types of instruction provided under the auspices of enrichment are indeed controversial (Cox et al., 1985). Most people, however, endorse the notion that gifted students should receive instruction that broadens their horizons.

Part of the difficulty in evaluating enrichment as an alternative for gifted students is the fact that so many different practices are thought to be enriching. Definitions of enrichment reflect the confusion. For example, some authors consider enrichment in its broadest application. According to Gowan and Demos (1964, p. 138), enrichment "embraces all the curricular adjustments made for gifted students. These include experiences in breadth and depth, and those connected with grouping, acceleration, and individualization of instruction in heterogeneous classes."

Other authors accept a more narrow definition. Epstein (1979), for instance, defines horizontal enrichment as lateral expansion of the curriculum. She characterizes enrichment as instruction in which:

> . . . the gifted children do not move up any faster, but their learning is enriched by different curriculum materials, individual instruction, emphasis on the higher mental processes of divergent thinking and creativity, independent study, problem-solving projects with real products, and any number of techniques that give youngsters a welcome change from the routine of the regular classroom. (Epstein, 1979, p. 69)

In order to gain a greater understanding of enrichment options for gifted students, it is important to evaluate several of the instructional alternatives that are typically used in enrichment programs. These alternatives represent three different approaches to enrichment: process-oriented approaches, content-oriented approaches, and product-oriented approaches.

Process-Oriented Approaches

Many enrichment programs are directed toward the goal of developing students' higher-order thinking skills. These skills may include problem-solving techniques, divergent thinking skills, or metacognitive strategies. Many enrichment programs attempt to develop higher-order thinking skills in isolation from academic or artistic content. The rationale for this approach is that, once students are proficient in these skills, they will be able to apply them to all content areas (see e.g., Clark, 1986). This approach has been criticized by a number of educators (e.g., Copley, 1961; Marzano & Hutchins, 1985; Van Tassel-Baska, 1985) who maintain that higher-order thinking skills must be taught within a curriculum based on content in the disciplines.

Problem-solving techniques. Many enrichment programs offer instruction in problem-solving techniques. Among the techniques that purport to increase higher-order thinking skills are the following:

1. library research projects,
2. problem-solving sessions,
3. instruction about the scientific method,
4. future problem-solving competitions, and
5. practice in games of strategy, such as chess and backgammon.

Divergent thinking skills. Instruction in divergent thinking skills differs from instruction in problem-solving because it emphasizes the significance of multiple, creative solutions to a problem rather than the significance of one, correct solution. Several techniques have been developed for teaching divergent thinking. Most prominent among these techniques are creative problem solving (Osborn, 1953) and synectics (Gordon, 1961).

Although these techniques do enable students to be more fluent in their generation of ideas, they may have no influence on students' ability to produce original theories or works of art. Certainly the impact of such training is seriously compromised when students are not exposed to content in mathematics, science, and the arts. Without a comprehensive understanding of content in these fields, students cannot possibly suggest creative solutions to *relevant* problems.

Metacognitive strategies. Several educational psychologists (e.g., Newell & Simon, 1972; Sternberg, 1977) have begun to identify information processing strategies that supposedly undergird all learning. According to some psychologists and educators, students can improve their problem-solving skills by becoming aware of these metacognitive strategies and their use.

At this point in time, however, research into metacognitive strategies is formative and inconclusive, and programs based on such research are necessarily experimental (see e.g., Feuerstein et al., 1981). The recommendation that gifted programs teach these strategies should probably be viewed as precipitous.

Content-Oriented Approaches

Enrichment programs that emphasize academic content rather than cognitive processes are popular in some districts. Such programs offer academic courses that are not typically included in the regular curriculum. The format for the delivery of such courses varies, but the nature of the courses is often similar.

Course delivery.   Some content-oriented enrichment programs enable gifted students to participate in academic courses that are not offered during the regular school day. After-school, Saturday, and summer workshops can provide academic instruction in subjects such as computer science, astronomy, archeology, and art. Although these learning experiences may be valuable for many gifted students, they rarely provide an adequate substitute for relevant academic instruction delivered through the regular curriculum. Enrichment courses do not constitute an articulated curriculum; they almost never carry academic credit. For these reasons, Stanley (1981, p. 263) regards such enrichment as "both the best short term and one of the worst long term approaches to the education of the gifted."

Course content.   Often, minicourses are used as the vehicle for delivering academic enrichment. Such minicourses may be topical, thematic, or skill-oriented. Topical minicourses tend to be based on the traditional disciplines. An example of a topical minicourse in mathematics would be a summer math course in elementary statistics. Thematic minicourses provide an interdisciplinary view of a particular issue. A course that explores the issue of air pollution from the perspectives of chemistry, biology, and sociology exemplifies such an offering. Skill-oriented minicourses provide intensive instruction in skills that enhance academic learning. These courses may teach skills such as typing, library research, or test taking.

Product-Oriented Approaches

Product-oriented enrichment programs direct students toward the production of significant products. Most notable among these approaches is Renzulli's (1977) Enrichment Triad model. The ultimate goal of this program is to enable students to prepare real products for presentation to appropriate audiences. Such programs rely heavily on independent study and research.

Some enrichment programs emphasize products that are less tangible. Programs that focus on career education, affective activities, and leadership training have as their products certain behavioral outcomes. In such programs students are expected to mimic the constellations of behavior that are assumed to characterize gifted leaders in business, science, and the professions.

Why Enrichment is Controversial

Enrichment *is* controversial for a number of reasons. Because it rarely can address the most significant academic needs of gifted students, its value as the sole option for such students is questionable. Because it may be appropriate for many average students as well as for gifted students, its exclusive province in the gifted program can be questioned.

The resolution of these controversies seems to be in the return to a broad definition of enrichment. When enrichment encompasses the total program for gifted students, including acceleration, grouping, and relevant instructional methods, it no longer is a controversial provision. Such a broad conception of enrichment, however, might better be referred to as "curriculum." The description of this sort of curriculum for gifted students is considered in the next section of the chapter.

CURRICULUM: ACADEMICS AND THE ARTS

Educators often disagree on what constitutes the best school curriculum. We think that the curriculum for gifted students should be based on academic and artistic *disciplines*. Not everyone shares our view.

Very liberal educators believe that the curriculum can and should include everything that life has to teach. They believe that any other view is narrow and harmful to children (e.g., Clark, 1986). This view is appealing to many who understand the shortcomings of formal schooling.

Very conservative educators, on the other hand, believe that some topics in the academic curriculum undermine traditional values (e.g., Lines, 1986). Others think that teaching the values of the Protestant ethic is an overlooked priority (Bennett, 1986). Still other observers—including the authors—believe that teaching intellectual skills, rather than all life has to offer, should take priority over any other instruction in *any* value system (Katz, 1971). Advocates of this view understand that some values adhere to any act of teaching and learning. The kind of values that adhere to the teaching of intellectual skills and knowledge are the generic values of hard work, mutual respect of teacher and student, and appreciation of meaningful statements.

Children, we believe, must become skilled readers and thinkers. It is an article of faith with us that children who accomplish these goals will become good citizens—in the best sense of the phrase—and will inevitably shape their *own* values.

Academics, the Arts, and Social Reconstruction

Schools have shown that their effectiveness is more limited than the great reformers of the past—educators like John Dewey, George Counts, and Leta Hollingworth—would have liked (Jencks et al., 1979). These educational reformers believed the schools could "reconstruct" a flawed industrial social order (Cremin, 1961; Tyack, 1974). Nonetheless, it seems clear that the schools *dare not* make a new social order (cf. Counts, 1932). In fact, they cannot.

At the same time, if they supply students with good intellectual tools, schools can contribute *indirectly* to the reconstruction of society in accordance with democratic ideals. To do so, they must nurture students who understand history, literature, mathematics, and science. The arts also play an important role in this endeavor by supplying alternative images of reality in music, dance, drama, painting, and sculpture (Arendt, 1981; Marcuse, 1978).

If, however, schools produce students who know little, read little, and never examine their assumptions, then they will fail to contribute to social progress. If schools cultivate only the politically safe disciplines of math and science, they will also fail to contribute meaningfully to social progress.

The observations presented here apply to all children, not just to an elite group. More children must have access to the tools of reason. Schools should teach basic skills, of course, but they also should enable students to engage in more sophisticated learning.

That gifted children are among those who can make rapid progress through the academic curriculum is a fact that has been confirmed by a large body of research. In our view, it makes sense to accommodate these students' confirmed potential.

Curriculum, Instruction, and Individual Differences

Before taking a brief look at what things the gifted ought to learn and when, we need to develop some sense of how curriculum relates to teachers and to students. First, we distinguish between curriculum and classroom instructional practice. Second, we examine the relationship of individual differences in students to both the curriculum and to instructional practice. This discussion applies to all children, but it has particular implications for gifted children.

Curriculum and classroom instructional practice. A curriculum is a course of study meant to *generalize* a body of knowledge to be taught to a given student population. In our view, the curriculum must be an organization of *disciplined knowledge.* (Some handicapped students require another sort of curriculum, however.) Disciplined knowledge is traditional academic knowledge, especially as conceived by those who practice the discipline.

The curriculum is one source—probably the most important source—of classroom practice. If instruction does not contain an adequate *interpretation* of disciplined knowledge, then students fail to acquire the intellectual tools they need. The tools of instruction—instructional formats and techniques—are the means by which teachers interpret disciplined knowledge to students. Teachers have a choice of instructional formats and techniques, and they are free to improvise their own. To teach composition, for example, a teacher may develop a program of cultural journalism (Wigginton, 1985), or assign weekly essays, or incorporate separate writing "units" in an English course.

Educational research and common sense suggest, of course, that some choices are better than others, depending on a teacher's circumstances. Whereas traditional (i.e., disciplined) knowledge is the best source of curriculum, traditional teaching methods are not necessarily the best source of instructional practice. Wigginton, who originated and published the *Foxfire* books with his students, for example, despaired of the traditional tools of instruction and developed a method that is clearly not traditional. His students do not work only in classrooms, and they do not produce the standard sorts of student essays; yet his students learn to write and to think well.

Obviously, teachers need both sets of knowledge, knowledge of the disciplines and knowledge of teaching methods. However, without the former, the latter is useless. In fact, we doubt if expertise in teaching method is possible without disciplined knowledge, just as we suspect that sophisticated thinking and reasoning cannot exist without disciplined knowledge.

Curriculum and individual differences. In the United States educators have placed a great deal of emphasis on accommodating individual differences within the generality of a common curriculum for all students. There are ideological and practical reasons for this development. The traditions of our culture bequeath to all of us a belief in the importance of liberty and individuality. Appreciation of these values, for example, is at the heart of support for free enterprise in the United States. At the same time, however, a counter tendency has influenced public education in the United States. During the early and middle nineteenth century our "common schools" were viewed as "melting pots" to Americanize immigrants and as agencies to dissolve the distinctions of social class (Katz, 1968; Tyack, 1974).

During the late nineteenth century, educators came increasingly to realize that schools did not treat children very much like individuals—or very much like children, for that matter (Cremin, 1961). Progressive educators (including reformers like Dewey) saw the shortcomings of the public schools and proposed a "child-centered" approach to both curriculum and instruction. Part of this approach entailed observation and accommodation of individual differences.

Over the years, many American educators have misunderstood what was meant by "child-centered." At one point, Dewey himself impatiently noted that he had seen many "really stupid" responses to his proposals (Cremin, 1961, p. 259). Dewey did not intend that curriculum be constructed for each child, or that each child's interests should determine a curriculum. Instead, he intended that children's natural proclivities for learning should be recognized and exploited by teachers in their efforts to make disciplined knowledge accessible to children (Dewey, 1902/1956).

Although teachers must be sensitive to children's interests, their role as educators is to lead children out of a naive conception of the world into a richer, better-informed, and more sophisticated conception. They *cannot* fulfill this role if they put children in charge of determining the curriculum.

Implications for gifted students. Three implications can be drawn from the preceding discussion. These implications help define important features of the curriculum and of instructional practice for gifted students.

First, curriculum based on disciplined knowledge is appropriate for gifted students, as it is for almost all other students. As we noted earlier, because giftedness indicates an exceptional potential for academic learning, however, the academic curriculum is the *curriculum of choice* for gifted students. Other curricula may be especially appropriate for other types of children. The curriculum for severely handicapped children, for example, usually includes self-help skills.

Second, like other children, gifted students need instruction that piques their natural curiosity and provides challenges that build both knowledge and self-esteem. They do not, any more than other children, need to have their interests consulted in the construction of a curriculum that is tailor-made for them. They do not need a "gifted curriculum."

Third, gifted students can typically master the academic curriculum in several years less time than other students. Instructional practice, therefore, should provide for the acceleration of these children through the academic curriculum. Other instructional modifications (certain kinds of teaching strategies, of special courses, of grouping arrangements, of instructional materials) can also help gifted students achieve their academic potential.

Curriculum for the Gifted

The previous discussion indicates that teachers of the gifted need to know what elements of the academic curriculum gifted children should encounter and when they should encounter them. Readers should remember, in considering the following discussion, that gifted children vary as much as other children. This discussion concerns what is typical, *not* what is universal. Many gifted students will need instructional modifications if the following guidelines are to be implemented responsibly.

Elementary level.   Research about gifted students suggests that it is reasonable to expect that many such students—perhaps 60 percent—could begin high school at the age of 12 if they received suitable instruction in elementary school. Basic skills should be taught up to about age ten—at as much as twice the pace of ordinary instruction.

By about the age of ten, most gifted children will no longer require instruction in reading per se; and, with guidance from an expert teacher, they can begin to consider serious literature. We recommend that the literature curriculum be established by a committee of teachers in a district. The committee should establish a reading list from which to draw perhaps four of five complete works for a year's classroom work in literature. English instruction should also involve regular writing assignments that move students toward the production of good quality essays of 1,500 to 2,500 words in length by about the age of 12.

By about the same age, gifted students should have mastered fractions, decimals, and measurement concepts. Many gifted students will be ready to start algebra at this time. Before beginning algebra, however, students should have mastered the critical concepts of *proportion* and *ratio*. These concepts are related to fractions and decimals, but they need to be understood *conceptually* if students are to succeed in algebra. That is, students should understand the meaning of proportion and ratio. They should, for example, be able to appreciate the way in which proportions resemble analogies. A two-year algebra sequence (or a half-year pre-algebra and three-semester algebra sequence) is one way to provide algebra to young gifted and mathematically able students.

Foreign languages are not taught well in American schools because foreign language instruction is not considered essential. Nevertheless, we think that, beginning in the elementary school, the curriculum for gifted students should include foreign language instruction. To accomplish this goal, it might be a good idea for teachers of the gifted at the elementary level to be prepared to offer instruction in one foreign language.

It is a reasonable instructional goal to prepare many gifted children to enter high school with one year's credit in mathematics (a first course in algebra), in foreign language (one year's credit), and in English (one year's credit). Fulfillment of this goal would, in most cases, require the persistent effort of a dedicated group of teachers, and the assistance of an administrator who understood why it was reasonable.

Secondary level. Many, if not most, gifted children should complete high school (i.e., Grades 9–12) in three years. A number of accelerative options are available to implement this recommendation.

A critical educational issue confronts the adults responsible for gifted students during the high-school years. At this time, many able students begin to internalize an academic self-image. Some will be generalists, and they will consider themselves equally interested in mathematical disciplines and in the humanities (literature, history, and the arts). An equal number, however, will want to specialize in one kind of study (e.g., mathematics courses or literature courses). Yet, students of this age (12–16) need to acquire a background in *both* mathematical disciplines and in the humanities.

It is essential to establish a distribution requirement to guide students' selection of courses. As we have suggested elsewhere (Howley et al., 1986), a 2 to 1 ratio between courses in more favored disciplines and less favored disciplines seems to make sense. This provision is important to observe, because it would be possible, in constructing flexible instructional practices for gifted students, to overlook the need to provide program balance.

Finally, gifted students in high school should follow programs that expose them to *original sources* in history and literature. Part of such exposure should include regular writing assignments about the works that are read. We can find no better preparation for work in competitive colleges and universities. We also believe that a second course in algebra (which includes trigonometry) is the minimum level of course taking in mathematics that should be required of gifted students; most gifted students, however, should also take one year of calculus during high school.

The Arts

The study of art and music does not fare well in our schools—substantially worse, perhaps, than the study of foreign languages. Neither the arts nor foreign languages is considered very useful, but knowledge of each is critically important to a deeper understanding of the world. All children should learn about the arts; and gifted students seem particularly interested in the philosophical (aesthetic and metaphysical) implications of the arts (Tidwell, 1980).

The arts and artists in society. The lack of a well-defined curriculum in the arts has been cited as one of the reasons for the lowly status of the arts in our schools. However, there are other reasons that the arts are not supported and do not receive the attention that reading and mathematics receive. The arts are not so useful as reading and mathematics, and the American ethos values most those skills that are most useful.

Artists tend to be aberrant individuals in our society and, in fact, in most Western societies. They live unconventional lives; they articulate views that offend those in power; and they often produce works that challenge common sense and popular tastes. Very few of us would be pleased to see our children grow up to be artists or musicians, if only because we know that such lives are so often filled with privation and hardship.

At the same time, many students, including large numbers of the gifted, express an abiding concern with aesthetics. Few of these students will seek to become professional artists or musicians, but the aesthetic interests of most will persist throughout their lives. For many of these students, the arts will become a source of continuous intellectual and emotional strength. Educators concerned with such students should recognize these facts and assist in the improvement of arts programs in the schools.

Improvement in school arts programs.   More instruction in the arts, particularly in the history of the arts, should be provided in public schools. Many art and music teachers in our schools today have nearly impossible jobs; some see hundreds of students (sometimes more than 1,000). They rarely teach the history of art or music in much detail. It is unfortunate that the only images and sounds most children grow up with are those found on television, billboards, and popular radio stations.

Art and music instruction are as intellectually important as literature, mathematics, history, and natural science. Art and music can help all students attain a quality of life that is not directly accessible in other disciplines.

Those students who are exceptionally talented in the arts also suffer from the fact that the arts are neglected in our schools. Such students must receive their most significant instruction (usually musical instruction) privately. Teachers of the gifted can contribute most to the education of exceptionally talented arts students by serving as advocates. In this role teachers can support school arrangements that accommodate these students' need for private instruction. In most cases, tests and assignments can be rescheduled or altered to accommodate the gifted student's practice or performance schedule.

For high-IQ and high-achieving gifted students, gifted programs can incorporate minicourses on art history and music—or perhaps a series of such courses—to help demonstrate to schools what is needed in aesthetic education. In addition to the gifted, such courses could include other able students.

CHARACTERISTICS OF INSTRUCTION FOR GIFTED STUDENTS

The topics of instruction and of curriculum are, of course, related. The point of the previous section was that the regular curriculum, conceived as disciplined knowledge organized for instruction, is the curriculum most appropriate for gifted students. We have emphasized throughout the discussion in this chapter, however, that the way in which the curriculum is presented to gifted children should differ from the way it is typically presented in regular classrooms.

The most efficient and—so far as we know—the most effective way to accomplish this goal is through acceleration. At the same time, acceleration falls very far short of being a complete response to the question of how to teach gifted children. We know that gifted students, more than other students, benefit from certain instructional formats and techniques. Those who teach gifted students, whether regular educators or teachers of the gifted, should at least be aware of such findings. Moreover, teachers of the gifted, in particular, need to conduct lessons that make use of these formats and techniques.

Finally, these instructional formats and techniques have *not*, in most cases, been developed especially for gifted students. They are probably beneficial to other students as well. None of them is *harmful* to other students. We know only that gifted students benefit more from them than other students. This finding may be more a characteristic of gifted students than it is a characteristic of these instructional formats and techniques.

Instructional Formats

Instructional formats come in two basic types, expository and inductive. The formats most commonly used in schools are expository. Lectures, directed reading, programmed instruction, and individual learning activities are expository formats appropriate for gifted students. Inductive formats are less seldom used than are expository formats, perhaps because their use requires more effort from teachers. Tutorials, seminars, independent study, simulations, inquiry training sessions, and laboratory and field studies are inductive formats appropriate for gifted students.

Inductive formats for teaching are presumed to lead to more active learning. Expository formats, on the other hand, sometimes fail to involve students in active learning as much as they might. Whereas induction is the construction of meaning for oneself, exposition is a reconstruction intended to make meaning accessible to others. Obviously, it is more difficult for teachers to induce learning than to expound knowledge. Similarly, practicing induction is often more difficult for students than listening to an exposition.

Induction is the essential act of learning; exposition is the essential act of teaching. From the viewpoint of the one who learns, almost everything that is learned is experienced as induction. From the viewpoint of the one who teaches, almost everything that is taught is experienced as exposition. In the classroom, the two should go hand-in-hand. Good teachers see that they do. In the discussion that follows, educators should recall that both induction and exposition are essential activities of the human mind. The most effective instruction blends both induction and exposition.

Which format is best?   Answering this question depends on a teacher's sense of self, students, curriculum, and instructional aims. Most research on teaching suggests that almost any method selected freely and used vigorously by a knowledgeable and experienced teacher will be effective.

At the same time, we know that when teachers are given the opportunity to select ways to teach a part of the curriculum, they do not proceed on the basis of whimsy. Nor do they all make identical choices. In making their choices, they think about such things as the following:

- the instructional activities that have been most successful for them in the past (teacher's instructional preferences);
- the students in their class now—their needs and the quality of their classroom interaction with one another and with the teacher (students' characteristics);
- the nature of what is to be taught (curriculum, instructional objectives of the program); and, finally,
- the time, place, and materials available to them (instructional resources of the program).

Such reflections determine the answer to "Which format is best?" That is, no format is best in all cases, and each can serve a useful purpose.

Inductive formats.   Inductive formats are thought to help students "induce" their own learning. Actually, when inductive formats are successful, students are led by their teachers carefully through a series of challenging events, propositions, or paradoxes. Through activities such as these, students, if successful, acquire new concepts. They often do, and well-constructed inductive learning experiences are memorable, both for students and teachers.

Inductive formats are especially pertinent to concept development, because in successful inductive activities, students participate actively in the development of the concept. Good inductive lessons often require that students engage in cycles of analysis, synthesis, evaluation, comprehension, and application (Bloom et al., 1956). Hence, inductive formats seem to meet the need to teach "higher-order thinking" to gifted students.

Whether this need is actually met by inductive formats is difficult to determine. Clearly, all students need practice in such intellectual work, and it is equally clear that much of their time in school is *not* spent in such activity (Marzano & Hutchins, 1985).

Inductive formats *are* a powerful tool to help teach important concepts to students. Gifted children *will* benefit greatly from some inductive instruction. However, inductive formats are *not* an alternative to gifted programs based on acceleration; they are *not* a remedy for inappropriate placement; and they are *not* appropriate for teaching many basic skills.

Expository formats. In general, expository formats are more efficient than inductive formats. Expository lessons are also easier for teachers to prepare than inductive lessons. These two facts account for the popularity of expository formats.

In fact, part of the appeal of inductive, as opposed to expository, formats centers on one's view of efficiency. The "cult of efficiency" has been viewed as an unhealthy and inhuman influence in American education (Callahan, 1962; Silver & DeYoung, 1986; Tyack, 1974). Inductive formats incorporate the view that efficiency is not the most important educational value (cf. Taba, 1965).

And yet, with gifted students, educators should recognize that considerations about the efficiency of instruction—or at least the efficiency of *learning*—are important. Time is too short for gifted students to learn everything for themselves, even if they might. "Learning by doing" is important, but so is learning by reading and learning by listening. It also makes good sense to teach many things, especially basic knowledge, using expository formats. For example, though students could learn the multiplication facts inductively, massed drill and practice is probably a more efficient and effective way to help students *memorize* these *facts*. The same point can be made about many topics in language arts, geography, science, and foreign languages.

Caveat magister (teacher beware). Educators concerned with gifted children should be wary of the claim that inductive formats are the method of choice for gifted students. This claim overstates research findings that show gifted children to benefit more than other children from this type of instructional format.

Though inductive formats provide an opportunity to engage in uncommon instructional activities, they will nurture higher-order thinking only to the extent that they are used in an overall scheme of curriculum and instruction that makes sense. No research exists that describes the features of such a scheme. We do know, however, that a comprehensive program rarely, if ever, exists for gifted students (Cox et al., 1985).

In a challenging academic program at the elementary level, no more than about 25 percent of the instructional time should be devoted to inductive formats. In a challenging academic program at the upper secondary level (ages 14–16), some gifted students could perhaps spend as much as half their instructional time in tutorials, seminars, and laboratory work.

If, however, the academic program for gifted elementary and secondary students is less than rigorous, these recommended proportions are too high. On the other hand, teachers who do not incorporate inductive routines into their teaching—and short inductive routines can be incorporated even in lectures—will certainly fail to engage students actively in learning.

Instructional Techniques

Instructional techniques are the events through which teaching actually takes place. The same influences that determine instructional format can also affect the instructional techniques a teacher chooses. These influences can be the teachers' instructional preferences, the students' characteristics, the curriculum and objectives of the program, and the instructional resources of the program.

Either an expository or an inductive instructional format can accommodate similar instructional techniques. Inductive formats may incorporate techniques that call for explanations (exposition) by the teacher, and expository formats may incorporate techniques that call for open-ended (inductive) responses from students. However, for any instructional technique to be effective in a program for gifted students certain conditions must be in place:

* careful selection of students,
* program elements flexible enough to address individual needs,
* a match between curriculum level and students' achievement level,
* a curriculum relevant to students' longterm educational goals, and
* a teacher who serves as an intellectual model.

Teacher as intellectual model. The first four conditions were discussed in previous sections of this chapter. The last is a critical concern with respect to instructional techniques.

Expertise in disciplined knowledge is the basic requirement of teachers of the gifted (Gallagher, 1975). Expert teachers are the only ones who can implement successful academic programs for the gifted or develop existing programs further. Of course, expertise in an academic discipline is necessary in order to manage any academic program well or to engage in sensible program and curriculum development.

Teachers of the gifted should serve as intellectual models to their students. They should, for example, write (Koch, 1973), paint (Chetelat, 1981), or engage in continuing studies of their own (Brown, 1967). Whatever else they do, they should also continue to read widely. Cohn (1984) reports that such teachers influence not only the achievement of their students, but their intellectual values (appreciation of intellectual work) as well.

Perhaps one of the strengths of these teachers is that they have a well-informed sense of teaching method—instructional preferences that show a high degree of self-awareness, a discipline-relevant understanding of student characteristics, a knowledge of subject and flexibility in determining objectives, and a clear understanding of essential resources. Such an informed sense of teaching method helps these teachers establish successful instructional routines.

Techniques for concept development. The development of concepts in students, in all of us, really, is a subtle process of evolution. Though we refer to concepts by words (e.g., "literary genre," "apartheid," "input-output economics," "entropy") we do not *develop* concepts by memorizing definitions. Original thinkers, for example, can legitimately understand each of the preceding concepts in very different ways. That is, thinkers induce their own concepts. Readers must realize that, in some sense, all human beings are original thinkers. The concepts to which we refer here, however, are primarily *academic* concepts.

Students' concepts are often quite naive. This observation applies even to successful students (Mestre & Gerace, 1986). According to Mestre and Gerace, students' *misconceptions* are commonplace. That is, students are prone to the same sorts of misconceptions.

When teachers seek to correct these misconceptions, they are really engaging in the business of concept development. Note that concept development in this view is rather like the behaviorist notion of "successive approximation." It respects students as thinking beings, and it is based on confidence in students' ability to refine the concepts they possess.

Successful concept development can employ both expository and inductive techniques. An expository lesson:

- supplies a definition,
- supplies examples, and
- contrasts examples with close nonexamples.

Note that these activities can be carried out with no active student participation at all. However, a basically expository format (e.g., a lecture format that also uses expository *techniques*) could be amplified to include an inductive routine in which students propose examples and nonexamples. As part of this activity a class discussion might result in the generation of related concepts to account for close nonexamples.

Inductive techniques for concept development lead students to abstract rules that define a concept. Instead of being told what the rules are, students:

- differentiate the qualities of objects and events,
- abstract shared qualities, and
- categorize objects and events on the basis of their observations.

Teaching about concepts with inductive techniques relies on good examples of the concept. In this case "examples" are not usually *verbal descriptions* of objects or events. The examples used in inductive techniques are typically real-life situations in the environment. Suchman's (1975) inquiry training sessions, for example, use an inductive *format* in which students confront scientific paradoxes (real-life examples) that seem to defy common sense. Students abstract the concepts that explain the paradox through a carefully structured series of observations and questions, (inductive techniques). Whenever possible, inductive techniques bring the "real" world into the classroom. Inductive lessons are thought by some educators to be a good antidote for schoolwork that relies too heavily on printed materials and on rote learning.

Inductive techniques include a good many "hands-on" activities. Hands-on activities involve students with concrete experiences and manipulative skills. Students acquire "operational" concepts (that is, nonverbal concepts) by observing what happens when they manipulate the environment. This characteristic of inductive techniques suggests that concrete experience informs even verbal concept development. Concrete experiences and abstract perceptions make up a completely understood concept.

In a similar way, induction and exposition make up a whole mental act. (Note that we said previously that students "explain" paradoxes in Suchman's inquiry training sessions.) The end product of induction is an explanation—a specifically formulated statement that can be communicated verbally to another person.

Finally, teachers should be aware of the empirical research on question asking. Good questioning skills are essential techniques for either inductive or expository lessons. The kind of questioning that nurtures students as thinkers is very different, for example, from questioning used to control student misbehavior. In a way, the techniques of questioning that help students think are teachers' most important tools (cf. Adler, 1982).

Here are some suggestions for teachers, based on the research about questioning:

- Do not convey the impression that classroom questions are a kind of test in which answers will be judged quickly for correctness.
- Questions that help dispel misconceptions or build new concepts are *neces-*

sarily ambiguous to students. Accommodate students' uncertainty or tentativeness.

- Give *individual* students ample time to respond to questions.
- If you get no reply in fifteen seconds, you may wish to rephrase the question. As much as possible, help the student tolerate the uneasiness of dealing with *necessarily ambiguous* questions.
- If a student's response is not satisfactory, address the ideas raised by the student in the response, and invite the student to provide a revised or extended answer. Do not simply judge the correctness of the student's answer.
- You can follow up an incomplete response or a response that indicates a misconception with a "probe" to help the student consider contradictory or misunderstood information.
- Give the *class* ample time to respond to a question. Pose the question to several students before you help them to evaluate the answers.

Questions should, above all else, serve to stimulate students' thinking. They should never be used as a technique of classroom management (cf. Good & Brophy, 1987). Asking rapid-fire questions and judging the correctness of results may appear to exert control over children, but it is a counterproductive kind of control (Anyon, 1980; Giroux, 1983). This misuse of questioning is a common practice in some schools that serve working-class students (Wilcox & Moriarity, 1977).

Sometimes, of course, a teacher may want to know if students have understood a point in a lecture or in a reading. Such questioning helps the teacher adjust lesson plans so that instruction matches students' needs. It should not be overused, and it should *never* be used to assess students' classroom performance.

Techniques for academic skill development. We implied above that the development of skills is related to the development of concepts. We also noted that concept development could be approached by teachers in either an inductive mode or in an expository mode. So it is with skill development. The acquisition of new skills leads inevitably to concept development, and new skills may also be taught in inductive or expository modes.

There is one important difference. Skills are *habitual* behaviors—for example, the skill of proofing text, or the skill of solving trigonometric equations, or the skill of declining Latin nouns. Skills become habitual only with a certain amount of practice. The acquisition of a new skill probably depends as much on practice as on anything else (providing, of course, that students are conceptually or developmentally prepared to learn the new skill.)

The acquisition of new skills requires exposure to and analysis of skill models. Students need to pattern their new behaviors after good models. A teacher's role is to use professional judgment in selecting skill models that are appropriate for students. A good example of this process can be found in Kenneth Koch's (1970) introduction to *Wishes, Lies, and Dreams*. Koch encourages teachers to consider models that seldom find their way into the classroom.

Koch's work is of the type Stanley (1976a) calls "relevant academic enrichment." The kind of judgment exemplified by Koch, however, needs to be applied to curriculum development across all subjects and instructional levels. Educators concerned with gifted students also need to consider the issues of pace and comprehensive educational planning when they design units that are intended to teach new skills.

Before students can practice the skills we want them to learn, they need to understand the features that make the selected models good. Again, both expository and inductive techniques can help students reach such an understanding. In geometry, for example, the features of a good proof can be explained in a lecture and demonstration. On the other hand, students might be asked to compare several proofs, and in the process the teacher could pose questions that lead students to abstract for themselves the features of a good proof.

Because students usually practice skills independently, teachers are often concerned to monitor the quality of students' practice work. Very often, teachers assign grades for practice work. This approach to students' practice is not defensible, however (Good & Brophy, 1987). There are better techniques for monitoring the quality of students' practice work. Among these techniques are the following:

- giving ungraded practice quizzes to help students evaluate their own progress,
- selecting appropriate practice materials that challenge students and have the potential to engage their interest,
- using task cards to differentiate assignments (Good & Brophy, 1987),
- using peer tutors,
- using cooperative learning techniques (Slavin, 1986),
- letting students complete written assignments using word processing,
- using instructional software, and
- establishing classroom routines that give students ample opportunity to ask questions of the teacher.

SUMMARY

This chapter provided an overview of methods for educators concerned with gifted students. The discussion was guided by empirical research about teaching these students. This research concerned alternative methods of identification, methods to ensure appropriate placement and program planning, methods of acceleration and enrichment for gifted students, and methods of curriculum and instructional design thought to be appropriate for gifted students. We acknowledge, however, that this approach has its shortcomings. Therefore, at the end of this chapter and of this book, a note about the place of methods in the real world of the classroom seems to be in order.

Despite our insistence on heeding the findings of research, we believe that teaching is more art than science. Nathaniel Gage (1978) has summarized the "scientific basis" of *the art of teaching*. If you read his work, you will perhaps agree that the best that can be said about the scientific basis of the art of teaching is that there is one. Whether it informs the practice of teaching is another matter. And the *ordinary* practice of teaching is a bit different from the art of teaching.

The *art of teaching* is the *adept* practice of teaching. Excellent teachers—like gifted children—are comparatively rare. Clearly we need to know more about them than we do at present; we would all like to be excellent teachers. Most of us who work hard, however, *do* get the chance to be considered good teachers by our students. Very few of us, we suspect, are capable of being consistently excellent.

The *good* teachers we have known do many of the things cited in this chapter—they have a grasp of disciplined learning, they make good plans, they ask questions well, and they make students feel cared for. They achieve these ends, however, in many different ways. Some favor inductive methods, some stick to expository methods, and still others improvise an effective combination. All of them put a great deal of effort into their work.

Teaching is the kind of job that takes all your skill if you wish to be good at it, no matter how talented you might be. No matter how talented you might be, there is always more to do, and there is always some portion of your routine to improve. In addition, the conditions of a teacher's work usually change over the course of a career; teachers often encounter different neighborhoods, different students, and different colleagues in the course of a career. They may accept different teaching assignments at different levels.

Perhaps a teacher's best resource in all of this flux is a sense of the alternatives: how to change a particular feature of a lesson, how to offer alternate explanations to students who seem to have missed the point, how to adapt a new technology to good instructional purpose, or how to switch from an expository to an inductive approach in the middle of a lesson. Such resourcefulness looks a lot like creativity—fluency, flexibility, originality, and elaboration. Take heart! Research on creativity says it is easy to learn!

In any case—kidding aside—a holistic sense of method is preferable to an atomistic, textbook sense of method. A holistic sense of method can be acquired by all teachers to some degree over time. It is also the sort of thing that can only be acquired inductively; so we hope that you will accept our expository approach (a textbook) as an invitation to read, act, and reflect further on the nature and needs of students, gifted or not, and on the educational arrangements that best accommodate their nurture.

References

ABELSON, P. (1967). Relation of group activity to creativity in science. In J. Kagan (Ed.), *Creativity and learning* (pp. 191–202). Boston: Beacon Press.

ADAMS, J. E., & ROSS, C. O. (1932). Is skipping grades a satisfactory method of acceleration? *American School Board Journal, 85,* 24–25.

ADLER, M. (1982). *The Paidea proposal: An educational manifesto.* New York: Macmillan.

ALBERT, R. S., & RUNCO, M. A. (1986). The achievement of eminence: A model based on a longitudinal study of exceptionally gifted boys and their families. In R. J. Sternberg & J. E. Davidson (Eds.), *Conceptions of giftedness* (pp. 332–357). Cambridge: Cambridge University Press.

ALBRIGHT, H. (1967). *Acting: The creative process.* Belmont, CA: Dickenson.

ALEXANDER, P. A. (1985). Gifted and nongifted students' perceptions of intelligence. *Gifted Child Quarterly, 29*(3), 137–142.

ALEXANDER, P. A., & SKINNER, M. (1980). The effects of early entrance on subsequent social and academic development: A follow-up study. *Journal for the Education of the Gifted, 3*(3), 147–150.

ALEXANDER, R. (1981). An historical perspective on the gifted and the talented in art. *Studies in Art Education, 22*(2), 38–48.

ALGOZZINE, B., YSSELDYKE, J., & SHINN, M. (1982). Identifying children with learning disabilities: When is a discrepancy severe? *Journal of School Psychology, 20*(4), 299–305.

ALLPORT, G., VERNON, P., & LINDZEY, G. (1951). *Study of values: Manual of directions.* Boston: Houghton Mifflin.

ALTER, J., DENMAN, D., & BARRON, F. (1972). Dancers write of themselves and dance education. In F. Barron (Ed.), *Artists in the making* (pp. 86–112). New York: Seminar Press.

ALVINO, J., MCDONNEL, R. C., & RICHERT, S. (1981). National survey of identification practices in gifted and talented education. *Exceptional Children, 48*(2), 124–132.

ALVINO, J., & WEILER, J. (1979). How standardized testing fails to identify the gifted and what teachers can do about it. *Phi Delta Kappan, 61*(2), 106–109.

AMES, L. B. (1968). Learning disabilities: The developmental point of view. In H. R. Myklebust (Ed.), *Progress in learning disabilities,* (Vol. 1, pp. 39–74). New York: Grune & Stratton.

ANASTASI, A., & SCHAEFER, C. E. (1971). Note on the concepts of creativity and intelligence. *Journal of Creative Behavior, 5*(2), 113–116.

ANDREWS, F. M. (1975). Social and psychological factors which influence the creative process. In I. A. Taylor & J. W. Getzels (Eds.), *Perspectives in creativity* (pp. 117–145). Chicago: Aldine.

ANOLIK, S. (1979). Personality, family, educational, and criminological characteristics of bright delinquents. *Psychological Reports, 44,* 727–734.

ANSBACHER, H. L., & ANSBACHER, R. R. (1956). *The individual psychology of Alfred Adler.* New York: Basic Books.

ANYON, J. (1980). Social class and the hidden curriculum of work. *Journal of Education, 162*(1), 67–92.

ANYON, J. (1980/1987). Social class and the hidden curriculum of work. In E. Stevens & G. H. Woods (Eds.), *Justice, ideology, and education: An introduction to the social foundations of education* (pp. 210–226). New York: Random House.

ARENDS, J., & KIRKPATRICK, J. (Eds.). (1987). *Building on excellence.* Washington, DC: Council for Educational Development and Research.

ARENDT, H. (1981). *The life of the mind.* New York: Harcourt Brace Jovanovich.

ARNHEIM, R. (1966). Growth. In E. W. Eisner & D. W. Ecker (Eds.), *Readings in art education* (pp. 85–96). Waltham, MA: Blaisdell.

ARNHEIM, R. (1972). *Toward a psychology of art: Collected essays.* Berkeley, CA: University of California Press.

ARONOFF, F. (1965). *Music and young children.* New York: Holt, Rinehart & Winston.

ASO, K. (1984). What is the source of art? *Journal of Education, 166*(2), 188–195.

ASTIN, H. S. (1974). Sex differences in mathematical and scientific precocity. In J. C. Stanley, D. P. Keating, & L. H. Fox (Eds.), *Mathematical talent: Discovery, description, and development* (pp. 70–86). Baltimore, MD: Johns Hopkins Univerity Press.

AUSTIN, A. B., & DRAPER, D. C. (1981). Peer relationships of the academically gifted: A review. *Gifted Child Quarterly, 25*(3), 129–133.

BACHMAN, J. G. (1970). *The impact of family background and intelligence on tenth-grade boys. Youth in transition* (Vol. 2). Ann Arbor, MI: Braun-Brumfield.

BACKMAN, M. E. (1972). Patterns of mental abilities: Ethnic, socioeconomic, and sex differences. *American Educational Research Journal, 9*(1), 112.

BAER, D., & BUSHELL, D. (1981). The future of behavior analysis in the schools? Consider its recent past, and then ask a different question. *School Psychology Review, 10*(2), 259–270.

BAIRD, L. L. (1985). Do grades and tests predict adult accomplishment? *Research in Higher Education, 23*(1), 3–85.

BALDWIN, A. Y. (1978). The Baldwin identification matrix. In A. Y. Baldwin, G. H. Gear, & L. J. Lucito (Eds.), *Educational planning for the gifted: Overcoming cultural, geographic, and socioeconomic barriers.* Reston, VA: Council for Exceptional Children.

BAMBERGER, J. (1986). Cognitive issues in the development of musically gifted children. In R. J. Sternberg & J. E. Davidson (Eds.), *Conceptions of giftedness* (pp. 388–413) Cambridge: Cambridge University Press.

BARBE, W., & MILONE, M. (1985). Reading and writing. In R. Swassing (Ed.), *Teaching gifted children and adolescents* (pp. 276–313). Columbus, OH: Merrill.

BARKER, R., & GUMP, P. (1964). *Big school, small school.* Stanford, CA: Stanford University Press.

BARNETTE, L. A., & FISCELLA, J. (1985). A child by any other name. . . A comparison of the playfulness of gifted and nongifted children. *Gifted Child Quarterly, 29*(2), 61–66.

BARRON, F. (1963). *Creativity and psychological health.* Princeton, NJ: Van Nostrand.

BARRON, F. (1969). *Creative person and creative process.* New York: Holt, Rinehart & Winston.

BARRON, F., & DENMAN, D. (1972). Students in the theater arts. In F. Barron (Ed.), *Artists in the making* (pp. 75–83). New York: Seminar Press.

BARRON, F., KRAUS, J., & CONTI, I. (1972). Six highly regarded students in interview. In F. Barron (Ed.), *Artists in the making* (pp. 19–32). New York: Seminar Press.

BAR-TAL, D. (1978). Attributional analysis of achievement-related behavior. *Review of Educational Research, 48*(2), 259–271.

BARTHE, C. L. (1980, May). *Program for academically talented students.* Paper presented at the Annual Meeting of the International Reading Association, St. Louis, MO.

BARYLICK, M. (1983). Both artist and instrument: An approach to dance education. *Daedelus, 112*(3), 113–127.

BARZUN, J. (1965). *Music in American life.* Bloomington, IN: Indiana University Press.

BASS, B. (1981). *Stogdill's handbook of leadership.* New York: Free Press.

BATEMAN, B. D. (1965). An educator's view of a diagnostic approach to learning disorders. In J. Hellmuth (Ed.), *Learning disorders* (Vol. 1). Seattle, WA: Special Child Publications.

BAVELAS, A. (1984). Leadership: Man and function. In W. E. Rosenbach & R. L. Taylor (Eds.), *Contemporary issues in leadership* (pp. 117–123). Boulder, CO: Westview Press.

BAYLEY, N. (1970). Development of mental abilities. In P. Mussen (Ed.), *Carmichael's manual of child psychology* (pp. 1163–1210). New York: Wiley.

BELL, E. T. (1965). *Men of mathematics*. New York: Simon & Schuster.

BENBOW, C. P. (1983). Adolescence of the mathematically precocious: A five-year longitudinal study. In C. P. Benbow & J. C. Stanley (Eds.), *Academic precocity: Aspects of its development* (pp. 9–37). Baltimore, MD: Johns Hopkins University Press.

BENBOW, C. P., PERKINS, S., & STANLEY, J. C. (1983). Mathematics taught at a fast pace: A longitudinal evaluation of SMPY's first class. In C. P. Benbow & J. C. Stanley (Eds.), *Academic precocity: Aspects of its development* (pp. 51–78). Baltimore, MD: Johns Hopkins University Press.

BENBOW, C., & STANLEY, J. (1980). Sex differences in mathematical ability: Fact or artifact? *Science, 210*(12), 1262–1264.

BENBOW, C., & STANLEY, J. (1981). The devil's advocate: Sex differences in mathematical reasoning ability. *Journal for the Education of the Gifted, 4*(3), 169–176, 239–243.

BENBOW, C., & STANLEY, J. (1982). Intellectually talented boys and girls: Educational profiles. *Gifted Child Quarterly, 26*(2), 82–88.

BENNETT, W. J. (1986). *What works: Research about teaching and learning*. Pueblo, CO: Office of Educational Research and Improvement.

BERG, I. (1972). Rich man's qualifications for poor man's jobs. In R. Lejune (Ed.), *Class and conflict in American society* (pp. 186–196). Chicago: Markham.

BERLINGHOFF, W. (1968). *Mathematics: The art of reason*. Boston: D. C. Heath.

BERNSTEIN, B. (1961). Social structure, language, and learning. *Educational Research, 3*(3), 163–176.

BEST, D. (1980). Art and sport. *Journal of Aesthetic Education, 14*(2), 69–80.

BIRCH, J., TIDSALL, W. J., PEABODY, R., & STERRETT, R. (1966). *School achievement and effect of type size on reading in visually handicapped children* (Cooperative Research Project No. 1766). Pittsburgh, PA: University of Pittsburgh.

BIRNBAUM, M. (n.d.). Educational problems of rural education for the gifted. In *Ideas for urban/rural gifted/talented* (pp. 67–69). Ventura, CA: National/State Leadership Training Institute on the Gifted and the Talented and the Office of the Ventura County Superintendent of Schools.

BLACHLY, P. H., DISHER, W., & RODUNER, G. (1968, December). Suicide by physicians. *Bulletin of Suicidology*, 1–18.

BLAU, P., & DUNCAN, O. (1967). *The American occupational structure*. New York: Wiley.

BLAUBERGS, M. S. (1978). Overcoming the sexist barriers to gifted women's achievement. In *Advantage: Disadvantaged gifted* (pp. 7–38). Ventura, CA: National/State Leadership Training Institute on the Gifted and the Talented and the Office of the Ventura County Superintendent of Schools.

BLOLAND, R., & MICHAEL, W. (1984). A comparison of the relative validity of a measure of Piagetian cognitive development and a set of conventional prognostic measures in the prediction of the future success of ninth- and tenth-grade students in algebra. *Educational and Psychological Measurement, 44*(4), 925–943.

BLOOM, B. (Ed.). (1956). *Taxonomy of educational objectives, Handbook I: Cognitive domain*. New York: David McKay.

BLOOM, B. (1964). *Stability and change in human characteristics*. New York: Wiley.

BLOOM, B. (1971). Learning for mastery. In B. Bloom, J. Hastings, & G. Madaus, *Handbook on formative and summative evaluation of student learning* (pp. 43–57). New York: McGraw-Hill.

BLOOM, B. (1976). *Human characteristics and school learning*. New York: McGraw-Hill.

BLOOM, B. (1977). Affective outcomes of school learning. *Phi Delta Kappan, 59*(3), 193–198.

BLOOM B. (1982). The role of gifts and markers in the development of talent. *Exceptional Children, 48*(6), 510–522.

BLOOM, B. (1985). *Developing talent in young people*. New York: Ballantine Books.

BLOOM, B., & SOSNIAK, L. (1981). Talent development vs. schooling. *Educational Leadership, 39*, 86–94.

BOEHM, L. (1962). The development of conscience: A comparison of American children of different mental and socioeconomic levels. *Child Development 33*, 575–590.

BOLES, D. (1980). X-linkage of spatial ability: A critical review. *Child Development, 51*, 625–635.

BOSS, R., & McCONKIE, M. (1981). The destructive impact of a positive team-building intervention. *Group & Organizational Studies, 6*(1), 45–56.

BOWEN, J. (1972). *A history of Western education*, (Vol. 1). New York: St. Martin's Press.

BOWERS, J. (1969). Interactive effects of creativity and IQ on ninth-grade achievement. *Journal of Educational Measurement, 6*(3), 173–177.

BOWLES, S., & GINTIS, H. (1976). *Schooling in capitalist America*. New York: Basic Books.

BRADY, F. (1973). *Profile of a prodigy: The life and games of Bobby Fischer*. New York: David McKay.

BRAGA, J. (1971). Early admission: Opinion versus evidence. *The Elementary School Journal, 72*(1), 35–46.

BRANDWEIN, P. (1955). *The gifted student as future scientist: The high school student and his commitment to science*. New York: Harcourt Brace Jovanovich.

BRAUNSCHWEIG, P. (1981). Training the young dancer. *Design for Arts in Education, 83*(1), 70–74.

BREKKE, B., JOHNSON, L., WILLIAMS, J. D., & MORRISON, E. (1976). Conservation of weight with the gifted. *Journal of Genetic Psychology, 129*, 179–184.

BRICKLIN, B., & BRICKLIN, P. M. (1967). *Bright child—poor grades: The psychology of underachievement*. New York: Delacorte Press.

BROCKWAY, W., & WEINSTOCK, H. (1958). *Men of music: Their lives, times, and achievements*. New York: Simon & Schuster.

BRONFENBRENNER, U., & CROUTER, H. C. (1982). Work and family through time and space. In S. B. Kamerman & C. D. Hayes (Eds.), *Families that work: Children in a changing world* (pp. 39–83). Washington, DC: National Academy Press.

BROUDY, H. (1958). A realistic philosophy of music. In N. Henry (Ed.), *Basic concepts in music education* (pp. 62–87). The Fifty-Seventh Yearbook of the National Society for the Study of Education, Part I. Chicago: University of Chicago Press.

BROWN, A. L. (1978). Knowing when, where, and how to remember: A problem of metacognition. In R. Glaser (Ed.), *Advances in instructional psychology*, (Vol. 1). Hillsdale, NJ: Erlbaum.

BROWN, J. D. (1967). The development of creative teacher-scholars. In J. Kagan (Ed.), *Creativity and learning* (pp. 164–180). Boston: Beacon Press.

BRUCH, C. (1975). Children with intellectual superiority. In J. Gallagher (Ed.), *The application of child development research to exceptional children*. Reston, VA: Council for Exceptional Children.

BRUNER, J. S. (1960). *The process of education*. New York: Vintage Books.

BRYAN, T. H., & BRYAN, H. J. (1978). *Understanding learning disabilities* (2nd ed.). Sherman Oaks, CA: Alfred.

BUCHMANN, M. (1987). Reporting and using research. In J. I. Goodlad (Ed.), *The ecology of school renewal* (pp. 170–191). Chicago: National Society for the Study of Education.

BUENNING, M., & TOLLEFSON, N. (1987). The cultural gap hypothesis as an explanation for the achievement patterns of Mexican-American students. *Psychology in the Schools, 24*, 264–272.

BULL, B. L. (1985). Eminence and precocity: An examination of the justification of education for the gifted and talented. *Teachers College Record, 87*(1), 1–19.

BULL, K. S. (1987). *The learning disabled gifted child: Educational procedures in rural settings*. Paper presented at the Seventh Annual Conference of the American Concil on Rural Special Education, Asheville, NC.

BURKS, B., JENSEN, D., & TERMAN, L. (1930). *The promise of youth: Genetic studies of genius* (Vol. 3). Stanford, CA: Stanford University Press.

BURNS, J. M. (1978). *Leadership*. New York: Harper & Row.

BURT, C. (1966). The genetic determination of differences in intelligence: A study of monozygotic twins reared together and apart. *British Journal of Statistical Psychology, 57*, 137–153.

BURT, C. (1975). *The gifted child*. New York: Wiley.

BUTTERFIELD, F. (1986, August 3). Why Asians are going to the head of the class. *New York Times*, pp. 18–23.

BUTTS, R. F. (1973). *The education of the West*. New York: McGraw-Hill.

CALLAHAN, C., & RENZULLI, J. (1981). The effectiveness of a creativity training program in the language arts. In W. Barbe & J. Renzulli (Eds.), *Psychology and education of the gifted* (3rd ed., pp. 394–400). New York: Irvington.

CALLAHAN, R. E. (1962). *Education and the cult of efficiency.* Chicago: University of Chicago Press.

CALLAWAY, W. R. (1970). Modes of biological adaptation and their role in intellectual development. In *The Galton Institute Monograph Series*, No. 1, 1–34.

CAMPBELL, J. (1971). *The portable Jung.* New York: Penguin Books.

CARRIER, J. G. (1983). Masking the social in educational knowledge: The case of learning disability theory. *American Journal of Sociology, 88*(5), 948–974.

CARROLL, J. B. (1963). Research on teaching foreign languages. In N. L. Gage (Ed.), *Handbook of research on teaching* (pp. 1060–1100). Chicago: Rand McNally.

CARROLL, J. B. (1976). Psychometric tests as cognitive tasks: A new structure of intellect. In L. B. Resnick (Ed.), *The nature of intelligence* (pp. 27–56). Hillsdale, NJ: Erlbaum.

CARTER, K., & KONTOS, S. (1982). An application of cognitive-developmental theory to the identification of gifted children. *Roeper Review, 5*(2), 17–20.

CARTER, K., & ORMROD, J. (1982). Acquisition of formal operations by intellectually gifted children. *Gifted Child Quarterly, 26*(3), 110–115.

CARTER, R. S. (1952). How invalid are marks assigned by teachers? *Journal of Educational Psychology, 43,* 218–228.

CARTWRIGHT, G. P., CARTWRIGHT C. A., & WARD, M. E. (1981). *Educating special learners.* Belmont, CA: Wadsworth.

CASSERLY, P. L. (1979). Helping able young women take math and science seriously in school. In N. Colangelo & R. T. Zaffrann (Eds.), *New voices in counseling the gifted* (pp. 346–369). Dubuque, IA: Kendall/Hunt.

CASTIGLIONE, L. V. (1984, June 6). The education of the gifted and talented: Nurturing a natural resource. *Education Week*, p. 40.

CATON, H. R. (1985). Visual impairments. In W. H. Berdine & A. E. Blackhurst (Eds.), *An introduction to special education* (2nd ed., pp. 235–282). Boston: Little, Brown.

CATON, H. R., & RANKIN, E. (1980). Variability in age and experience among blind students using basal reading materials. *Journal of Visual Impairments and Blindness, 74,* 147–149.

CATTELL, R. B. (1950). *Culture fair intelligence test: Scale 1.* Champaign, IL: Institute for Personality and Ability Testing.

CATTELL, R. B. (1971). *Abilities: Their structure, growth, and action.* Boston: Houghton Mifflin.

CATTELL, R. B., & CATTELL, A. K. S. (1960). *Culture fair intelligence test: Scale 2.* Champaign, IL: Institute for Personality and Ability Testing.

CATTELL, R. B., & CATTELL, A. K. S. (1963). *Culture fair intelligence test: Scale 3.* Champaign, IL: Institute for Personality and Ability Testing.

CHALL, J. (1967). *Learning to read: The great debate.* New York: McGraw-Hill.

CHIARI, J. (1960). *Realism and imagination.* London: Barrie and Rockliff.

CHANSKY, N. (1964). A note of the grade point average in research. *Educational and Psychological Measurement, 24,* 95–99.

CHETELAT, F. (1981). Visual arts education for the gifted elementary level art student. *Gifted Child Quarterly, 25*(4), 154–158.

CLARIZIO, H. F., & MEHRENS, W. A. (1985). Psychometric limitations of Guilford's structure-of-intellect model for identification and programming of the gifted. *Gifted Child Quarterly, 29*(3), 113–120.

CLARIZIO, H. F., & PHILLIPS, S. E. (1986). Sex bias in the diagnosis of learning disabled students. *Psychology in the Schools, 23*(1), 44–52.

CLARK, B. (1979). *Growing up gifted.* Columbus: OH: Merrill.

CLARK, B. (1983). *Growing up gifted* (2nd ed.). Columbus, OH: Merrill.

CLARK, B. (1986). *Optimizing learning: The integrative education model in the classroom.* Columbus, OH: Merrill.

CLARK, B. (1988). *Growing up gifted* (3rd ed.). Columbus, OH: Merrill.

CLARK, G., & ZIMMERMAN, E. (1983). Identifying artistically talented students. *School Arts, 83*(3), 26–31.

CLARK, G., & ZIMMERMAN, E. (1984a). *Educating artistically talented students.* Syracuse, NY: Syracuse University Press.

CLARK, G., & ZIMMERMAN, E. (1984b). Toward a new conception of talent in the visual arts. *Roeper Review, 6*(4), 214–216.

CLARKE, E. L. (1916/1968). *American men of letters: Their nature and nurture.* New York: AMS Press.

CLEMENTS, S. D. (1966). *Minimal brain dysfunction in children: Terminology and identification, Phase one of a three phase project* (NINDS Monograph No. 3, U. S. Public Health Service Publication No. 1415). Washington, DC: U.S. Government Printing Office.

COHN, S. J. (1984). Project F. U. T. U. R. E.: A progress report after three prototype years of serving intellectually gifted students. *Journal for the Education of the Gifted, 7*(2), 103–119.

COLANGELO, N., & PFLEGER, L. R. (1979). Academic self-concept of gifted high school students. In N. Colangelo & R. T. Zaffrann (Eds.), *New voices in counseling the gifted* (pp. 188–193). Dubuque, IA: Kendall/Hunt.

COLEMAN, J. (1961). *The adolescent society.* New York: Free Press of Glencoe.

COLEMAN, J., CAMPBELL, E., HOBSON, C., McPARTLAND, J., MOOD, A., WEINFELD, F., & YORK, R. (1966). *Equality of educational opportunity report.* Washington, DC: U.S. Government Printing Office.

COMMITTEE FOR ECONOMIC DEVELOPMENT. (1985). *Investing in our children: Business and the public schools.* New York: Committee for Economic Development.

COPLEY, F. O. (1961). *The American high school and the talented student.* Ann Arbor, MI: University of Michigan Press.

CORNELL, D. G. (1984). *Families of gifted children.* Ann Arbor, MI: UMI Research Press.

COUNCIL OF STATE DIRECTORS OF GIFTED PROGRAMS. (1985). *The state of the states' gifted and talented education.* Augusta, ME: Maine Department of Education.

COUNTS, G. (1930). *The American road to culture: A social interpretation of education in the United States.* New York: John Day. (Facsimile reprint edition by Arno Press-New York Times, 1971)

COUNTS, G. (1932). *Dare the school build a new social order?* New York: John Day.

COX, C. (1926). *The early mental traits of three hundred geniuses: Genetic studies of genius* (Vol. 2). Stanford, CA: Stanford University Press.

COX, J., & DANIEL, N. (1983). Specialized schools for high ability students. *G/C/T, 28,* 2–9.

COX, J., DANIEL, N., & BOSTON, B. (1985). *Educating able learners: Programs and promising practices.* Austin, TX: University of Texas Press.

CREMIN, L. (1961). *The transformation of the school.* New York: Vintage Books.

CREMIN, L. (1980). *American education: The national experience.* New York: Harper & Row.

CROSS, D. P. (1985). Physical and health-related disabilities. In W. H. Berdine & A. E. Blackhurst (Eds.), *An introduction to special education* (2nd ed., pp. 283–332). Boston: Little, Brown.

CUBAN, L. (1982). Persistence of the inevitable: The teacher-centered classroom. *Education and Urban Society, 15*(1), 26–41.

CUMMINGS, S., BRIGGS, R., & MERCY, J. (1977). Preachers versus teachers: Local-cosmopolitan conflict over textbook censorship in an Appalachian community. *Rural Sociology, 42*(1), 7–21.

CURTIN, M., AVNER, A., & SMITH, L. (1983). The Pimsleur Battery as a predictor of student performance. *The Modern Language Journal, 67*(1), 33–40.

DACEY, J. S., & MADAUS, G. F. (1971). An analysis of two hypotheses concerning the relationship between creativity and intelligence. *Journal of Educational Research, 64*(5), 213–216.

DARWIN, C. (1859/1958). *The origin of species.* New York: Mentor Books. (Original work published 1859)

DAURIO, S. P. (1979). Educational enrichment versus acceleration: A review of the literature. In W. George, S. Cohn, & J. Stanley (Eds.), *Educating the gifted: Acceleration and enrichment* (pp. 13–63). Baltimore, MD: Johns Hopkins University Press.

DAVIDSON, H. P. (1931). An experimental study of bright, average, and dull children at the four-year mental level. *Genetic Psychology Monograph, 9,* 119–289.

DAVIDSON, H., & BALDUCCI, D. (1956). Class and sex differences in verbal facility of bright children. *Journal of Educational Psychology, 47*(8), 476–480.

DAVIS, G., & RIMM, S. (1982). Group inventory for finding interests (GIFFI) I and II: Instruments for identifying creative potential in the junior and senior high school. *Journal of Creative Behavior, 16*(1), 50–57.

DAVIS, H. B., & CONNELL, J. P. (1985). The effect of aptitude and achievement status on the self-system. *Gifted Child Quarterly, 29*(3), 131–136.

DAVIS, J. (1929). A study of 163 outstanding communist leaders. *American Sociological Review, 24*, 42–55.

DAVIS, P., & HERSH, R. (1981). *The mathematical experience.* Boston: Houghton Mifflin.

DE GROOT, A. D. (1978). *Thought and choice in chess* (2nd ed.). The Hague: Mouton.

DE LEON, J. (1983). Cognitive style differences and the underrepresentation of Mexican Americans in programs for the gifted. *Journal for the Education of the Gifted, 6*(3), 167–177.

DELISLE, J. R. (1986). Death with honors: Suicide among gifted adolescents. *Journal of Counseling and Development, 64*(9), 558–560.

DENBOW, T. (1984). Rhodes recipe. *MSU Today, 3*(3).

DEUTSCH, M. (1968). Environment and perception. In M. Deutsch, I. Katz, & A. Jensen (Eds.), *Social class, race, and psychological development* (pp. 58–85). New York: Holt, Rinehart & Winston.

DEWEY, J. (1902/1956). *The child and the curriculum.* Chicago: University of Chicago Press.

DeYOUNG, A. (1987). The status of American rural education research: An integrated review and commentary. *Review of Educational Research, 57*(2), 123–148.

D' HEURLE, A., MELLINGER, H., & HAGGARD, E. (1959). Personality, intellectual, and achievement patterns in gifted children. *Psychological Monographs, 13*, 1–24.

DIMITROVSKY, L., & ALMY, M. (1975). Early conservation as a predictor of arithmetic achievement. *Journal of Psychology, 91*, 65–70.

DOBZHANSKY, T., & MONTAGU, A. (1975). Natural selection and the mental capacities of mankind. In A. Montagu (Ed.), *Race and IQ* (pp. 104–113). London: Oxford University Press.

DOLAN, L. (1983). The prediction of reading achievement and self-esteem from an index of home educational environment: A study of urban elementary students. *Measurement and Evaluation in Guidance, 16*(2) 86–94.

DOMAN, G. J. (1964). *How to teach your baby to read: The gentle revolution.* New York: Random House.

DOWDALL, C., & COLANGELO, N. (1982). Underachieving gifted students: Reviews and implications. *Gifted Child Quarterly, 26*(4), 179–184.

DREWS, E. M. (1961). A critical evaluation of approaches to the identification of gifted students. In E. Arthur (Ed.), *Measurement and research in today's school* (pp. 109–121). Washington, DC: American Council on Education.

DULEE, R. (1983). Interview with John Holt. *Aegis: Newsletter of the WVGEA, 2*(1), 6–8. Charleston, WV: West Virginia Gifted Education Association. Available from Education Department, University of Charleston, Charleston, WV

DUNCAN, A. D. (1969). *Behavior rates of gifted and elementary school children* (Monograph). Cincinnati, OH: The National Association for Gifted Children.

DUNCAN, I. (1927). *My life.* New York: Liveright.

DUNCUM, P. (1985). How 35 children born between 1724 and 1900 learned to draw. *Studies in Art Education, 26*(2), 93–102.

DUNN, L., & MARKWARDT, F. (1970). *Peabody individual achievement test.* Circle Pines, MN: American Guidance Service.

DUPUIS, M., & CARTWRIGHT, G. (1979, April). *The writing of gifted children.* Paper presented at the American Educational Research Association Annual Conference, San Francisco, CA.

DURDEN, W. (1980). Gifted programs: The Johns Hopkins program for verbally gifted youth. *Roeper Review, 2*(3), 34–37.

DURKIN, D. (1966). *Children who read early.* New York: Teachers College

DURR, W. K. (1981, January). *Reading and the gifted student.* Paper presented at the Annual Meeting of the Southwest Regional Conference of the International Reading Association, San Antonio, TX.

ECCLES, J. (1985). Model of students' mathematics enrollment decisions. *Educational Studies in Mathematics, 16*, 311–314.

EDGE, O., & FRIEDBERG, S. (1984). Factors affecting achievement in the first course in calculus. *Journal of Experimental Education, 52*(3), 136–140.

EDMISTON, R. (1943). Do teachers show partiality? *Peabody Journal of Education, 20*, 234–238.

EDMONDS, R. (1979). Effective schools for the urban poor. *Educational Leadership, 37*(1), 15–18.

EDUCATIONAL TESTING SERVICE. (1926–1987). *College entrance examination board scholastic aptitude test.* Princeton, NJ: Educational Testing Service.

EDUCATIONAL TESTING SERVICE, COOPERATIVE TEST DIVISION. (1956–1972). *Sequential tests of educational progress.* Princeton, NJ: Educational Testing Service.

EPSTEIN, C. B. (1979). *The gifted and talented: Programs that work.* Arlington, VA: National School Public Relations Association.

ERLICH, V. Z. (1979). *The Astor program for gifted children prekindergarten through the primary grades, five years later—Evaluation and problems of transition.* (ERIC Document Reproduction Service No. ED 171 054.)

EHRLICH, V. Z. (1982). *Gifted children: A guide for parents and teachers.* Englewood Cliffs, NJ: Prentice-Hall.

EYSENCK, H. J. (1983). The roots of creativity: Cognitive ability or personality trait? *Roeper Review, 5*(4), 10–12.

EYSENCK, H. J., & EYSENCK, S. B. G. (1975). *Manual of the Eysenck personality questionnaire.* San Diego, CA: Edits.

FEARN, L. (1981, March–April). Writing: A basic and developmental skill for gifted learners. *G/C/T,* 26–27.

FEARN, L. (1982). Underachievement and rate of acceleration. *Gifted Child Quarterly, 26*(3), 121–125.

FEIS, O. (1910). *Studien über die Genealogie und Psychologie der Musikers.* Weisbaden, Germany: Bergmann.

FELDHUSEN, J. F., & KLAUSMEIER, H. J. (1962). Anxiety, intelligence, and achievement in children of low, average, and high intelligence. *Child Development, 33,* 403–409.

FELDHUSEN, J., & KOLLOF, M. (1979). An approach to career education for the gifted. *Roeper Review, 2*(2), 13–17.

FELDMAN, D. (1979). The mysterious case of extreme giftedness. In A. H. Passow (Ed.), *The gifted and talented: Their education and development,* The Seventy-Eighth Yearbook of the National Society for the Study of Education, Part II (pp. 335–351). Chicago: University of Chicago Press.

FELDMAN, D. (1984). A follow-up of subjects scoring above 180 IQ in Terman's "Genetic Studies of Genius." *Exceptional Children, 50*(6), 518–523.

FEUERSTEIN, R., MILLER, R., HOFFMAN, M. B., RAND, Y., MINTZKER, Y., & JENSEN, M. R. (1981). Cognitive modifiability in adolescence: Cognitive structures and the effects of intervention. *Journal of Special Education, 15*(2), 269–287.

FINE, B. (1967). *Underachievers: How they can be helped.* New York: Dutton.

FINK, M. B. (1962). Self-concept as it relates to academic underachievement. *California Journal of Educational Research, 13,* 57–62.

FISHER, K. (1987, November). *Cognitive development in real children: Levels and variations.* Paper presented at Teaching Thinking and At-Risk Students, an Invitational Cross-Laboratory Conference, Philadelphia, PA.

FISHER, R. (1973). *Musical prodigies, masters at an early age.* New York: Association Press.

FLAVELL, J. H. (1977). *Cognitive development.* Englewood Cliffs, NJ: Prentice-Hall.

FLEMING, E. (1985). Career preparation. In R. Swassing (Ed.), *Teaching gifted children and adolescents* (pp. 340–375). Columbus, OH: Merrill.

FONTEYN, M. (1979). *The magic of dance.* New York: Knopf.

FORNESS, S. R., SINCLAIR, E., & GUTHRIE, D. (1983). Learning disabilities discrepancy formulas: Their use in actual practice. *Learning Disability Quarterly, 6,* 107–114.

FOSTER, W. (1981). Leadership: A conceptual framework for recognizing and educating. *Gifted Child Quarterly, 25*(1), 17–25.

FOSTER, W. (1985). Helping a child toward individual excellence. In J. Feldhusen (Ed.), *Toward excellence in gifted education* (pp. 135–162). Denver, CO: Love.

FOSTER, W. (1986). The application of single subject research methods to the study of exceptional ability and extraordinary achievement. *Gifted Child Quarterly, 30*(1), 33–37.

FOWLKES, J. G. (1930). Adjusting the curriculum to the needs of superior pupils. *Nation's Schools, 5,* 82–84, 85.

FOX, L. H. (1976a). Facilitating educational development of mathematically precocious youth. In J. C. Stanley, D. P. Keating, & L. H. Fox (Eds.), *Mathematical talent: Discovery, description, and development* (pp. 47–69). Baltimore, MD: Johns Hopkins University Press.

Fox, L. H. (1976b). Sex differences in mathematical precocity: Bridging the gap. In D. P. Keating (Ed.), *Intellectual talent: Research and development* (pp. 183–214). Baltimore, MD: Johns Hopkins University Press.

Fox, L. H. (1976c). The values of gifted youth. In D. P. Keating (Ed.), *Intellectual talent: Research and development* (pp. 273–284). Baltimore, MD: Johns Hopkins University Press.

Fox, L. H. (1978). Scientists and mathematicians of the future. In *Advantage: Disadvantaged gifted* (pp. 47–52). Ventura, CA: National/State Leadership Training Institute on the Gifted and the Talented, Office of the Ventura County Superintendent of Schools.

Fox, L. (1983). Gifted students with reading problems: An empirical study. In L. Fox, L. Brody, & D. Tobin (Eds.), *Learning disabled/gifted children* (pp. 117–139). Baltimore, MD: University Park Press.

Fox, L. H., & Cohn, S. J. (1980). Sex differences in the development of precocious mathematical talent. In L. H. Fox, L. Brody, & D. Tobin (Eds.), *Women and the mathematical mystique* (pp. 94–112). Baltimore, MD: Johns Hopkins University Press.

Fox, L. H., & Denham, S. A. (1974). Values and career interests of mathematically and scientifically precocious youth. In J. C. Stanley, D. P. Keating, & L. H. Fox (Eds.), *Mathematical talent: Discovery, description, and development* (pp. 140–175). Baltimore, MD: Johns Hopkins Univerity Press.

Fox, L. H., Pasternak, S. R., & Peiser, N. L. (1976). Career-related interests of adolescent boys and girls. In D. P. Keating (Ed.), *Intellectual talent: Research and development* (pp. 242–261). Baltimore, MD: Johns Hopkins University Press.

Fox, M. N. (1981). Creativity and intelligence. *Childhood Education, 57*(4), 227–232.

Frauenheim, J. (1978). Academic achievement characteristics of adult males who were diagnosed as dyslexic in childhood. *Journal of Learning Disabilities, 11,* 476–483.

Freedman, D. G., & Freedman, N. C. (1969). Behavioral differences between Chinese-American and European-American newborns. *Nature, 244,* 1227.

Freeman, J. (1979). *Gifted children.* Baltimore, MD: University Park Press.

Freeman, J. (1983). Emotional problems of the gifted child. *Journal of Child Psychology and Psychiatry, 24,* 481–485.

French, J. L., & Cardon, B. W. (1968). Characteristics of high mental ability dropouts. *The Vocational Guidance Journal, 16*(3), 162–168.

Friend, R. (1939). Influences of heredity and musical environment on the scores of kindergarten children on the Seashore Measures of Musical Ability. *Journal of Applied Psychology, 23,* 347–357.

Fund for the Advancement of Education. (1957). *They went to college early* (Evaluation Report No. 2). New York: Fund for the Advancement of Education.

Gaddes, W. H. (1980). *Learning disabilities and brain function: A neurophysiological approach.* New York: Springer-Verlag.

Gage, N. (1978). *The scientific basis of the art of teaching.* New York: Teachers College Press.

Gage, N., & Berliner, D. (1975). *Educational psychology.* Chicago: Rand McNally.

Gallagher, J. (1958). Peer acceptance of highly gifted children in elementary school. *The Elementary School Journal, 58,* 465–470.

Gallaher, J. (1975). *Teaching the gifted child* (2nd ed.). Boston: Allyn & Bacon.

Gallagher, J. (1985). *Teaching the gifted child* (3rd ed.). Boston: Allyn & Bacon.

Gallagher, J., & Crowder, T. (1957). The adjustment of gifted children in the classroom. *Exceptional Children, 23,* 306–319.

Galluci, N. T. (1988). Emotional adjustment of gifted children. *Gifted Child Quarterly, 32*(2), 273–276.

Galton, F. (1869/1962). *Hereditary genius.* London: Fontana.

Galton, F. (1883). *Inquiries into human faculty and its development.* London: Macmillan.

Gardner, H. (1973). *The arts and human development.* New York: Wiley.

Gardner, H. (1982). *Art, mind, and brain: A cognitive approach to creativity.* New York: Basic Books.

Gardner, H. (1983). *Frames of mind: The theory of multiple intelligences.* New York: Basic Books.

Gardner, J. (1961). *Excellence.* New York: Harper & Row.

Gaug, M. (1984). Reading acceleration and enrichment in the elementary grades. *Reading Teacher, 37*(4), 372–376.

Getzels, J. W. (1979). From art student to fine artist: Potential, problem finding, and performance. In A. H. Passow (Ed.), *The gifted and talented: Their education and development* (pp. 372–387). The Seventy-eighth Yearbook of the National Society for the Study of Education, Part 1. Chicago: University of Chicago Press.

GETZELS, J. W., & CSIKSZENTMIHALYI, M. (1968). The value orientation of art students as determinants of artistic specialization and creative performance. *Studies in Art Education, 10,* 5–16.

GETZELS, J. W., & CSIKSZENTMIHALYI, M. (1976). *The creative vision: A longitudinal study of problem finding in art.* New York: Wiley.

GETZELS, J. W., & JACKSON, P. W. (1962). *Creativity and intelligence: Explorations with gifted students.* New York: Wiley.

GHISELLI, E. E. (1963). Intelligence and managerial success. *Psychological Reports, 12,* 898.

GINZBERG, E. (1971). *Career guidance: Who needs it, who provides it, who can improve it.* New York: McGraw-Hill.

GIROUX, H. A. (1983). *Theory and resistance in education: A pedagogy for the opposition.* South Hadley, MA: Bergin Garvey.

GLASS, G. (1983). Effectiveness of special education. *Policy Studies Review, 2* (Special 1), 65–78.

GLIDEWELL, J., KANTOR, M., SMITH, L., & STRINGER, L. (1966). Socialization and social structure in the classroom. In L. Hoffman & M. Hoffman (Eds.), *Review of child development research* (pp. 221–256). New York: Russell Sage.

GOERTZEL, V., & GOERTZEL, M., (1962). *Cradles of eminence.* Boston: Little,

GOLD, M. (1965). *Education of the intellectually gifted.* Columbus, OH: Merrill.

GOOD, T., & BROPHY, J. (1987). *Looking in classrooms* (4th ed.). New York: Harper & Row.

GOODNOW, J. J. (1984). On being judged "intelligent." *International Journal of Psychology, 19*(4–5), 391–406.

GOODWIN, W. L., & DRISCOLL, L. A. (1980). *Handbook for measurement and evaluation in early childhood education.* San Francisco: Jossey-Bass.

GORDON, E. E. (1965). *Music aptitude profile.* Boston: Houghton-Mifflin.

GORDON, E. E. (1979). *Primary measures of music audiation.* Chicago: GIA.

GORDON, E. E. (1980). The assessment of music aptitudes of very young children. *Gifted Child Quarterly, 24*(3), 107–110.

GORDON, W. J. (1961). *Synectics: The development of creative capacity.* New York: Harper & Row.

GOTZ, K. O., & GOTZ, K. (1973). Introversion-extraversion and neuroticism in gifted and ungifted art students. *Perceptual and Motor Skills, 36,* 675–678.

GOTZ, K. O., & GOTZ, K. (1979). Personality characteristics of professional artists. *Perceptual and Motor Skills, 49,* 327–334.

GOULD, S. J. (1980). Women's brains. In S. J. Gould (Ed.), *The panda's thumb* (pp. 152–159). New York: Norton.

GOULD, S. (1981). *The mismeasure of man.* New York: Norton.

GOULDNER, A. W. (1979). *The future of intellectuals and the rise of the new class.* New York: Oxford University Press.

GOWAN, J. (1978). The facilitation of creativity through meditational procedures. *Journal of Creative Behavior, 12*(3), 156–160.

GOWAN, J., & DEMOS, G. (1964). *The education and guidance of the ablest.* Springfield, IL: Thomas.

GRAY, R. A., SASKI, J., MCENTIRE, M. E., & LARSEN, S. C. (1980). Is proficiency in oral language a predictor of academic success? *Elementary School Journal, 80*(5), 261–268.

GREEN, W. W. (1985). Hearing disorders. In W. H. Berdine & A. E. Blackhurst (Eds.), *An introduction to special education* (2nd ed., pp. 183–234). Boston: Little, Brown.

GREENFIELD, P. (1972). Oral or written language: The consequences of cognitive development in Africa, the United States, and England. *Language and Speech, 15,* 169–178.

GRIFFIN, L., KALLEBERG, A., & ALEXANDER, K. (1981). Determinants of early labor market entry and attainment: A study of labor market segmentation. *Sociology of Education, 54*(3), 206–221.

GRIFFITH, D. R., & CLARK, P. M. (1981). Motivation, intelligence, and creative behavior in elementary school children of low-creative ability. *Journal of Experimental Education, 49*(4), 229–234.

GROST, A. (1970). *Genius in residence.* Englewood Cliffs, NJ: Prentice-Hall.

GROTH, N. (1975). Mothers of gifted. *Gifted Child Quarterly, 19*(3), 217–222.

GUILFORD, A. M., SCHEUERLE, J., & SHONBURN, S. (1981). Aspects of language development in the gifted. *Gifted Child Quarterly, 25*(4), 159–163.

GUILFORD, J. P. (1950). Creativity. *American Psychologist, 5,* 444–454.

GUILFORD, J. P. (1959). Three faces of intellect. *American Psychologist, 14,* 469–479.

GUILFORD, J. P. (1967). *The nature of human intelligence.* New York: McGraw-Hill.

GUILFORD, J. P., & CHRISTENSEN, P. R. (1973). The one-way relation between creative potential and IQ. *Journal of Creative Behavior, 7*(4), 247–252.

GUSKEY, T. (1984). *Implementing mastery learning.* Belmont, CA: Wadsworth.

HAGGARD, E. (1957). Socialization, personality, and academic achievement in gifted children. *The School Review, 65,* 388–414.

HAIER, R. J., & DENHAM, S. A. (1976). A summary profile of the nonintellectual correlates of mathematical precocity in boys and girls. In D. P. Keating (Ed.), *Intellectual talent: Research and development* (pp. 225–241). Baltimore, MD: Johns Hopkins University Press.

HALLER, E. J., & DAVIS, S. A. (1980). Does socioeconomic status bias the assignment of elementary school students to reading groups? *American Educational Research Journal, 17*(4), 409–418.

HARNESS, B., EPSTEIN, R., & GORDON, H. W. (1984). Cognitive profiles of children referred to a clinic for reading disabilities. *Journal of Learning Disabilities, 17,* 346–351.

HARRIS, M., MORGENBESSER, S., ROTHSCHILD, J., & WISHY, B. (Eds.). (1960). *Introduction to contemporary civilization in the West* (3rd ed., 2 vols.). New York: Columbia University Press.

HASKELL, S. H., BARRETT, E. K., & TAYLOR, H. (1977). *The education of motor and neurologically handicapped children.* New York: Wiley.

HATHAWAY, S. R., & MEEHL, P. E. (1951). *An atlas for the clinical use of the Minnesota multiphasic personality inventory.* Minneapolis, MN: University of Minnesota Press.

HAUCK, B. B., & FREEHILL, M. F. (1972). *The gifted: Case studies.* Dubuque, IA: Brown.

HAYES, C. D., & KAMERMAN, S. B. (Eds.). (1983). *Children of working parents: Experiences and outcomes.* Washington, DC: National Academy Press.

HEATH, S. B. (1982). Questioning at home and at school: A comparative study. In G. Spindler (Ed.), *Doing the ethnography of schooling* (pp. 96–101). New York: Holt, Rinehart & Winston.

HEID, M. K. (1983). Characteristics and special needs of the gifted student in mathematics. *Mathematics Teacher, 76*(4), 221–226.

HELSON, R. (1971). Women mathematicians and the creative personality. *Journal of Consulting and Clinical Psychology, 36*(2), 210–220.

HENSON, F. O. (1976). *Mainstreaming the gifted.* Austin, TX: Learning Concepts.

HERSBERGER, J., & WHEATLEY, G. (1980). A proposed model for a gifted elementary school mathematics program. *Gifted Child Quarterly, 24*(1), 37–40.

HERRNSTEIN, R. (1973). *IQ in the meritocracy.* Boston: Little, Brown.

HERSEY, J. (1960). *The child buyer.* New York: Knopf.

HETHERINGTON, E. M., CAMARA, K. A., & FEATHERMAN, D. L. (1981). *Cognitive performance, school behavior, and achievement of children from one-parent households* (Report prepared for Families as Educators Team). Washington, DC: National Institute of Education. (ERIC Document Reproduction Service No. ED 221 780)

HIEBERT, E. H. (1980). The relationship of logical reasoning ability, oral language comprehension, and home experiences to preschool chldren's print awareness. *Journal of Reading Behavior, 12*(4), 313–324.

HILDRETH, G. (1966). *Introduction to the gifted.* New York: McGraw-Hill.

HOCEVAR, D. (1979). Ideational fluency as a confounding factor in the measurement of originality. *Journal of Educational Psychology, 71*(2), 191–196.

HOCEVAR, D. (1980). Intelligence, divergent thinking, and creativity. *Intelligence, 4*(1), 25–40.

HOFSTADTER, R. (1963). *Anti-intellectualism in American life.* New York: Knopf.

HOLLAND J. L. (1973). *Making vocational choices: A theory of careers.* Englewood Cliffs, N. J.: Prentice-Hall.

HOLLAND, J. L., & ASTIN, A. W. (1962). The prediction of academic, artistic, scientific, and social achievement of undergraduates of superior scholastic aptitude. *Journal of Educational Psychology, 53,* 132–143.

HOLLAND, J. L., & RICHARDS, J. M. (1965). Academic and nonacademic accomplishment: Correlated or uncorrelated? *Journal of Educational Psychology, 56,* 165–174.

HOLLANDER, L. (1978). Extemporaneous speech presented at the National Forum on the Arts and the Gifted, Aspen, CO, June 1978. In E. Larsh (Ed.), *Someone's Priority.* Denver, CO: Colorado State Department of Education. (ERIC Document Reproduction Service No. ED 181 663)

HOLLINGWORTH, L. (1926). *Gifted children: Their nature and nurture.* New York: Macmillan.

HOLLINGWORTH, L. (1942). *Children above 180 IQ.* New York: World Book.

HOLLINGWORTH, L., & COBB, M. V. (1928). Children clustering at 165 IQ and children clustering at 146 IQ compared for three years in achievement. In G. M. Whipple (Ed.), *Nature and nurture: Their influence upon achievement,* Yearbook of the National Society for the Study of Education, Part II (pp. 3–33). Bloomington, IL: Public School Publishing.

HORN, J. M., LOEHLIN, J. C., & WILLERMAN, L. (1979). Intellectual resemblance among adoptive and biological relatives: The Texas Adoption Project. *Behavior Genetics, 1,* 133–148.

HORNER, V. (1965). *Music education: The background of research and opinion.* Victoria, Australia: Australian Council for Educational Research.

HORODEZKY, B., & LABERCANE, G. (1983). *Educational and psychological measurement, 43*(2), 657–662.

HOWLEY, A. (1986). Gifted education and the spectre of elitism. *Journal of Education, 168*(1), 117–125.

HOWLEY, A., & HOWLEY, C. (1985). A personal record: Is acceleration worth the effort? *Roeper Review, 8*(1), 43–45.

HOWLEY, A., HOWLEY, C., & PENDARVIS, E. (1986). *Teaching gifted children: Principles and strategies.* Boston: Little, Brown.

HOWLEY, C. (1982). *Relationship between structural class background and intelligence.* Unpublished master's thesis, West Virginia College of Graduate Studies, Institute, WV.

HOWLEY, C. (1986). *Intellectually gifted students: Issues and policy implications.* Charleston, WV: Appalachia Educational Laboratory.

HOWLEY, C. (1987a). Anti-intellectualism in programs for able students (Beware of gifts): An application. *Social Epistemology, 1*(2), 175–181.

HOWLEY, C. (1987b). It's controversial, but "acceleration" could bring gifted kids up to full speed. *American School Board Journal, 174*(6), 32–33, 40.

HOYT, K., & HEBELER, J. (1974). *Career education for gifted and talented students.* Salt Lake City, UT: Olympus.

HUFF, V. E. (1978). Creativity and transactional analysis. *Journal of Creative Behavior, 12*(3), 202–208.

HUME, M. (1987, April 20). Statistical picture of special education shows commitment, but problems. *Education Daily,* pp. 1, 3–4.

HUNT, E. B. (1978). Mechanics of verbal ability. *Psychological Review, 85,* 109–130.

HUNT, J. McV. (1961). *Intelligence and experience.* New York: Ronald.

HUXLEY, A. (1962). *Island.* New York: Harper & Row.

JACKENDOFF, R., & LERDAHL, F. (1981). A grammatical parallel between music and language. In M. Clynes (Ed.), *Music, mind, and brain: The neuropsychology of music* (pp. 83–118). New York: Plenum Press.

JACKSON, P. (1981). Secondary schooling for the privileged few: A report on a visit to a New England boarding school. *Daedelus, 110*(4), 117–130.

JACOB, E. (1981). *Dancing.* Reading, MA: Addison-Wesley.

JACOBS, J. C. (1971). Effectiveness of teacher and parent identification of gifted children as a function of school level. *Psychology in the Schools, 8,* 140–142.

JANOS, P. J., FUNG, H. C., & ROBINSON, N. M. (1985). Self-concept, self-esteem, and peer relations among gifted children who feel "different." *Gifted Child Quarterly, 29*(2), 78–82.

JANOS, P. J., MARWOOD, K. A., & ROBINSON, N. M. (1985). Friendship patterns in highly intelligent children. *Roeper Review, 8*(1), 46–49.

JASTAK, J., & JASTAK, S. (1978). *Wide range achievement test.* Wilmington, DE: Jastak Associates.

JENCKS, C., SMITH, M., ACLAND, H. BANE, M. J., COHEN, D., GINTIS, H., HEYNS, B., & MICHELSON, S. (1972). *Inequality: A reassessment of the effect of family and schooling in America.* New York: Harper & Row.

JENCKS, C., BARTLETT, S., CORCORAN, M., CROUSE, J., EAGLESFIELD, D., JACKSON, G., McCLELLAND, K., MUESER, P., OLNECK, M., SCHWARZ, J., WARD, S., & WILLIAMS, J. (1979). *Who gets ahead? The determinants of economic success in America.* New York: Basic Books.

JENKINS, M. D. (1943). Case studies of Negro children of Binet IQ 160 and above. *Journal of Negro Education, 12,* 159–166.

JENKINS, M. D. (1950). Intellectually superior negro youth: Problems and needs. *Journal of Negro Education, 22*(2), 322–332.

JENKINS-FRIEDMAN, R. (1982). Myth: Cosmetic use of multiple selection criteria. *Gifted Child Quarterly, 26*(1), 24–26.

JENNINGS, H. H. (1943). *Leadership and isolation.* New York: Longmans, Green.

JENSEN, A. (1969). How much can we boost IQ and scholastic achievement? *Harvard Educational Review, 39,* 1–123.

JENSEN, A. (1973). *Educability and group differences.* New York: Harper & Row.

JENSEN, A. (1980). *Bias in mental testing.* New York: Free Press.

JENSEN, J. (1973). Do gifted children speak an intellectual dialect? *Exceptional Children, 39*(4), 337–338.

JOHNSON, D., & MYKLEBUST, H. (1967). *Learning disabilities.* New York: Grune & Stratton.

JOHNSON, P. (1965). Art for the young child. In W. R. Hastie (Ed.), *Art education* (pp. 51–85). The Sixty-fourth Yearbook of the National Society for the Study of Education, Part II. Chicago: University of Chicago.

JONES, L. (1971). *Black music.* New York: Morrow Press.

KALINOWSKY, A. G. (1985). The development of Olympic swimmers. In B. S. Bloom (Ed.), *Developing talent in young people* (pp. 139–192). New York: Ballantine Books.

KAMIN, L. (1981). Separated identical twins. In H. J. Eysenck & L. Kamin (Eds.), *The intelligence controversy* (pp. 106–113). New York: Wiley.

KAMPHAUS, R. W., & REYNOLDS, C. R. (1984). Development and structure of the Kaufman Assessment Battery for Children. *Journal of Special Education, 18*(3), 213–228.

KANOY, R. C., JOHNSON, B. W., & KANOY, K. W. (1980). Locus of control and self-concept in achieving and underachieving bright elementary students. *Psychology in the Schools, 17*(1), 395–399.

KARNES, F. A., & CHAUVIN, J. (1986). The leadership skills: Fostering the forgotten dimension of giftedness. *G/C/T, 9*(3), 22–23.

KARNES, M. B. (1978). *Nurturing academic talent in early childhood.* (ERIC Document Reproduction Service No. 161 528)

KATCHADOURIAN, H., & BOLI, J. (1985). *Careerism and intellectualism among college students.* San Francisco: Jossey-Bass.

KATZ, M. (1968). *The irony of early school reform.* Cambridge, MA: Harvard University Press.

KATZ, M. (1971). *Class, bureaucracy, and schools.* New York: Praeger.

KAUFFMAN, J. M. (1977). *Characteristics of children's behavior disorders.* Columbus, OH: Merrill.

KAUFFMAN, J. M. (1981). *Characteristics of children's behavior disorders* (2nd ed.). Columbus, OH: Merrill.

KAUFFMAN, J. M. (1985). *Characteristics of children's behavior disorders* (3rd ed.). Columbus, OH: Merrill.

KAUFMAN, A., & KAUFMAN, N. (1983). *Kaufman assessment battery for children: Sampler manual.* Circle Pines, MN: American Guidance Service.

KAVALE, K. A., & FORNESS, S. R. (1985). Learning disability and the history of science: Paradigm or paradox? *Remedial and Special Education, 6*(4), 12–24.

KEATING, D. P. (1974). The study of mathematically precocious youth. In J. C. Stanley, D. P. Keating, & L. H. Fox (Eds.), *Mathematical talent: Discovery, description, and development* (pp. 23–46). Baltimore, MD: Johns Hopkins University Press.

KEATING, D. P. (1975). Precocious cognitive development at the level of formal operations. *Child Development, 45,* 276–280.

KEATING, D. P. (1976a). Creative potential of mathematically precocious boys. In D. P. Keating (Ed.), *Intellectual talent: Research and development* (pp. 262–272). Baltimore, MD: Johns Hopkins University Press.

KEATING, D. P. (1976b). Discovering quantitative precocity. In D. P. Keating (Ed.), *Intellectual talent: Research and development* (pp. 23–31). Baltimore, MD: Johns Hopkins University Press.

KEATING, D. P. (1976c). A Piagetian approach to intellectual precocity. In D. P. Keating (Ed.), *Intellectual talent: Research and development* (pp. 90–102). Baltimore, MD: Johns Hopkins University Press.

KEATING, D. P. (1980a). Four faces of creativity: The continuing plight of the intellectual underserved. *Gifted Child Quarterly, 24*(2), 56–61.

KEATING, D. P. (1980b). Thinking processes in adolescence. In J. Adelson (Ed.), *Handbook of adolescent psychology* (pp. 211–247). New York: Wiley.

KEATING, D. P., & STANLEY, J. C. (1972). Extreme measures for the exceptionally gifted in math and science. *Educational Researcher, 1,* 3–7.

KELLY, M. P. (1985). Unique educational acceleration: The dilemma of John Stuart Mill and contemporary gifted youths. *Gifted Child Quarterly, 20*(1), 87–89.

KELLY, T. K., BULLOCK, L. M., & DYKES, M. K. (1977). Behavioral disorders: Teachers' perceptions. *Exceptional Children, 43*(5), 316–318.

KEPHART, J., KEPHART, C., & SCHWARTZ, G. (1974). A journey into the world of the blind child. *Exceptional Children, 40,* 421–429.

KERSH, M., & REISMAN, F. (1985). Mathematics for gifted students. In R. Swassing (Ed.), *Teaching gifted children and adolescents* (pp. 136–180). Columbus, OH: Merrill.

KHATENA, J. (1978). *The creatively gifted child: Suggestions for parents and teachers.* New York: Vantage Press.

KIMBALL, B. (1952). The sentence completion technique in a study of scholastic underachievement. *Journal of Consulting Psychology, 16,* 353–358.

KIMBALL, B. (1953). Case studies in educational failure during adolescence. *American Journal of Orthopsychiatry, 23,* 406–415.

KING, M. (1981). *Rural delinquency proneness: Its relationship to giftedness, environmental support, and environmental availability.* Unpublished master's thesis, University of Wisconsin, Platteville.

KIRK, B. (1952). Test versus academic performance in malfunctioning students. *Journal of Consulting Psychology, 16,* 213–216.

KIRK, S. A., & GALLAGHER, J. J. (1983). *Educating exceptional children* (2nd ed.). Boston: Houghton Mifflin.

KIRSTEIN, L. (1983). Classic ballet: Aria of the aerial. In R. Copeland & M. Cohen (Eds.), *What is dance? Readings in theory and criticism* (pp. 238–243). Oxford: Oxford University Press.

KITANO, M., & KIRBY, D. (1986). *Gifted education: A comprehensive view.* Boston: Little, Brown.

KLAUSMEIER, H. J., & LOUGHLIN, L. T. (1961). Behavior during problem solving among children of low, average, and high intelligence. *Journal of Educational Psychology, 52,* 148–152.

KLEIN, R. D. (1982). An inquiry into the factors related to creativity. *Elementary School Journal, 82*(3), 256–265.

KLEINSASSER, A. M. (1986, October). Explorations of an ambiguous culture: Conflicts facing gifted females in rural environments. Paper presented at the annual conference of the National Rural and Small Schools Consortium, Bellingham, WA. (ERIC Document Reproduction Service No. ED 278 522).

KOCH, K. (1970). *Wishes, lies, and dreams.* New York: Vintage Books.

KOCH, K. (1973). *Rose, where did you get that red?* New York: Vintage Books.

KOESTLER, A. (1964). *The act of creation.* New York: Macmillan.

KOHL, H. (1967). *Thirty-six children.* New York: Signet Books.

KOHN, M. L. (1977). *Class and conformity: A study in values* (2nd Ed.). Chicago: University of Chicago Press.

KORTEN, D. C. (1972). Situational determinants of leadership structure. In G. D. Paige (Ed.), *Political leadership: Readings for an emerging field* (pp. 146–164). New York: Free Press.

KORZENIK, D. (1981). Is children's work art? Some historical views. *Art Education, 34*(5), 20–24.

KRAUS, R. (1969). *History of dance in art and education.* Englewood Cliff, NJ: Prentice-Hall.

KRUTETSKII, V. (1976). *The psychology of mathematical abilities in schoolchildren.* I. Wirszup & J. Kilpatrick, (Eds.). J. Teller (Trans.). Chicago: University of Chicago Press. (Original work published 1968)

KUBISZYN, T., & BORICH, G. (1984). *Educational testing and measurement: Classroom application and practice.* Glenview, IL: Scott, Foresman.

KULIK, J., & KULIK, C. (1984). Effects of accelerated instruction on students. *Review of Educational Research, 54*(3), 409–425.

KURTZMAN, K. A. (1967). A study of school attitudes, peer acceptance, and personality of creative adolescents. *Exceptional Children, 34,* 157–162.

KUVLESKY, W. P. (1973). Rural youth: Current status and prognosis. In D. Gottlieb (Ed.), *Youth in contemporary sociey* (pp. 321–345). Beverly Hills, CA: Sage.

KWALWASSER, J. (1955). *Exploring the musical mind.* New York: Coleman-Ross.

LABERGE, D., & SAMUELS, J. (1974). Toward a theory of automatic information processing in reading. *Cognitive Psychology, 6,* 293–323.

LABOV, W. (1972). The logic of nonstandard English. In P. P. Giglioi (Ed.), *Language and social context* (pp. 179–216). New York: Penguin Books.

LACHAPELLE, J. R. (1983). Creativity research: Its sociological and educational limitations. *Studies in Art Education, 24*(2), 131–139.

LANE, Y. (1960). *The psychology of the actor.* New York: John Day.

LANGWAY, L. (1983, March 28). Bringing up superbaby. *Newsweek,* pp. 62–68.

LAWLER, L. B. (1964). *The dance in ancient Greece.* Middletown, CT: Wesleyan University Press.

LAYCOCK, F. (1979). *Gifted children.* Glenview, IL: Scott, Foresman.

LEACOCK, E. (1969). *Teaching and learning in city schools.* New York: Basic Books.

LEE, E. S. (1951). Negro intelligence and selective migration: A Philadelphia test of the Klineberg hypothesis. *American Sociological Review, 16,* 227–233.

LEHMAN, E., & ERDWINS, C. (1981). The social and emotional adjustment of young, intellectually gifted children. *Gifted Child Quarterly, 25*(3), 134–137.

LEHMAN, N. (1986). The origins of the underclass. *The Atlantic, 257*(6), 31–43, 47–55.

LEITER, J., & BROWN, J. S. (1985). Determinants of elementary school grading. *Sociology of Education, 58,* 166–180.

LEONTIEF, W. (1982). The distribution of work and income. *Scientific American, 247* (3), 188–204.

LESGOLD, A. M., & PERFETTI, C. A. (1978). Interactive processes in reading comprehension. *Discourse Processes, 1,* 323–336.

LESSER, G., DAVIS, F. B., & NAHEMOW, L. (1962). The identification of gifted elementary school children with exceptional scientific talent. *Educational and Psychological Measurement, 22*(2), 349–364.

LESSER, G. S., FIFER, G., & CLARK, D. H. (1965). Mental abilities of children from different social-class and cultural groups. *Monographs of the Society for Research in Child Development, 30*(4).

LEWIS, C. L., & KANES, L. G. (1980). Gifted IEPs: Impact of expectations and perspectives. In D. M. Jackson (Ed.), *Readings in curriculum development for the gifted* (pp. 70–76). Guilford, CT: Special Learning Corporation.

LEWIS, R. B., & DOORLAG, D. H. (1983). *Teaching special students in the mainstream.* Columbus, OH: Merrill.

LEWONTIN, R., ROSE, S., & KAMIN, L. (1984). *Not in our genes.* New York: Pantheon Books.

LINES, P. (1986). *Home instruction: An overview.* Charleston, WV: Appalachia Educational Laboratory.

LIPSET, S., & DOBSON, R. (1972). The intellectual as critic and rebel: With special reference to the United States and the Soviet Union. *Daedalus, 101,* 137–198.

LITZINGER, W., & SCHAEFER, T. (1984). Leadership through followership. In W. E. Rosenbach & R. L. Taylor (Eds.), *Contemporary issues in leadership* (pp. 138–143) Boulder, CO: Westview Press.

LOBAN, W. (1967). *The language of elementary school children.* Champaign, IL: National Council of Teachers of English.

LOMBROSO, C. (1891). *The man of genius.* London: Walter Scott.

LOPATE, P. (1978). Children, productivity, and creativity: The artist in the schools. *Social Policy, 9*(2), 42–47.

LOWENFELD, V., & BRITTAIN, W. L. (1970). *Creative and mental growth* (5th ed.). New York: Macmillan.

LUCITO, L. (1964). Independence-conformity behavior as a function of intellect: Bright and dull children. *Exceptional Children, 31*(1), 5–13.

LYON, H. C. (1971). *Learning to feel: Feeling to learn.* Columbus, OH: Merrill.

MACCOBY, E. E., & JACKLIN, C. N. (1974). *The psychology of sex difference.* Stanford, CA: Stanford University Press.

MACINTOSH, D. K., & DUNN, L. M. (1973). Children with major specific learning disabilities. In L. M. Dunn (Ed.), *Exceptional children in the schools: Special education in transition* (2nd ed.). New York: Holt, Rinehart & Winston.

MACKINNON, D. W. (1975). IPAR's contribution to the conceptualization and study of creativity. In I. A. Taylor & J. W. Getzels (Eds.), *Perspectives in creativity* (pp. 60–89). Chicago: Aldine.

MACKINNON, D. W. (1978). *In search of human effectiveness: Identifying and developing creativity.* Buffalo, NY: Creative Education Foundation.

MACKINNON, D. W. (1962/1981). The nature and nurture of creative talent. In W. B. Barbe & J. S. Renzulli (Eds.), *Psychology and education of the gifted* (3rd ed., pp. 111–127). New York: Irvington. (Original article published 1962)

MACLEISH, R. (1984). Gifted by nature, prodigies are still mysteries to man. *Smithsonian, 14*(12), 70–79.

MADDI, S. R. (1975). The strenuousness of the creative life. In I. A. Taylor & J. W. Getzels (Eds.), *Perspectives in creativity* (pp. 173–190). Chicago: Aldine.

MADDUX, C. D., SCHEIBER, L. M., & BASS, J. E. (1982). Self concept and social distance in gifted children. *Gifted Child Quarterly, 26*(2), 77–81.

MAINES, D. (1985). Preliminary notes on a theory of informal barriers for women in mathematics. *Educational Studies in Mathematics, 16*(3), 314–317.

MAKER, C. J. (1982). *Teaching-learning models for gifted education.* Rockville, MD: Aspen Systems.

MAKER, C. J., REDDEN, M. R., TONELSON, S., & HOWELL, R. M. (1978). *The self-perceptions of successful handicapped scientists.* Albuquerque, NM: University of New Mexico, Department of Special Education.

MANN, D. (1986). Thinking about the undoable: Dropout programs. In P. Penn (Ed.), *Children at risk: An Urban Education Network conference proceedings* (pp. 1–11). Charleston, WV: Appalachia Educational Laboratory.

MARCUSE, H. (1978). *The aesthetic dimension.* Boston: Beacon Press.

MARJORIBANKS, K. (1972). Achievement orientation of Canadian ethnic groups. *Alberta Journal of Educational Research, 18*(3), 162–173.

MARJORIBANKS, K. (1976). Academic achievement, intelligence, and creativity: A regression surface analysis. *Multivariate Behavioral Research, 11*(1), 105–118.

MARK, M. (1978). *Contemporary music education.* New York: Schirmer Books.

MARLAND, S. (1972). *Education of the gifted and talented: Report to the Congress of the United States by the U.S. Commisioner of Education.* Washington, DC: U.S. Government Printing Office.

MARLAND, S. (1974). *Career education: A proposal for reform.* New York: McGraw-Hill.

MARSHALL, B. (1985). Career decision-making patterns of gifted and talented adolescents: Implications for career education. *Journal of Career Education, 7*(4), 305–310.

MARTINSON, R. (1968). *Curriculum enrichment for the gifted in the primary grades.* Englewood Cliffs, NJ: Prentice-Hall.

MARTINSON, R. (1972). Background papers. In S. Marland's *Education of the gifted and talented* (Vol. 2) Washington, DC: U.S. Department of Health, Education, and Welfare.

MARZANO, R., & HUTCHINS, C. (1985). Thinking skills: A conceptual framework. A special issue of *Noteworthy.* Aurora, CO: Midcontinent Regional Laboratory.

MASLOW, A. H. (1954). *Motivation and personality.* New York: Harper & Row.

MATHER, N., & UDALL, A. J. (1985). The identification of gifted underachievers using the Woodcock-Johnson Psycho-Educational Battery. *Roeper Review, 8*(1), 54–56.

MAY, F. (1982). *Reading as communication.* Columbus, OH: Merrill.

McASKIE, M., & CLARKE, A. (1976). Parent-offspring resemblance in intelligence. *British Journal of Psychology, 67,* 243–273.

McCALL, M. W., JR. (1984). Conjecturing about creative leaders. In W. E. Rosenbach & R. L. Taylor (Eds.), *Contemporary issues in leadership* (pp. 271–280). Boulder, CO: Westview Press.

McCLELLAND, D., ATKINSON, J., CLARK, R., & LOWELL, E. (1953). *The achievement motive.* New York: Appleton-Century-Crofts.

McConnell, F. (1973). Children with hearing disabilities. In L. M. Dunn (Ed.), *Exceptional children in the schools: Special education in transition* (2nd ed., pp. 351–412). New York: Holt, Rinehart, & Winston.

McCracken, R. A. (1960). Accelerating the reading speed of sixth grade children. *Exceptional Children, 27*, 27–28.

McKayle, D. (1966). The art of theatre. In S. J. Cohen (Ed.), *The modern dance: Seven statements of belief* (pp. 53–61). Middletown, CT: Wesleyan University Press.

McKinney, J. D., & Forman, S. G. (1977). Factor structure of the Wallach-Kogan tests of creativity and measures of intelligence and achievement. *Psychology in the Schools, 14*(1), 41–44.

McNemar, Q. (1964). Lost: Our intelligence. Why? *American Psychologist, 19*, 871–882.

Mednick, S. A. (1962). The associative basis of the creative process. *Psychological Review, 69*, 220–232.

Mednick, S. A., (1962). The associative basis of the creative process. *Psychological Review, 69*, 220–232.

Meier, N. C. (1939/1966). Factors in artistic aptitude: Final summary of a ten-year study of special ability. In E. W. Eisner & D. W. Ecker (Eds.), *Readings in art education* (pp. 105–116). Waltham, MA: Blaisdell.

Mercer, J. (1981). The system of multicultural pluralistic assessment: SOMPA. In *Balancing the scale for the disadvantaged gifted: Presentations from the Fourth Biennial National Conference on Disadvantaged Gifted/Talented* (pp. 29–57). Ventura, CA: Ventura County Superintendent of Schools.

Messe, L., Crano, W., Messe, S., & Rice, W. (1979). Evaluation of the predictive validity of tests of mental ability for classroom performance in elementary grades. *Journal of Educational Psychology, 71*(2), 233–241.

Mestre, J., & Gerace, W. (1986). *A study of the algebra acquisition of Hispanic and anglo ninth graders: Research findings relevant to teacher training and classroom practice.* Unpublished manuscript, University of Massachusetts: Amherst.

Metcalfe, R. J. (1978). Divergent thinking "threshold effect"–IQ, age, or skill? *Journal of Experimental Education, 47*(1), 4–8.

Meyer, J. (1977). The effects of education as an institution. *American Journal of Sociology, 83*(1), 55–71.

Michael, W. B. (1983). Manifestions of creative behaviors by maturing participants in the Study of Mathematically Precocious Youth. In C. P. Benbow & J. C. Stanley (Eds.), *Academic precocity: Aspects of its development* (pp. 38–50). Baltimore, MD: Johns Hopkins University Press.

Miles, D. L. (1986). Why do more boys than girls receive special education? *Contemporary Education, 57*(2), 104–106.

Miller, C., & Heeren, V. (1986). *Mathematical ideas* (5th ed.). Glenview, IL: Scott, Foresman.

Miller, R. V. (1956). Social status and socioempathic differences among mentally superior, mentally typical, and mentally retarded children. *Exceptional Children, 22*, 114–119.

Miller, S. D. (1979). Wolfgang Amadeus who? The neglect of music literature. *Music Educators Journal, 65*(8), 50–53.

Mills, C. W. (1959) *The power elite.* New York: Oxford University Press.

Milne, A., Myers, D., Rosenthal, A., & Ginsburg, A. (1986). Single parents, working mothers, and the educational achievement of school children. *Sociology of Education, 59* (July), 125–139.

Mitchell, J. V. (1959). Goal-setting behavior as a function of self-acceptance, over- and underachievement and related personality variables. *Journal of Educational Psychology, 50*(3), 93–104.

Mitchell, P. B. (1981). *An advocate's guide to building support for gifted and talented education.* Washington, DC: National Association of State Boards of Education.

Mitchell, R. (1979). *Less than words can say.* Boston: Little, Brown.

Mitchell, S. (1976, April). *Parental perceptions of their experiences with due process in special education: A preliminary report.* Paper presented at the annual meeting of the American Educational Research Association. San Francisco, CA. (ERIC Document Reproduction Service No. ED 130 482)

Mjoen, J. (1926). Genius as a biological problem. *Eugenics Review, 17*, 242–257.

MONSAAS, J. A. (1985). Becoming a world-class tennis player. In B. S. Bloom (Ed.), *Developing talent in young people* (pp. 211–269). New York: Ballantine Books.

MOORE, C., NELSON-PIERCY, C., ABEL, M., & FRYE, D. (1984). Precocious conservation in context: The solution of quantity tasks by nonquantitative strategies. *Journal of Experimental Child Psychology, 38,* 1–6.

More women in education but men earn more, report says. (1987, August). *The Huntington Herald Dispatch,* p. D5.

MORGENSTERN, S. (Ed.). (1956). *Composers on music: An anthology of composers' writings from Palestrina to Copland.* New York: Pantheon Books.

MORSE, W. C., CUTLER R. L., & FINK, A. H. (1964). *Public school classes for the emotionally handicapped: A research analysis.* Washington, DC: Council for Exceptional Children.

MOSTELLER, F., & MOYNIHAN, D. (Eds.). (1972). *On equality of educational opportunity.* New York: Random House.

MUNSINGER, H. (1975). The adopted child's IQ: A critical review. *Psychological Bulletin, 82,* 623–659.

MURPHY, J. (1980). Conflict, consensus, and communication: An interpretive report on the Ann Arbor Symposium on the applications of psychology to the teaching and learning of music. *Music Educators Journal, 66*(7), S1-S32.

MURSELL, J. (1958). Growth processes in music education. In N. Henry (Ed.), *Basic concepts in music education* (pp. 140–162). The Fifty-Seventh Yearbook of the National Society for the Study of Education, Part I. Chicago: University of Chicago Press.

MYERS, J. T. (1982). Hemisphericity research: An overview with some implications for problem solving. *Journal of Creative Behavior, 16*(3), 197–211.

MYKLEBUST, H. R., & BOSHES, B. (1960). Psychoneurological learning disorders in children. *Archives of Pediatrics, 77,* 247–256.

NACHTIGAL, P. (1982). *Rural education: In search of a better way.* Boulder, CO: Westview Press.

NATIONAL COMMISSION ON EXCELLENCE IN EDUCATION. (1983). *A nation at risk: The imperative for educational reform.* Washington, DC: U. S. Department of Education.

NATIONAL RURAL DEVELOPMENT INSTITUTE. (1986). *Toward a definition of rural and small schools.* Bellingham, WA: National Rural Development Institute.

NELSON, C. M. (1985). Behavior disorders. In W. H. Berdine & A. E. Blackhurst, (Eds.), *An introduction to special education* (2nd ed., pp. 427–468). Boston: Little, Brown.

NEWELL, A., & SIMON, H. (1972). *Human problem solving.* Englewood Cliffs, NJ: Prentice-Hall.

NORTON, D. (1980). Interrelationships among music aptitude, IQ, and auditory conservation. *Journal of Research in Music Education, 28*(4), 207–217.

NYE, R., & NYE, V. (1970). *Music in the elementary school* (3rd. ed.). Englewood Cliffs, NJ: Prentice-Hall.

OAKES, J. (1985). *Keeping track: How schools structure inequality.* New Haven, CT: Yale University Press.

ODEN, M. (1968). *The fulfillment of promise: Forty-year follow up of the Terman gifted group.* Stanford, CA: Stanford University Press.

ODIN, A. (1895). *Genese des grands hommes: Gens de lettres francais modernes.* Paris.

OLLER, J., & KYLE, P. (Eds.). (1978). *Language in education: Testing the tests.* Rowley, MA: Newburg.

OLSON, M. B. (1984). What do you mean by spatial? *Roeper Review, 6,* 240–244.

ORFF, K. (1955). *Music for children.* Translated and adapted by A. Walter & D. Hall. New York: Associated Music Publishers.

ORTON, S. T. (1937). *Reading, writing and speech problems in children.* New York: Norton.

OSBORN, A. F. (1953). *Applied imagination.* New York: Scribner's.

OSBORN, A. F. (1963). *Applied imagination* (3rd. ed.). New York: Scribner's.

OSBURN, W. J., & ROHAN, B. J. (1931). *Enriching the curriculum for gifted children: A book of guidance for educational administrators and classroom teachers.* New York: Macmillan.

OWEN, F. (1978). Dyslexia—Genetic aspects. In A. Benton & D. Pearl (Eds.), *Dyslexia: An appraisal of current knowledge* (pp. 266–284). New York: Oxford University Press.

Oxford English Dictionary (compact ed., Vols. 1–2). (1971). New York: Oxford University Press.

PAFFENBARGER, R. S., & ASNES, D. P. (1966). Chronic disease in former college students. *American Journal of Public Health, 56,* 1026–1936.

PAGE, E. B. (1976). A historical step beyond Terman. In D. P. Keating (Ed.), *Intellectual talent:*

Research and development (pp. 295–315). Baltimore, MD: Johns Hopkins University Press.

PAIVIO, M. (1971). *Imagery and verbal processes.* New York: Holt, Rinehart & Winston.

PARNES, S. (1975). CPSI—A program for balanced growth. *Journal of Creative Behavior, 9*(3), 23–29.

PARNES, S. (1981). CPSI: The general system. In W. Barbe & J. Renzulli (Eds.), *Psychology and education of the gifted* (3rd ed., pp. 304–314). New York: Irvington.

PARTRIDGE, E. (1934). Leadership among adolescent boys. *Teachers College contributions to Education* (No. 608). New York: Teachers College Press.

PASSOW, A., GOLDBERG, M., & TANNENBAUM, A. (1967). *Education of the disadvantaged.* New York: Holt, Rinehart & Winston.

PASTORE, N. (1949). *The nature-nurture controversy.* New York: Columbia University, Kings Crown Press.

PEARLMAN, C. (1983). A theoretical model for creativity. *Education, 103*(3), 294–305.

PEGNATO, C. W., & BIRCH, J. W. (1959). Locating gifted children in junior high school. *Exceptional Children, 25*(7), 300–304.

PENDARVIS, E. (1983). *The written language of gifted children.* Unpublished doctoral dissertation, University of Kentucky, Frankfort, KY.

PERKINS, D. N. (1981). *The mind's best work.* Cambridge, MA: Harvard University Press.

PERRY, L. (1984). *Intellectual life in America.* New York: Franklin Watts.

PETZOLD, R. G. (1978). Identification of musically talented students. In E. Larsh (Ed.), *Someone's priority* (pp. 58–64). Denver, CO: Colorado State Department of Education. (ERIC Document Reproduction Service No. ED 181 663)

PFEIFFER, S. (1980). The school-based interprofessional team: Recurring problems and some possible solutions. *Journal of School Psychology, 18*(4), 388–394.

PHIPPS, P. M. (1982). The LD learner is often a boy—Why? *Academic Therapy, 17*(4), 425–430.

PHOTIADAS, J. (1983). *Community and family change in rural Appalachia.* Charleston, WV: Appalachia Educational Laboratory.

PIMSLEUR, P., MOSBERG, L., & MORRISON, A. V. (1962). Student factors in foreign language learning: A review of the literature. *Modern Language Journal, 46,* 160–170.

PIROZZO, R. (1982). Gifted underachievers. *Roeper Review, 4*(4), 18–21.

PLOWMAN, P. (n.d.). What can be done for rural gifted and talented children and youth? In *Ideas for urban/rural gifted/talented* (pp. 71–87). Ventura, CA: National/State Leadership Training Institute on the Gifted and the Talented and the Office of the Ventura County Superintendent of Schools.

POULANTZAS, N. (1974). *Classes in contemporary capitalism.* London: Verso.

PRESSEY, S. (1955). Concerning the nature and nurture of genius. *Scientific Monthly, 81,* 123–129.

PRESSEY, S. (1967). Fordling accelerates: Ten years after. *Journal of Counseling Psychology, 14*(1), 73–80.

PRICHARD, A., & TAYLOR, J. (1980). *Accelerating learning: The use of suggestion in the classroom.* Novato, CA: Academic Therapy.

PRINGLE, M. K. (1970). *Able misfits.* London: Longman.

PYRYT, M. (1979). Inner-city students' perceptions of the gifted. *Journal for the Education of the Gifted, 2*(2), 99–105.

RAPH, J. B., GOLDBERG, M. L., & PASSOW, A. H. (1966). *Bright underachievers.* New York: Teachers College Press.

RASKIN, M. (1972). The channeling colony. In M. Carnoy (Ed.), *Schooling in a corporate society* (pp. 23–35). New York: David McKay.

READ, H. (1959). *A concise history of modern painting.* London: Thames & Hudson.

READ, H. (1960). The third realm of education. In *The creative arts in American education: The Inglis and Burton lectures.* Cambridge, MA: Harvard University Press.

REID, D. K., HRESKO, W. P., & HAMMILL, D. (1983). *Test of early reading ability.* Los Angeles: Western Psychological Services.

REKDAL, C. K. (1979). Genius creativity and eminence. *Gifted Child Quarterly, 23*(4), 837–854.

RENZULLI, J. S. (1977). *The enrichment triad model: A guide for developing defensible programs for the gifted and talented.* Wethersfield, CT: Creative Learning Press.

RENZULLI, J. S. (1978). What makes giftedness? *Phi Delta Kappan, 60*(3), 180–184, 261.

RENZULLI, J. S., & HARTMAN, R. K. (1971). Scale for rating the behavioral characteristics of superior students. *Exceptional Children, 38,* 243–248.

RENZULLI, J. S., SMITH, L. H., WHITE, A. J., CALLAHAN, C. M., & HARTMAN, R. K. (1977). *Scales for rating the behavioral characteristics of superior students.* Mansfield Center, CT: Creative Learning Press.

RESNICK, L., & FORD, W. (1981). *The psychology of mathematics for instruction.* Hillsdale, NJ: Lawrence Erlbaum Associates.

RESTAK, R. M. (1979). *The brain: The last frontier.* New York: Warner Books.

REYNOLDS, C. R. (1985). Critical measurement issues in learning disabilities. *Journal of Special Education, 18*(4), 451–476.

REYNOLDS, C. R., & RICHMOND, B. O. (1985). *The revised children's manifest anxiety scale.* Los Angeles: Western Psychological Services.

RIDDEL, F. S. (1971). *Related aspects of the social and economic problems, cultural tradition, and educational system of rural Appalachia: An analysis based on the concept of scale.* Unpublished doctoral disseration, Ohio State University, Columbus, OH.

RIMM, S., & DAVIS, G. (1980). Five years of international research with GIFT: An instrument for the identification of creativity. *Journal of Creative Behavior, 14*(1), 20–24.

THE RIPON SOCIETY. (1969). *The lessons of victory.* New York: Dial Press.

RIST, R. (1970). Student social class and teacher expectations: The self-fulfilling prophecy in ghetto education. *Harvard Educational Review, 40,* 411–451.

RITVO, E. R. (1977). Biochemical studies of children with the syndromes of autism, childhood schizophrenia, and related developmental disabilities: A review. *Journal of Child Psychology and Psychiatry, 18,* 373–379.

ROBINSON, N., & JANOS, P. (1986). Psychological adjustment in a college-level program of marked academic acceleration. *Journal of Youth and Adolescence, 15*(1), 51–60.

ROE, A. (1943/1975). Painters and painting. In I. A. Taylor & J. W. Getzels (Eds.), *Perspectives in creativity* (pp. 157–172). Chicago: Aldine.

ROE, A. (1952). A psychologist examines 64 eminent scientists. *Scientific American, 187*(5), 21–25.

ROE, A. (1953). *The making of a scientist.* New York: Dodd, Mead.

ROE, A. (1956). *The psychology of occupations.* New York: Wiley.

ROEDELL, W. C. (1978, August). *Social development in intellectually advanced children.* Paper presented at the Annual Convention of the American Psychological Association, Toronto. Canada.

ROEDELL, W. C., JACKSON, N. E., & ROBINSON, H. B. (1980). *Gifted young children.* New York: Teachers College Press.

ROEPER, A. (1966). Finding the clue to children's thought processes. *Young Children, 21,* 335–348.

ROEPER, A. (1978). Some thoughts about Piaget and the young gifted child. *Gifted Child Quarterly, 22,* 252–257.

ROGERS, C. (1959). Toward a theory of creativity. In H. Anderson (Ed.), *Creativity and its cultivation* (pp. 69–82). New York: Harper & Row.

ROSE, L. H., & LIN, HS-T. (1984). A meta-analysis of long-term creativity training programs. *Journal of Creative Behavior, 18*(1), 11–22.

ROSE, R. (1979). A program model for altering children's consciousness. *Gifted Child Quarterly, 23*(1), 109–117.

ROSE, S. J. (1986). *The American profile poster: Who owns what, who makes how much, who works where, and who lives with whom.* New York: Pantheon Books.

ROSENBAUM, J. (1975). The stratification of the socialization process. *American Sociological Review, 40,* 48–54.

ROSENWALD, P. J. (1984). Breaking away '80's style. *Dancemagazine, 58*(4), 70–74.

ROTH, R. M., & PURI, P. (1967). Direction of aggression and the underachievement syndrome. *Journal of Counseling Psychology, 14*(3), 277–281.

RUBOVITS, P., & MAEHR, R. (1973). Pygmalion black and white. *Journal of Personality and Social Psychology, 25*(2), 210–218.

RUMBERGER, R. (1984). The job market for college graduates, 1960–1990. *Journal of Higher Education, 55*(4), 433–454.

RYAN, W. (1976). *Blaming the victim.* New York: Vintage Books.

RYSER, C. P. (1964). The student dancer. In R. N. Wilson (Ed.), *The arts in society* (pp. 97–121). Englewood Cliffs, NJ: Prentice-Hall.

SALOME, R. A. (1974). Identifying and instructing the gifted in art. *Art Education, 27*(3), 16–19.

SALVIA, J., & YSSELDYKE, J. E. (1987). *Assessment in special and remedial education* (3rd ed.). Boston: Houghton Mifflin.

SALZER, R. T. (1984). Early reading and giftedness. *Gifted Child Quarterly, 28*(2), 95–96.

SAMUDA, R. J. (1975). *Psychological testing of American minorities: Issues and consequences.* New York: Dodd, Mead.

SATTLER, J. M. (1982). *Assessment of children's intelligence and special abilities* (2nd ed.). Boston: Allyn & Bacon.

SAUNDERS, R. J. (1982). Screening and identifying the talented in art. *Roeper Review, 4*(3), 7–10.

SAWYER, R. N. (1988). In defense of academic rigor. *Journal for the Education of the Gifted, 11*(2), 5–19.

SCARR, S. (1981). *Race, social class, and individual differences in IQ.* Hillsdale, NJ: Lawrence Erlbaum Associates.

SCARR, S., & WEINBERG, R. (1976). IQ test performance of black children adopted by white families. *American Psychologist, 31,* 726–739.

SCHLOSSER, L., & ALGOZZINE, B. (1980). Sex, behavior, and teacher expectancies. *Journal of Experimental Education, 48,* 231–236.

SCHOLWINSKI, E., & REYNOLDS, C. R. (1985). Dimensions of anxiety among high IQ children. *Gifted Child Quarterly, 29*(3), 125–130.

SCHONBERG, H. C. (1970). *The lives of the great composers.* New York: Norton.

SCHUBERT, D. (1973). Intelligence as necessary but not sufficient for creativity. *Journal of Genetic Psychology, 122*(1), 45–47.

SCHULTZ, R. E. (1958). Comparison of Negro pupils ranking high with those ranking low in educational achievement. *Journal of Educational Sociology, 31,* 265–270.

SCOTT, B. (1986). The decline of literacy and liberal learning. *Journal of Education, 168*(1), 105–116.

SCOTT, E., & BRYANT, B. (1978). Social interactions of early-reading and non-reading kindergarten students with high intellectual abililty. *Catalog of Selected Documents in Psychology, 8,* 95.

SCRIPTURE, E. W. (1891). Arithmetical prodigies. *American Journal of Psychology, 4,* 1–59.

SEAGOE, M. V. (1975). *Terman and the gifted.* Los Altos, CA: Kaufmann.

SEARS, P., & BARBEE, A. (1977). Career and life satisfactions among Terman's gifted women. In J. Stanley, W. George, & C. Solano (Eds.), *The gifted and the creative: A fifty-year perspective* (pp. 28–65). Baltimore, MD: Johns Hopkins University Press.

SEASHORE, C. (1967). *Psychology of music.* New York: Dover. (Original work published 1938)

SEELEY, K. R. (1984). Perspectives on adolescent giftedness and delinquency. *Journal for the Education of the Gifted, 8*(1), 59–72.

SEGAL, S., BUSSE, T., & MANSFIELD, R. (1980). The relationship of scientific creativity in the biological sciences to predoctoral accomplishments and experiences. *American Educational Research Journal, 17*(4), 491–501.

SELLS, L. W. (1976, February). *The mathematics filter and the education of women and minorities.* Paper presented at the Annual Meeting of the American Association for the Advancement of Science, Boston, MA. (ERIC Document Reproduction Service No. ED 121 663)

SENF, G. M. (1983). The nature and identification of learning disabilities and their relationship to the gifted child. In L. H. Fox, L. Brody, & D. Tobin (Eds.), *Learning disabled/gifted children.* Baltimore, MD: University Park Press.

SESSIONS, R. (1965). *The musical experience of composer, performer, and listener.* New York: Atheneum. (Original work published 1950)

SESSIONS, R. (1979). *Roger Sessions on music: Collected essays.* Princeton, NJ: Princeton University Press.

SEXTON, P. (1969). *The feminized male: Classrooms, white collars, and the decline of manliness.* New York: Random House.

SHADE, B. J. (1978). Social-psychological characteristics of achieving black children. *Negro Educational Review, 29*(2), 80–86.

SHADE, B. J. (1981). Personal traits of educationally successful black children. *Negro Educational Review, 32*(2), 6–11.

SHANTZ, C. (1975). The development of social cognition. In E. M. Hetherington (Ed.), *Review of child development research* (Vol. 5). Chicago: University of Chicago Press.

SHAW, M. C., & GRUBB, J. (1958). Hostility and able high school achievers. *Journal of Counseling Psychology, 5*(4), 263–266.

SHAW, M. C., & McCUEN, J. T. (1960). The onset of academic underachievement in bright children. *Journal of Educational Psychology, 53*(3), 103–108.

SHER, J. (Ed.). (1977). *Education in rural American: A reassessment of the conventional wisdom.* Boulder, CO: Westview Press.

SHERWOOD, J., & NATAUPSKY, M. (1968). Predicting the conclusions of Negro-white intelligence research from biographical characteristics of the investigator. *Journal of Personality and Social Psychology, 8*(1), Part 1, 53–58.

SHETLER, D. (1985). Prenatal music experiences. *Music Educators Journal, 71*(7), 26–27.

SHIELDS, J. (1978). MZ twins: Their use and abuse. In W. Nance (Ed.), *Twin research psychology and methodology.* New York: Liss.

SHIELS, M., WEATHERS, D., HOWARD, L., & GIVENS, R. (1983, January 17). A portrait of America. *Newsweek,* pp. 20–33.

SHILS, E. (1972). *The intellectuals and the powers and other essays.* Chicago: University of Chicago Press.

SHNEIDMAN, E. (1981). Suicide among the gifted. *Suicide and Life-Threatening Behavior, 11*(4), 254–282.

SHUTER, R. (1964). *An investigation of hereditary and environmental factors in musical ability.* Unpublished doctoral dissertation, University of London.

SHUTER, R. (1968). *The psychology of musical ability.* London: Methuen.

SILVER, L. A. (1971). A proposed view on the etiology of the neurological learning disability syndrome. *Journal of Learning Disabilities, 4,* 123–132.

SILVER, R., & DeYOUNG, A. (1986). The ideology of rural/Appalachian education, 1895–1935: The Appalachian education problem as part of the Appalachian life problem. *Educational Theory, 36*(1), 51–65.

SILVERMAN, R., & LANIER, V. (1965). Art for the adolescent. In W. R. Hastie (Ed.), *Art education* (pp. 115–152). The Sixty-fourth Yearbook of the National Society for the Study of Education. Chicago: University of Chicago Press.

SIMON, A., & WARD, L. O. (1973). The performance of high and low ability groups on two measures of creativity. *Journal of Experimental Education, 42*(1), 70–73.

SIMONTON, D. K. (1984). *Genius, creativity, and leadership.* Cambridge, MA: Harvard University Press.

SIPOLA, E., & HAYDEN, S. (1965). Exploring eidetic imagery among the retarded. *Perceptual and Motor Skills, 21,* 275–286.

SISK, D. A., & BIERLY, K. (1979). Every child in a gifted program? *Instructor, 88*(9), 84–86, 90, 92.

SIZER, T. (1984). *Horace's compromise.* Boston: Houghton Mifflin.

SKODAK, M., & SKEELS, H. (1949). A final follow-up study of one hundred adopted children. *Journal of Genetic Psychology, 75,* 85–125.

SLAVIN, R. (1986). Learning together. *American Educator: The Professional Journal of the American Federation of Teachers, 10*(2), 6–11.

SMITH, C. R. (1983). *Learning disabilities: The interaction of learner, task, and setting.* Boston: Little, Brown.

SMITH, S. B. (1983). *The great mental calculators.* New York: Columbia University Press.

SMOLAK, L. (1982). Cognitive precursors of receptive vs. expressive language. *Journal of Child Language, 9,* 13–22.

SNUGG, D. (1938). The relation between the intelligence of mothers and of their children living in foster homes. *Journal of Genetic Psychology, 52,* 401–406.

SOLANO, C. H. (1977). Teacher and pupil stereotypes of gifted boys and girls. *Talents and Gifts, 19,* 4–8.

SORREL, W. (1967). *The dance through the ages.* New York: Grosset & Dunlap.

SOSNIAK, L. (1985). Learning to be a concert pianist. In B. S. Bloom (Ed.), *Developing talent in young people* (pp. 19–67). New York: Ballantine.

SPEARMAN, C. (1927). *The abilities of man.* New York: Macmillan.

SPRINGER, S., & DEUTSCH, G. (1981). *Left brain, right brain.* San Francisco: Freeman.

STALKER, M. Z. (1981). Identification of the gifted in art. *Studies in Art Education, 22*(2) 49–56.

STANISLAVSKI, C. (1948). *My life in art.* New York: Meridian Books.

STANLEY, J. (1976a, September). *Brilliant youth: Improving the quality and speed of their education.* Paper presented to the Eighty-fourth Annual Conference of the American Psychological Association, Washington, DC. (ERIC Document Reproduction Service No. ED 136 536)

STANLEY, J. C. (1976b). Use of tests to discover talent. In D. P. Keating (Ed.), *Intellectual talent: Research and development* (pp. 3–22). Baltimore, MD: Johns Hopkins University Press.

STANLEY, J. (1977). The predictive value of the SAT for brilliant seventh- and eighth-graders. *The College Board Review, 106,* (Winter, 1977–1978), 31–37.

STANLEY, J. (1981). Rationale of the study of mathematically precocious youth (SMPY) during its first five years of promoting educational acceleration. In W. Barbe & J. Renzulli (Eds.), *Psychology and education of the gifted* (3rd ed., pp. 248–283). New York: Irvington.

STANLEY, J. C. (1985). A baker's dozen of years applying all four aspects of the Study of Mathematically Precocious Youth (SMPY). *Roeper Review, 7*(3), 170–173.

STANLEY, J. C. (1986, April). *Some characteristics of SMPY's "700—800 on SAT-M before age 13" group.* Paper presented at the Sixty-Seventh Annual Conference of the American Educational Research Association, San Francisco, CA. (ERIC Document Reproduction Service No. 277 206)

STANLEY, J., & BENBOW, C. (1983). SMPY's first decade: Ten years of posing problems and solving them. *The Journal of Special Education, 17*(1), 11–25.

STANLEY, J., KEATING, D., & FOX, L. (Eds.). (1974). *Mathematical talent: Discovery, description, and development.* Baltimore, MD: Johns Hopkins University Press.

STANOVICH, K. E., CUNNINGHAM, A. E., & FEEMAN, D. J. (1984). Intelligence, cognitive skills, and early reading progress. *Reading Research Quarterly, 19*(3), 278–303.

STEDMAN, L. (1924). *Education of gifted children.* Yonkers-on-Hudson, NY: World Book.

STERN, H. H., & CUMMINS, J. (1981). Language teaching/learning research: A Canadian perspective on status and directions. In J. K. Phillips (Ed.), *Action for the 80's: A politic, professional, and public program for foreign language education* (pp. 195–248). Skokie, IL: National Textbook.

STERN, W. (1914). *The psychological methods of testing intelligence* (G. M. Whipple, Trans.). Baltimore, MD: Warwick & York.

STERNBERG, R. (1977). *Intelligence, information processing, and analogical reasoning: The componential analysis of human abilities.* Hillsdale, NJ: Erlbaum.

STERNBERG, R. (1981). A componential theory of intellectual giftedness. *Gifted Child Quarterly, 25,* 86–93.

STERNBERG, R. (1982a). Lies we live by: Misapplication of tests in identifying the gifted. *Gifted Child Quarterly, 26,* 63–67.

STERNBERG, R. (1982b, April). Who's intelligent? How the layperson defines intelligence. *Psychology Today, 16,* 30–33.

STERNBERG, R. (1985). *Beyond IQ: A triarchic theory of human intelligence.* Cambridge: Cambridge University Press.

STERNBERG, R., & GARDNER, M. K. (1983). Unities in inductive reasoning. *Journal of Experimental Psychology: General, 112,* 80–116.

STEVENS, E., & WOODS, G. H. (Eds.). *Justice, ideology, and education: An introduction to the social foundations of education.* New York: Random House.

STOCKARD, J., LANG, D., & WOOD, J. W. (1985). Academic merit, status variables, and students' grades. *Journal of Research and Development in Education, 18*(2), 12–20.

STOCKARD, J., & MAYBERRY, M. (1986). *The relationship between school environment and student achievement: A review of the literature.* Eugene, OR: Center for Educational Policy and Management.

STODGILL, R. (1974). *Handbook of leadership: A survey of theory and research.* New York: Free Press.

STODOLSKY, S. S., & LESSER, G. (1967). Learning patterns in the disadvantaged. *Harvard Educational Review, 37,* 546–593.

STRACHEY, J. (Ed.). (1961). *Sigmund Freud's "Civilization and its discontents."* New York: Norton.

STRANG, R. (1954). Reading development of gifted children. *Elementary English, 31,* 35–40.

STRANG, R. (1956). Gifted adolescents' views of growing up. *Journal of Exceptional Children, 23,* 10–15.

STRANG, R. (1963). Psychology of gifted children and youth. In W. Cruickshank (Ed.), *Psychology of exceptional children and youth* (2nd ed., pp.484–525). Englewood Cliffs, NJ: Prentice-Hall.

STRAUSS, A. A., & LEHTINEN, L. E. (1947). *Psychopathology and education of the brain-injured child.* New York: Grune & Stratton.

STROMEYER, C. (1970). Eidetikers. *Psychology Today, 4*(6) 76–80.

SUCHMAN, R. (1975). A model for the analysis of inquiry. In W. Barbe & J. Renzulli (Eds.), *Psychology and education of the gifted* (2nd ed., pp. 336–345). New York: Irvington.

SULLIVAN, E. (1967). *Piaget and the school curriculum: A critical appraisal.* Bulletin No. 2 of The Ontario Institute for Studies in Education. Toronto: Ontario Institute for Studies in Education.

SUTARIA, S. D. (1985). *Specific learning disabilities: Nature and needs.* Springfield, IL: Thomas.

SWARD, K. (1933a). Jewish musicality in America. *Journal of Applied Psychology, 17*(6), 675–712.

SWARD, K. (1933b). Temperament and direction of achievement. *Journal of Social Psychology, 4,* 406–429.

SWASSING, R. H. (Ed.). (1985). *Teaching gifted children and adolescents.* Columbus, OH: Merrill.

SYPHERS, D. (1972). *Gifted and talented children: Practical programming for teachers and principals.* Arlington, VA: The Council for Exceptional Children.

TABA, H. (1965). Learning by discovery: Psychological and educational rationale. In J. J. Gallagher (Ed.), *Teaching gifted students: A book of readings* (pp. 177–186). Boston: Allyn & Bacon.

TANNENBAUM, A. (1962). *Academic attitudes toward academic brilliance.* New York: Bureau of Publications, Teachers College, Columbia University.

TANNENBAUM, A. (1981). Pre-sputnik to post-Watergate concern about the gifted. In W. Barbe & J. Renzulli (Eds.), *Psychology and education of the gifted* (3rd. ed., pp. 20–37). New York: Irvington.

TANNENBAUM, A. (1983). *Gifted children: Psychological and educational perspectives.* New York: Macmillan.

TAO, B. (1986). Parental involvement in gifted education. *Educational Studies in Mathematics, 17,* 313–321.

TAYLOR, D. W., & ELLISON, R. L. (1975). Moving toward working models in creativity: Utah creativity experiences and insights. In I. A. Taylor & J .W. Getzels (Eds.), *Perspectives in creativity* (pp. 191–223). Chicago: Aldine.

TAYLOR, J. (1966). To do and not to see: The teacher of art. In E. W. Eisner & D. W. Ecker (Eds.), *Readings in art education* (pp. 238–245). Waltham, MA: Blaisdell.

TAYLOR, M. L. (1975). *Idea people.* Chicago: Nelson-Hall.

TERFERTILLER, C. (1986). Family characteristics of gifted versus non-gifted students. *Graduate Monographs, 4*(1), 37–40.

TERMAN, L. (1925). *Mental and physical traits of a thousand gifted children: Genetic studies of genius* (Vol. 1). Stanford, CA: Stanford University Press.

TERMAN, L. M. (1973). *Concept mastery test.* New York: Psychological Corporation.

TERMAN, L. M., & MERRILL, M. A. (1973). *Stanford-Binet intelligence scale: Manual for third revision* (Form L-M). Boston: Houghton-Mifflin.

TERMAN, L. M., & ODEN, M. H. (1947). *The gifted child grows up: Genetic studies of genius* (Vol 4). Stanford, CA: Stanford University Press.

TERMAN, L. M, & ODEN, M. (1959). *The gifted group at mid-life: Genetic studies of genius* (Vol V). Stanford, CA: Stanford University Press.

THORNDIKE, R. (1972). Review of Torrance Tests of Creative Thinking. In O. K. Buros (Ed.), *The seventh mental measurement yearbook* (pp. 838–839). Highland Park, NJ: Gryphon.

THORNDIKE, R., & HAGEN, E. (1959). *Ten thousand careers.* New York: Wiley.

THRASHER, F. (1927). *The gang.* Chicago: University of Chicago Press.

THUROW, L. (1987). A surge in inequality. *Scientific American, 256*(5), 30–37.

THURSTONE, L. L. (1938). *Primary mental abilities* (Psychometric Monographs No. 1). Chicago: University of Chicago Press.

TIDWELL, R. (1980). A psycho-educational profile of 1,593 gifted high school students. *Gifted Child Quarterly, 24*(2), 63–68.

TIMAR, T., & KIRP, D. (1987). Educational reform and institutional competence. *Harvard Educational Review, 57*(3), 308–330.

TISDALL, W. J., BROWN, D. L., BYNUM, C. D., & ROBINSON, S. (1972). Junior—Gifted and disadvantaged. In B. B. Hauck & M. F. Freehill (Eds.), *The gifted—Case studies* (pp. 86–104). Dubuque, IA: Brown.

TONEMAH, S. (1987). Assessing American Indian gifted and talented students' abilities. *Journal for the Education of the Gifted, 10*(3), 181–194.

TORRANCE, E. P. (1962). *Guiding creative talent.* Englewood Cliffs, NJ: Prentice-Hall.

TORRANCE, E. P. (1963). *Education and the creative potential.* Minneapolis, MN: University of Minnesota Press.

TORRANCE, E. P. (1965). *Rewarding creative behavior.* Englewood Cliffs, NJ: Prentice-Hall.

TORRANCE, E. P. (1966). *Torrance tests of creative thinking: Research edition.* Princeton, NJ: Personnel Press.

TORRANCE, E. P. (1974). *Norms-technical manual: Torrance tests of creative thinking.* Lexington, MA: Ginn.

TORRANCE, E. P. (1979). Unique needs of the creative child and adult. In A. H. Passow (Ed.), *The gifted and talented: Their education and development.* The Seventy-eighth Yearbook of the National Society for the Study of Education (pp. 352–371). Chicago: University of Chicago Press.

TORRANCE, E. P. (1980). Growing up creatively gifted: A 22-year longitudinal study. *Creative Child and Adult Quarterly, 5*(3), 148–158, 170.

TORRANCE, E. P. (1984). The role of creativity in identification of the gifted and talented. *Gifted Child Quarterly, 28*(4), 153–156.

TORRANCE, E. P., & MYERS, R. E. (1971). *Creative learning and teaching.* New York: Dodd, Mead.

TRAVERS, K., & McKNIGHT, C. (1985). Mathematics achievement in U.S. schools: Preliminary findings from the second IEA mathematics study. *Phi Delta Kappan, 66*(6), 407–413.

TREZISE, R. (1978). What about a reading program for the gifted? *Reading Teacher, 31,* 742–746.

TYACK, D. (1974). *The one best system: A history of American urban education.* Cambridge, MA: Harvard University Press.

TYLER, F. (1962). Intraindividual variability. In N. B. Henry, *Individualizing instruction.* The Sixty-first Yearbook of the National Society for the Study of Education (pp. 164–174). Chicago: University of Chicago Press.

VAN TASSEL-BASKA, J. (1981). A comprehensive model of career education for the gifted and talented. *Journal of Career Education, 7,* 325–331.

VAN TASSEL-BASKA, J. (1983). Statewide replication in Illinois of the Johns Hopkins Study of Mathematically Precocious Youth. In C. P. Benbow & J. C. Stanley (Eds.), *Academic precocity: Aspects of its development* (pp. 179–191). Baltimore, MD: Johns Hopkins University Press.

VAN TASSEL-BASKA, J. (1985). Appropriate curriculum for the gifted. In J. Feldhusen (Ed.), *Toward excellence in gifted education* (pp. 45–68). Denver, CO: Love.

VAUGHAN, D. (1984). Twyla Tharp: Launching a new American classicism. *Dancemagazine, 58*(5), 54–58.

VERNON, P. E. (1979). *Intelligence, heredity, and environment.* San Francisco: Freeman.

VERNON, P., ADAMSON, G., & VERNON, D. (1977). *The psychology and education of gifted children.* Boulder, CO: Westview Press.

WAGNER, H., & ZIMMERMAN, B. (1986). Identification and fostering of mathematically gifted students. *Educational Studies in Mathematics, 17*(3), 243–259.

WALLACE, A. (1986). *The prodigy: A biography of William James Sidis, America's greatest child prodigy.* New York: Dutton.

WALLACH, M. A., & KOGAN, N. (1965). *Modes of thinking in young children.* New York: Holt, Rinehart & Winston.

WALLAS, G. (1926). *The art of thought.* New York: Harcourt, Brace.

WALBERG, H., & FOWLER, W. (1987). Expenditure and size efficiencies of public school districts. *Educational Researcher, 16*(7), 5–13.

WALBERG, H., RASHER, S., & PARKERSON, J. (1979). Childhood and eminence. *Journal of Creative Behavior, 13*(4), 225–231.

WARD, L. F. (1906). *Applied sociology.* Boston: Ginn.

WARD, W. C. (1975). Convergent and divergent measurement of creativity in children. *Educational and Psychological Measurement, 35,* 87–95.

WATT, I. (1957). *The rise of the novel.* London: Chatto & Windus. (Paperback edition published 1967 by the University of California Press)

WECHSLER, D. (1958). *The measurement and appraisal of adult intelligence.* Baltimore, MD: Williams & Wilkins.

WECHSLER, D. (1974). *Wechsler intelligence scale for children–revised.* New York: Psychological Corporation.

WECHSLER, D. (1981). *Manual for the Wechsler adult intelligence scale-revised.* New York: Psychological Corportation.

WEEKS, T. E. (1974). *The slow speech development of a bright child.* Lexington, MA: Lexington Books.

WEILER, D. (1978). The alpha children: California's brave new world for the gifted. *Phi Delta Kappan, 60*(3), 185–187.

WEINER, N., & ROBINSON, S. (1986). Cognitive abilities, personality, and gender differences in math achievement of gifted adolescents. *Gifted Child Quarterly, 30*(2), 83–87.

WEINSTEIN, J. B., & BOBKO, P. (1980). The relationship between creativity and androgyny when moderated by an intelligence threshold. *Gifted Child Quarterly, 24*(4), 162–166.

WEISS, D. S., HAIER, R. J., & KEATING, D. P. (1974). Personality characteristics of mathematically precocious boys. In J. C. Stanley, D. P. Keating, & L. H. Fox, *Mathematical talent: Discovery, description, and development* (pp. 126–139). Baltimore, MD: Johns Hopkins Univerity Press.

WELCH, W., ANDERSON, R., & HARRIS, L. (1982). The effect of schooling on mathematics achievement. *American Educational Research Journal, 19*(1), 145–153.

WELSH, G. S. (1949). *A projective figure-preference test for diagnosis of psychopathology.* Unpublished doctoral dissertation, University of Minnesota, Minneapolis.

WELSH, G. S. (1975). *Creativity and intelligence: A personality approach.* Chapel Hill, NC: Institute for Research in Social Science.

WELSH, G. S., & BARRON, F. (1963). *Barron Welsh art scale.* Palo Alto, CA: Consulting Psychologists Press.

Where are they now? (1969, April 28). *Newsweek,* p. 18.

WHIPPLE, G. M. (Ed.). (1941). *Art in American life and education.* The Fortieth Yearbook of the National Society for the Study of Education. Chicago: University of Chicago Press.

WHITE, M. A. (Ed.). (1966). *School disorder, intelligence, and social class.* New York: Teachers College Press.

WHITMORE, J. (1980). *Giftedness, conflict, and underachievement.* Boston: Allyn & Bacon.

WHITMORE, J. (1981). Gifted children with handicapping conditions: A new frontier. *Exceptional Children, 48*(2), 106–113.

WHITMORE, J. (1982). Recognizing and developing hidden giftedness. *Elementary School Journal, 82*(3), 274–283.

WHITMORE, J., & MAKER, C. J. (1985). *Intellectual giftedness in disabled persons.* Rockville, MD: Aspen.

WHORTON, J. E., KARNES, F. A., & CURRIE, B. B. (1985). Comparing ability and achievement in three academic areas for upper elementary gifted students. *Journal for the Education of the Gifted, 8*(2), 149–154.

WIENER, N. (1954). *The human use of human beings: Cybernetics and society* (rev. ed.). New York: Avon.

WIGGINTON, E. (1985). *Sometimes a shining moment.* Garden City, NY: Anchor Press/Doubleday.

WILCOX, K. (1982). Differential socialization in the classroom: Implications for equal opportunity. In G. Spindler (Ed.), *Doing the ethnography of schooling* (pp. 268–309). New York: CBS College.

WILCOX, K., & MORIARITY, P. (1977). Schooling and work: Social constraints on equal educational opportunity. *Social Problems, 24*(2), 204–213.

WILKINS, W. L. (1936). High school achievement of accelerated pupils. *School Review, 44,* 268–274.

WILLIAMS, F. (Ed.). (1970). *Language and poverty.* Chicàgo: Markham.

WILLIAMS, F. (1972). *A total creativity program.* Englewood Cliffs, NJ: Educational Technology.

WILLIAMS, R. (1976). *Keywords: A vocabulary of culture and society.* New York: Oxford University Press.

WILLINGS, D. (1985). The specific needs of adults who are gifted. *Roeper Review, 8*(1), 35–38.

WILLITS, F. F., BEALER, R. C., & CRIDER, D. M. (1973). Leveling of attitudes in mass society: Rurality and traditional morality in America. *Rural Sociology, 38*(1), 36–45.

WILSON, F. T. (1953). Some special ability test scores of gifted children. *Journal of Genetic Psychology, 82,* 69–90.

WILSON, R. N. (Ed.). (1964). *The arts in society.* Englewood Cliffs, NJ: Prentice-Hall.

WINEFORDNER, D. (Ed.). (1988). *Career exploration and planning program.* Bloomington, IL: Meridian.

WING, H. (1948). Tests of musical ability and appreciation. *British Journal of Psychology Monograph Supplement* (No. 27).

WING, H. (1954). Some applications of test results to education in music. *British Journal of Educational Psychology, 24,* 161–170.

WING, H. (1955). Musical aptitude and intelligence. *Education Today, 5*(1).

WIRSZUP, I. (1981). The Soviet challenge: The new mathematics curriculum required of all students in the USSR is superior to that of any other country. *Educational Leadership, 38*(5), 358–360.

WITTY, P. (1930). *A study of one hundred gifted children.* Lawrence, KS: Bureau of School Service and Research.

WITTY, P. (1958). Who are the gifted? In N. Henry (Ed.), *Education of the Gifted,* The Fifty-seventh Yearbook of the National Society for the Study of Education, Part II (pp. 41–63). Chicago: University of Chicago Press.

WOLF, J., & GYGI, J. (1981). Learning disabled and gifted: Success or failure? *Journal for the Education of the Gifted, 4*(3), 199–206.

WOLF, M. H. (1981). Talent search and development in the visual and performing arts. In *Balancing the scale for the disadvantaged gifted* (pp.103–115). Ventura, CA: National/State Leadership Training Institute on the Gifted and the Talented and the Office of the Ventura County Superintendent of Schools.

WOODCOCK, R. (1973). *Woodcock reading mastery tests.* Circle Pines, MN: American Guidance Services.

WOODCOCK, R., & JOHNSON, M. (1977). *Woodcock-Johnson psychoeducational battery.* Boston: Teaching Resources.

WOODDELL, G. (1984). Gifted children in general music. *Music Educators Journal, 70*(5), 43–46.

WOODMAN, R., & SHERWOOD, J. (1980). The role of team development in organizational effectiveness: A critical review. *Psychological Bulletin, 88*(1), 166–186.

WRIGHT, E. (1979). *Class structure and income determination.* New York: Academic Press.

YSSELDYKE, J., & ALGOZZINE, B. (1982). Bias among professionals who erroneously declare students eligible for special services. *Journal of Experimental Education, 50*(4), 223–228.

YSSELDYKE, J., ALGOZZINE, B., & MITCHELL, J. (1982). Special education team decision making: An analysis of current practice. *Personnel and Guidance Journal, 60*(5), 308–313.

ZAFFRANN, R. T., & COLANGELO, N. (1979). Counseling with gifted and talented students. In N. Colangelo & R. T. Zaffrann (Eds.), *New voices in counseling the gifted* (pp. 142–153). Dubuque, IA: Kendall/Hunt.

ZALEZNIK, A. (1984). Charismatic and consensus leaders: A psychological comparison. In W. E. Rosenbach & R. L. Taylor (Eds.), *Contemporary issues in leadership* (pp. 255–270). Boulder, CO: Westview Press.

ZANDER, A., & VAN EGMOND, E. (1958). Relationship of intelligence and social power to the interpersonal behavior of children. *Journal of Educational Psychology, 49*(5), 257–268.

Index

AUTHOR INDEX

SUBJECT INDEX